RICH MAN'S WAR

David Williams

RICH MAN'S
WAR

CLASS, CASTE, AND CONFEDERATE DEFEAT IN THE LOWER CHATTAHOOCHEE VALLEY

Sponsored by the
Historic Chattahoochee Commission

The University of Georgia Press   Athens and London

© 1998 by the University of Georgia Press

Athens, Georgia 30602

All rights reserved

Designed by Sandra Strother Hudson

Set in 10 on 13 Sabon with Trajan display by G & S Typesetters, Inc.

Printed and bound by Maple-Vail

The paper in this book meets the guidelines for permanence and
durability of the Committee on Production Guidelines for Book
Longevity of the Council on Library Resources.

Printed in the United States of America

02 01 00 99 98 C 5 4 3 2 1

Library of Congress Cataloging in Publication Data

Williams, David, 1959–

Rich man's war : class, caste, and Confederate defeat in the Lower
Chattahoochee Valley / by David Williams.

p. cm.

Includes bibliographical references and index.

"Sponsored by the Historic Chattahoochee Commission."

ISBN 0-8203-2033-1 (alk. paper)

1. Chattahoochee River Valley—History—19th century.

2. Georgia—History—Civil War, 1861–1865—Social aspects.

3. United States—History—Civil War, 1861–1865—Social aspects.

I. Historic Chattahoochee Commission.   II. Title.

F292.C4W54   1998

975.8—dc21   98-20312

British Library Cataloging in Publication Data available

For my parents

This has been "a rich man's war and a poor man's fight."
It is true there are a few wealthy men in the army, but nine tenths
of them hold positions, always get out of the way when they think
a fight is coming on, and treat the privates like dogs. . . .
there seems to be no chance to get this class to carry muskets.

Early County News, April 5, 1865

·

CONTENTS

ACKNOWLEDGMENTS

It would be difficult to overstate the gratification I felt when the Historic Chattahoochee Commission first contacted me about doing a history of the lower Chattahoochee Valley during the Civil War. I looked forward to the project as something of a homecoming. Nearly all my early years were spent in the valley, and my roots there go back almost two centuries. Born in Chattahoochee County, I lived for some years in neighboring Muscogee County, then across the river in Lee County, Alabama, before moving with my parents to their home county of Miller, in southwest Georgia. After graduating from Miller County High, I attended North Georgia College, where I met another deep-rooted valley native, Teresa Crisp of Columbus. Two years later we were married in the little stone chapel at Harris County's Callaway Gardens. A few years later we moved to Lee County, where, with sustaining encouragement from family, friends, and professors, I completed a Ph.D. in history at Auburn University. Though Teresa and I have been away for over a decade now, our thoughts are constantly drawn back to the valley. Every few months, we still make the journey home.

Like the doctoral degree, this project would not have been possible without continued support from many quarters. Doug Purcell, executive director of the Historic Chattahoochee Commission, not only reviewed the work but promoted it through any number of hazards to submission for publication. Once at the University of Georgia Press, Karen Orchard, the press director, and Kristine Blakeslee, my project editor, skillfully guided it into print. Other helpful folks at the press include Jane Kobres, David E. Des Jardines, Tricia Stuart, and Kelly Caudle, former managing editor. Thanks also to Ellen Goldlust-Gingrich for her excellent work as copy editor. Lee Formwalt, graduate dean at Albany State University and editor of the *Journal of Southwest Georgia History*, helped make significant improvements when he published an earlier version of the manuscript in article form. So did Jeff Jakeman of Auburn University, editor of *Alabama Review*, during the editorial process for an article dealing with slave resistance in the lower Chattahoochee Valley. Thanks also go to the staff and readers of the *Journal of Southwest Georgia History*, *Alabama Review*, and the University of Georgia Press.

Other readers whose comments proved extremely valuable were Nash Boney and Emory Thomas of the University of Georgia, Edmund L. Drago of the University of Charleston, James Lee McDonough of Auburn University, Junius Rodriguez of Eureka College, Mike Fitzgerald of St. Olaf College, Billy Winn of the *Columbus Ledger-Enquirer,* and John Lupold of Columbus State University. Additional thanks go to Lupold for his thorough two-volume bibliography, *Chattahoochee Valley Sources and Resources,* which was essential to tracking down much of the source material. I am especially grateful to Frank Lawrence Owsley Jr., professor emeritus at Auburn University, who recommended me to the Historic Chattahoochee Commission for this project. He went on to review the first draft and gave further guidance on dealing with the valley's plain folk. Years earlier, he directed my doctoral dissertation and now has graciously served something of the same function again. Much of what I am as a scholar I owe to him.

Several colleagues in Valdosta also contributed to the manuscript's many revisions. Joe Tomberlin, head of the Valdosta State University history department and a specialist in southern history, not only supported teaching-load reductions that allowed me time to write the book but gave his own time to reviewing the manuscript. Cathy Badura, also of the history department, selflessly brought her extraordinary talents as a southern historian to bear on the manuscript at a time when she was struggling to get her own fine scholarship ready for print. Trish Mincy, the history department's senior secretary, read the manuscript and picked up on numerous errors the rest of us missed. Sheri Gravett of the English department, a specialist in southern and Civil War literature, contributed significantly to the work in both a literary and a historiographical sense. Tracy Meyers of the sociology department lent her statistical expertise to the appendices and helped arrange the tables in such a way that they would make sense. Her husband, Chris Meyers, head of the social science department at Georgia Military College in Valdosta, deserves special thanks. A fellow nineteenth-century historian with whom I shared countless conversations and several research trips, Chris helped me work out a number of interpretational matters with keen insight and scholarly brilliance.

Students who read the manuscript in my Civil War courses substantially improved the first draft by raising important questions and helping me better communicate my ideas. Especially helpful were Alan Bernstein, David Carlson, Courtney Churchville, Jim Carter, Kim Evans, Michael Cox, Coretta Udell, Tom Cribb, Clay Crump, Jess Hornsby, Charles Powell, Darlene Register, Pam Sherman, Saul Taylor, Bobbie Warren,

Cliff Nichols, Michael Croom, Tiffany Norwood, Robert Couey, Olivia Dallas, Stephanie Enfinger, James Lunsford, Alan Morgan, Tom Nodar, Phil Painter, Jon Payne, Gina Strong, Don Taylor, and Mary Taylor. John Davis, whose master's thesis I directed, proved to be particularly astute during our many conversations about the Civil War's larger meaning and impact. His comments were always highly regarded.

Those who rendered personal assistance during the research process have my highest appreciation. A few of the most helpful were Robert Holcombe Jr. of the Confederate Naval Museum; Kaye Minchew and Randy Allen of the Troup County Archives; Miriam Syler of the Cobb Memorial Archives; Craig Lloyd and David Daniel of the Columbus State University Archives; Mark Ellis of Albany State University's Pendergrast Library; Joyce Massey of Eufaula's Carnegie Library; Bev Powers of the Auburn University Archives; Dale Foster of Auburn University Special Collections; Tim Dodge of Auburn University Microforms and Documents; Mark Palmer and Ken Tilley of the Alabama Department of Archives and History; Sally Moseley, Alice James, Andy Phrydas, and Anthony Winegar of the Georgia Department of Archives and History; and Anne Bailey of Georgia College and State University. I owe my greatest debt in the area of research assistance to Denise Montgomery of Valdosta State University's Odum Library. She cheerfully tolerated my constant requests for interlibrary loan material and even led me to sources of which I was unaware. She defines the term *professional* in the field of library science.

For assistance with the illustrations I am indebted to Richard Porter, proprietor of Hi-Plains Features in Plainview, Texas; Rex Devane and Terrence Nolley of Valdosta State University's Media Services; Bebe Overmiller of the Library of Congress; Gail Miller DeLoach of the Georgia Department of Archives and History; and Jody Norman of the Florida State Archives. Financial support was provided by the Historic Chattahoochee Commission and Valdosta State University.

Finally, a very special thanks to long-suffering family members who have supported me through the project in countless ways. My aunt, Jeanette Daniels Williams, my great-aunt, Martha Bush Kirkland, my mother-in-law, Margaret "Peggy" Crockett Crisp, and my grandmother, Helen Kirkland Daniels, all led me to old photos and memorabilia that helped make this book, in small part, a family as well as a regional history. My brother, Scott, who did his graduate work at the University of Georgia, constantly pushed me to enliven the manuscript. He still thinks the prologue is a bit dry but encourages readers not to be deterred. The rest of the book, he says, is much better. My wife, Teresa, was a little gentler in her reading of the manuscript, though no less insistent on good writing. Her dedication to and sacrifice for this project was every bit as great as my own. My parents, Harold O. "Buck" and Anita D. Williams, also read the manuscript and provided insights that can come only from those who have lived through poverty and suffered through war both on the battle-field and on the home front. This book is gratefully and lovingly dedicated to them.

RICH MAN'S WAR

PROLOGUE:
SOONER THAN ALL LINCOLNDOM

The Civil War is by far the most studied event in American history. Scholars and laity alike have written tens of thousands of books and articles about this era that so enthralls the popular imagination. In film as well as print, the war continues to be a prime factor shaping the American self-image. The Civil War is widely seen as the nation's epic, its turning point, its defining moment. *Legacy, heritage, cause,* and *crusade* are all terms still used to describe the character of that distant conflict.

But somehow, despite the great chasm that exists between our world and the mid–nineteenth century, that distant struggle does not feel so distant. We like to think that those Americans who endured such hardship and sacrifice for a cause—any cause—were not so different from ourselves. We like to feel that such strength of character says something about us. The war does for us what we often seem unable to do for ourselves. It defines us. It validates us. So it should not be surprising that, in many ways, the war is still with us. In the persistence of racial divisions, in the struggle for civil rights, in the quest for economic justice, elements of the Civil War appear familiar. Of course, these issues are in a sense timeless, especially in the South. William Faulkner wrote that for southerners the past is not dead, it is not even past.

For all the attention lavished on the Civil War and all about it that feels familiar, the war's pervasive socioeconomic nature is lost to the popular mind. It remains elusive even in academic circles. A supreme irony of American history is that its most studied event is also among its most misunderstood. Perhaps this is because so many of those who are drawn to that era come not so much to learn the lessons it can teach but to confirm preconceived notions. That we still tend to refight so many of the war's issues politically and symbolically is testimony to lessons unlearned. Our skewed image of the conflict may in part stem from an overemphasis on its military and political aspects. Sadly, that dominant focus still obscures the more decisive social and economic elements of the crisis that brought it about and determined its outcome.[1]

Perhaps, finally, it is our reluctance to deal frankly with issues of class and caste that most forcefully stands between our popular image of the war and a clear understanding of its causes and course. Recognizing how elements of racism, nationalism, and religion were used to suppress class conflict hits uncomfortably close to home. Examining the ways in which common folk have historically been manipulated to their own disadvantage reminds us of our own vulnerability. Even in our modern American "democracy," monetary wealth still determines who is represented and who is not—and the extent to which they are represented. It determines who is free and who is not—and the extent to which they are free. It determines who can purchase "justice" and who cannot. All too often, it determines who lives and who dies.[2]

Despite our discomfort with these realities of the class system, it was, in the end, class conflict that proved to be the crucial factor in deciding the contest between union and secession. The side that could most successfully, within its own socioeconomic confines, suppress or redirect class antagonism would emerge the victor. It was the most important challenge faced by either camp.

President Abraham Lincoln had a terribly difficult time gaining and maintaining enough popular support in the North to conduct the war. Most northerners seemed willing to let secession stand rather than resort to war. Just two days after Lincoln's election, Horace Greeley of New York, one of the country's most influential newspaper editors, insisted on letting the cotton states go in peace, as did the editors of the *New York Herald,* the *Detroit Free Press,* and the *Bangor (Maine) Union.* The *Albany (New York) Argus* encouraged Lincoln to allow all functions of the federal government to be suspended in the seceded states. "Any other course," said the paper, "would be madness." Even the fiery abolitionist William Lloyd Garrison called for separation without war, telling the South, "Organize your own confederacy, if you will, based on violence, tyranny, and blood, and relieve us from all responsibility for your evil course!"[3]

It was mainly business elites having economic ties to the South, especially those with cotton interests, who pressured Lincoln to hold the Union together. Only after the Confederacy's bombardment of Fort Sumter fired enough nationalistic fervor did Lincoln get the volunteers he needed to combat secession. But that fervor quickly died down after the Union defeat at First Manassas, or Bull Run, as it was called in the North. The flow of recruits slowed to a trickle and desertion was a constant drain on the army's manpower.

By late 1862 Lincoln found it necessary to do what he had resisted for over a year—announce the Emancipation Proclamation and accept the services of black volunteers. Most white northerners were similarly resistant, even hostile, to emancipation. Though racism was a primary motivating force, it was strongly bolstered by economic concerns. Business elites worried that the flow of cheap southern cotton might end with slavery's downfall. The working classes feared that freedom for the slaves would mean greater job competition and lower wages. With emancipation now an official war aim, it seemed that this perceived threat might soon become a reality.

Anxiety among common folk rose to a fever pitch in 1863 after Congress enacted a military draft. Now people would be forced to fight in a war they did not want for an objective they did not support. Even worse, men of means could avoid the draft by hiring a substitute or paying a three hundred dollar exemption fee. Cries of "Rich man's war!" swept the North, and Lincoln faced the worst riots in American history. In New York, mobs of working-class men and women roamed the streets chanting "Kill the niggers!" They torched the draft office, looted and destroyed the homes of prominent Republicans, burned a home for black orphans, and lynched at least a dozen blacks. Federal troops straight from the Battle of Gettysburg were rushed in to stop the rampage.[4]

A year later, in summer 1864, Henry J. Raymond, head of the Republican National Committee, assured Lincoln that he could not win a second term. Lincoln agreed. The belief that the war had become a crusade against slavery was simply too prevalent. Public opinion turned in Lincoln's favor that September when Atlanta fell. The war's end finally seemed to be in sight with this major Union victory. Even so, Lincoln defeated his Democratic rival, George McClellan, by only 10 percent of the popular vote.

Difficult as they were, Lincoln's problems with northern class conflict pale in comparison to those faced by his Confederate counterpart, Jefferson Davis. Even before the Confederacy came into being, signs that a southern republic would lack popular support were clear. More than half the South's white population, three-fourths of whom owned no slaves, opposed secession.[5] Ignoring the majority's will, state conventions across the Deep South, all of them dominated by slaveholders, pushed their states out of the Union even before Lincoln's inauguration. One prominent southern politician conceded in his diary that ambitious colleagues had engineered secession without strong backing from "the mass of the people." A staunch South Carolina secessionist admitted the same: "But whoever waited for the common people when a great move was to be made—We must make the move and force them to follow."[6]

Still, there was some general enthusiasm for the war in the wake of Lincoln's call for volunteers to invade the South. But southern enlistments, like those in the North, declined rapidly after the first major battle at

Manassas. The Confederacy's response to its recruitment problem was an early indicator of the role class and caste issues would play in the wartime South.

In April 1862 the Confederate Congress passed the first national draft act in American history. Like the North's later draft, men of wealth could avoid service by hiring a substitute or paying an exemption fee. Later that year, slaveholders with twenty or more slaves were automatically excused from the draft. This twenty-slave law was perhaps the most widely hated act ever imposed by the Confederacy and was especially reviled by poor soldiers already in the ranks. Private Sam Watkins later wrote, "It gave us the blues; we wanted twenty negroes. Negro property suddenly became very valuable, and there was raised the howl of 'rich man's war, poor man's fight.'" He continued, "From this time on till the end of the war, a soldier was simply a machine. We cursed the war . . . we cursed the Southern Confederacy. All our pride and valor had gone." Not surprisingly, desertion became an even greater problem for the Confederacy than for the Union. By September 1864, Davis publicly admitted that "two-thirds of our men are absent . . . most of them without leave." To make matters worse, more than 100,000 southern whites served in the Union armies, and thousands more formed anti-Confederate guerrilla bands.[7]

Another official practice that helped turn many southerners against the Richmond government was confiscation of private property, or impressment. Farmers deeply resented being forced to give up a portion—sometimes a major part—of their meager produce to the government. That they had to sell at prices set by the government was even more galling. But for most, prices did not matter: farmers received promissory notes, usually unredeemable, or inflated paper currency that was nearly as worthless. Very often they got nothing at all. One Georgia woman grumbled, "the country is plum full of [Confederate] cavalry . . . stealing all the time."[8]

Barely a year into the war, one southern newspaper editor wrote, "We often hear persons say, 'The *Yankees cannot do us any more harm than our own soldiers have done.*'" John Hagan, a soldier from southwest Georgia, confirmed that assertion in a letter to his wife: "I beleave our troops are doing as much harm in this country as the yankees . . . and in fact wheare this army goes the people is ruined." He was certain that the Confederacy could never survive while handling its own people so roughly.[9]

Poor and middling farmers bore the brunt of impressment since they were easier targets than the more politically influential planters. Furthermore, smaller farmers were more likely to grow food products, which was what the impressment agents wanted. For the planters, old habits were hard to break. They continued to devote much of their land to cotton production while soldiers and civilians were starving. The result was an overwhelming food shortage that led to increasing desertion rates in the army and food riots throughout the South. As early as March 1862 a concerned southwest Georgia man wrote to Governor Joseph E. Brown begging him to restrain the planters, "for they will whip us sooner than all Lincolndom combined could do it." [10]

That planters could avoid not only the draft but impressment as well was further evidence to the common folk that this was a rich man's war. When a Confederate impressment agent took two cows from one farmer in 1863, the man fumed that "the sooner this damned Government fell to pieces the better it would be for us." [11]

Even more alienated than yeomen and poor whites were southern blacks. Though they made up a third of the population, they could hardly be counted on to support a government dedicated to the principle that slavery was, as Confederate Vice President Alexander H. Stephens put it, their "natural and normal condition." Blacks had been socially and economically relegated to a lower caste as early as the eighteenth century. The cotton gin's development and widespread application in the early nineteenth century threatened to make slavery a perpetual institution. By the time of the Civil War, more than 100,000 slaves had escaped bondage, and the number of escapees continued to rise as the war went on. [12]

Clearly, the South entered the secession crisis with barely a third of its population lending support. The Confederacy could not survive with so little backing, and that fact was widely acknowledged during the war. "If we are defeated," said one Atlanta newspaper, "it will be by the people at home." And so the Confederacy was defeated—by selfish planters, greedy speculators, corrupt officials, disaffected whites, and desperate slaves. [13]

After the war, in an effort to mask that reality and justify themselves in the wake of defeat, the still dominant planter class produced a body of revisionist literature that has defined the Old South's popular image ever since. It is, of course, that familiar portrait of an idyllic South populated by a chivalric race of cavaliers who were kind masters to happy slaves— a utopian South, beaten and broken by superior northern numbers and industry while defending an ill-defined Lost Cause. That image reached its peak with the 1939 film *Gone with the Wind,* which won ten Academy Awards and became one of the most widely viewed motion pictures in the history of cinema. But the Lost Cause mythology, reflected so well in *Gone with the Wind* and Margaret Mitchell's book on which the movie was based, contains no hint of the class divisions that tore the South apart between 1861 and 1865—nothing of conscription, desertion, impressment, or disaffection. The literary Lost Cause image is, like its celluloid offspring, not fact but fiction.

If the Lost Cause tradition ignored discontent and disaffection among the common folk, it actively fostered the impression that slaves were happy with their lot in life. It assumed servitude to be the natural condition of black people and slavery to be their highest ambition. Yet even as apostles of the Lost Cause preached their doctrine of black docility, they knew better. Many were former slaveholders and had firsthand knowledge of their slaves' longing for freedom. To slaves, the Civil War was a struggle against slavery long before Lincoln announced the Emancipation Proclamation. Thousands fled to Union lines in the war's first year. Thousands more escaped after the Proclamation and joined Union armies. Still more deserted plantations to follow Yankee troops as they moved through Alabama and Georgia in the war's last year.

Perhaps nowhere can the divisive role of the economic class system and the caste system of slavery be viewed more clearly than in the lower Chattahoochee River Valley of Georgia and Alabama.[14] Though primarily an agricultural region, it held one of the Confederacy's major manufacturing centers. River and rail linked the valley to the outside world. Its population ran the socioeconomic scale from planters down through lesser slaveholders, yeomen, tenant farmers, sharecroppers, farm laborers, and slaves. Besides the rural farming folk, there were merchants, factory workers, skilled artisans and craftspeople, urban professionals, and industrial entrepreneurs.[15] The valley was, in short, as representative a slice of the Cotton Kingdom as one is likely to find. And nestled as it was in the heart of the Deep South, far from the front lines and coastal regions, it did not feel the direct sting of battle until the war was nearly over. Most studies of southern disaffection with the Confederacy have focused on the South's more homogeneous and battle-scarred hill country.[16] But examining the same phenomenon in a socially and economically diverse area like the lower Chattahoochee Valley, upon which the Confederacy so depended for men and materiel, may tell us even more about why the Civil War ended as it did.

By 1860 the lower Chattahoochee Valley was one of the South's most prosperous regions, producing almost a quarter of a million cotton bales annually. About half those bales went out by rail. The rest made their way downriver to Apalachicola for export. At the head (or upper limit) of navigation on the Chattahoochee River, Columbus became a thriving cotton market. After 1855, this inland port city handled more than 100,000 bales a year. With its population of more than nine thousand, Columbus was the largest urban center in the valley. Manufacturing employed nearly a thousand of the townspeople, two-thirds the number of industrial workers in the entire valley. With a total estate value of more than $155 million, both real and personal, per capita wealth in the lower Chattahoochee Valley was 15 percent higher than the combined averages of Georgia and Alabama.[17]

That prosperity, however, was hardly shared by all valley residents. Most lived in conditions that were regarded even at the time as abject poverty. Of the region's more than 200,000 people, half were slaves. The great majority of the valley's free inhabitants were directly engaged in agriculture, but only half owned three or more acres of land. Most of the rest were tenant farmers, sharecroppers, or day laborers, all working land owned by someone else. Of those farmers who owned three acres or more, a majority also held slaves, but nearly half owned fewer than five. Most of these farmers worked the fields along with their slaves and had a lifestyle not so different from that of many nonslaveholding yeomen. Only the planters (who owned twenty or more slaves) and their families benefited significantly from an economic system based on cotton and slavery. This group made up less than 4 percent of the valley's population.[18]

What most small farmers wanted, of course, was to become big landholders. That had been possible for some in the 1820s and '30s when land was relatively cheap following the brutal expulsion of the native Creeks. By the 1850s, however, land and slaves were so expensive that few small farmers had any real hope of ever living in the "big house." Both socially and economically, the class system as it existed was taking on an air of permanence. The South's socioeconomic hierarchy was so rigid that even the white social structure might be more accurately defined as a caste system in which yeomen and poor whites had little chance for upward mobility. Yet once the war began, these plain folk had to be convinced of their stake in the system for the Confederacy to survive. As both a regional portrait and an interpretive exploration, this book suggests how difficult that task really was. In fact, so great was the South's latent class antagonism that the job would ultimately prove impossible.

CHAPTER

1

Not One Foot
Was Owned by a Poor Man

John Horry Dent was one of the richest planters in the lower Chatta-hoochee Valley. By 1860, his Barbour County plantation had almost five hundred acres in cotton, and he was one of the few valley planters who owned more than one hundred slaves. His sons fought for the Confeder-acy, and one died for it. Still, in spite of his wealth and personal involve-ment in the cause of southern independence, Dent was a reluctant Rebel. He had warned a northern friend in 1856 that the election of a "Black Re-publican" president would lead to secession. The South had to protect its "honor and self respect." But four years later, faced with the realities of secession and civil war, Dent had second thoughts. Though he expressed an earnest hope for compromise, Dent was not optimistic. In his journal, he privately lamented that "troubles and hard times are anticipated in every part of the once United States. And no man can predict what is to come to pass." [1]

Only a few months into the war, Dent himself was ready to predict its outcome. Both the Confederacy and the institution of slavery, he thought, were doomed. Slaves would seek freedom at the earliest opportunity, and poor whites' hatred of the rich would boil to the surface in "lawless vio-lence." [2] He saw much more clearly than most of his class that, given the ambivalence and hostility of common folk, their planter republic with its cornerstone of slavery would be impossible to maintain.

Prospects for the valley's planter class had not seemed so bleak just a generation earlier. On the contrary, hopes for a perpetual Cotton King-dom along the lower Chattahoochee ran high. Between 1814 and 1836 the Creek Indians were killed or driven out of west Georgia and east Alabama. The land they left behind was plentiful, fertile, and cheap. Much of it was already cleared by the natives, who had farmed the land for centuries before Europeans arrived. In 1822, the bustling port city of Apalachicola exported its first cotton shipment. Within a few years it was the third largest cotton port on the Gulf Coast, behind New Orleans and Mobile.[3] Farther north, whites began moving into the village of Yufaula by 1823. Ten years later the settlement was chartered as Irwinton, and in 1857 it was incorporated as the town of Eufaula. A visitor from Mobile described it in 1849 as "a pretty and thriving town of about two thousand inhabitants . . . a clean, comfortable, respectable looking town. There are three churches, Methodist, Baptist, and Presbyterian, and a male and female academy. The population is a sober, industrious, and orderly one; and, for the number of inhabitants, there is a degree of education and refinement not usually found in so newly settled a country." By the time of its incorporation, Eufaula was the center of cotton trade in southeast Alabama.[4]

The busiest cotton market on the Chattahoochee was Columbus, Georgia. Located at the fall line about fifty miles upriver from Eufaula, Columbus was the northernmost inland port on the Chattahoochee– Apalachicola River system. As such, it was a major junction of economic activity, which had been true of the area long before the coming of Europeans. For centuries it was the site of Coweta and Cusseta, major centers of political and economic power in the Creek nation. Continental trade routes dating back at least three thousand years converged there.

In July 1828, less than a year after Georgia forced the Creeks out, town lots were put up for auction. A year later Columbus had a population of more than one thousand, and the city boasted a busy river wharf, a weekly newspaper, a theater, and a hotel. By 1833 the town had five hotels and a population of more than two thousand. Columbus was, as one enthusiast called it, the "boom town of west Georgia."[5]

Just two decades after its founding, the town had more than two hundred businesses, five cotton warehouses, and five textile factories. By 1860 Columbus was one of the two leading textile manufacturing centers in the South. Only Richmond, Virginia, produced more. The city also boasted two ironworks and facilities for making steam engines, cotton gins, firearms, and iron railing. In all of Georgia, Columbus was second only to Savannah in total manufacturing. So important were cotton textiles to the region's economy that leading Columbus residents began promoting their city as the "Lowell of the South." Tyrone Power, a visitor from Ireland, said of antebellum Columbus, "Nowhere in this South country have I yet seen a place which promises more of the prosperity increasing wealth can bestow than this."[6]

If the town's industrial capacity impressed visitors, its people frequently did not. They were mostly a rough-hewn lot much like those who later populated the frontier towns of the West. In 1833 a Swedish traveler wrote that "the manners of the people were uncouth. . . . Many individuals, there called gentlemen, would in other places receive a very different appellation." Twenty years later, another visitor wrote that he had never seen "so much gambling, intoxication, and cruel treatment of servants in public, as in Columbus." He advised those traveling for pleasure or health to avoid the town if at all possible.[7]

Just across the river from Columbus, the settlement of Girard (now Phenix City) had an even worse reputation. Local residents commonly called it "Sodom" after the decadent city of biblical infamy. One account noted that the town swarmed with drunks and prostitutes. According to another, "scarcely a day passed without some human blood being shed in its vicinity."[8] Clearly, neither Columbus nor Girard had reputations as centers of cultural refinement. But that was hardly the objective of their antebellum residents. Most were too poor or too busy to have much regard for social elegance. As for the local elites, their primary interest was economic development. What their neighbors did outside that realm was of little concern to them.

Transportation was key to the valley's economic growth, and the transportation system centered on the river, as much from necessity as from convenience. The region's dirt roads were poorly kept and impassable much of the year, as one tourist discovered on his way from Columbus to Fort Mitchell, Alabama: "I had often been told that this was the worst piece of ground in the Southern states, and this account I found, by woeful experience, to be by no means exaggerated." According to one account, the roads in southeast Alabama were "indebted for their improvement to nothing but the wheels that run over them."[9] Little wonder that most people preferred to travel on the river when they could.

In 1827 the steamer *Fanny* became the first riverboat to reach Columbus. Within a year three others were plying the Chattahoochee's waters. By 1835 there were as many as two dozen. In the 1840s and '50s the number of steamers working the river at any given time averaged between twenty and thirty. The total number may have been nearly two hundred.[10]

The round-trip between Columbus and Apalachicola usually took five days, but stumps, roots, sandbars, strong currents, low water, flooding, and fire made regular schedules hard to keep. Still, some captains liked to think of themselves as more than a match for the river's hazards. In 1841, when flooding made it impossible for ships to go under the bridge at Eufaula, the 110-ton steamer *Siren* simply went around it. A Columbus paper reported that the *Siren* had reached the city by making the trip "for the greater part over submerged plantations." Other ships were noted for their shallow drafts and ability to negotiate the river in dry seasons. Some river men said that the steamer *Ben Franklin* could navigate the Chattahoochee as long as the river bottom was moist.[11]

Despite such claims, the dangers of river traffic remained very real. On January 2, 1860, water levels fell so quickly at the Columbus wharf that the *Oswichee* and *Munnerlyn* were left high and dry. It took more than a week to dislodge the *Munnerlyn,* and the *Oswichee* could not be floated again for nearly a month. In 1853 the *Retrieve* hit a rock while carrying 1,200 bales of cotton. The *Viola* sank with a loss of more than a thousand bales. When the *Fanny Ellsler* went up in flames, it lost a shipment worth three thousand dollars. One of the worst accidents on the river occurred in 1840 when the *LeRoy*'s boiler exploded and engulfed the ship in flames. Within fifteen minutes it was a smoldering wreck. The explosion threw the *LeRoy*'s pilot a hundred yards upriver along with parts of the smokestacks and wheelhouse. Somehow he survived with no serious injuries. One of the passengers was never found. Insurance rates for river cargoes ran as high as 3 percent of the freight's value. This reflected the Chattahoochee's dangerous nature, which made it one of the most expensive water systems in the country on which to operate. Rates on the Mississippi were a third lower, and cargoes bound for any European port from Apalachicola could be insured for half the Chattahoochee rate.[12]

High insurance rates and the dangers of navigation were major reasons that some cotton growers and merchants began to see railroads as a cheaper alternative. Efforts to raise funds for railroad construction were made as early as the 1830s. But the Panic of 1837 and resulting economic depression put so many local banks out of business that capital was impossible to raise. In the wake of this crisis, all six Columbus banks went under. The planned rail lines had to be delayed. The late 1840s and early 1850s saw a renewed interest in rail construction for several reasons. Light rains caused lower water levels, making river transport even more dangerous and expensive than before. The shipping channel in Apalachicola Bay, dredged out twenty years earlier, was beginning to silt up. Besides, shipyards were building bigger river steamers every year. Some could barely negotiate the snags and sandbars up to Columbus. A few could not make it at all. The advantages of railroad transportation seemed clear.[13]

The first rail line built into the valley was the Montgomery and West Point. Incorporated in 1837, the line finally reached the Chattahoochee from Montgomery in 1851. A bridge spanning the river was completed two years later, and a year after that the Atlanta and LaGrange Railroad reached West Point. The meeting of these two lines established the first interstate rail link between Alabama and Georgia. Columbus made its first rail connection in 1853 with a line to Butler, which put the city in direct rail contact with the port of Savannah. This connection had such an impact on cotton transport that within a year cotton bale receipts at Apalachicola fell by 27 percent. Savannah saw an increase of 36 percent during the same period. A second rail line from Columbus was completed in 1855, connecting the city with the Montgomery and West Point Railroad via the Opelika Branch. Within five years a third line ran from Girard to Union Springs. By the time of the Civil War, Cuthbert, Georgetown, and Fort Gaines all had rail connections as well.[14]

Whether trade, manufacturing, or transportation, most of the valley's economic activity was directly or indirectly driven by cotton. The towns depended on plantations and served the needs of planters. Local cotton fed the textile mills. Workers at train depots and river docks loaded cotton. Wagoners, steamer crews, and railroad workers hauled cotton. Carpenters and masons built cotton warehouses. Merchants and manufacturers sold their goods to townspeople and to plantations. Cotton brokers, for an average 2.5 percent commission, provided planters with access to the textile mills of the North and Europe. The cotton market's relative stability in the 1850s made the dependence of so many people on cotton possible. Cotton prices remained steady at ten to twelve cents a pound and were rising by the end of the decade. The first bale auctioned at Columbus in 1860, produced by Russell County planter C. B. Taliaferro, brought 12.5 cents a pound.[15]

Rising prices reflected a huge demand for southern cotton. Much of the valley's cotton made its way to New England textile mills through commission firms like Hall and DeBlois of Columbus. This agency purchased so much cotton for the Lowell mills in Massachusetts that its storage building became known locally as the "Lowell Warehouse." Other cotton brokers, like the Englishman Samuel Cassin, represented firms on both sides of the Atlantic. From his office in Apalachicola, Cassin funneled cotton to textile manufacturers through agencies based in New York and Liverpool. Most cotton shipments out of Apalachicola were bound for the British port of Liverpool, which served the great textile manufacturing center of Manchester.[16]

Cotton was the nation's leading export in 1860, accounting for more than half of all exports. Little wonder that so many planters thought of cotton as king and themselves as something of an aristocracy. One visitor to the south vividly described the obsession with cotton: "People live in cotton houses and ride in cotton carriages. They buy cotton, sell cotton, think cotton, eat cotton, drink cotton, and dream cotton. They marry cotton wives, and unto them are born cotton children. In enumerating the charms of a fair widow, they begin by saying she makes so many bales of cotton." Cotton was, in short, "the great staple, sum and substance" of life for most southern planters and their associates.[17]

Though cotton brought great wealth to the valley, that prosperity was concentrated in the hands of a very few. Only the planters traveled in "cotton carriages." The oxcart was much more common; horses and mules were too expensive for most people. Personal transportation was only one reflection of what had by 1860 become a rigid socioeconomic scale headed by planters, along with a few industrialists and financiers. At the bottom were poor whites and slaves.[18]

In the South as a whole, the planter class made up about 2.5 percent of the population. That figure was slightly higher for the lower Chattahoochee Valley at 3.8 percent, but planter holdings in land and slaves represented a much greater percentage of the valley's wealth. There were 1,518 heads of household who owned twenty slaves or more, placing the planters at only 17 percent of the valley's slaveholders. Yet these few people held 58 percent of the region's slaves. Most of the planters (1,200) owned between twenty and forty-nine slaves; 271 held from fifty to ninety-nine. Only forty-seven planters owned more than one hundred slaves, and only five had more than two hundred. A single valley planter, James Wright of Russell County, held more than three hundred slaves.[19]

On the eve of the Civil War, Wright was perhaps the richest man in the valley. His five thousand–acre plantation, valued at more than $100,000, was worked by 389 slaves. His farm machinery was appraised at eight thousand dollars and his livestock at twelve thousand dollars. In 1860, his farming operations produced 1,228 bales of cotton, ten thousand bushels of corn, and five hundred bushels of oats. Wright's income that year from the cotton crop alone was around sixty thousand dollars. Such wealth was, of course, unusual even among planters. Wright was one of only ten Alabama planters who owned more than three hundred slaves, and just eight Georgia planters fell into that category.[20]

Still, as a class, the planters could afford a somewhat aristocratic lifestyle compared to that of their less fortunate neighbors. Even those whose wealth was only indirectly related to cotton enjoyed some degree of gentility. Eufaula banker John McNabb and his family rode in a silver-trimmed carriage, wore Irish linen and Scottish tweeds, drank Chinese tea, and vacationed abroad every year. But for sheer ostentation, the big planters were hard to beat. The most affluent modeled themselves after the landed gentry of Britain. The Shacklefords of Early County were renowned for the extravagance they displayed at every opportunity. One guest at "The Pines," as the Shackleford plantation was called, arrived by horseback at dusk and was "ushered to a room where a body servant prepared his bath and laid out fresh linen. Downstairs, candles and an open fire illuminated a large room with French windows opening onto a veranda. There were comfortable chairs, tables for reading by lamplight, a secretary for writing, a piano piled high with music. A dinner table [was] laid with the finest silver, china and crystal." At "The Refuge" on the Flint River near Bainbridge, the Munnerlyns lived and entertained in similar fashion at their "lovely mansion set in an English garden." As if to emphasize the aristocratic nature of the planter self-image, Mrs. Munnerlyn was referred to by friends and family as the "Empress." [21]

The vast majority of planters did not live in as lavish surroundings as the Shacklefords and Munnerlyns. Even fewer adorned themselves with false titles of nobility. Most lived not in opulent mansions but in large frame houses of eight to ten rooms. Some did not even reside on their plantations, preferring the comforts and conveniences of town life. Most were educated, but they usually lacked the social and cultural refinement so often associated in popular literature with the planter class. The great majority viewed themselves primarily as businessmen whose status as large slaveholders happened to confer upon them a certain social prestige. Despite variations in lifestyle and self-image among the planters, nearly all took pains to set themselves apart in one way or another from the common folk. [22]

On the next rung down the valley's social ladder stood a comfortably well-to-do class made up of prosperous slaveholding farmers owning between five and nineteen slaves, together with a smattering of merchants and urban professionals. These slaveholders and their families totaled about twenty thousand people, nearly a fifth of the valley's white population or about one-tenth the total population. [23] Their primary cash crop was cotton, but many also raised livestock and grew oats and corn for market. They lived in moderate homes of five to six rooms and were better fed, clothed, and educated than the yeoman farmers and poor whites.

Roughly 27,000 valley residents comprised the region's yeoman class. Most of these folk, just over 19,000, were members of small slaveholding households owning fewer than five slaves. The other eight thousand owned

no slaves at all.[24] Yeomen generally lived in small frame houses of two to
four rooms. Few had any formal education, and many were illiterate. They
usually grew some cotton as a cash crop, but much of their acreage was
devoted to subsistence farming, especially for nonslaveholding yeomen.
Many depended more on herding than horticulture, particularly in the
lower parts of the valley.[25] Whatever their individual economic focus, their
main concern was having enough food on the table from day to day. For
most yeomen, cotton did not figure prominently in their economic lives.
With their limited farmland and labor force, devoting all or even most of
their acreage to cotton was a luxury they could not afford. It was unlikely
that they ever would. There was only so much farmland to go around,
and most of it was already owned by the planters and more affluent slaveholders. Hopes of moving into the planter class or even reaching the ranks
of the comfortably secure were not high, especially among the lesser nonslaveholding yeomen.

In most cases, these lesser yeomen were only marginally better off than
the poor whites, often called "white trash" by the planters and more prosperous slaveholders. Poor whites made up close to half the valley's white
population. They included urban laborers who one observer described as
"in such a condition that, if temporarily thrown out of employment, great
numbers of them are at once reduced to a state of destitution, and are
dependent upon credit or charity for their daily food," although charity
could not have been a very dependable source of sustenance. Columbus
factory workers were so despised that some of their more fortunate neighbors hatched a plan to have them all housed on the Alabama side of the
river. The idea was eventually rejected, probably because of its inconve-
nience to factory owners, but it was a prominent issue in the 1852 city
elections.[26]

Most of the valley's poor whites were landless farm laborers and tenants. Some hired themselves out to landholders for meager wages. Others
worked land owned by someone else for a share of the crop.[27] What vegetables they had were grown with their own hands in small gardens. What
meat there was came from hunting, fishing, or small herds of free-roaming
(or open-range) livestock. Illiteracy rates ran high among these people,
most of whom lived in log structures with one or two rooms and dirt floors.
Like the lesser yeomen, few of the valley's sharecroppers could ever hope
to improve their condition in a society run by cotton money and planter
politics.

Opportunities for upward mobility along the lower Chattahoochee had
been much better only a generation earlier. Land prices in the 1820s and

1830s were low after the indigenous Creeks were pushed out. Wealthy men from the increasingly crowded coastal regions bought much of the land, but small farmers had little trouble getting loans with which to buy land and slaves. Cotton prices were on the rise, and there was every expectation that loans could easily be repaid. Many of these small farmers who were lucky enough to have rich land and adequate rain soon became affluent slaveholders and even planters.

But a severe economic depression, the Panic of 1837, put an end to the hopes of thousands. Cotton prices fell dramatically overnight and continued falling into the early 1840s. Aspiring yeomen found it impossible to keep up with loan payments. Their land and slaves were repossessed and sold at auction, usually to wealthy planters. The sheriff in Henry County auctioned off so many small farms that enraged yeomen demanded his resignation. Some farmers were able to keep a few acres and eked out a living as lesser yeomen. Many, however, lost everything and fell into tenancy and sharecropping. When the cotton market finally recovered in the 1840s, affluent slaveholders held nearly all the valley's better agricultural land. By that time, most valley farmers found themselves trapped in a system of poverty from which few could ever escape, even with a move to cheaper western lands.[28]

The gap between rich and poor continued to grow through the 1850s not only along the lower Chattahoochee but throughout the South. Planters bought up more and more land, forcing a rapid rise in land prices and making it nearly impossible for smaller farmers to increase their holdings or for sharecroppers to buy any land at all. Wealth in terms of slaveholding was also becoming concentrated in fewer hands. During the last decade of the antebellum era, the proportion of slaveholders in the free population dropped by 20 percent. Only the distribution of land and slaves to the heirs of deceased planters kept social mobility from being far more limited than it was.[29]

By 1860 the top 10 percent in the cotton states held 53 percent of the region's agricultural wealth. The bottom half owned only 5 percent. In Early County alone, according to an antebellum resident, "there was a body of land east of Blakely . . . which made 216 square miles, and not one foot of it was owned by a poor man." The more affluent slaveowners and planters not only held more land than their yeoman neighbors but held better land as well. Economic circumstances beyond their control forced many yeomen into landless tenancy—so many in fact that the editor of one southern newspaper predicted a complete disappearance of the South's small independent farming class. By 1860 at least 25 percent of southern farmers were tenants, and more were joining their landless ranks every day.[30]

At the bottom of the social scale, in a caste of their own, separate and distinct from the white class structure, were those of African descent. Numbering well over one hundred thousand, they made up half the valley's population. Virtually all were slaves: the 1860 census listed only 401 as free.

Though blacks and whites lived side by side and interacted on a daily basis, there was a vast chasm separating them. It was a chasm not simply of institutional slavery but of racial attitude. In 1863, the *Columbus Daily Sun*'s editor reacted to Lincoln's Emancipation Proclamation by wondering, "is a negro really a white man with a black skin, or is there a moral *caste* existing between the two races?" The question was more sarcastic than serious, meant only to illustrate for his thoroughly racist readers how ridiculous the notion of emancipation was. Entitling his article "NIGGERS VS. WHITE MEN," the editor left little doubt what he thought the answer should be. Few whites of the nineteenth century, North or South, took seriously the suggestion that black males might be men as well.[31]

Despite the enormous social chasm between them, in a material sense, living and working conditions for slaves were not altogether different from those of poor whites. In describing a typical day's labor, one slave remembered getting up every morning before sunrise to go to work in the fields. After a short dinner break at noon, it was back to the fields until dark. And the women worked just like the men.[32] The same was true for tenants, sharecroppers, and lesser yeomen of both sexes. Similarly, neither slaves nor poor whites had much hope of ever improving their economic condition. The poor whites may have been free in the strictest sense, but freedom meant little in practical terms without opportunities for economic advancement. Conversely, those held as chattel slaves did bear physical and psychological burdens from which the poor whites were mercifully free. Threats of personal violence and separation from loved ones were ever present in the slaves' world.

Despite planter claims to the contrary, the "wise master," as historian Kenneth Stampp put it, "did not take seriously the belief that Negroes were natural-born slaves. He knew better. He knew that Negroes freshly imported from Africa had to be broken into bondage; that each succeeding generation had to be carefully trained. This was no easy task, for the bondsman rarely submitted willingly. Moreover, he rarely submitted completely. In most cases there was no end to the need for control—at least not until old age reduced the slave to a condition of helplessness." Control of elderly slaves was hardly ever a concern anyway. Less than four in a hundred ever lived to see age sixty.[33]

Slave resistance took a variety of forms ranging from work slowdowns to running away. Murder and suicide were not unheard of. Some slaves were treated so badly that death was a welcome relief. In 1856, a Cuthbert slave belonging to Lizzie McWilliams took her own life by swallowing strychnine. When threatened with a whip, an Alabama slave decided that enough was enough. Crying out that he would take no more beatings and knowing he risked death, the desperate slave turned and ran. Seconds later he was shot to death by his overseer.[34]

Occasionally, the slaves turned against and killed their oppressors. One valley slave set fire to the riverboat *Van Buren* after being flogged. Passengers and crew alike jumped into the Chattahoochee's churning waters to escape the flames. Two people drowned. The survivors were stranded in a swamp for four days before being rescued by a passing steamer. In 1849, a Chambers County slave shot his master. Near Notasulga in Macon County, an overseer named James Davis was "violently attacked with a knife and cut to pieces" by a slave on the N. W. Cocke plantation.[35]

Such brutality on the part of slaves was rare. More often they were on the receiving end of violence. Slaves were defined as private property by both state and federal courts. As such, they were generally subject to their masters' absolute authority and to whatever controls the owners chose to employ. As one member of the Georgia Supreme Court said, "Subordination can only be maintained by the right to give moderate correction—a right similar to that which exists in the father over his children." There were, however, enforceable laws forbidding parents to murder their children. What slight legal protection slaves had was largely ineffective since, in practice, the definition of "moderate correction" was left almost entirely to the slaveholder. "Should death ensue by accident while this slave is thus receiving moderate correction," recalled one visitor to the lower Chattahoochee Valley, "the constitution of Georgia kindly denominates the offence justifiable homicide." The Reverend W. B. Allen, a former Russell County slave, personally knew slaves who were beaten to death for no other reason than being off the plantation without written permission. Other offenses that might result in capital punishment included lying, loitering, stealing, and "talking back to—'sassing'—a white person."[36]

Because slaves had monetary value, death as a direct result of discipline was unusual. More often, the objective of physical punishment was to inflict as much pain as possible without doing permanent damage. Scarring or mutilation might decrease the slave's resale value or ability to work.

Wide leather straps or perforated wooden paddles were more common than whips. They were just as painful but left no permanent marks that might identify the slave as a troublemaker to potential buyers. In 1859, a student at East Alabama Male College (now Auburn University) wrote home advising his mother not to purchase a slave that obviously had "been very much abused." [37]

Overseers frequently administered beatings to slaves in the "buck" or "rolling Jim" positions. In each case the slave was stripped naked and bound tight. Rias Body, a Harris County slave, remembered the buck as "making the Negro squat, running a stout stick under his bended knee, and then tying his hands firmly to the stick—between the knees. Then the lash was laid on his back parts." A Russell County slave recalled that with the rolling Jim the slave was "stretched on his stomach at full length on a large log, about eight feet long. Into holes bored in the end of this log, wooden pegs were driven. The feet were securely tied to one set of these pegs—at one end of the log, and the hands to the pegs at the other end. The victim was then ready to be worked on." [38]

Another common method of punishment was to string slaves up by their thumbs, with only their toes touching the ground, and whip them. The slave might be "further tormented by having his wounds 'doctored' with salt and red pepper." Rhodus Walton of Stewart County was regularly brutalized by an overseer "whose favorite form of punishment was to take a man (or woman) to the edge of the plantation where a rail fence was located. His head was then placed between two rails so that escape was impossible and he was whipped until the overseer was exhausted. This was an almost daily occurrence, administered on the slightest provocation." After recalling the variety of tortures inflicted on slaves, one Columbus freedman told an interviewer in the 1930s, "Sir, you can never know what some slaves endured." [39]

Georgia and Alabama slave codes defined the limitations of life for slaves far beyond their status as personal property. No slave could legally carry a gun, own property, travel without a pass, testify against whites in a court of law, or learn to read or write. Slave marriages had no legal status, and slave gatherings, even for religious services, were forbidden without a white person present. In the words of historian James Oakes, "It was like turning the Bill of Rights upside down." [40]

Despite their portrayal of slaves as happy and contented, slaveholders lived in constant fear of slave rebellion. One of the most terrifying aspects of the slaves' miserable existence was the slave patrol, designed to guard against the possibility of insurrection. Justices of the peace in most county precincts assigned companies of white men to patrol duty. In some counties, slaves found away from their plantations without written permission could be given up to twenty lashes on the spot. In Barbour County, the limit was thirty-nine.[41] Though service in slave patrols was often compulsory, some took a perverse pleasure in riding down slaves. Decades after the war, W. H. Andrews fondly remembered the excitement of serving on a slave patrol in Early County:

> There were patrol gangs in every community. I belonged to a gang of six . . . and sure we were a jolly band of night riders. . . . We usually rode on Saturday nights, as that was the time the negroes wanted to meet at some quarter for an all night dance. We would hitch our horses some distance from the quarter and try to slip up on them, but they always had out sentries and when one of them saw us would yell "Buckra, Buckra!" which was like throwing a rock into a covey of partridges. . . . The next thing was a chase. Rube Gilmore owned a pack of six young hounds that he was training to trail negroes with, and they were put on the trail. Now, if there is any finer sport than riding after hounds on a hot trail under full cry, I have never found it.[42]

Slaveholders feared an educated slave nearly as much as an armed slave. As early as 1832, the Alabama legislature passed an act making it illegal to teach slaves "to spell, read or write, upon penalty of not less than two hundred and fifty dollars nor more than five hundred." Georgia enacted a similar law the following year. And slaveholders themselves might subject their chattel to severe punishment for the crime of literacy. Louis Meadows, born a slave in Russell County, remembered that slaves on the Porter Meadows plantation were whipped if they even looked at a book. On other plantations, punishment could be even more severe. Lucindy Jurdon recalled that on her owner's plantation in what is now Lee County, slaves might lose a forefinger for trying to read or write. Another former Lee County slave, Abraham Chambers, seemed surprised when asked about literacy among slaves. "Learn to read? Honey, you better read and write them cotton rows." [43]

Besides the constant threat of physical punishment, masters usually found the family to be the most effective means of keeping slaves under control. Any slave might be provoked beyond the point of regard for his or her own safety and attempt to fight or escape, but when slaveholders threatened to punish family members, slaves were more likely to hold their anger in check. Though marriages within slave communities were the

norm, cemented by such ceremonies as jumping the broom, they had no
recognition in law. That would have established a state-sanctioned bond
between members of slave families that implicitly infringed on the property rights of the owner, specifically the right to deal with and dispose of
his property as he saw fit. Nevertheless, masters allowed and even encouraged slaves to marry at an early age and raise children on the plantations.
At the same time, owners used a variety of means to drive home the point
that even within the slave family, the master was still master. Some personally presided over marriage ceremonies. Others, like Peter Heard in
Troup County, did not even allow parents to name their own children, re-
serving that privilege for themselves.[44]

In naming the children of slave women, many slaveholders were actually exercising their own parental rights. For a planter to have any number
of mistresses among his slaves was not uncommon. Some masters viewed
rape as another method of enforcing psychological dominance within the
slave community. Others did it simply because they viewed slaves as property to be used at the owner's pleasure. Whatever the motive, slaves of light
complexion were present on nearly every plantation. In 1833, the *Columbus Enquirer* ran an advertisement offering twenty dollars for the return
of a runaway slave named Mabin. The paper described him as "a bright
mulatto, with grey eyes—hair straight and sandy. . . . He will pass for a
white man where he is not known." A former Alabama slave noted that
those of fair skin often received special treatment from the master, even to
the point of living in the slaveholder's house.[45]

Mary Chesnut, the wife of one of the largest planters in the South, wrote,
"Like the patriarchs of old our men live all in one house with their wives
and their concubines, and the mulattoes one sees in every family exactly
resemble the white children—and every lady tells you who is the father
of all the mulatto children in everybody's household, but those in her own
she seems to think drop from the clouds, or pretends so to think." With
the legal and political status of white women only marginally better than
that of slaves, plantation mistresses had little choice but to endure the
infidelity of their husbands. In referring to Harriet Beecher Stowe's *Uncle
Tom's Cabin,* Chesnut suggested that the author "did not hit the sorest
spot. She makes [Simon] Legree a bachelor." When the slaves finally gained
their freedom, a planter's wife in Barbour County said of Lincoln, "he has
freed us, too."[46]

No matter how the children were sired, masters usually encouraged slave
women to have as many as possible. More children, of course, meant more
field hands, but they also gave the slaveholder an effective tool of control.
Not only did slaves fear punishment for family members, but there was also

the additional concern that they might be sold at any time. As the slaves well knew, an owner's threat to sell spouses or children was no idle one. One valley observer wrote that "such separations as these are quite common, and appear to be no more thought of, by those who enforce them, than the separation of a calf from its brute parent." [47]

The slaves' monetary value made threats of selling family members even more menacing. In the 1850s, slave prices were on the rise. A field hand could cost over a thousand dollars, and a skilled slave was more. One ex-slave remembered slave traders driving groups of children to market "the same as they would a herd of cattle." [48] Slaves were not anxious to see their families, especially their children, put through such misery and were less likely to escape since that too would mean permanent separation from their loved ones.

By the mid–nineteenth century, slavery based on African ancestry was a firmly entrenched institution in the South. But it had not always been so. Two centuries earlier there had been no distinctions in law or custom between white and black servants. In fact, the term *slave* was applied to whites as well as to blacks. Like white servants, blacks typically gained freedom after serving a number of years in what was legally defined as indentured servitude. The servants themselves were, as Stampp put it, "remarkably unconcerned about their visible physical differences." They were very familiar with the confines of their class system, but rigid caste lines based on race were unknown. Black and white servants worked together, played together, lived together, ran away together, and married each other. The brand of racism all too common among later generations was absent in the seventeenth century. [49]

That began to change in the eighteenth century as the upper classes, fearing rebellion from below, took steps to divide poor whites and blacks both socially and economically. As colonial planters well knew, the threat of rebellion was very real. The great majority of southerners were servants or slaves. Most of the rest were landless tenants who were practically slaves themselves. And there were a few small landholding farmers who held mostly poorer lands that the gentry did not want. None could vote or hold office. Those privileges were reserved for the wealthy. In 1676, these various groups in Virginia united against their oppressors in what came to be known as Bacon's Rebellion. They established fortifications all along the James River, marched on the capital at Jamestown, and came close to seizing power in the colony before they were put down by Crown forces. Among the last rebels to surrender was a band of eighty blacks and twenty whites. [50]

Bacon's Rebellion sent shock waves through the ranks of the ruling classes. Many feared that some such future insurrection, perhaps larger and better organized, might actually succeed. What could be done to avert such a calamity? The strategy adopted was something akin to the military maxim "divide and conquer." In the words of historian Edmund Morgan, "for those with eyes to see, there was an obvious lesson in the rebellion. Resentment of an alien race might be more powerful than resentment of an upper class." [51] To create a social distance between poor whites and blacks, and hence a feeling of superiority on the part of whites, would make the two groups less likely to unite in rebellion.

In the late seventeenth and early eighteenth centuries, colonial legislatures throughout British North America passed a series of laws designed to do just that. Interracial marriages were outlawed. Penal codes were amended to deal more harshly with blacks than with whites. Blacks became legally defined first as "servants for life" and later as slaves outright. The Virginia assembly mandated that white servants, upon completion of their term of indenture, be given fifty acres of land, ten bushels of corn, thirty shillings, and a musket worth at least twenty shillings. In urban areas, only whites could hold certain occupations, such as carpenter, blacksmith, mechanic, and the like. [52] None of these measures was enough to qualify lower-class whites for voting or holding office, which would not come for another century. But these changes did instill in whites of all classes a sense that they were somehow better than those with even a drop of African blood—though many of them had a few such drops in their own bloodlines whether they knew it or not.

The strategy worked even better than the elites had hoped. Racism, they found, was a self-perpetuating thing passed on from generation to generation, keeping the poor divided and easier to control. Lower-class whites still resented the elites who kept them politically powerless and heaped on them a disproportionate tax burden. There were any number of eighteenth-century insurrections aimed at redressing these grievances— Shays's Rebellion, the Whiskey Rebellion, and the Regulator Movement among them. Slaves too occasionally rose in rebellion. But never again did poor whites and blacks unite against their common oppressors as they had in 1676.

Ironically, the eighteenth century was also a time of changing attitudes toward slavery. The Scientific Revolution had shown that there were natural laws governing the physical universe. Some reasoned that perhaps there were also natural laws governing human interaction. It may even be that people had natural rights. The most basic of these, as Thomas Jefferson wrote, would surely be "life, liberty, and the pursuit of happiness." [53]

If so, was not slavery a violation of human rights? The idea troubled many planters of Jefferson's generation, schooled as they were in Enlightenment philosophy. Most, like Jefferson himself, were not willing to give up their slaves, but they did not defend slavery on moral grounds. Some, like George Washington and Virginia's archconservative John Randolph of Roanoke, freed their slaves in their wills.

Aside from the moral issues involved, many Americans of that era saw slavery as an economic dead end. The institution thrived only in the tobacco fields of the Chesapeake region and the rice country of coastal Carolina and Georgia. As the nation expanded, slavery would become proportionally less important to the nation's economy and would eventually die a natural death. But the development of a cotton engine (or gin) in the 1790s changed the situation. The cotton gin became the vehicle by which slavery was carried south and west across South Carolina and Georgia into Florida, Alabama, Mississippi, Arkansas, Louisiana, and finally Texas. Not surprisingly, planter attitudes toward slavery changed with the institution's growing economic importance.[54]

That change did not occur overnight. Antislavery sentiment in the South remained strong and openly expressed into the early 1830s. Any number of abolitionist societies were active in Georgia and Alabama. To discourage the use of slave labor, some groups paid above-market prices for cotton produced by free labor. Alabama editor James G. Birney started an abolitionist newspaper in the state. In 1827 the Alabama legislature passed a law prohibiting the importation of slaves from other states, and at every session throughout the decade members proposed legislation favoring gradual emancipation.[55]

But this was also the era of Indian removal from the South. In 1827 Georgia forced out its few remaining Creeks, and nine years later Alabama did the same. The early 1830s saw the Choctaws and Chickasaws driven out. And in 1838 the Cherokees were herded westward on the Trail of Tears following the discovery of gold on their land. In 1842 the Seminoles became the last of the southern nations to be violently relocated to land that they were promised would be theirs for "as long as grass grows or water runs." At the time it was simply called Indian Territory. Today it is the state of Oklahoma.[56]

Indian removal completed the transition in planter attitudes begun a generation earlier by the cotton gin. Not only did they have the technology and labor force with which to make cotton king, they now had the land on which to do it. Slaveholders no longer viewed slavery as a temporary evil but held it forth as a positive good for both master and slave. Ideas regarding slavery held by the Founding Fathers, they said, were completely erroneous. In the words of Alexander H. Stephens, a preeminent Georgia politician and vice president of the Confederacy, "the prevailing ideas entertained by . . . the leading statesmen at the time of the formation of the old Constitution were that the enslavement of the African was in violation of the laws of nature; that it was wrong in *principle,* socially, morally and politically. It was an evil they knew not well how to deal with, but the general opinion of the men of that day was that somehow or other in the order of Providence, the institution would be evanescent and pass away. . . . Those ideas, however, were fundamentally wrong." But the slaveholders' new position presented them with a serious problem. Just a quarter of southern whites owned slaves, and outside the United States chattel slavery survived only in Brazil, Cuba, Puerto Rico, Dutch Guiana, and parts of Africa.[57] How were the masters to guarantee the survival of slavery in a society where most people did not own slaves and in a world where slaveholders were a dying breed?

In the 1830s planters launched a campaign designed to educate their fellow southerners, and the world, on the virtues of slavery. First, planters argued, the world could not do without southern cotton. English and northern mills depended too much upon it. Benjamin Hill of Troup County, later a senator in the Confederate Congress, insisted that "the world can never give up slavery until it is ready to give up clothing." Besides, planters said, chattel slaves on southern plantations were much better off than "wage slaves" in northern factories. They were better housed and better clothed and did lighter work than laborers in the North—indeed, than laborers anywhere in the world. They lived in cottages that were, in their humble way, as comfortable as the master's house. After the day's chores were done, the slaves ate a fine supper of meat and vegetables, sang and danced, played the banjo, and went to bed contented and happy. People of African descent were happy in slavery because it was their "natural and normal condition." They were, in the words of one apologist for slavery, "utterly incapable of self-culture and self-government." No less a figure than the eminent Harvard scientist Louis Agassiz confirmed that Africans were a "degraded and degenerate race" lacking the intelligence necessary for independent thought and action.[58]

Dr. Samuel A. Cartwright of New Orleans attributed that lack of intelligence to small brains and a disease peculiar to those of African descent, which he called *dysesthesia:* "It is the defective atmospherization of the blood," he said, "conjoined with a deficiency of cerebral matter in the cranium . . . that is the true cause of that debasement of mind which has rendered the people of Africa unable to take care of themselves." If slaves lacked intelligence, could not care for themselves, and were happy in slavery, why then did so many try to escape? Cartwright had an answer for that too—*drapetomania,* or "the insane desire to run away."[59]

Other supporters of slavery turned to a historical defense. The classical civilizations of Greece and Rome, the greatest the world had ever seen, had large slave populations. The institution must therefore necessarily be a hallmark of high culture. James Henry Hammond of South Carolina argued that the existence of slavery had always been necessary to make possible an upper class that "leads progress, civilization, and refinement."[60]

And, of course, there was the biblical defense. How could slavery be an evil institution when the patriarchs of the Old Testament had owned slaves? Were these not men ordained by God? Were their institutions, including slavery, not holy? Was not slavery the result of Noah's curse on his younger son, Ham, and all his descendants, whose skin was assumed to have turned black as a mark of the curse? In the New Testament, did not both the apostles Paul and Peter make it clear that servants should be obedient to their masters? The Reverend Thornton Stringfellow, in his 1856 defense of slavery, argued that Christ himself "recognized this institution as one that was lawful among men." Stringfellow cited 1 Tim. 6, in which Paul, after counting masters as "worthy of all honor," warns that "if any man teach otherwise, and consent not to wholesome words, even the words of our Lord Jesus Christ, and to the doctrine which is according to godliness, he is proud, knowing nothing, but doting about questions and strifes of words, whereof cometh envy, strife, railings, evil surmisings." There could be no question: slavery was a hallowed institution ordained by God himself. Opposition to it was nothing more than "evil surmisings."[61]

Throughout the South, clergymen emerged as some of the most eager and influential allies of the planter class in defending slavery. Those who held that Scripture must be taken literally had been for some time disturbed by a strong opposing trend in Christianity. By the early nineteenth century, science had clearly shown that the Bible contained many factual errors and omissions. The sun did not revolve around the earth, as the story of Joshua suggested, and the earth was much older than the Bible implied. Furthermore, suggestions were beginning to surface that plants and animals might not have been created in their present form but had somehow evolved. In any case, hundreds of species had obviously become extinct. Many influential clergymen and laity began to argue that the Bible must be understood symbolically, not literally. Thomas Jefferson predicted that within a generation most southerners would abandon the literalist doctrines in favor of a more enlightened Unitarianism.[62]

But if the Bible was to be interpreted symbolically, what might that mean for its treatment of slavery? Was that to be taken symbolically as well? Could Paul have been using the relationship of servant to master as a metaphor for the relationship of humanity to God? No, such symbolism would not do. If Scripture was to be used effectively as a moral defense of slavery, it must be taken literally—not just in part, but in its entirety. As the slaveholding South changed its attitude toward slavery's morality in the early nineteenth century, it became ever more closely tied to a literalist view of the Bible.[63]

Nowhere was the union of religion and slavery more evident than in the popular press. As tensions between North and South rose during the 1850s, slavery's editorial apologists increasingly relied on divine sanction to reassure their patrons and justify the South's "peculiar institution." In an 1856 issue, the *Cuthbert Reporter* reminded its readers that where threats to slavery were concerned, there was "no need for the South to be alarmed. . . . She did not create slavery—God did it. His law is immutable until time shall cease to be."[64] What better security could slavery have than the eternal word of almighty God?

As much weight as the biblical argument carried among a God-fearing people, the most effective tactic adopted by slaveholders was their encouragement of racist fears among whites. By playing on these fears, slavery's defenders hoped to make all whites feel they had a stake in preserving the slave system whether they owned slaves or not. Poor whites especially were encouraged to think of what slavery's demise in the South might mean for them. No longer would they be in a position of social superiority to the slaves. Poor whites would occupy the bottom rung on the class ladder along with blacks, who would be their equals. One Columbus man stated the case clearly: "It is African slavery that makes every white man in some sense a lord. . . . Here the division is between white free men and black slaves, and every white is, and feels that he is a MAN." At a political rally in Colquitt during the 1856 presidential campaign, J. F. M. Caldwell delivered an hour-long speech in which he stressed the social importance of slavery for poor whites. According to Isaac Bush, who chaired the rally and was a member of one of the area's most politically active planter families, Caldwell's "arguments on the slavery question, and the reason why *poor* men at the South, above all others, ought to be enlisted under the banner of Southern Rights, were convincing."[65]

In many ways, the planters argued, slavery was good, not just for masters, but for slaves, poor whites, the North, and the world. It was, after all, an institution ordained by God himself. "Whoever doubts that it is a blessing," wrote one apostle of slavery, "has no right to hold any opinion at all on the subject." [66] Other proslavery men said the same—and meant it. By the 1830s it was becoming dangerous to express antislavery views in the South. Those who opposed slavery either kept their opinions hidden or were driven out. The Grimké sisters of South Carolina, Sarah and Angelina, fled to the North, where they were active in both the abolitionist and women's rights movements. James G. Birney left Alabama to form the Liberty Party, the nation's first antislavery political organization, and in 1840 he became its first presidential candidate.

Intolerance on the slavery question and the use of religion to bolster it had a particularly chilling effect on southern institutions of higher learning. One southern newspaper editor boldly declared that "the professorships should be sifted and weeded of those who may covertly circulate opinions not in sympathy with our social institutions." Horace Holley, president of Kentucky's Transylvania University and a religious liberal, was removed from his post. The free-thinking president of South Carolina College, Thomas Cooper, was likewise driven from office. Professor Benjamin Hendrick lost the chair of agricultural chemistry at his alma mater, the University of North Carolina, because he dared express unorthodox views on slavery. The university justified Hendrick's removal on the grounds that his "political opinions . . . are not those entertained by any member of this body." Even the University of Virginia, founded by Thomas Jefferson as a haven of free thought and inquiry, introduced sectarian religious ceremonies. [67]

In less than a generation, southern academia lost many of its finest intellectuals. Those who remained dared not challenge the view that slavery was a positive good and that the King James Bible was God's literal word. To the contrary, men like Matthew Fontaine Maury—aristocratic Virginian, pioneer oceanographer, and founder of the U.S. Weather Bureau—upheld the Bible as the greatest book of science. In responding to opponents who viewed the Bible as "no authority in matters of science," Maury proclaimed, "the Bible is authority for everything it touches." [68]

Though religion, racism, pride, and fear were all used by planters to bolster slavery at home and justify it abroad, the driving force behind their proslavery campaign was the same one that caused their change of attitude in the first place—economic self-interest. Some planters, like Hill, were candid enough to admit it. "In our early history," he said, "the Southern statesmen were antislavery in feeling. So were Washington, Jefferson, Madison, Randolph, and many of that day who never studied the argument of the cotton gin, nor heard the eloquent productions of the great Mississippi Valley. Now our people not only see the justice of slavery, but its providence too."[69] Cotton, cultivated by slave labor, gave planters their economic power, and that power gave planters the political strength with which to control the South's lower classes and silence or exile slavery's opponents.

Though all white males could vote, and many did, there was little for them to decide. Then as now, any successful bid for high political office depended as much on money as votes, and planters controlled the money. Both major parties, Whig and Democrat, centered more on personalities than issues, and both represented slaveholding interests. Slave rebellions and abolitionism were always central campaign themes, with each candidate trying to "out-nigger" the other. But by the mid-1830s, slavery's morality was no longer a topic of political debate in the South.[70]

The influence of planter wealth in politics was not lost on the lower classes. As one yeoman observed, the planter "used money [to win votes] whenever he could. This fact usually elected him." In Columbus, a process of buying votes known as "penning" was so common that it was called the "peculiar institution of Muscogee County." On the day before an election, campaign workers would round up men off the streets, lodge them in local hotels, get them drunk, and then march them to the polls the next morning. The party with the largest "pen" usually won the election. Obviously, these men felt that their right to vote meant very little in elections that primarily represented upper-class interests. In his study of antebellum Georgia's political culture, Donald DeBats made a similar observation: "Far from encouraging citizen participation in the party system, the leaders of both parties discouraged grassroots politics. . . . Beyond the simple casting of a ballot, the role of the citizen in the party system was passive by design." Some party bosses tried to keep poorer citizens out of the political process entirely with a poll tax.[71]

Planter control of southern politics was nearly absolute. One southerner observed that although the majority of those eligible to vote owned no slaves, "they have never yet had any part or lot in framing the laws under which they live. There is no legislation except for the benefit of slavery and slaveholders." Although many nonslaveholders held high public office, they were nearly always backed directly or indirectly by planter money, and some even married into planter families. During the 1850s, though the proportion of slaveholders in the general population was falling, their numbers in southern state legislatures were on the rise.[72] It seemed that planter dominance of the South was secure and that slavery as an institution was secure as well. But even as slaveholders consolidated their political control, cracks began to appear at the base of the South's social pyramid. The fissures had always been there, suppressed and controlled, but as wealth became concentrated in fewer hands and opportunities for economic advancement were increasingly closed to yeomen and poor whites, those cracks began to grow.

Antislavery sentiment never completely died in the South despite efforts to wipe it out. Some whites continued to view slavery as a moral evil, others opposed it on economic grounds, and still others opposed slavery simply because they were too poor ever to own slaves themselves. Whatever the reason, antislavery feeling was on the rise in the late 1850s. And though it was very risky, a few brave souls were even willing to speak out or take action. Perhaps the most dangerous way in which southerners expressed displeasure with slavery was through their participation in the Underground Railroad. Thousands of sympathetic whites, like William Allen of Troup County, wrote fake passes for slaves. Others gave them transportation. Some even turned their homes into safe houses along the Underground Railroad. The system could not have operated effectively without the cooperation of southern whites.[73]

One of the most outspoken southern opponents of slavery was Hinton Rowan Helper. The son of a yeoman farmer in North Carolina, Helper moved to New York, where he wrote what one historian has called "the most important single book, in terms of its political impact, that has ever been published in the United States." In *The Impending Crisis of the South,* published in 1857, Helper argued vigorously that the "lords of the lash are not only absolute masters of the blacks . . . but they are also the oracles and arbiters of all nonslaveholding whites, whose freedom is merely nominal, and whose unparalleled illiteracy and degradation is purposely and fiendishly perpetuated."[74]

Slavery, Helper pointed out, benefited only a few. Its very existence kept most white southerners in ignorance and poverty. The region's economic development was so inadequate that it was nothing more than a colony of the North, providing raw materials and buying back manufactured goods.

The North is the Mecca of our merchants, and to it they must and do make two pilgrimages per annum—one in the spring and one in the fall. All our commercial, mechanical, manufactural, and literary supplies come from there. We want Bibles, brooms, buckets and books, and we go to the North; we want pens, ink, paper, wafer and envelopes, and we go to the North; we want shoes, hats, handkerchiefs, umbrellas and pocket knives, and we go to the North; we want furniture, crockery, glassware and pianos, and we go to the North; we want toys, primers, school books, fashionable apparel, machinery, medicines, tombstones, and a thousand other things, and we go to the North for them all. Instead of keeping our money in circulation at home by patronizing our own mechanics, manufacturers, and laborers, we send it all away to the North, and there it remains; it never falls into our hands again. . . . Slavery, and nothing but slavery, has retarded the progress and prosperity of our portion of the Union . . . [and] made us a tributary to the North.[75]

Planters had good reason to fear Helper's impact. They knew very well, perhaps better than the yeomen, that there was much truth in Helper's argument. It was, after all, the planters who bought many of the items imported from the North. All they had to do was look at the books on their shelves, the silverware on their tables, and the tools on their plantations to verify the accuracy of Helper's statements. With a circulation larger than any other nonfiction work of its day, *Impending Crisis* was matched only by *Uncle Tom's Cabin* as a target of slavery's defenders. They publicly burned copies of *Impending Crisis* in Greensboro, North Carolina. One Methodist preacher spent a year in jail for owning the book. Three of Helper's readers in Arkansas were hanged.[76]

Despite inherent dangers both for antislavery writers and their audience, Helper was not alone in pointing out the economic drawbacks of slavery. For those who looked beyond the Old South's aristocratic facade, the system's disadvantages were obvious enough. Like other visitors of his time, Englishman James Stirling, who passed through the lower Chattahoochee Valley in the 1850s, wondered why the southern states were lagging behind in "development and prosperity." He could find only one answer—slavery. "When Southern statesmen count up the gains of slavery," warned Stirling, "let them not forget also to count its cost. They may depend upon it, there is a heavy 'per contra' to the profits of niggerdom."[77]

Not only did slavery hinder economic growth, but the concentration on cotton production forced the South to import foodstuffs. Georgia's comptroller-general lamented that, with regard to food, the state was "every day becoming more dependent upon those 'not of us.'" Livestock production was declining. The corn crop was stagnant. In just ten years, the oat crop had dropped by more than half. One Eufaula newspaper complained about huge shipments of high-priced foodstuffs from the Midwest coming into the valley. The editorial blamed planters who, more concerned with growing cotton, preferred to import produce rather than to grow it. Another valley paper urged planters to grow more corn and less cotton. Such pleas accomplished little. During 1861, southwest Georgia alone imported at least half a million bushels of corn.[78]

Only a few years earlier, Helper had calculated that the value of the North's food production outstripped that of the South by almost $45 million annually. In light of that fact alone, he said, "the first and most sacred duty of every southerner who has the honor and the interest of his country at heart is to declare himself an unqualified and uncompromising abolitionist." Helper even suggested that nonslaveholders form a southern abolitionist political party and sweep proslavery politicians out of office. But as a class they had neither the leisure nor the capital to take a leading role in politics.[79]

Still, growing discontent within the Cotton Kingdom, of little concern to the planters only a decade earlier, was by the 1850s causing panic among many of them. As if to confirm Helper's arguments, one planter asked, "If the poor whites realized that slavery kept them poor, would they not vote it down?" Many were beginning to fear the possibility. How could support for slavery be maintained among poor whites if they owned no slaves and had no prospects of ever owning any? Some suggested state laws mandating that each white family be given at least one slave. Others demanded a slave for every white person. The *Eufaula Express* suggested reopening the slave trade from Africa, with or without the approval of Congress, to bring the price of slaves down. If slavery was constitutional, then so was the slave trade. Any laws restricting it should be ignored.[80]

Those who took a larger view realized that the problem was not just the expense of slaves but the lack of land. There was only so much prime farmland to go around, and the more affluent slaveholders already had most of it. Such people saw the future security of slavery in terms of territorial expansion. To them it was clear—slavery must expand or die. That issue would dominate national politics for more than a decade.

CHAPTER

2

I Don't Want Any War

The issue of slavery's expansion was not a new one. It was older than the nation itself. Shortly after Georgia's founding in 1732, the trustees excluded a number of evils from their colony, among them hard liquor, lawyers, and slavery. But they did not remain outlawed for long. There was too much money to be made. Pressure from South Carolina rice planters to permit slavery in Georgia was constant, and slaves were smuggled into the colony despite the trustees. They finally gave in and lifted the ban in 1750. By the time of the American Revolution a quarter century later, nearly half of Georgia's forty thousand inhabitants were slaves.[1]

At the same time, chattel slavery as a viable economic institution was dying in the North. In the 1780s individual states began to abolish slavery within their borders. New York became the last state north of the Mason-Dixon line to outlaw slavery in 1827. Congress too made an early stand against the expansion of slavery. In a move suggested by Thomas Jefferson, the Northwest Ordinance of 1787 permanently excluded slavery from territory that later became the states of the western Great Lakes.[2] South of the Ohio River and the Mason-Dixon line, however, the cotton gin and progressive removal of Native Americans from rich cotton lands gave slavery an economic vitality that grew in strength with each new slave state added to the Union. Opponents of slavery both North and South wondered where—or if—it would end.

Congress reached a temporary settlement of the question in 1820 with the Missouri Compromise. Missouri was admitted to the Union as a slave state and Maine as a free state, thus preserving the balance of free and slave states in the Senate. More significantly, a line extending from the southern border of Missouri to the Rocky Mountains (then the western limit of the United States) established a boundary between slavery and freedom. All future states created north of the line would be free. Those south of the line would be slave. The compromise settled the issue as far as the federal government was concerned. There was even a gag rule forbidding any official discussion of slavery in Congress. But as the aggressively expansive United States pushed its way to the Pacific Ocean, politicians could not ignore the slavery question for long.

When the United States took the upper half of Mexico in 1848 following a two-year war of conquest, slavery was again thrust onto the nation's political stage. Mexico had abolished slavery two decades earlier. Would it now be reintroduced in the new U.S. territories? Many, like President Zachary Taylor, hoped the government could continue to ignore the question entirely. But in 1849 California requested admission to the Union as a free state, and Congress was forced to address the issue. The next year California entered the Union under the Compromise of 1850, giving the free states a two-seat advantage in the Senate. As compensation, slaveholders got the Fugitive Slave Act mandating the return of slaves who escaped to the North. As for the remaining territories of the Mexican cession, "popular sovereignty" would prevail. Voters in both the New Mexico and Utah territories would make the decision on slavery themselves.

Reaction to the Compromise of 1850 in politically active circles was mixed throughout the South. Slaveholders liked the Fugitive Slave Act but were concerned that a loss of parity in the Senate would relegate them to second-class status in national politics. Popular sovereignty made slavery's expansion into the territories questionable. Many believed that withdrawal from the Union would be a better option and had thought so for a long time. As early as the 1830s, some were convinced that slavery could never be completely safe within the Union. One Milledgeville, Georgia, newspaper, ironically called the *Federal Union,* said in 1830, "The moment any improper interference is attempted with our slaves, we say, let the Union be dissolved." [3]

In 1850 many slaveholders and their allies, especially those in the press, denounced popular sovereignty as improper interference. With its October 15, 1850, issue, the *Eufaula Democrat* boldly changed its name to *Spirit of the South.* The paper labeled southerners who supported compromise "submissionists" and took as its motto "Equality in the Union, or Independence out of it." The *Columbus Sentinel's* rhetoric was even more inflammatory: "We despise the Union and the North as we do hell itself." [4]

Barbour County, Alabama, was a major center of opposition to the Compromise of 1850. Soon after its enactment, 150 county residents signed a petition calling on the governor to convene the state legislature for a discussion of secession. An association of Eufaula citizens, composed mostly of younger men in their late twenties and early thirties, demanded the immediate formation of a secession convention. On July 25, 1850, a mass meeting took place at Abbeville, the seat of Henry County, to protest the compromise. According to one account, nearly three thousand people from southeast Alabama and southwest Georgia attended. Several speakers were from Eufaula, including John Gill Shorter, who would become Alabama's governor in 1861. Resolutions adopted at the meeting called the act entirely unworthy of being called a compromise and urged all southerners to oppose it.[5]

When Alexander Stephens and Robert Toombs, two Whig supporters of the compromise, showed up for a debate in Columbus, they were met by a hostile crowd and burning effigies. When Toombs insulted the assembly, claiming he wore the only clean shirt ever seen at a gathering of Democrats, pandemonium erupted. By one account, "knives and pistols appeared and fist fights broke out in the crowd." With some degree of understatement the *Columbus Times* reported, "Toombs and Stephens have operated like sparks on a tinder box in this community. . . . We deem it fortunate there was no serious accident to report."[6]

Despite such violent opposition, there was considerable support for the compromise among valley residents. Citizens of Henry County held a rally in Lawrenceville to demonstrate their support for the document, and even an opponent conceded that those in attendance were "quite respectable in character." Another procompromise mass meeting in Montgomery had as its featured speaker James Abercrombie of Russell County. This assembly maintained a "firm conviction that the issue of secession, now before the public, on account of the late compromise acts of Congress, was in no wise demanded, either on the score of justice, policy, or the honor of the South." The *Columbus Enquirer*'s editor had some reservations about the compromise but was generally supportive. Another Columbus man, Samuel W. Flournoy, pleaded with Congressman Howell Cobb to visit the city and help "silence the disunionists, secessionists, and that whole breed of croaking agitators with whom we have to contend."[7]

Alabama's governor was not entirely happy with the compromise but considered the matter settled nevertheless. No popular vote on the issue was held in Alabama and no convention was called. Secession would almost certainly have been voted down in any case since pro-Union candidates carried the state elections in 1851. Georgia did hold a popular vote for delegates to a convention, which the unionists won by an overwhelming 46,000 to 24,000 margin. When the delegates met in December 1850 they voted to accept the compromise but warned that states' rights—

specifically rights involving slavery—took priority over the Union. In what came to be called the Georgia Platform, the convention declared Georgia ready to secede if Congress restricted the domestic slave trade, refused to admit new slave states to the Union, or interfered with slavery in the territories. Furthermore, the convention insisted that the Union's preservation depended on "the faithful execution of the Fugitive Slave Bill by the proper authorities." Given the ambiguities of popular sovereignty, not to mention the ambivalence of northern officials toward enforcement of the Fugitive Slave Act, the Georgia Platform was a sure formula for the Union's eventual collapse. John Cochran, a Eufaula lawyer and recently defeated secessionist candidate for Congress, predicted as much: "I do not think the Union will be dissolved immediately," he wrote in 1851, "but I believe, and rejoice in the belief, that at this moment there is amongst us here a leaven of disunion, which by a more or less rapid, but perceptibly certain process, will leaven the whole lump." [8]

Popular sovereignty's inherent complications became clear soon after passage of the Kansas-Nebraska Act in 1854. In exchange for southern congressional votes favoring organization of these territories through which northerners hoped to build the first transcontinental railroad, Kansas was opened to the possibility of slavery under popular sovereignty. Kansas actually lay north of the old Missouri Compromise line, which would have barred slavery from the area. But northern congressmen wanted their railroad and they needed southern votes to get it. Repeal of the Missouri Compromise was the price for those votes. It seemed to many at the time a small price to pay. Most northern legislators were certain there was no real danger of Kansas becoming a slave state since its geography was not suitable for large-scale cotton agriculture.

But Kansas was just west of Missouri, a slave state. "Free Soilers" and abolitionists rushed to get settlers into Kansas as quickly as possible. Proslavery men did the same. In Barbour County, Jefferson Buford and Henry Clayton, both of the so-called "Eufaula Regency," financed proslavery expeditions to Kansas. They provided settlers with wagons, horses, oxen, and, most importantly, land. In exchange, the new arrivals were expected to vote for a proslavery state constitution.[9]

Not all Barbour County planters were so enthusiastic about the project. Though he contributed financially to Buford's effort out of friendship, John Horry Dent feared its consequences. "Two such opposite elements," he wrote, "meeting with opposite aims will apt to result in bitter strife and contentions which will create in the two sections of this union a bitter sectional animosity." Dent's words were prophetic. When Kansas held its first elections, thousands of "border ruffians" crossed over from Missouri to vote, giving the proslavery faction a victory. The territorial governor called the election a fraud but let the results stand. The new proslavery legislature quickly expelled its few antislavery members and proposed a state constitution allowing slavery. Under the new government, to question the legality of slavery in Kansas was a felony. To aid or encourage an escaping slave was a capital offense. In response, antislavery men formed their own government and drew up a constitution excluding both slavery and free blacks from the territory. As Dent had predicted, the controversy was by no means limited to political bickering. A proslavery raid on the town of Lawrence left one man dead. In retaliation, an antislavery band led by John Brown, later of Harper's Ferry fame, killed five proslavery men along Pottawatomie Creek. By the end of 1856 more than two hundred settlers from both sides were dead.[10]

In May of that year violence over Kansas broke out in Congress itself. Abolitionist Senator Charles Sumner of Massachusetts, in a two-day speech entitled "The Crime against Kansas," went beyond the bounds of decorum when he called one of his colleagues, Andrew P. Butler of South Carolina, a liar and made thinly veiled sexual accusations against him. Sumner's comments might have brought him discredit had it not been for Butler's nephew, Preston Brooks, a member of the House of Representatives. Two days after Sumner's speech, Brooks attacked him on the Senate floor, beating him nearly to death with a cane. It was two years before Sumner was well enough to return to the Senate. In the heat of sectional crisis, many slaveholders defended Brooks, and few dared to openly criticize his actions. One exception was the *Columbus Enquirer*'s editor, who called the attack "disgraceful" and rightly feared that it could only lend momentum to the antislavery cause.[11]

If Brooks's caning of Sumner provided abolitionists with a martyr for their cause, John Brown's raid on Harper's Ferry gave southern secessionists an incident they could use to their own advantage. In October 1859, Brown led an attempt to seize the federal arsenal at Harper's Ferry, Virginia, and arm the state's slaves. The effort failed and a state court sentenced Brown to hang for treason. Abolitionism now had another martyr, but the South's fire-eating secessionists had something even more important.

Despite a lack of evidence for their position, secessionists had been claiming for years that the North was plotting to end slavery by encouraging and assisting slave rebellion. In reality, few northerners called themselves abolitionists. Many of those who did were actually antislavery southerners who had fled their native region. Most northerners were by no means opposed to slavery where it existed. Laborers feared that freedom for slaves would mean more competition for already low-paying jobs. Northern factory owners and financiers, particularly those with interests in textiles or transportation, feared that the end of slavery would mean the end of cheap southern cotton. What they opposed, and all they opposed, was an extension of slavery into the western territories.[12] Nevertheless, southern fire-eaters easily played on fears of northern-backed slave revolt in the aftermath of Harper's Ferry.

The encouragement of such fears among poor whites went as far back as the colonial era. Those fears soared in the 1830s after Nat Turner's rebellion and remained high through the Civil War. As early as 1835, slaveholders organized an antiabolition meeting in Stewart County, where the main topic of discussion was slave revolt. By the mid-1850s newspapers serving the lower Chattahoochee Valley carried alarming news of rebellion plots throughout the South. They advised an increase in slave patrols and warned that "citizens should always have their arms ready for service."[13]

Some newspapers went even further. By 1858 the *Eufaula Express* carried beneath its heading this motto: "A Southern Confederacy—The Sooner the Better." After the raid at Harper's Ferry, the editor urged immediate secession even if it meant war: "Since blood has commenced to flow, we say let it flow on until the question is settled once and for all." The editor called on slave states to "form a separate confederacy, and then let the Abolitionists whip us if they can." The *Opelika Southern Era* saw Brown's attack as an outright declaration of war against the South. The paper insisted that thousands of northerners must have known of Brown's plans yet gave no warning of this "conspiracy to murder and plunder the free white citizens of the South."[14]

Columbus papers carrying news of the Harper's Ferry raid stressed that some of the rebels were blacks, organized and led by "blatant 'freedom shriekers.'" Some valley residents were sure this incident was the start of a general slave uprising designed "for the extermination of the Southern whites." A Barbour County woman imagined that "the three places in our own county which were known . . . to be most thickly peopled with slaves were marked on John Brown's map of blood and massacre as the first spots for the negro uprising."[15]

In Early County, slaveholders were terrified by wild rumors that their chattel planned to "rise on a certain night" and "murder, pillage and burn." Other reports held that groups of Brown's men were hiding in the

valley, ready to strike. One Opelika newspaper insisted that the whole
South was infested with "agents of the Black Republican Party." Several
fires in November 1859 were blamed on rebellious blacks and abolitionists. One fire destroyed an estimated six thousand dollars worth of corn,
fodder, and cotton on a Muscogee County plantation. Another swept
through a gin house two miles from Columbus, destroying twenty-five
cotton bales along with the gin. The *Daily Sun*'s editor called it "Kansas
Work in Georgia." [16]

On December 6, the *Opelika Southern Era* applauded a group of young
men who hanged an effigy of Brown near the town's depot. A few of the
zealots, testing their marksmanship, quickly shot the likeness to pieces.
The *Era*'s editor thought it would have been much better to leave the figure swinging on its gallows as an example to "skulking Abolitionists who
are prowling about our place." "In fact," he continued, "nothing would
gratify us more than to see one of these copper-headed reptiles elevated to
a like honorable position. Boys, can't you capture one for a Christmas
frolick?" [17]

Any northern visitor, regardless of his business in the valley, was automatically suspected of collusion with Brown. William Scott, who represented a New York textile firm, was run out of Columbus after displaying
"more interest in the 'nigger question' than in the real object of his visit."
A vigilante committee decided "that he was an abolitionist 'dyed in the
wool,' and an unsafe man for any Southern community." Scott was lucky
to escape unharmed. Others were not as fortunate. At Society Hill near
Auburn, a Montgomery man was accused of being a "Brownite" just for
talking with several slaves. Local vigilantes gave him four hours to leave
the state. Not far out of town, the man was caught by "parties unknown"
and whipped nearly to death. A few days later, an Opelika paper com-
mented that the "Southern climate is becoming entirely too warm for
Abolition sympathizers. . . . We hear of suspected persons being notified
to migrate to more congenial regions." [18]

Free blacks and slaves bore the brunt of the Brown hysteria along the
lower Chattahoochee. "Confessions" of involvement in the Harper's Ferry
plot were beaten out of blacks all across the South. Free blacks especially
felt the impact of the anti-Brown backlash. Slaveholders had long been
concerned about the presence of 250,000 free blacks in the South. They
posed a danger as potential leaders of slave rebellions and as counter-
weights to the argument that blacks could not take care of themselves.
Now, with fear of insurrection reaching a panic stage, slaveholders were
ready to take action. One apostle of slavery in Alabama insisted that a

free black person was "not only a nuisance, but a loathsome pest" and called on the state legislature to take action against the "morbid growth of free-niggerdom." In December 1859, two months after the Harper's Ferry raid, a Columbus paper reported that "there seems to be a growing sentiment in favor of the removal of this class of population" even though there were just 141 free blacks in the city and only 260 more in the whole valley.[19]

That same month the Georgia General Assembly made it illegal for owners to free slaves in their wills. It also forbade "free persons of color" to enter the state. Those who did would be sold into slavery. Free blacks already in Georgia who were found "wandering or strolling about, or leading an idle, immoral or profligate course of life" could be charged with vagrancy and sold into slavery. Alabama already had an act barring free blacks from the state but went even further than Georgia when it came to owners freeing slaves in their wills. The 1859–60 legislative session not only outlawed this practice but, with the Reenslavement Act, voided all such previous wills. Slaves who had gained freedom in this way were required to leave the state or become slaves once again.[20]

This volatile atmosphere of panic and paranoia formed the backdrop of the presidential campaign in 1860. The Democrats met in Charleston, South Carolina, but could not agree on a policy regarding slavery in the territories. Southern delegates insisted on adherence to the Supreme Court's Dred Scott decision, which opened the territories to slavery.[21] Northerners held to popular sovereignty, arguing that territorial legislatures could still effectively bar slavery simply by refusing to enact slave codes protecting the institution. Unable to find common ground in Charleston, the party reconvened in Baltimore later that year. Again it reached an impasse and most southerners walked out. The remaining delegates nominated Stephen A. Douglas of Illinois, who had championed popular sovereignty in the Senate for more than a decade. Southern Democrats held their own convention and nominated Vice President John C. Breckinridge of Kentucky for the nation's highest office.

The Republicans meeting in Chicago seemed to agree on everything but a candidate. Of the leading contenders, none controlled enough delegates to ensure nomination going into the convention. The party finally settled on a dark horse from Illinois who seemed to be everyone's second choice, Abraham Lincoln. As for slavery, the party's platform aimed not to abolish it but only to limit its expansion.[22] Some southern politicians, concerned by the developing sectional nature of the campaign, formed the Constitutional Union Party. To represent their ticket, they nominated John

Bell of Tennessee for president and Edward Everett of Massachusetts for vice president. Their only platform was "the Constitution of the Country, the Union of the States, and the Enforcement of the Laws." Of the four presidential candidates, none commanded a national following. Douglas was the only one who really tried.

As the campaign season progressed, the political atmosphere along the lower Chattahoochee became increasingly heated. Edward Norton wrote from Fort Browder in Barbour County that "some of our citizens have almost become maniacs on the subject of politics." The valley's most vocal campaigners were those supporting Breckinridge. Most were secessionists (though Breckinridge himself was not) and clearly hoped that the split among Democrats foreshadowed a national division. Calling themselves the Southern Rights Party, they held rallies throughout the valley at which staunch secessionists like Robert Toombs delivered fiery orations to large, boisterous crowds. In Barbour County, as elsewhere, Breckinridge men demanded immediate secession in the event of Lincoln's election. Bell partisans were not as entertaining or impetuous, but they were able to draw fair numbers to their rallies and even had some support in the press. Conservative newspapers called Bell and his running mate "sound national men, as against [the Southern Rights Party,] which had broken its pledges and was continuing its warfare against the Union." Douglas drew sizable crowds himself as he passed through Columbus on November 1, 1860, headed for Montgomery. During a delay between trains, Douglas gave two speeches at the courthouse and the Oglethorpe Hotel. At a Douglas rally in Temperance Hall the next evening, Alexander H. Stephens drew cheers when he insisted that a Douglas victory was the only way to preserve the Union.[23]

Though no Lincoln rallies were held in the valley, Republicans apparently had some support among voters. There may have been at least a few in Stewart and Randolph Counties. But with slaveholders dominating the political process and almost everything else, it was not wise to support openly a party whose primary platform called for excluding slavery from the territories. One Columbus firm's business was hurt so much by its rumored support for Lincoln that it printed a strong denial in the *Daily Sun*.[24]

Lincoln's most passionate support in the South came from those who could not vote—the slaves. Though only a child at the time, former Russell County slave Louis Meadows remembered hearing talk of the election among adult slaves. All agreed that a Lincoln victory was in their best interest. The valley's black residents, both slave and free, did all they could to learn about the campaign and what it might mean for them. They attended so many public campaign rallies in Columbus that white citizens became alarmed by the blacks' "unusual interest in politics, and the result of the Presidential election." The mayor issued an order in September barring all blacks from future rallies. In Eufaula, "vigilant committees" kept a close watch on blacks who gathered in the streets to discuss the upcoming election.[25]

A heightened sense of anticipation among the valley's slaves was clearly evident as election day approached. But having no right to express themselves through free speech or the ballot box, blacks found other outlets for their frustrations. At 2:30 A.M. on the night before the election, much of Fort Gaines was consumed by fire. Among the buildings destroyed were Paullin's drugstore, Jones's grocery store, Pearson's bank, the Masonic building, and C. N. Johnston's dry goods store. Total damage was estimated at $50,000. Not long after residents brought the flames under control, two blacks were shot in the act of trying to restart the blaze.[26] The incident was but one example of the many challenges faced by slaveholders in trying to maintain control. The results of the next day's election could only make control more difficult, and the slaveholders knew it.

On November 7, 1860, the Southern Rights Party carried eleven of the lower Chattahoochee Valley's fifteen counties. Only Chambers, Troup, Harris, and Muscogee failed to return Breckinridge majorities. Bell came in a close second, with Douglas a distant third. Lincoln's name was not even on the ballot.[27] Nonetheless, Lincoln did carry all of the more populous free states except Rhode Island, which went to Douglas, giving Lincoln 180 electoral votes and the presidency.

With Lincoln poised to enter the White House, secessionists felt that it was time to push hard for disunion. Most slaveholders would certainly support such a move. If lesser yeomen and poor whites could be made to see Lincoln as a John Brown writ large, they too might support withdrawal from the Union. Secessionist leaders had to act quickly, before Lincoln took office, or they might never have another chance.

On the day after the election Hubert Dent, a young attorney from Eufaula, announced his intention to join a local militia company. "I feel like the South now expects every man to do his duty," he said. Dent had hoped that Breckinridge would carry the entire South, but if the slave states seceded he would be satisfied. As far as Dent was concerned there was no alternative to secession. "It is absolute submission to Black Republican Rule," he said, "or absolute resistance." Others in Barbour County felt the same way. On November 8, 1860, a mass meeting was held in Clayton, where, according to one account, "the people were all united in approving immediate secession." Three days later, J. E. Hall, a student at Auburn, wrote to his father, "Don't you think it is the duty of every slave state to secede?" The young man was sure secession would mean war: "If we don't fight now, when shall we fight?" In Abbeville, crowds gathered at the post office every day waiting for any news about the crisis. When word of South Carolina's secession arrived just before Christmas, leading Whigs and Democrats of Henry County held a "burying the hatchet" ceremony on the town square. Both sides resolved to support South Carolina and secession.[28]

Some of secession's most vocal supporters came from the ranks of the clergy, which was hardly surprising since the major denominations had long since split along sectional lines. Reverend James R. Thomas of Georgia warned that if the South did not secede, it would remain nothing more than a colony of the North. In December, a meeting of Methodist ministers in Montgomery declared full support for withdrawal from the Union. The Alabama Baptist Convention passed a resolution "in defense of the sovereignty and independence of Alabama and of her sacred right as a sovereignty to withdraw from this Union."[29]

Well-to-do women also added their voices to the rising chorus for disunion. Companies of them roamed the streets of Eufaula handing out cockades to be worn in support of secession. When one man refused the offer, the women loudly condemned him as a coward. One turned to a gathering crowd and ordered the men "to protect that man's wife and children should the South have to resort to arms in defense of its rights."[30]

Parthenia Hague of Barbour County was sure the Republican Party "felt that the people of the South were fit only for the pikes hidden at Harper's Ferry." How, she insisted, could the South not secede with Lincoln in the White House? The *Clayton Banner* went so far as to call for "the immediate outlawry of all who after [December 13, 1860,] may come among us from the land where they educate and send forth emissaries to incite insurrections, secret poisonings, murders and house burnings at the South." This action was, said the *Banner,* "necessary and justifiable on the ground that *most of those who come have more or less connection* with the criminal objects mentioned."[31]

In Columbus, a regiment calling itself the Southern Guard formed shortly after Lincoln's election. The city's secessionists put together a committee of fifty, led by Henry L. Benning, Paul J. Semmes, F. W. Dillard, and Martin J. Crawford, to organize a local anti-Union campaign. Columbus secessionists celebrated news of South Carolina's secession with a torchlight parade. It was, said one witness, "a magnificent sight.

Bonfires blazed in the streets, fireworks sparkled and hissed, and altogether it was an extraordinary and most exciting and impressive spectacle." [32]

Among the valley's most ardent fire-eaters was Columbus attorney Henry Lewis Benning. A strong advocate of secession as early as 1849, Benning warned that Lincoln's election meant the end of slavery. All who resisted slavery's demise, he said, would be hanged by Lincoln and his "Black Republican Party." The only way to avoid the "horrors of abolition" was immediate secession. "Why hesitate?" Benning asked. "The question is between life and death." [33] Benning's cousin, Augusta Evans, was just as zealous. She urged Benning to read a statement at Georgia's secession convention in which she called immediate disunion "the only door of escape from the . . . bondage of Black Republicanism." Even if it meant war and devastation, southerners should sever all ties with "the waves of Abolitionism" that had swept Lincoln into the presidency. "The Union has become a misnomer. . . . We of the South will Samson-like lay hold upon its pillars, and if need be, perish in its ruins." [34]

Congressman Martin J. Crawford of Columbus was just as passionate in his support for secession. A decade earlier he had worked against immediate secession following the Compromise of 1850, but while representing his west Georgia district from 1855 to 1861, Crawford came to embrace the secessionist cause. At a political rally in Albany, Georgia, a month before Lincoln's election, Crawford acknowledged the strength of secession's opponents in southwest Georgia when he said, "we hear the cry of Union among us—Union at all hazzards." But, he asked, "are we to cry Union when surrounded by enemies? Out of 117 Black Republicans in Congress, 68 endorsed the [Hinton Rowan] Helper book." For Crawford, that was reason enough to secede. A few weeks later when the "Black Republican" Lincoln (who actually denounced parts of Helper's book) became president-elect, one of Crawford's congressional colleagues called him "crazy" and "insane" for secession. "He would prefer to see the whole South from the Delaware to the Rio Grande, one charnel house of destruction, to submitting a single day to Lincoln's administration." [35]

Perhaps the most vocal organization in the valley supporting secession was the Eufaula Regency. Formed in the 1850s to support "southern rights," its members consistently pushed for the formation of a southern confederacy. It included such locally prominent planters and lawyers as Henry Clayton, Jere N. Williams, Jefferson Buford, Sterling G. Cato, Edward Courtney Bullock, and John Gill Shorter, soon to be governor of Alabama. In October 1860 the regency wrote to Governor A. B. Moore urging him to schedule an election for delegates to a secession convention at the earliest possible date following the presidential election. The shorter the interval between the two elections, the less time antisecessionists would have to organize.[36]

As for the question of war, Shorter calmly assured his followers that it would never come to that. South Carolina would soon leave the Union, he wrote on December 9, 1860, to be followed quickly by the other slave states. The Lincoln administration would not dare make war on a united South. Others, like Sarah Bacon of LaGrange, felt that immediate secession was in fact the only way to avoid war. If the South hesitated, it would have no time to prepare for defense before Lincoln took office. An ill-prepared South might only encourage northern aggression. But Bacon, like Shorter, was certain that a union of the slave states would ultimately prove invincible.[37]

Other valley residents were not as sure, and they were not eager to test the issue by a hasty resort to secession. The *Columbus Enquirer*'s editor was strongly against it, as was John Horry Dent, who continued to hope for compromise even after secession was an established fact. The *La-Grange Reporter* condemned "that imprudence which would wildly precipitate us out of the Union without making the last effort to maintain our rights and honor in it." When one man tried to hoist a prosecession flag in LaFayette, a unionist cut the rope to keep it from being raised.[38]

Like their opponents, antisecessionists held rallies throughout the lower Chattahoochee Valley to urge caution among their fellow citizens. In Harris County they held an open meeting arguing that every effort should be made "to preserve the honor and rights of the South" without resorting to secession. In Stewart County, "a large number of citizens" attended an antisecession meeting led by P. H. Gregory, L. Bryan, and James L. Wimberly. They nominated three of the county's most prominent citizens, John C. Byrd, Simon Holt, and Charles H. Warren, to represent their views in the upcoming campaign.[39]

Columbus unionists, led by such men as N. L. Howard, Porter Ingram, and Hines Holt (later elected to the First Confederate Congress), formed a committee of one hundred to organize local antisecession efforts. On December 15 they held a mass meeting that called for "redressing the South's grievances within the Union." In Barbour County, at least sixteen people canceled their subscriptions to the *Clayton Banner* because of the paper's extreme secessionist views.[40]

Antisecession sentiment was so strong in Randolph County that secession men feared the tide was turning against them. In a letter to Howell Cobb they asked, "Where are all our speakers? We have done what little we can here but there is great need for missionaries [of secession] in every part of the State." They urged Cobb to take a short tour through southwest Georgia to bolster the waning enthusiasm for secession. Their fears were not unfounded. Efforts to weaken the appeal of disunion were being made throughout the region. Three prominent Bainbridge citizens, Lew Griffin, John Law, and Alexander Murphy, had already written to Lincoln begging him not to take office. They urged Lincoln to throw his support to Bell when the electoral college met in December. For Lincoln to step aside was, they believed, the surest way to avoid secession and civil war.[41]

The leading opponent of secession in the lower Chattahoochee Valley was Troup County planter Benjamin Harvey Hill. A former Whig politician who had supported Bell and the Constitutional Union ticket, Hill was a strong voice for union in Georgia. He argued that Lincoln's election posed no real threat to slavery either in the South or in the territories. "Mr. Lincoln cannot do us damage," Hill asserted. "He cannot even form his Cabinet unless he make it acceptable to a Democratic Senate. And I go further and say that he cannot get even his salary—not a dime to pay for his breakfast—without the consent of Congress." Therefore, he said, "the wisest policy, the most natural remedy, and the surest way to vindicate our honor and self-respect, is to demand the unconditional observance of the Constitution." [42]

Among the yeomen and poor whites, opinions on secession were ambiguous. Slaveholding yeomen certainly saw Lincoln as a potential threat. And though lesser yeomen and poor whites owned no slaves, they still had their racist pride. Would Lincoln really try to free the slaves, as secessionists claimed? No less a figure than Governor Joe Brown of Georgia, self-proclaimed friend of the common man, said it was true. He warned that poor whites would suffer even more than planters if Lincoln freed the slaves. Former slaves would, Brown insisted, "come into competition with [poor whites], associate with them and their children as equals—be allowed to testify in court against them—sit on juries with them, march to the ballot box by their sides, and participate in the choice of their rulers—claim social equality with them—and ask the hands of their children in marriage." Was this really Lincoln's intent? Of course, said Brown. The ultimate aim of the "Black Republican Party" was to set the slaves free and place them on an equal footing with whites.[43]

Still, many plain folk were leery of secessionist motives. For years they had been told to think of themselves as the planter's equal. Brown said that they belonged "to the only true aristocracy, the race of *white men*." Kinship ties across class lines were often used to reinforce the point. But

the fact remained that the plain folk did not live as the planters' equals
and by the 1850s could never hope to do so. Most saw the planters themselves as responsible for that situation. It was just as clear to yeomen and
poor whites that planters did not view them as equals no matter what
they said in public. As one Tennessee yeoman put it, "Slaveholders always
acted as if they were of a better class and there was always an unpleasant
feeling between slaveholders and those working themselves."[44]

By the 1850s many planters had indeed come to view themselves as
something of an aristocracy and the poor whites as little better than slaves.
One planter, in a private letter to a friend, wrote of the poor whites, "not
one in ten is . . . a whit superior to a negro." Most tried to keep such opinions concealed lest their hypocrisy be exposed. Occasionally, though, suggestions of planter arrogance slipped into print. In his classic defense of
slavery, *Sociology for the South, or the Failure of Free Society,* George
Fitzhugh not only insisted that slavery was "the best form of society yet
devised for the masses" but also "that slavery, *black or white,* was right
and necessary." Could white slavery be just around the corner? Perhaps
some poorer whites were beginning to fear it might be. It certainly seemed
to many of them that one way or the other, under Republican or planter
rule, they were condemned to occupy the lowest rung of the social ladder
along with the slaves.[45]

As early as 1849, one Georgia carpenter openly declared his opposition
to slavery. Competition with slave labor, he believed, kept his wages low.
A poor Georgia farm laborer confided to a friend that if it came to a war
over slavery, he was going to "black himself" and fight for emancipation.
Without slavery, perhaps he could get better wages. Some nonslaveholders were already taking action against slavery. In 1859, another Georgia
farmer was convicted of hiding a runaway slave for three months. Yet another was found making out bogus passes for slaves and "teaching them
to write and cipher."[46]

Could growing numbers of people like these, along with the legions of
poor whites who already resented the planters, be potential recruits for
the Republican Party? Slaveholders dreaded the thought. With Lincoln in
the White House and discontent rising in the South, a truly national Republican Party might become a reality. One defender of slavery warned
that if men like Hinton Rowan Helper were allowed to speak freely in the
South, as they surely would be under a Lincoln administration, "they will
have an Abolition party in the South, of Southern men." Another frankly
admitted, "I mistrust our own people more than I fear all of the efforts of

the Abolitionists." Yet another man wrote to Alexander Stephens warning that if it were left to the poor whites, slavery would soon be ended.[47]

And what of the slaves themselves? Though planters argued otherwise, they knew very well that slavery did not come naturally to those of African descent. Slaves ran away, they resisted, they had to be controlled through fear and violence. They wanted to be set free, and they believed Lincoln would do just that. How could they think otherwise with secessionists trumpeting throughout the South that Lincoln's ultimate goal was to free the slaves? One Russell County man remembered that slaves "hoped and prayed he would be elected. They wanted to be free and have a chance."[48] How much more difficult might controlling slaves be with Lincoln in the White House and expectations for freedom running so high?

More than popular sovereignty, more than the abolitionists, more than Lincoln himself, planters feared the South's lower classes. General dissatisfaction was on the rise by the 1850s. A Lincoln presidency could only encourage internal dissent. If the cotton states remained in the Union, many slaveholders feared that their "peculiar institution" might be in serious jeopardy from within. Controlling the lower classes might be easier and slavery might be more secure in an independent confederacy of slaveholding states. Other factors certainly helped fuel the crisis. Overestimates of abolitionist strength in the North, the issue of slavery's expansion, and personal political ambitions all played their part. But slaveholders' fear of their fellow southerners was a primary, though publicly unacknowledged, force driving secession.[49]

Even so, slaveholders were far from united behind secession. Though most recognized the dangers to slavery from within, wealthier and more conservative "old money" planters tended to view secession as much more risky than remaining in the Union. With a greater stake in preserving the status quo, they were more cautious on the issue of secession than lesser slaveholders. Should withdrawal from the Union lead to civil war, success would depend on widespread support from the lower classes. Many planters wondered how long that support could last. Secession might actually hasten the end of slavery rather than preserve it. This danger seemed clear enough to Ben Hill. He warned that a divided South could not possibly survive a civil war. The southern government would fall and slavery with it.[50]

Many of Hill's colleagues had similar fears. A few weeks after Lincoln's election, in "a large meeting of the Members of the General Assembly" at the Georgia capitol, legislators called for thoughtful restraint on the secession issue. They appointed a committee of twenty-two, including Hill, Hines Holt of Muscogee County, and R. R. Terrell of Decatur County, to draft a resolution urging their fellow Georgians not to give their votes to secessionists in the upcoming election for convention delegates. Immediate secession would, they insisted, be hasty and ill advised, creating "nothing but divisions among our people, confusion among the slaveholding States, strife around our firesides, and ultimate defeat to every movement for the effective redress of our grievances."[51]

On the other side, those favoring secession found their most enthusiastic support among the more numerous "new money" planters and lesser slaveholders. Their spokesmen were young up-and-coming lawyer/politicians trying to carve out a niche for themselves at the expense of the old establishment. Few were more ambitious than Henry L. Benning. "I am no Calhoun man," wrote Benning in 1849. "He in fact is off the stage; the coming battle is for other leadership than his, a leadership that is of this generation, not of the past." Russell County attorney Milton S. Latham, an unsuccessful candidate for state office, was even less generous than Benning in his opinion of the old guard: "It certainly is cramping to an ardent and desirous mind to find so many avenues to success blocked by Dam Asses." The politically ambitious increasingly took up secession's banner and, to the dismay of more conservative colleagues, carried it high into the late 1850s. This division of opinion among the South's leading politicians set the stage for intense controversy at the state secession conventions.[52]

In November 1860, Governor Brown signed a bill providing for the election of delegates to Georgia's secession convention. Balloting would take place the following January 2, and the convention would meet two weeks later in Milledgeville to decide the issue. The Alabama legislature had already passed a nearly unanimous resolution in February, nine months before Lincoln's election, providing for a convention and secession rather than submit to the rule of a "foul sectional party."[53] On December 24, 1860, Alabama citizens went to the polls and returned a 35,693 to 28,181 vote in favor of secession, giving the secessionists a fifty-four to forty-six edge at the convention. On the Alabama side of the lower Chattahoochee, all five counties returned secessionist majorities. In Georgia, the statewide vote was even closer than Alabama's, with a slight majority of 42,744 to 41,717 *opposing* secession. Of Georgia's eleven lower Chattahoochee counties, eight voted to leave the Union. Only Troup, Harris, and Chattahoochee sent antisecession (or cooperationist) delegates to the state convention. The balloting in Decatur County was very close, with only 105 votes separating the secession and antisecession candidates.[54]

It is impossible to view the election returns as representative of the popular will one way or the other. Voter turnout was surprisingly low considering the gravity of the issue involved. In the entire lower Chattahoochee Valley, only half the eligible voters went to the polls. Perhaps because of the cold and rainy weather, voting was heaviest in and around urban areas, where opinions more strongly favored secession. Most of the rural folk who bothered to vote were probably planters and lesser slaveholders. The poorer yeomen and landless whites were, as always, less likely to feel that their votes counted for much, and some surely stayed at home because they could not afford to pay the poll tax. Whatever the reason, it seems clear that the views of more affluent voters carried a much greater weight at the polls.[55]

There was an even more basic concern about how democratic the initial nominating process had been. One disgusted west Georgia man complained bitterly that delegates were "nominated by mass conventions assembled at the county sites; and it is plain that not half of the citizens attend these nominations. But few men living ten or fifteen miles from [the] county site go to such conventions . . . and as it is an admitted fact that the secession sentiment is much stronger in and around the cities than it is among the common people in the country, it is easy to see the advantage the 'immediate secessionist' will have in the Convention."[56] Despite such objections, the state convention formed on the basis of the balloting as it stood.

At the Alabama convention, antisecession proposals were voted down by a fifty-four to forty-five vote, with one abstention. By January 11, when the final vote on secession came up, the outcome seemed inevitable. Several cooperation men switched sides, giving secessionists a sixty-one to thirty-nine majority.[57] A week later at the Georgia convention, Eugenius A. Nisbit proposed a test resolution supporting secession to gauge the feeling of the delegates. Enough delegates who had been elected on a promise to vote against immediate secession were enticed by the promise of a slaveholder republic to pass the resolution by a 166 to 130 vote. The next day, January 19, with more delegates switching sides, the convention approved an ordinance of secession 208 to 89. On the final vote, even Hill cast his ballot for secession as a show of unity.[58] It could hardly have been surprising that the convention ultimately favored secession in spite of the popular vote. While only 37 percent of Georgia's electorate owned slaves, 87 percent of the convention delegates were slaveholders.[59]

At both the Alabama and Georgia conventions the few remaining antisecession delegates urged that their secession ordinances be put to a vote

of the people. Fearing the outcome of such a move, the secessionist majorities refused. Both states left the Union without submitting the issue to
a direct popular vote.[60] In February, Georgia and Alabama delegates, along
with others from South Carolina, Florida, Mississippi, Louisiana, and
Texas, met in Montgomery to form the Confederate States of America.

News of secession touched off wild celebrations in every town along
the lower Chattahoochee. One valley resident recalled that in Opelika
and Auburn, "the people were perfectly crazy with enthusiasm." Elizabeth
Rhodes wrote in her diary that "there was never such a time in Eufaula
as that night, a gala night, with the booming of cannon in our ears. Flags
were floating in the breeze in all directions. . . . The most gloriously
magnificent sight I ever beheld. Almost every home appeared as if stud-
ded with diamonds in a glorious sunlight, so brilliant were the bonfires."
She went on to say that "the cannons fired sixty salutes. The bells rang
forth many peals."[61]

Not everyone saw the Confederacy's formation as cause for celebra-
tion. For many it was a time of sober reflection. Said one Georgia man of
the merrymakers, "Poor fools! They may ring their bells now, but they
will wring their hands—yes, and their hearts, too—before they are done
with it." A Barbour County woman remembered that "feelings of sadness,
rather, something akin to those of Peri outside the gate of Paradise, overcame us." John Horry Dent worried about his business interests and the
stability of the cotton market. "Business matters are completely depressed
and deranged," he wrote. "Cotton dull and little or none selling."[62]

Then there was the question of war. Hubert Dent of the Eufaula Rifles
wrote from Montgomery on February 14, "The common opinion here is
that we will not have a general war." Elizabeth Rhodes wrote shortly after Lincoln's election, "I do trust that a merciful ruling Providence may so
order our every movement that all things may be settled without blood-
shed." But on February 11, she wrote, "War is impending. Our people
have made a formal demand for Forts Sumter and Pickens. If not granted,
they will be taken, if possible, by force." John Horry Dent also worried
about the probability of war and predicted that "the dreadful conflict . . .
must take place in Charleston harbor in the storming of fort Sumpter."[63]

The common folk, North and South, were by no means eager for war
in March 1861. One Alabama fire-eater noted with alarm that there were
enough antisecessionists in his state to vote it back into the Union. Southern whites, particularly the poor whites, were so ambivalent about the
Confederacy that staunch secessionists like Hubert Dent actually hoped
for war because he believed it was just what the Confederacy needed to

boost domestic support. "It will," he said, "unite the South better than anything else." [64]

In the North, Lincoln was under intense pressure from his financial backers and other northern industrialists to keep the cotton states in the Union. How else could they guarantee continued access to southern markets and cheap cotton? The *Boston Herald* warned that the Confederacy would "impose a heavy tax upon the manufactures of the North, and an export tax upon the cotton used by northern manufacturers. In this way she would seek to cripple the North." [65]

Such arguments carried little weight among the northern working classes. Most of them had nothing against slavery in the South, only its extension. Many were glad to be free of their political ties to the obstinate slaveholders. They certainly had no desire to put their lives in danger trying to keep the cotton states in the Union by force. One newspaper in Rochester, New York, reported on the difficulties officers had getting recruits despite the availability of unemployed, able-bodied men by the thousands. "We hear a great deal of talk," said the editors, "among the ardent platform Republicans about coercing the secessionists of the south by means of Northern soldiers, but the indications are that the fighting is to be done mostly with the tongue." [66]

How could Lincoln get the men he needed to keep the cotton states in the Union with such attitudes so prevalent? A military draft was out of the question. Popular reaction might mean the end of the Republican Party. Lincoln considered issuing a call for volunteers, but that too was unrealistic. Not only would it be likely to drive more slave states out of the Union, it would also be political suicide in the free states. What Lincoln needed was an incident to fire northern patriotism and draw volunteers to the army.

On April 12, 1861, the Confederate government gave Lincoln just what he needed by firing on the federal garrison at Fort Sumter. John Horry Dent wrote in his journal ten days later that "the people of the North are exasperated at the news of the surrender of Fort Sumter and are volunteering by thousands to subjugate the South; a bloody war may be anticipated." As Hubert Dent had hoped, reaction was similar in the South. With war a certainty, four more slave states—Arkansas, Tennessee, North Carolina, and Virginia—left the Union. Displays of unity were common on the local level too. In Early County, the Democrats and Whigs held a mass meeting on the Blakely town square. Judge James Bush, speaking for the Democrats, and Colonel James Buchannon, representing the Whigs, together promised an end to local political bickering. Henceforth all their efforts would be devoted to opposing the Yankees instead of each other. Near the close of the meeting, Judge Bush dug a hole under the courthouse steps in which he buried a hatchet to symbolically cement the agreement.[67]

All across the South, so many men rushed to military service that the Confederacy could not arm them all. Many volunteers had to provide their own weapons or secure the backing of wealthy patrons. William H. Young, founder of the Eagle Manufacturing Company and president of the Bank of Columbus, outfitted an entire artillery battery at a personal cost of $65,000. Like most other units, however, the Miller County Wildcats were left to arm themselves "with every death-dealing instrument that could be procured." Each recruit carried a Bowie knife along with an old rifle or shotgun. One elderly man who had tried without success to talk his son out of going to war with the Wild Cats finally gave in and presented him with what was surely a prized possession—a single-barrel shotgun. "I don't want any war," the old man told his boy, "but . . . here's old Betsy; take her and give the Yankees hell."[68]

Several factors account for the widespread surge of volunteering, fear of Yankee invasion perhaps foremost among them. There was also regional identity, desire for upward mobility, peer pressure, and even a sense of adventure. Whatever their misgivings about slaveholders and slavery, thousands of slaveless yeomen and poor whites took up arms in spring 1861. Georgia alone had furnished 18,000 volunteers for Confederate service by May 7, second only to Virginia. Little wonder that the state's rail system was in chaos. According to one source, lines were clogged with trainloads of raw recruits "whose enthusiasm for the Confederate cause was equaled only by their lack of any clear conception as to the authority under which they were to serve, or of their destination." And enthusiastic they were. Just fourteen days after the firing on Fort Sumter, the LaGrange Light Guards and the West Point Guards were on their way to the front. During the war's first year, more than 1,300 men from Troup County volunteered.[69]

The Columbus Guard left that city for Savannah in late April 1861. According to one account, Columbus sent eighteen companies—1,200 men in all—to the front in the war's first year. Other sources credit the city with twenty-two companies. Whatever the exact figure, there were enough volunteers in the war's first weeks to keep five recruiting officers busy. From Stewart County came six companies, including the Stewart Greys, Rawson Rangers, and Xollicoffer's Guards. The Henry Grays left Abbeville on May 11, followed two months later by the Henry Pioneers. The Fort Gaines Guards sent 120 men off to fight under the command of

Captain R. A. Turnipseed, and three other companies from Clay County soon joined the Guards. The Quitman Grays, named after their home county, left for the front in June. Even tiny Loachapoka, in what is now Lee County, contributed four units to the war effort.[70]

Letters to southern governors poured in from volunteer companies requesting orders to active duty. Some even came from neighboring states. Captain Peter Brenan, commanding the Starke Guards of Quitman County, wrote to Governor Brown that the company would consider it an "everlasting favor" to be ordered into service as soon as possible, adding, "we would be greatly obliged by being furnished with arms and accouterments by your Excellency at the shortest possible time." Some companies did not even need that help. Thomas Flournoy of Opelika wrote to Brown that there was a company of one hundred men "armed with Shot Guns and Rifles who is anxious to go to Savannah for her defense." All they asked was "transportation from Columbus to Savannah and feed us while in Service and transportation back home."[71]

For eagerness to serve, no company surpassed the Cuthbert Rifles. On March 28, 1861, two weeks before the firing on Sumter, they wrote to the governor that "several companies have been ordered to different stations, but much to our disappointment, ours was not included in the number." They pleaded "that if any more troops from Georgia are needed that you will bear in mind that there is still in existence a company called the Cuthbert Rifles, and trust that they will have an equal showing with the balance."[72]

Perhaps the youngest and surely one of the most persistent soldiers from the Chattahoochee Valley was Robert Reynolds of Henry County. Only fifteen years old, he ran away from home in the first year of the war to enlist with W. C. Oates's regiment. Rejected because of his age, he was sent home. Again he ran off, this time all the way to Virginia, where he joined a Henry County unit, the Irwin Invincibles. He almost died soon after from an attack of measles and typhoid fever. He returned home in December 1861 "almost a skeleton." The following May, he enlisted in the Twenty-seventh Alabama Infantry and served until wounded during the Atlanta Campaign in July 1864. Young Reynolds returned to his unit after a three-month recuperation, serving until the war's end.[73]

It seemed in spring 1861 that almost everyone was caught up in the excitement of what they were sure would be a short conflict. Assuming as they did that one southern boy could whip ten Yankees, how could it be otherwise? Even men who could not join the army offered to serve in other areas. Thomas Coleman of Cuthbert, a physically impaired bookkeeper, wrote to Governor Brown asking for "a situation in some place to enable me to help support the government."[74]

There were even a few slaves and free blacks who offered their support. Joe Clark, a free black barber from Columbus, asked Governor Brown for permission to raise a militia company of free black volunteers. Though some questioned the wisdom of employing members of his "cast" as soldiers, Georgia newspapers praised Clark for his patriotism and remarked that he still limped from a wound received in the Seminole War of 1836. In an open letter to Jefferson Davis published in the *Clayton Banner,* Bowman Seals of Barbour County asked to help defend "the best poor man's country in the world" from invasion by the "intermeddling and domineering" Yankees. It is difficult to say what motivated those of African descent to offer service to the Confederacy, a government having as its "cornerstone," in the words of Vice President Stephens, "the great truth that the negro is not the equal of the white man." Some slaves certainly associated military service with freedom and may have viewed it as the shortest route to their ultimate goal. And while some free blacks like Clark and Seals may have been motivated by local loyalties, they also knew that the offer of military service alone could invite favor from the white community. In any case, no such offers were accepted.[75]

Like slaves and free blacks, women were barred from the military. But the enthusiasm of many females for the cause was just as great as that of the men. It seemed that for every young man who left home, there was a young woman to see him off. Throughout the valley, women organized farewell ceremonies, formed sewing circles, and otherwise donated time and energy to the war effort. On May 14, 1861, the ladies of Whitesville in Harris County presented a flag to the departing Whitesville Guards during a public ceremony held at the local Methodist church. Women of Randolph County did the same for the Cuthbert Rifles and said that they hoped the Rifles "would be ordered to Washington, and that they could place that flag on the Capitol first, and that Lincoln and his host could find another roost." In Newton, Dale County recruits were treated to a flurry of speech making, drum beating, flag waving, and young ladies singing patriotic songs. M. B. Houghton, only sixteen at the time, recalled that "those of us who had enlisted felt that we were great heroes and were going forth to participate in a kind of holiday excursion, soon to return crowned with victorious laurels."[76]

All through summer 1861, men of military age felt tremendous pressure to join others already at the front. One zealous group of young women in Columbus went so far as to form the Ladies' Home Guard for the "special protection of young men who have concluded to remain at home during the existence of war." Some of the city's older women were critical of such coercive recruiting tactics. After all, their sons were feeling the pressure. One woman who signed herself "A Matron" argued in a letter to the *Daily Sun,* "It is time that the ladies should check, not spur, the zeal of our young men, who are too ready to leave important duties at home and fly to more exciting, though not more honorable employment." [77] But the Ladies' Home Guard continued to harass the less enthusiastic men of Columbus.

Some Columbus women organized drives to sell Confederate war bonds. Others collected scarce metals like copper, bronze, and steel for the war effort. One group collected enough brass to make a twelve-pound howitzer known as the "Ladies' Defender." Elizabeth Rhodes of Eufaula welcomed the war because it would force the South into just such a mobilization of its resources. In doing so, she said, the South would establish its "independence not only in name but reality. We have too long relied on the Yankees for nearly almost everything." [78]

Perhaps the most valued service women provided early in the war was sewing uniforms. There were so many volunteers in 1861 that the Confederate government could not provide uniforms for them all. In August, when F. W. Dillard was placed in charge of establishing a quartermaster depot in Columbus, he had to depend on the volunteer work of local women to make his first shipment of uniforms. A group of Opelika women combined their efforts with those of young ladies at the local female academy to clothe every member of the Opelika True Volunteers. The Ladies' Relief Society of West Point made uniforms for the West Point Guards and other local companies. An Auburn woman, Mrs. William Collins, offered to sew a hundred uniforms for one local unit singlehandedly.[79]

In homes all along the lower Chattahoochee, women made clothing of every sort for the soldiers. Mary Fleming of Dale County recalled how the women of her family gathered to make "uniforms, socks, and gloves, etc." Mrs. Willie W. Foreman of Stewart County remembered that even the young girls "helped card, spin, sew, knit and even went into the swamps to collect barks . . . to dye the cloth for the soldiers clothes and comforts." [80]

Ironically, the rush to war was heartily endorsed by leading apostles of the Prince of Peace. Even before his state seceded, Stephen Elliot, bishop of the Episcopal Diocese of Georgia, told his clergy to delete from their prayers "president of the United States" and insert an invocation for the governor. The Episcopal Convention of Alabama did the same. In May 1861, delegates to the Southern Baptist Convention meeting in Savannah unanimously voted their support for the war. The Southern Methodists, meeting in Atlanta, offered prayers to God for "brilliant victories." Catholic clergymen urged their parishioners to pray for southern deliverance from the "northern barbarians." At the local level, Reverend C. W. Key of LaGrange urged young men of his congregation into battle against the "fanatical enemy." As an expression of its patriotism, the Methodist church in Hamilton sent thirty-three dollars to Governor Brown as a contribution to the war effort. And in a complete reversal of the "swords into plowshares" doctrine, the LaGrange Methodist Church offered to cast its church bells into cannons.[81]

Despite mass volunteering, general excitement, and even divine sanction, there were early signs that support for the war and for the Confederacy itself might not last long. A few citizens openly supported the Union. One man was lynched a few miles west of Auburn for speaking out against secession. George Martin, a southwest Georgia man, was arrested for "uttering treasonable sentiments against the Southern Confederacy." Perhaps fearing for his life, Martin nearly killed an army lieutenant while making his escape. Authorities offered a $250 reward for Martin's capture, dead or alive.[82]

While a few southern unionists gave voice to their opinions, hundreds of others did not. For safety's sake they outwardly expressed support for disunion when they had to and remained silent when they could. The slightest suggestion that someone might be a unionist could lead to violence, and it was just as likely to be directed at the accuser as the accused. In Hamilton, a gunfight broke out when one man called another's father an abolitionist.[83]

In the face of threats to their personal safety, many southerners openly expressed doubts about the legitimacy of secession. In Georgia, Governor Brown did not announce the results of the January 2 vote for convention delegates until late April, and then only at the insistence of influential voters—and he lied about the figures. Brown insisted that the secessionists had won by more than 13,000 votes when in fact they were most likely defeated by a margin of just over one thousand. Brown was not alone in his determination to see Georgia out of the Union regardless of the popular will. In speaking for secession just after Lincoln's election, Robert Toombs demanded of his fellow Georgians, "Give me the sword! But if you do not place it in my hands, before God *I will take it!*"[84] Toombs, Brown, and their secessionist allies did just that.

Secession's opponents could be even more biting with their rhetoric. Responding to Toombs's threat, an antisecessionist editor from west Georgia wrote, "Toombs says that if Georgia does not give him the sword he will take it.—Let him take it, and, by way of doing his country a great service, let him run about six inches of it into his left breast." But by spring 1861, the war of words was over and the Confederacy was an established fact. Southerners were now more concerned about how the war might affect the South in general, and themselves in particular, if it did not end quickly. Elizabeth Rhodes noted that "the prospect seems increasing for a long bloody war. It makes me sad to think of it." John Horry Dent warned fellow planters that if the war continued for very long the Yankees would surely overrun Alabama and Georgia, but few believed him. They scoffed at Dent's concerns and insisted that the Yankees would never make it past Virginia and Tennessee if they decided to fight at all. Some were taking no chances. In June 1861, long before any major fighting took place, Henry Mabin and D. W. Roach of Henry County sidestepped the wave of volunteerism by forming of a company called the Home Guards—for local defense only. Frontline duty was not for them.[85]

The notion that Yankees would not fight or would be easily beaten if they did was common in early 1861. When asked about the dangers of going to war, one Stewart County man replied that he was not the least bit afraid. In a play on the "money-grubbing Yankee" stereotype, he said that if he saw a Yankee pointing a gun at him, he would simply offer to buy the weapon and thereby end the fight. S. S. Curry of the Henry Grays was also certain that the North would not fight. From Fairfax, Virginia, he wrote to his wife on June 22 that the Confederates there faced several thousand Yankees, "but they won't fight. . . . I believe peace will be made soon, for they see that they cannot fight the South." Jerry Boykins, a Troup County slave, recalled his master saying that he was going to "whip those sons of bitches and would be back 'fore breakfast." It was two years before he returned home. Many would never see home again.[86]

On July 21, 1861, Curry and the Henry Grays learned that the Yankees would indeed fight when they struck the Confederates early that Sunday morning at Manassas. Though the Yankees were beaten back, it was no easy task. Nearly a thousand men from both sides died on the field, and hundreds more died later of their wounds. It was the bloodiest battle in American history up to that time, but it would soon pale in comparison to the killing fields of Shiloh, Antietam, Fredericksburg, and Gettysburg.

When soldiers of the Fifteenth Alabama arrived in Virginia and visited Manassas a month later, they found hundreds of shallow graves scattered over the battlefield. Rain had washed much of the dirt away and skeletal remains protruded from the ground. Hogs were feeding on the dead. It was not what the young men had expected to find when they left Fort

Mitchell just a few days before. Few had allowed themselves to imagine what the horrors of war were really like in the immediate post-Sumter excitement. But after Manassas, the soldiers had no choice. Private J. W. Lokey of Muscogee County, only fifteen years old at the time, later remembered that Manassas "made me realize that this war was no child's play."[87]

The violent nature of war was not so obvious back home. Hundreds of miles from the battlefield, Eufaula's *Spirit of the South* could imagine that the victory at Manassas might "cause the patriot fires to burn higher . . . and every one to dare and do more than ever." Most whites along the lower Chattahoochee were certainly glad to see the Yankees turned back, but post-Manassas enthusiasm did not last long. Before the year was out, hundreds of valley folk, rich and poor, joined John Horry Dent in reflecting on the war's human costs. "How many widows and orphans . . . has this war brought about?" asked Dent. "See what destruction and ruin has taken place at the seat of war in Virginia. To us, who have not witnessed it, it is incomprehensible." Little wonder that so many soldiers began to reexamine their motives for volunteering. Some deserted even before the fighting started. Several members of the Opelika True Volunteers deserted shortly after they arrived at the Virginia front in May 1861. In late July, just ten days after Manassas, Joel Crawford of Quitman County wrote to Governor Brown wanting to know "if after the signing of a written instrument binding the signer to go to the present war, if any signer thereof has the legal right to withdraw his name." On August 15, the *Albany Patriot* printed a list of deserters from the "Miller [County] Grays" that included men with such names as Calhoun, Hendley, Bush, Grimes, Cowart, Roberts, Braswell, and Davis.[88]

Besides the ebbing enthusiasm among soldiers, there was a growing awareness among plain folk that their personal sacrifices were likely to be much greater than those of the elites. This class disparity became clear early on when the Confederate government, lacking weapons enough for all its volunteers, allowed those who could provide their own to enlist for only one year instead of three. That proviso meant purchasing the expensive .577-caliber Enfield rifles, which few common soldiers could afford. Most volunteers were not informed until they reached the front lines that their shotguns and squirrel rifles would not do for military service. Many poor soldiers found that their one-year enlistments had suddenly turned into three. As historian Paul Escott noted, "The price of being a patriot was higher for the common man than for the rich man, three times higher to be exact." In October 1861, Captain Edward Croft of the Columbus

Artillery reported that it was almost impossible to find volunteers for long-term service.[89]

The yeomen had other concerns as well. Who would care for their families and farms while they were in the army? Planters had fewer such worries because they had slaves to work their plantations. And taxes were rising on everything except slaves. As the 1861 state elections approached, these issues remained uppermost in the minds of poorer voters. In September, one Georgia farmer addressed an open letter to candidates for the legislature: "Please give your views concerning our present condition—about the war, and the cause of the war . . . and our present condition of taxation for the support of the war. Is it right that the poor man should be taxed for the support of the war, when the war was brought about on the slave question, and the slave at home accumulating for the benefit of his master, and the poor man's farm left uncultivated, and a chance for his wife to be a widow, and his children orphans? Now, in justice, would it not be right to levy a direct tax on the species of property that brought about the war, to support it?" A week later, the editor of the newspaper that printed the letter apologized for doing so because, he said, that kind of talk might cause class division.[90] In fact, such letters did not cause division but simply expressed an underlying class resentment that already existed. Before the war, that resentment had been directed against numerous inequities, only one of which involved slavery. During the first year of the war, however, slavery became the focus of class conflict. To poor whites it was the symbol of everything they hated about the planters.

In May 1861 William Brooks, who had served as president of Alabama's secession convention, expressed his concerns about class divisions in an urgent letter to Jefferson Davis. Too many common folk believed that "nothing is now in peril in the prevailing war but the title of the master to his slaves." Already some had openly "declared that they will 'fight for no rich man's slaves.'" More and more plain folk were beginning to express their class resentment. If this trend continued, Brooks told the president, "I leave you to imagine the consequences."[91]

Davis should have listened. But it was still early in the war and the Confederacy had more immediate concerns. Along the lower Chattahoochee, Confederate officials busied themselves with creating an industrial base at Columbus and pondered the inevitable labor shortages. They fretted about transportation difficulties and worried over the possibility of Yankee gunboats steaming up the Chattahoochee River. In the early months of the war, reports of discontent seemed insignificant. They would not seem so for long.

CHAPTER

3

For the Benefit of the Aristocrats

Rumors of an impending Yankee assault up the Chattahoochee terrified people in the lower part of the valley, especially the planters. Some were sure such an invasion would come. It could only be a matter of time. One resident of Steam Mill in Decatur County felt certain an attack was imminent. He was just as certain it would succeed. "I am fully warranted," he told the governor, "in saying that under present circumstances no adequate resistance could be offered. . . . Something ought to be done, and done at once, if not, this part of our beloved state will be overrun by the hated Yankees." John M. Potter of Gatesville in Early County shared the Decatur man's fears. He too was sure that Union forces would shortly steam up the Chattahoochee "and endeavor to lay waste . . . the fairest portion of Georgia with fire and sword."[1]

Such letters from the rich cotton country of southwest Georgia poured into Governor Joe Brown's office begging for assistance. Forty members of the Early County home guard wrote to Brown requesting rifles for the soldiers and side arms for the officers. They had been drilling for some time without weapons of any kind. J. A. Zeigler, clerk of court in Bainbridge, informed the governor that Decatur County citizens, "particularly those having plantations on or near the river," feared being "visited" by Yankee gunboats. He urged Brown to send powder and shot for a local volunteer company. "Unless you can supply it, the company will be entirely without ammunition."[2]

Fears of invasion seemed justified in summer 1861. Lincoln had ordered a blockade of all southern ports that April. Two months later, the USS *Montgomery* took its station off the port of Apalachicola. No American vessels were allowed in or out, and all foreign ships were given ten days to leave. This early phase of the blockade was in fact little more than a nuisance. There was only one Union warship to guard the two main passes and two shallower channels into Apalachicola Bay. City officials were much more concerned that a Union landing force might try to take the city and built three miles of defensive works by the end of the year. But only 1,200 soldiers were stationed in Apalachicola. If the Yankees attacked in force, the city would need at least five thousand defenders.

The USS *Cuyler* arrived in August to strengthen the blockade, but a few blockade-runners continued to elude the Yankees. Still, the noose was tightening. In November the *Rain,* loaded with cotton, was captured as it made a run for open water. Three more schooners, the *Onward,* the *Franklin,* and the *Phoenix,* were caught trying to slip back into Apalachicola Bay. Only one runner, the *Benson,* made a successful round trip. The arrival of more Union vessels over the next few months made free traffic in or out of Apalachicola Bay almost impossible. In March 1862 Confederate forces abandoned the nearly useless port city.[3]

Worried officials now began to focus their energies on keeping the Yankees from moving upriver. Governors John Milton of Florida, John Gill Shorter of Alabama, and Joe Brown of Georgia appealed to Jefferson Davis for help. The president responded by creating a new military district in the region and placed General Howell Cobb, a native Georgian, in command. Cobb's first priority was river defense, and he immediately placed fortifications and obstructions along the inland waterway. Georgia's legislature contributed more than half a million dollars to the effort.[4]

Cobb's chief engineer, Captain Theodore Moreno, placed three enormous chains across the Apalachicola River at the Narrows to catch logs and other floating debris. This obstruction, along with its adjacent artillery, constituted the first line of defense. Further upriver, Cobb placed fortifications at Ricko's Bluff, Alum Bluff, Rock Bluff, and Chattahoochee. He even built a small fort armed with three cannons on the bluff at Fort Gaines. These upper forts were only precautions. Cobb was certain that the defensive works at the Narrows alone could block any assault.[5] And Cobb had one other obstacle to a Union advance upriver—the CSS *Chattahoochee.*

The *Chattahoochee* was originally conceived as part of a larger plan to break the Union blockade. The Confederate Navy Department hoped to construct many of these small oceangoing gunboats on inland waterways to challenge the Union fleet. But when the Confederates abandoned Apalachicola, the *Chattahoochee*'s mission changed from breaking the blockade to river defense.[6]

On October 19, 1861, Lieutenant Augustus McLaughlin, commanding the Confederate Navy Yard in Columbus, contracted with planter and entrepreneur David S. Johnston for construction of the *Chattahoochee* at

Saffold in Early County. Saffold was selected as the building site for several reasons. The area had abundant timber, and the local sawmill could turn out five thousand board feet of lumber a day. Johnston also had a labor force of ninety slaves. The contract called for the *Chattahoochee*'s delivery within 120 days at a cost of $47,500.[7]

From the very beginning, Johnston ran into construction problems. Though his slaves could handle the heavy manual labor, Johnston needed skilled workers as well, and they were in very short supply. The February 17, 1862, completion deadline came and went, and the *Chattahoochee* was little more than a skeletal frame. On March 4, Johnston placed an advertisement in the *Columbus Daily Sun* promising "steady employment and good wages" for ship carpenters, joiners, caulkers, and "hands accustomed to Ship and Steamboat work." As a further incentive, Johnston added that "all hands employed at the Confederate States Navy Yard are exempt from military duty, and any one in the Army can be furloughed to work there."[8]

Spring passed into summer and still the *Chattahoochee* was nowhere near ready for service. In June, Lieutenant McLaughlin asked the captain of the *Kate Bruce* to stop by Saffold on his next trip downriver and check into the delays. McLaughlin was beginning to suspect Johnston of using Saffold's navy yard more for his private business operations than for work on the *Chattahoochee*. McLaughlin demanded a full construction report and a solid timetable for completion. Shortly thereafter, McLaughlin wrote, "The department is very much annoyed at the manner in which things have been conducted at that yard. There seems no disposition on the part of the contractor to complete the work, his main view being to construct a permanent arrangement at his place for future operations of a private nature, which is highly detrimental to our cause." As the war continued, it would become increasingly commonplace for planters and wealthy businessmen to place personal gain above all else. Johnston finally delivered the ship on December 8, 1862, nearly ten months after its originally scheduled completion date. Even then, it took navy carpenters another two and a half months to finish work on the boat.[9]

Mechanical problems and plain bad luck continued to plague the *Chattahoochee*. In May 1863, after only three months of active service, it sunk when its boiler exploded near Blountstown, Florida. But damage to the structure was surprisingly light, and it was raised in August and taken to Columbus for repairs. Work did not begin until December but went quickly after that. By the end of April 1864 the refitted gunboat was again ready to sail.[10] That the *Chattahoochee* ever floated again at all was something of a minor miracle. That it was readied for active service was an even more impressive feat considering the scarcity of construction material available in the Confederacy by 1864. But the War Department had come to expect this sort of thing from McLaughlin. With the construction of the ironclad ram *Jackson* (also known as the *Muscogee*) and the torpedo boat *Viper,* not to mention the *Chattahoochee*'s repair, McLaughlin earned a reputation for superhuman organizational and production skills that even he was hard pressed to live up to.

From the war's outset, the War Department recognized Columbus as a natural location for war-related industries. It was deep in the southern heartland, far from the major theaters of combat. It had rail connections to every major city in the South, and it was at the head of navigation on the Chattahoochee River. Besides, it was already a thriving industrial center. With only minor modifications, its boatyard and factories could be put to service in the war effort. Columbus was only one of more than a dozen major industrial cities available for Confederate use, and there were dozens of smaller manufacturing centers. So successful was the Confederacy in quickly organizing its industrial base that its armies never lost a major battle for lack of munitions.

Of greatest industrial interest in the lower Chattahoochee Valley was the Columbus Iron Works, established by William R. Brown in 1848. The ironworks' first contribution to the Confederacy was the production of two three-inch rifled cannons for local militia units in July 1861. Within a few months it had orders from the Ordnance Department for brass Napoleon twelve-pounders and iron rifled artillery. Early in 1862 officials inspected the ironworks for possible transfer to the Navy Department and were impressed with what they saw. In June the navy took a lease on the facility and from then until the end of the war it was known as the Columbus Naval Iron Works. James Warner, former chief engineer at Gosport's navy yard in Virginia, took charge that fall. Under his direction, the ironworks became the Confederacy's leading producer of maritime machinery.[11]

Columbus manufacturing facilities attracted the attention of the Quartermaster Department as well. Uniforms were in short supply and Quartermaster General Abraham C. Myers hoped that the Columbus textile mills could help overcome the deficiency. In August 1861 he made local cotton merchant F. W. Dillard a quartermaster captain and put him in charge of contracting with Columbus firms for 20,000 uniforms. Incredibly, it took only a few months to complete the task. But as larger orders poured in during winter 1861–62, they became impossible to fill with the facilities at hand. To meet the crisis, the army promoted Dillard to the rank of major and gave him authority to oversee construction of the Confederate Quartermaster Depot. By June 1862 the depot was producing 240 crates of uniforms a month, enough to fill fourteen railroad cars. Within a year its production was second only to the quartermaster depot in Richmond. Dillard also established government tanneries and went into shoe manufacturing. In September 1862 he was granted permission to confiscate all hides in Columbus. By spring of the next year Dillard controlled all leather supplies in Georgia, Alabama, Tennessee, and South Carolina.[12]

The Confederate Ordnance Department established a permanent presence in the city with its Columbus Arsenal in June 1862. Headed by Captain F. C. Humphreys, the facility turned out knapsacks, harnesses, saddles, bridles, ammunition, and artillery pieces. By November, the Columbus Arsenal was using ten thousand pounds of lead monthly in the manufacture of ten thousand rounds of small-arms ammunition and seventy-five to one hundred artillery shells per day. Though this production rate lagged behind the operations in Atlanta and Augusta, it surpassed those at Charleston, Selma, and Macon. At the height of its operation, the arsenal employed roughly three hundred workers.[13]

Private manufacturers also took advantage of wartime opportunities. Requests for government contracts poured into the offices of state and Confederate officials. One jeweler, A. H. DeWitt, converted his shop into a sword factory. Madison Barringer and Joseph Merton, two Columbus mechanics, set up a facility to manufacture gun carriages. John D. Grey, who established a small rifle factory on Broad Street, supplied firearms to the Confederate government and to local militia companies. Eldridge S. Greenwood and William C. Gray, partners in a cotton warehouse firm, hired an English-born gunsmith and mechanic, J. P. Murray, to run their rifle factory. So many orders came in that Murray had to move the operation to a larger building and hire more workers. His labor force eventually reached 150.[14]

Perhaps the largest private weapons manufacturers in Columbus were Louis and Elias Haiman, immigrants from Prussia who had been in Columbus since the 1830s. By the 1850s the brothers were running a small tinsmith shop and hardware store that their father had established. When the war broke out, they leased the old Carter building and set up a sword factory. Within a year, they had purchased the Muscogee Iron Works to meet the rising demand. Keeping a supply of raw materials was such a problem that Elias spent most of the war in Europe running steel to Louis through the blockade.

By 1863 the factory employed four hundred workers, and Haiman swords were selling for twenty dollars each "when bought in quantity." Louis expanded his operation that year to include the manufacture of mess kits, tin cups, saddles, and bayonets. He also developed a pistol modeled after the Colt navy revolver. Large-scale production began in April 1863 after he received an order from the government for ten thousand pistols. An Ordnance Bureau estimate placed the Haiman factory's value at $80,000.[15]

Columbus firms supplied much more than weapons to the Confederacy. Nearly every type of military item imaginable rolled off the city's production lines. The firm of Manly and Hodges, which dealt in dry goods before the war, cleared space in the back of its store, bought several sewing machines, hired a few workers, and made tents for the Confederate army and the Georgia militia. A Columbus grocer, S. M. Sappington, turned his business into a shoe factory and eventually became the largest private shoe manufacturer in the South. The Rothchild brothers, who had been dry goods merchants, went into the uniform business when the war came. Within a year they had delivered more than five thousand uniforms to the Georgia militia and the Confederacy.[16]

Other major textile firms in Columbus included the Grant Factory and the Columbus Factory Company. The city's largest private textile mill, with 23,000 spindles, was the Eagle Manufacturing Company. It was, in fact, the largest private industrial operation of any kind in Columbus. Just before the war broke out the company merged with Howard Manufacturing, making it one of the largest textile mills in the South. By early 1862 the mill's daily production included two thousand yards of gray tweed for uniforms, 1,500 yards of tenting material, and $1,500 worth of cotton for army shirts, sheeting, and yarn. In its first year as a war-materials supplier, Eagle Manufacturing's production was valued at more than $600,000. As the war dragged on, it became more difficult to sustain this level of output with raw materials becoming harder to get by the day. Wool was particularly scarce because much had come from outside the South before the war. But the Eagle Company tapped into wool supplies throughout the lower Chattahoochee Valley and Florida so effectively that it was able to keep up a production of at least nine thousand yards of wool monthly through December 1862.[17]

Food production, especially flour and meal, was of great concern to the Confederate government, and Columbus filled a need here as well. Established in 1828, the City Mills expanded operations considerably in the first months of the war. The Palace Mills, founded in 1848, was the largest

producer in the city with an average early-war output of 250 barrels of
flour and meal per day.[18]

Though Columbus was by far the largest manufacturing center along the
lower Chattahoochee—indeed, one of the largest in the Confederacy—
other communities in the valley also served the South's industrial needs.
Some of the valley's industries fed directly into larger operations at
Columbus. J. W. Young, who ran a machine shop in Clayton, served as a
middleman for such supplies as wood, charcoal, and scrap iron bound for
the Columbus Naval Iron Works. A thriving timber industry sprang up in
Russell County to serve the Confederate Navy Yard just across the river.[19]

One of the most important industries in counties along the river was
textiles. The Troup Factory and Robertson Mill sent textiles all over the
Confederacy from Troup County. Gilbert and Forbes of LaGrange manufactured uniforms and boots on special order. There was a thread factory
near Saffold and a cotton mill on Harrod's Creek in Early County. A small
woolen mill was located near Columbia in Henry County. Across the river
in Decatur County, S. D. Tonge bought a three-story textile mill at the beginning of the war, and the Tonge Factory's 125 employees soon were
producing wide sheeting, ball thread, homespun, and rope.[20]

In Dale County, Jake Merritt manufactured tubs, buckets, looms, and
reels. Another Dale County man, a Mr. Ardis, ran a tannery at Westville
where he made shoes. Most of his workers were slaves. One shoe manufacturer, William Hendry of Cuthbert, wrote to Governor Brown in January 1862 boasting of his factory's ability to make up to four thousand
shoes annually. And P. T. Jackson of Stewart County promised the governor he could deliver as much as a thousand pounds of soap per week to
the state.[21]

The manufacture and delivery of such items as soap, uniforms, and artillery pieces depended on an adequate transportation system. Before the
war much of the lower Chattahoochee's import and export traffic flowed
along the river. But after Confederate troops abandoned Apalachicola
early in the war its port lost much of its commerce. Some raw materials
and manufactured products did continue to flow through Apalachicola
courtesy of blockade-runners, but the town's volume of exchange was not
what it had been before the war. Still, steamboating on the Chattahoochee
did not disappear by any means. Timber, cotton, wool, and other raw materials were regularly shipped to manufacturing centers along the river on
boats like the *Indian, Munnerlyn, Shamrock, Uchee,* and *Wave.*[22]

With Apalachicola lost as a dependable import-export center, the valley's rail connections became more important than ever. The Civil War

was the first in which railroads were of key strategic significance, and the Confederacy's nine thousand miles of track made it second only to the United States among railroading nations. Georgia had about one thousand miles of track, more than any other Confederate state except Virginia. But many southern rail lines, though relatively new, had been poorly built by companies more concerned with quick profits than quality construction. Trains could travel no faster than about twenty-five miles per hour on the rickety tracks, though engines were capable of much greater speeds. At the same time, traffic along these lines was increasing rapidly. In April 1862 the Montgomery and West Point Railroad had a net income of $143,995.46. A year later that figure was up by more than 430 percent to $628,528.56. But the company's repair costs were rising and its efforts to keep the line open were not always successful. Daniel H. Cram, the railroad's superintendent, reported that the increased traffic was "inflicting extraordinary wear upon the track." He warned that the rails on the upper part of the line near the Chattahoochee River were "very much worn and totally insufficient to sustain a business of any magnitude . . . the bars were almost daily breaking loose from their fastenings under the passage of trains, always endangering and very frequently causing accidents." It was impossible for him to say how much longer the rails might hold together, but it was only a matter of time, and a short time at that, before the company would have to replace them.[23]

Accidents were not uncommon along the valley's rail lines. Kate Cumming, a Confederate nurse who spent some time in the valley, recalled one mishap in her diary. Her train was a few miles from Opelika when the engine ran off the track. Seated in the last car, she felt a jerking motion "as if the train was about to upset," then heard screams from the forward cars. She looked out the window and saw people running from the train, fearful that the engine might explode. No explosion occurred, but the passengers had to spend the night on the train. They were rescued next afternoon by a wood car sent up from Columbus. Henrietta McLaughlin, wife of Augustus McLaughlin, was not so fortunate. While on her way back from Richmond, her train derailed and landed upside down after rolling down a fourteen-foot embankment. She was so badly injured that it was a month before she could travel again.[24]

The blockade and limited domestic supplies of scrap iron caused shortages in many areas for railroad companies all over the South as the war entered its second year. Locomotives were scarce, and the surge in rail traffic caused many to wear out early in the war. The cars were also wearing out quickly and, like the locomotives, were difficult to repair or replace.

The Confederacy had a few firms making rail cars, but they were never able to meet Southern needs. Hubert Dent wrote from his camp in Tennessee that the railroad cars there were "full of lice and no seats." And there were shortages of other essential equipment, such as axes, shovels, files, and framing tools.[25]

One of the most serious handicaps suffered by the Confederacy's railroads was a deficiency of lubricating oil. Before the war it had been imported, but substitutes now had to be found. Lard was the most common, and peanut oil and castor oil, which one Southerner called "the best lubricator known," were used as well. Commercial firms opened all over the South to manufacture lard, but they could never keep up with the demand. Railroads were so desperate that they placed ads offering "the highest market price" for lard in newspapers all over the South.[26]

Superintendent Cram of the Montgomery and West Point line attributed much of the supply problem to misguided Confederate policy. While he agreed that it was necessary for the government to seize as much of the South's iron as it could lay its hands on, more should go to the building and maintenance of railroads. As it was, much raw and scrap iron went into munitions production and remained "for months piled in those beautiful pyramids which adorn our Arsenal Yards" while the means of hauling these munitions went neglected. In his April 1863 report, Cram insisted that Confederate policy was doing more harm to the South's rail system than was the Yankee blockade: "It is the blockade imposed by our own rulers upon the resources of the country that is working our destruction."[27]

Railroad workers, both skilled and unskilled, also became scarce as the war dragged on. Such labor was legally exempt from military service, but by 1862 many railroad firms saw their employees siphoned off to the army. Brown was able to block the draft of employees on the Western and Atlantic Railroad, the only state-owned line in Georgia, by making them part of the state militia. He also warned Davis that "the military operations of the Government cannot be carried on without the use of all our railroads, and the same necessity exists for the exemption of all other railroad officers and workmen which exists in the case of the State Road." Some companies made up the labor deficiency with slaves, but even they were not enough to meet labor needs. There were so few axe men to cut cordwood for fuel that trains often sat idle on the tracks. The state militia sometimes helped cut wood so that trains could run.[28]

With hundreds of young men in military service, labor shortages were felt early in the war not only by the railroads but by most industrial concerns along the lower Chattahoochee. In September 1861 a single issue of one Columbus paper contained urgent appeals for twenty or thirty weavers and forty or fifty other workers at the Eagle factory along with twenty more for the Rothchilds. Much of the demand for labor in Columbus and other parts of the valley was met by thousands of farmers from surrounding counties as well as refugees from areas hit hard by the war. So many people flooded into Columbus that the city's population swelled to 17,000, nearly twice its prewar level.[29]

The labor shortage brought new opportunities for hundreds of workers, black as well as white. In the war's first months, blacks began moving into occupations that had previously been closed to them. Nearly a third of the Columbus Factory Company's workforce was black as early as spring 1861. Within a year or two, most of the draymen and teamsters in Columbus were free blacks or slaves. Free blacks were hired as clerks and bookkeepers for the first time. By 1863, 68 percent of the attendants at LaGrange's four hospitals were black. The Grant Factory of Columbus, which hired only white labor before the war, quickly began building a force of slave labor. So did the city's giant Eagle Manufacturing Company. By 1864 it was advertising for free black workers, promising "good wages and steady employment." Between 1861 and 1864 blacks made up half the labor force at the Rock Island paper mill just outside Columbus. Any number of highly skilled blacks, slave and free, had jobs at the Columbus Naval Iron Works. Horace King, a free black contractor, supplied more than 15,000 board feet of lumber for construction of the ironclad gunboat *Jackson*. Most of the five hundred employees in the shoe manufacturing division of the quartermaster depot were black. Scores of African American blacksmiths were employed at the Haiman factory. John D. Gray also recruited carpenters and blacksmiths for his Columbus armory from the city's black community.[30]

As the war continued into 1862 and '63, most slaveholders became reluctant to hire their slaves out either to private or government industries. Accidents were frequent, and if a slave were killed or could no longer work, the slaveholder usually received no compensation. Slaves were injured lifting heavy loads, fell from scaffolding, and were hit by trains and mangled in machinery. One slave was killed in a boiler explosion at the Columbus Naval Iron Works. So difficult did it become to hire slave labor that in August 1863 the secretary of war ordered the impressment of 20 percent of the slaves in Georgia alone. Their owners were paid twenty-five dollars a month for the labor of each slave and $2,500 if the slave was captured, killed, or injured. Slaves were impressed by the hundreds to repair rail lines and build fortifications around Columbus in 1864.[31]

Despite the dangers involved, many blacks saw industrial and clerical work as a way to achieve some measure of economic status. Perhaps a few saw such employment as a chance to prove themselves to the white community—an opportunity to destroy the arguments that justified oppression for all blacks and slavery for most. A major pillar of the proslavery argument had been that people of African descent were capable of performing only menial tasks. However, such was the skill and efficiency of the city's black bookkeepers, clerks, and mechanics that even the editor of the *Columbus Daily Sun,* once the city's most vocal opponent of black labor, called their performance "laudable." One white citizen remembered that black labor boosted morale in Columbus and was a "source of civic pride during the war." [32]

Despite such praise, there were few corresponding calls for an end to slavery or for black equality under the law. If any expected it, they were very much disappointed. The dynamics of a caste system based on race simply would not allow it. Those blacks who thought hard work alone was the path to civil and social equality failed to understand that the problem lay not with themselves but rather with the class-related self-image of whites and how they used blacks to bolster their image. No amount of hard work and dedication on the part of blacks could overcome that, and most were probably under no illusion that it would. Years after the war, one former Columbus slave said of the freedman, "you can't fool him about a white man! And you couldn't fool him when he was a slave! He knows a white man for what he is, and he knew him the same way in slavery times." [33]

That attitude among blacks was based on generations of being kept, by one means or another, "in their place." Rarely did that place include the factory. As early as the eighteenth century, white urban laborers had struggled to keep blacks out of their ranks in an effort to limit competition and maintain some degree of social status. When Georgia's legislature considered a bill outlawing racially restrictive trade unions in April 1863, white workers throughout the state howled in protest. They saw it as a first step toward placing them in direct competition with slaves. White laborers, especially skilled workers, were sure that after passage of the bill, "the wealthier classes would attempt to apprentice a lot of negroes, and place them in the various machine and workshops (thus placing the negro on an equality with the white man)." [34]

Along with other sources of urban unrest, high food prices among them, the controversy over unions and black labor sparked riots in cities throughout the South, Columbus included. "We feel that you would have us grovel in the dust beneath your aristocratic tread," wrote one group of enraged workers. They spoke for many common folk when they charged that the Confederate constitution had been "formed solely for the benefit (socially and pecuniarily) of the aristocrats," giving poor whites "no rights that are not guaranteed to the negro."[35] Many working-class whites were beginning to see the Confederacy as a threat to their economic and social status, further entrenching their "rich man's war" attitude.

If black industrial labor was a source of intense controversy, child labor was not. It had not been uncommon to see children of poor whites doing factory work even before the war, especially in textile mills. As with black labor, the war created new demands for child labor and dramatically expanded their exploitation. Industrial establishments like the Eagle factory advertised employment opportunities for "boys and young women." By 1863 most of the Haiman factory's workers were young boys. Even government facilities like the Columbus Naval Iron Works sought the financial advantages of inexpensive child labor. Because they were unskilled and economically less valuable, children often performed the most dangerous tasks. In February 1865, Jack McElrath and John Madden, aged twelve and thirteen respectively, were horribly mangled when an artillery shell they were working on exploded at the Columbus Naval Iron Works. Both suffered through more than an hour of agony before they mercifully died.[36]

Like slaves, free blacks, and children, women took up much of the slack in the valley's industrial labor force. The type of work done by individual women depended largely on their class status. Working-class women, both free and slave, held industrial and menial jobs. Nearly all Columbus industries employed poor women in some way. The quartermaster depot in Columbus could not have functioned without them, and fully half of the Columbus Arsenal's three hundred employees were women.[37]

More affluent women of the leisure classes formed ladies' aid societies and sewing circles. One of the first was the "Ladies' Soldier's Friend Society," organized in Columbus on May 21, 1861. Elizabeth Rhodes put together a similar soldiers' aid group in Eufaula. Such groups held fairs, plays, and other fund-raising activities in almost every town along the lower Chattahoochee. In Cuthbert, the "Thespian Corps" gave performances of well-known plays like *Richelieu,* but some of the productions were original and had war-related themes. One such play in Alabama depicted a wounded Confederate soldier being attended by a host of beautiful young women. A similar play at Notasulga brought in sixty-eight dollars. The women sent the proceeds to the governor's office to purchase hospital supplies.[38]

Columbus women were particularly fond of staging choral concerts in Temperance Hall. Such patriotic songs as "Let Me Like a Soldier Fall" and "Southrons, Hear Your Country Call You" were among their favorites. They also sponsored benefit concerts by a young slave piano prodigy, Thomas "Blind Tom" Bethune. His performances were, said one admirer, "calculated to excite, if not awe, wonderment in the very highest degree." During what one source called a typical month in 1861, the Columbus Ladies' Soldier's Friend Society raised $1,542 and furnished 2,503 articles of clothing to thirteen military companies. They also established the Wayside Home to provide meals for soldiers passing through the city, and by summer 1864 the home was serving between one hundred and three hundred meals a day.[39]

One method of fund-raising used by women's societies was the lottery. Prizes might be anything from cotton bales to livestock, and few saw any harm because the money went to support the troops. But some ministers and a few newspaper editors were outraged. One typical antilottery editorial from Opelika objected not only because of the lottery's morally subversive nature but also because it kept women from their primary duty of sewing clothes for the soldiers. The editor insisted that the women might as well open gambling houses as continue with lotteries. Such criticism was usually ignored and lotteries remained popular through the end of the war.[40]

Whatever other activities women may have engaged in, sewing societies flourished in the lower Chattahoochee Valley. The women of a Eufaula circle met once a week to make "socks, blankets, woolen coverlets, and even home-made bedquilts." The Whitesville Soldier Aid Society and the Cataula Ladies' Aid Society, both in Harris County, did the same. Another Harris County organization, the Soldiers Relief Association of Waverly Hall, collected potatoes, onions, squash, apples, beets, cakes, gingerbread, cucumbers, okra, chickens, and ham. When a shipment of food and clothing was ready for the soldiers, some member of the company received a furlough and went home to get the supplies.[41]

Perhaps the most appreciated service women provided to the soldiers was nursing. With doctors in short supply from the war's outset, women were badly needed as caretakers for wounded and dying men. There was no shortage of volunteers for nursing duties, especially in the lower Chattahoochee Valley. Only two weeks after the firing on Fort Sumter, twenty young "unengaged" women of Columbus published a notice in the *Daily Sun* offering their "humble services in the anticipated engagements, as Florence Nightingales to the brave companies who have so nobly marched from our city to the defense of our country and our homes." This was only the beginning for the city's women in the field of nursing. Two Columbus sisters followed the troops to Virginia in the first months of the war and according to one report made almost all the bandages used at the Battle of First Manassas. One city merchant found it difficult to keep a clean shirt in his house. Each time he searched for one he found that his wife had used it at the local hospital.[42]

Columbus became a major center for soldiers' long-term medical care and its importance expanded as the war dragged on. Hospital overcrowding, always a problem, became even worse during the Atlanta campaign of 1864. In May, Columbus hospitals were overwhelmed when the first trains of wounded soldiers began arriving. In one twenty-four-hour period seven hundred new patients flooded into town. The army rented buildings along Broad Street, including two saloons, to house all the wounded pouring in from the north Georgia battlefields. The courthouse itself was turned into a makeshift hospital. Surgeons placed wounded soldiers anywhere they could, even open railroad sheds at the city depot.[43]

Army surgeons also confiscated Columbus churches and turned them into hospitals, but they were careful not to offend the city's elite. Only churches of the poor, such as the factory churches near the river, were taken outright. The army preferred to have churches of the well-to-do voluntarily offer their facilities for hospital use in the spirit of Christian charity. No such offers came and officials did not press the issue. This blatant class discrimination in the face of wartime anguish served only to reinforce the "rich man's war" attitude, by then widespread among common folk. Even the *Columbus Times* recognized the incident's demoralizing impact: "It seems to us that it would have been far less subversive of the good of the community to have taken any or all of the handsome up town churches."[44]

Columbus was far from alone in its problems with housing the wounded. Eufaula had forty patients in its hospital by March 1864 but needed room for many more. There were plans to expand the existing facility to two hundred beds and build a second hospital for two hundred more.[45] Progress on the new facilities was much too slow and it was soon too late. On July 24, post surgeon Paul DeLacy Baker wrote, "Late last night, I had emptied upon me, without any sort of notice, between 200 and 300 wounded men. I am compelled to lay these men, filthy and lousy, upon the floor of the houses I have prepared for bunks, without any kind of appliance or convenience necessary to the required cleanliness. I have, for these men sent on in advance of all necessary materials, no pans, no tubs, no spittoons, no medicines, no nurses, no ward masters, no adequate medical assistance, no Hospital clothing, and, consequently, cannot have the clothing of these men washed without turning them naked in the Houses or in the streets." [46]

Throughout the valley, army surgeons took shelter for the wounded wherever they could find it. The seminary at Fort Gaines served as a hospital after the Battle of Olustee in north Florida. Andrew Female College in Cuthbert was converted to a Confederate army hospital. West Point and LaGrange both became hospital centers because of their location on the railroad. LaGrange had four major hospitals but they were not enough in the war's last year. Some of the more kindhearted folk living near the railroad tracks, like Sarah Clayton of Opelika, opened their homes to the wounded and dying. [47]

Few citizens were as sympathetic to the soldiers' plight as Clayton, especially in the war's last year. Many did not even want wounded men housed in their vicinity. Citing concerns over sanitation, the mayor and city council of Columbus unanimously passed a resolution calling on the army to move all its hospitals to some more "healthy location" outside the city. The surgeon in command, George B. Douglas, was outraged. Far from being a health risk, Douglas countered, the hospitals had actually reduced the threat of disease: hospital workers carried out a sanitation plan for the city that involved cleaning up huge piles of accumulated garbage. Douglas believed the real motive behind the resolution was that the mayor and city council wanted their courthouse back. In any case, he ignored all protests and the hospitals stayed. [48]

Baker had similar problems in Eufaula. He made arrangements with a Mrs. O'Harra to use her hotel as a hospital, but when Baker's steward arrived to clean the building Mrs. O'Harra had changed her mind. Surgeon William L. Nichol's experience with the people of Cuthbert was even more trying. From the time he set up his hospital at Andrew College in summer 1864 Nichol encountered constant resistance, even hostility, from town residents. "The people are totally insensible to the wants of the army," he wrote shortly after his arrival. "They are more essentially selfish than any set with whom I have been thrown." Nichol could find no one to rent him space for an office even though there were any number of available buildings in town. "I am entirely out of the world down here," he complained to his superiors. "If I swore at all I would say Damn this place." [49]

Not all townsfolk were set against having a hospital in their midst. But Nichol's comments do suggest that by 1864 people in the lower Chattahoochee Valley had lost patience with the war and the Confederacy in all their representative forms. Through it all, though, even in the face of open hostility, nurses continued to care for the soldiers. No matter where soldiers in need of care were housed, there too would be the nurses.

Women became so indispensable to the care of wounded soldiers that in fall 1862 the Confederacy provided for the position of hospital matron to "exercise a superintendence over the entire domestic economy of the hospital, to take charge of such delicacies as may be provided for the sick, to see that the food or diet is properly prepared, and all such other duties as may be necessary." Among those duties were "to superintend the laundry, to take charge of the clothing of the sick, and the bedding of the hospital." Hundreds of volunteers had been doing these things without pay for more than a year, but now chief matrons would receive forty dollars per month, assistant matrons thirty-five, and ward matrons thirty.[50]

In spite of the effort they put into helping soldiers, women found resistance to their assumption of nontraditional roles at nearly every turn. Columbus native Edward Henry Grouby, founder, proprietor, and first editor of Blakely's *Early County News,* compiled a list of things he did not like to see.

> There is too much travel on the rail roads by the women. Hundreds go where they have no business. . . .

> We have noticed that the ladies hold up their dresses—not in front to prevent the wearer from stepping on them, *but all round, and to an exceeding great height.* This is perfectly disgusting. . . .

> We have noticed another habit that is growing in the country—the habit of cutting the hair *short*—or, as the barbers say, "*shingling the hair.*" This is a sort of "disrespectable city cut," and don't look half as well as the old styles. . . .

> Some of the ladies, now that there are so few men in the country, are becoming *too familiar* with the few remaining. . . . We like to see ladies familiar, but not *disgustingly* familiar.[51]

Even in the hospitals many physicians objected to the "petticoat government" imposed by matrons. One doctor was overheard complaining to a colleague, "in a tone of ill-concealed disgust, that 'one of *them* had come.'" In the face of criticism from society in general and male doctors in particular, women continued to insist on their right to serve. As Cum-

ming put it, "The war is certainly ours as well as that of the men. We can
not fight, so must take care of those who do." [52]

Not all women who went to work in the hospitals were driven by patriotism. Cumming overheard one young widow saying how much she
liked working at the hospital because it was the perfect place to catch a
husband. Another nurse frankly admitted that she was quitting hospital
work because she had accomplished her objective there—to find a man.
Cumming remarked in her diary how little she thought of such motives
and how she hoped such women were rare. But flirtation was all too common on hospital wards throughout the war. [53]

Whether their motives involved patriotism or matrimony it took an in-
ner strength to work for any length of time in the hospitals. Some women
did not have the stomach for it. A few of the more "delicately bred" ladies
were put off by little more than a fear of immodesty. One Alabama woman,
when applying for a hospital position, asked if she would be required to
dress "stomach" wounds. Cumming held such women in low esteem,
saying that their "respectability must be at a low ebb when it can be en-
dangered by going into a hospital." But even she was at times distressed
by the conditions around her. Early in her career Cumming was taken
aback when she "saw a stream of blood running off an operating table
into a tub, which also held the patient's recently severed arm." Many new
nurses passed out when confronted with such horrors and subsequently
left the hospitals, never to return. Cumming accustomed herself to the realities of hospital work over time but she continued to write in her diary
of "the most soul-harrowing scenes that it has been the lot of mortals to
witness." [54]

The fortitude of women like Cumming gained the eternal admiration
and gratitude of the men in the ranks. One of the most impressive displays
of nursing skill and dedication came in the wake of the May 1863 *Chattahoochee* explosion. Wounded survivors were carried upriver to Columbus,
where women nursed many of them back to health and made comfortable
those who were beyond help. McLaughlin recalled how "the Home was
literally besieged with ladies, and for one week the street in front of the
Home was blocked up with vehicles of all descriptions. . . . The four worst
cases were placed together in the room upstairs." In a personal compli-
ment McLaughlin remarked, "It was with the utmost difficulty that I
could remain in the room sufficiently long to ascertain what was required
and to see what service I could render, the atmosphere was so unpleasant,
yet the ladies did not seem to notice it and remained at their post till the
last." [55]

This kind of endurance on the part of Columbus women in particular and of its population in general, along with its industrial base and rail connections, made the town vitally important to the Confederate cause. Union forces recognized its significance as well. In 1862 one officer on blockade duty near Apalachicola wrote to his superiors in Washington, "Columbus is one of the grand depots and sources of strength of the Confederacy. Besides the 60,000 to 70,000 bales of cotton stored there three cotton factories, one rolling mill, foundries to cast cannon, machine shops, and two gun shops are in active operation; from Columbus railroads diverge, communicating with Montgomery, Ala., Savannah, Ga., Augusta, and Milledgeville, the capital of Georgia." [56]

For the moment, Union forces could do little to stop the flow of war materials from Columbus. That inability gave Columbus residents a sense of security not enjoyed by the border states and coastal regions. It was one factor sustaining support for the Confederacy in Columbus during the war's early months. Other factors included a relative abundance of food in the city and, perhaps most significantly, the economic boom brought on by the war.

"No other city in the Confederacy has been so fortunate as Columbus," wrote the editor of one local paper. "There is perhaps no city in the Confederacy that has felt less the deprivations and inconveniences of war." Though prices were on the rise all over the South, wages initially kept pace with inflation in Columbus. By December 1862 wages at the Eagle mills alone were up 300 percent from a year and a half earlier. In fact, during the first year of the war the standard of living for many of the city's middle-class merchants and artisans was higher than it had ever been. Before the Confederate and state governments took control of raw materials flowing into the city, fabric and yarn were available to local residents at reasonable prices. So abundant were basic necessities that speculation and profiteering, so common in other parts of the Confederacy, were almost unknown in Columbus during the war's first year. [57]

The Columbus upper classes were particularly pleased with the new business opportunities. From their microeconomic perspective the blockade was a godsend that served only to boost demand for their products. For them, life and leisure went on much as they had before the war. They were entertained at Temperance Hall by traveling shows like the Holman Parlor Opera Troupe, the George Christy Minstrels, and the New Orleans and Metropolitan Burlesque Opera Troupe. While thousands were dying in Virginia and Tennessee some of Georgia's well-to-do held extravagant dinner parties and barbecues at their lavish homes in Wynnton, two miles east of Columbus. A few built vacation homes three miles north of the city across the river in Russell County.[58]

As for the valley's rural planters, their lifestyle too was little changed compared to their poorer neighbors. Demand for cotton was up at the valley's textile mills, producing a windfall for cotton growers throughout the region. Some planters raised more cotton than ever, hoping not only to take advantage of regional demand but also to hoard as much as possible for sale after the war. Manufacturers in England and the North would by then be desperate for southern cotton and paying top dollar for it.[59]

Not everyone in the lower Chattahoochee Valley could look on the war as favorably as the urban elite and planters. For yeomen and landless poor the hardships of war were felt from the beginning and became more intense as the war continued. Women on the farms were especially hard hit as early as fall 1861, when harvest time came and their men were not back from the war. One Georgia soldier expressed deep regret over leaving his wife alone to care for their farm but wrote to her from Virginia, "You must be man and woman both while the war lasts."[60] He had no idea that the war would last so long nor did he realize the price he and his family would have to pay. Few southerners understood the costs in the beginning but by the war's second year, inflation, hunger, conscription, and government confiscation were beginning to erode southern resolve—with fatal consequences for the Confederacy.

CHAPTER

4

What Will Become
of the Women and Children?

Hubert Dent of Eufaula earnestly hoped that the war would bring white southerners of all classes together in a common cause.[1] But as the war entered its second year the gap between rich and poor only became wider. The southern upper classes seemed completely unable to comprehend the magnitude of suffering among plain folk, or perhaps they simply did not care. In any case, they ignored both the misery of the lower classes and the consequences of their own callousness for far too long.

While thousands faced starvation, journals and letters of the affluent were filled with descriptions of dinner parties and splendid meals. On March 29, 1864, Dr. John Meriwether, an army surgeon stationed in Eufaula, wrote to his wife of a dinner party at the Pope residence. His hosts served "a very nice table indeed, meats of various kinds, cakes, fruits, custards, floats and plenty of pure coffee." A few days later he described another dinner at the Crawford home where there was "ham, dressed with salads, nice turkey, mutton, chicken salad, cakes, custards and a great many other niceties." At the same time hardly anything was available in town for the common folk. "All the stores are pretty well closed," Meriwether wrote, "and the few that are open contain nothing at all."[2]

As late as March 1865, only weeks before the war's end, one woman wrote of a meal at the Cook House in Columbus where the table was so heavy with food that it "actually groaned." There were sausages, roast pork, cold turkey, biscuits, hot rolls, cornbread, and even cake. The next morning's breakfast featured coffee with milk and sugar. Coffee was one of the rarest commodities in the Confederacy and so expensive that poorer folk used everything from peanuts to pecan shells as substitutes. Though most plain folk had run out of coffee by summer 1861, not until a year later did one plantation mistress notice with astonishment that some people were instead drinking a brew of parched rye.[3]

Of course, the southern elites were not able to escape the blockade's effects entirely. Young belles recycled hoopskirts by sewing new cloth onto old frames and cut up old carpet to make house slippers. Expensive curtains and draperies became dresses and homespun cotton undergarments replaced the usual silk finery. Even this small deprivation was too much for some of the more genteel young ladies. One Georgia girl wrote in her journal that although she was willing to wear make-do dresses, she just could not stand the homespun underwear. It made her feel "vulgar and common." Nevertheless, the upper classes endured and, wrote one woman on a Barbour County plantation, "even made merry over our inevitable privations and inconveniences. Indeed, we grew so accustomed to them that they scarcely seemed privations."[4]

While planters sacrificed luxuries and suffered inconveniences, plain folk faced a daily struggle just to stay alive. The situation was hardly a formula for unity among southern whites. When a "village belle" in Blakely said that she "could get along without stockings so long as she had fashionable dresses," Editor E. H. Grouby of the *Early County News* labeled her and others like her "a set of ignoramuses."[5] As Grouby clearly recognized, most planters had little understanding of the hardships suffered by common people.

One of the most severe misfortunes confronted by southerners, especially the poor, was excessive inflation. At first, few thought it would be a problem since the war was expected to end quickly. Even after First Manassas, some scoffed at the blockade and its economic threat. Others, however, were more farsighted. John B. Lamar, Howell Cobb's brother-in-law, wrote to the general in November 1861, "we can laugh at the blockade for a while if salt is $12 a sack," but he wondered what the impact would be if the blockade lasted another year. "It makes me hold my breath when I think of it." A year later the blockade was tighter than ever and salt was selling for eighty dollars a sack. It had been only fifty cents before the war.[6]

Such dramatic price increases for even the most basic commodities were not uncommon. Butter went from twelve cents a pound in 1861 to seventy-five cents in less than two years. By the end of the war it was five dollars or more. Two dollars a bushel in 1863, corn sold for fourteen by February 1865. Bacon went from twelve cents to fifty cents a pound in the war's first year and reached four dollars by war's end. Flour that sold for nine dollars a barrel before the war went to four hundred. Coffee rose to

TABLE I

Inflation during Civil War, from Columbus, Georgia, Newspapers

	Mar. 1862	Jul. 1863	Nov. 1863	Mar. 1865
Corn (bushel)	$1.10	$2.50	$5.00	$15.00
Sugar (pound)	.50	2.00	3.00	8.00
Butter (pound)	.40	1.00	3.00	7.00
Cotton (pound)	.16	.41	.60	.75
Tobacco (pound)	.60	1.75	—	7.10

thirty dollars a pound shortly after the war began and from there to sixty and seventy dollars. The cost of more potent beverages went up too. Rum purchased for just seventeen cents a gallon in Cuba sold for twenty-five dollars after being run through the blockade.[7]

Even in prosperous Columbus, prices were beginning to outstrip wages by the second year of the war. Table I charts inflation during the war as listed in Columbus newspapers.[8]

This inflationary spiral hit the city's working class especially hard. One Columbus paper remarked, "we see some of them with their families living for days on bread and water; their children barefooted and in rags." Some firms, like the Eagle mills, tried to help by selling provisions to their employees at cost. But with wages constantly lagging behind inflation, such gestures were little comfort to the working class. In April 1864 a city paper published a mechanic's letter that listed his family's monthly income and expenses.[9] Even after selling his bed, the man was in debt for the month. This cycle of increasing debt had been going on for months and would continue for much longer.

Though the blockade contributed to rising prices, even more damaging to the economy were profiteering and speculation by planters, merchants, and industrialists. In his study of Columbus during the war, Diffee Standard concluded that the blockade was more an excuse than a reason for inflated prices. That fact seemed obvious to contemporary residents. The Columbus Relief Association wrote to the Confederate secretary of war that "heartless extortioners" were "advancing the prices of all provisions to such rates as to place them beyond the reach of the laboring class and the families of absent soldiers." Though corn prices in Columbus had more than doubled in only a year, a March 1863 article in one city paper reported that there was twice as much corn stored in local warehouses as there had ever been before. Yet corn prices were high and getting higher. "It has been bought for speculation," complained the editor, "and the speculators are still buying." One Columbus man insisted that "the depreciation of our currency is only a trick of our enemies at home, else why should they strive so hard to secure it all?" Kate Cumming was sure that the South could sustain itself in spite of the blockade if not for the speculators who were "making *piles* of money out of the misfortunes of their country."[10]

The problem of inflation lay not just with town merchants. Captain A. M. Allen of Columbus wrote to the War Department in May 1863 complaining that southwest Georgia planters were not only charging too much for their corn but that they also were not growing enough. By then, corn supplies within twenty-five or thirty miles of the rail lines were nearly exhausted and planters were charging up to two dollars a bushel for what remained.[11]

As early as November 1861 a Georgia man complained to Vice President Alexander Stephens that "common farmers" were finding it difficult "to keep our heads above the flood of destruction" brought on by "the money thieves, those Speculators." With the war effort dependent as it was on the yeomen, if they were forced under by wild speculation the Confederacy might go with them. E. H. Grouby saw the danger as well. Those who engaged in profiteering (Grouby called them "home Yankees") were "by far greater enemies to the South and do more to injure her cause than ten times their number of Yankees in the field." Such people, said Grouby, "carry their patriotism in the *pocket-book*." James N. Bethune of Columbus agreed. In a letter to the *Daily Sun,* he warned that the avarice of southern elites was the Yankees' most powerful ally. Bethune urged planters to contrast their own inconveniences with the hardships of poor soldiers and their families who were suffering and dying to defend the planters' slave property. "And now you complain of making sacrifices if you furnish bread for him at less than you might get for it from somebody else."[12]

If the southern elites did not notice or care about disparities of sacrifice, the plain folk certainly did. One Georgia paper reflected the prevailing view among poor whites when it wrote, "There is one mode that would work most successfully in bringing down the prices of everything, and that is for the wealthier classes to practice, for awhile, the rigid self-denial that the poor are compelled to practice." A southwest Georgia man wrote to Governor Joe Brown in March 1862 begging him to do something about "those unpatriotic men in our midst who are engaged in buying up and holding the necissaries of life, and who fears not God nor sympathise with humanity." The *Opelika Southern Republic* reminded its readers of the biblical warning that "extortioners" could not "inherit the kingdom of God."[13]

As if private speculation was not bad enough, government contractors and high-ranking military officers were also guilty of profiteering. Duncan Jordan of the firm Lennard and Jordan, a small shoe-manufacturing company in Cuthbert, complained to Governor Brown in November 1861 about the practices of government purchasing agents. He had been selling his shoes to them at low prices, thinking they were going to the army. He later discovered that the agents were selling his shoes on the open market at inflated prices. Jordan suggested that the state make "application through honest agents" and void the contracts of "averacious Speculators."[14]

Less than a year later, scandal rocked the War Department when quartermaster officers were caught selling army rations to speculators. Congress responded by making it illegal for the public to buy military supplies from enlisted men but said nothing of officers. Small wonder that the act did little to stop corruption but served only to emphasize the South's pervasive class divisions. The *Early County News* denounced the legislation for its elitist overtones: "Why is it not also against the law to buy any of these articles from Quarter Masters, Commissaries, &c., when it is a well known fact that many of these swoll head gentry steal a great deal of this kind of Government property which they have in their possession, to be distributed among the needy Soldiers, sell them, and pocket the money? There is more rascality, according to the number, among officers than privates. Why are not officers bound up as tight as privates? There is altogether too much *favoritism* shown to little jackass officers by Congress." Another exasperated Georgian added his voice to the swelling chorus urging Governor Brown to take decisive action: "Do for God's sake put an end to this unrighteous war. We shall be eaten up by Confederate Office holders and Speculators."[15]

It was not long before inflation and speculation began to take their toll on Confederate currency. With prices going up every day, government notes became increasingly worthless. Many people abandoned the use of paper money altogether in favor of a barter system. Most were already accustomed to some degree of barter. In parts of the valley, according to one native, "cattle, cow hides, peas, pork, 'possum and potatoes were legal tender" even before the war.[16] But so serious was the inflation problem that livestock, farm equipment, corn, and cotton all became regular mediums of exchange by the war's second year.

Gadwell Jefferson Pearce, president of LaGrange Female College, advised a Troup County woman to "get all the thread you can. It is an article of necessity and good currency, vastly better than Confederate." Pearce knew what he was talking about. Newspapers throughout the valley advertised items for barter, and yarn was one of the most common. In Early County, Joel W. Perry offered to exchange yarn for pork. The *Early County News* got in on the barter system when its editor began selling one-year subscriptions in trade for eight pounds of bacon, lard, or sugar.[17]

The flood of pleas from anguished citizens and the impact of inflation on the currency could not long be ignored. As early as December 1861 Joe Brown signed legislation outlawing speculation in all sorts of basic commodities including "clothing, shoes, leather, cloth of any kind, provisions, wheat, flour, corn, corn-meal, meat, bacon, hogs, cattle, salt, bagging, rope, and twine." Penalties for violation ranged from five hundred dollars to five thousand dollars. In Alabama, Governor A. B. Moore issued a proclamation declaring speculation "unpatriotic and wicked" and approved legislation limiting profit on all goods to 15 percent. Any proceeds above that margin would go to the state treasury. In a similar effort Georgia passed a profit and income tax intended to funnel speculators' excess profits to the state. Confederate officials also tried to curb inflation by appointing price commissioners to fix prices on items deemed common and necessary. Even local citizens tried to rein in speculation and inflation by price fixing. M. T. Alexander and W. W. Fleming called a public meeting in Early County to discuss regulation of prices on local produce.[18]

Despite efforts to control it, profiteering continued unabated. Brown admitted that the antispeculation laws in Georgia were a "dead letter." One major reason was that profit and income taxes lacked proper administration and enforcement. Georgia's comptroller-general, Peterson Thweatt, estimated that the taxes brought in only one-fifth the amount due. Though there was little he could do against them, Brown was sure that speculators and profiteers were among the Confederacy's greatest enemies.[19]

Speculators were an obvious threat to the southern economy, but, as Brown seemed to recognize, they were an even greater threat to the war effort. Volunteering was down by winter 1861–62 and new recruits could hardly be expected to come from the ranks of the common folk. They already felt they were being starved by those who benefited most from the war. Kate Cumming asked of the southern elites, "How can they expect men to fight for them when they are taking the lives of their wives and children?" Cumming expressed the feelings of plain folk all over the South when she wrote that speculators were, "in the eyes of God," murderers destined for hellfire. "If they only suffer one half the pangs of which they have been the cause," she said, "their case will be sad indeed." [20]

Speculation became so excessive and widespread that the *Columbus Enquirer,* a paper not generally known for its sympathy for the poor, joined the attack on those who saw the war as an opportunity to line their pockets. The editor warned that for a man to grow rich during the war would forever dishonor him. "It will pass for robbery of the country at large, of the families of soldiers, of the poor. In other words, it will be seen *as it is.* No disguise will cover it up; no apology extenuate it." [21] But neither the force of law nor the threat of social disgrace could stem the rising tide of profiteering. There was simply too much money to be made.

By far the most precious goods hoarded by speculators were medicine and drugs, particularly chloroform, morphine, and quinine. Even speculators had a hard time getting their hands on these items. None were produced in the South, and as the blockade tightened they became increasingly rare. Quinine shot up to twenty dollars an ounce soon after the blockade went into effect. By the end of 1863 one ounce cost from four hundred dollars to six hundred dollars when it could be found at all. So anxious were people to get medicines at any price that when Alabama tried to limit profits on all commodities to 15 percent in 1862, drugs were specifically exempt. [22]

Nearly every blockade-runner carried medicine as part of its cargo. Like other goods, it was sold at auction in the South's coastal port cities and from there made its way to markets all over the Confederacy, prices doubling or tripling at every exchange. Smuggling drugs through enemy lines, sometimes called land blockade–running, was also common. Medicines could be hidden easily in garment linings and hoopskirts. One Alabama man ran medicine through the lines in an old hospital wagon flying a yellow flag with "smallpox" emblazoned on it. No one ever challenged him. [23]

With drugs so expensive and difficult to import, substitution became the order of the day whenever possible. There were no substitutes for morphine and chloroform, but any number of concoctions could replace quinine. Most common were brews of dogwood, willow, oak, poplar, or cherry tree bark that were sometimes boiled together with whiskey. Another popular quinine substitute, guaranteed to keep off the chill, was a blend of tea, table salt, and red pepper. [24]

Physicians and pharmacists developed their own substitutes for drugs no longer available from abroad. Though some had sincere motives, others were more interested in making fast money and outrageous claims abounded. The Columbus pharmaceutical company of Urquhart and Chapman ran an advertisement in valley papers announcing

WAR! WAR!
is declared against
PAINS OF ANY KIND
By Dr. A. W. Allen's
SOUTHERN LINIMENT
And every Southerner will be satisfied by using
ONE DOLLAR'S WORTH
that they have no further use for Northern liniments.

Also distributed by such firms as D. J. Dickinson and Company and E. R. Peabody and Company of Bainbridge, this "miracle" liniment was offered as a cure for "Rheumatisms, Neuralgia, Strains, Burns, Bruises, Fresh Cuts, Pains in the Back or Limbs, Colic in Man or Beast, and Blind Staggers in Horses." [25]

Valley residents, especially rural folk, depended more on themselves and each other to produce medical treatments. One desperate woman, fearful of going blind, wrote to her sister at West Point asking what she had done for a similar eye problem. The physicians could apparently offer no help. Most people had little choice but to be self-sufficient. For some like the Edwards family in Dale County, the nearest drugstore was forty miles away in Troy. Considering the state of medical science at the time, it was probably just as well. Store-bought remedies sometimes did more harm than good. Aside from the expense, this was perhaps a major reason why rural people preferred, for example, their own liniment of turpentine and homemade vinegar to prepackaged brands like Dr. Allen's. It was cheaper and almost certainly as potent. The vinegar was produced by mixing a pint of molasses with a gallon of warm water and letting it ferment for two months. One of the most dreaded home tonics, though widely regarded as a cure-all, was made of vinegar with nails or iron filings mixed in. It was so effective, according to one account, that "no second dose was ever needed. . . . It was enough to show the patient the bottle." [26]

Most home remedy ingredients were gathered from the natural surroundings. As one Barbour County woman said, the woods served as drugstores and had done so for slaves and poor whites long before the war. A Troup County slave remembered using "everything for medicine that grew in the ground." Perhaps the most popular of the medicinal plants were poppies, from which laudanum and opium were made. So scarce did laudanum become early in the war that the Confederate government encouraged its citizens to plant as many poppies as possible and even provided poppy seeds. Though told to collect its sticky juice and hand it over to the government, most people kept it to make their own laudanum. Like castor oil, the domestic laudanum was said to be as pure as any imported variety. Nevertheless, the Confederacy's laudanum production program was a dismal failure. One disappointed official wrote that "large quantities of poppies were raised, but very little opium was gathered."[27]

Some of the most persistent physical discomforts suffered by people along the lower Chattahoochee were intestinal ailments. But here too, the gardens and woods provided relief. One valley woman recommended to her husband in the army, "Eat just as many Spanish potatoes as you want. They say they are the best thing you could eat for your bowels." Constipation could be hazardous if not quickly alleviated, but laxatives were easily made by boiling the roots or leaves of a variety of such trees as the peach, mayapple, or butternut. Diarrhea could be cured by drinking a brew of raspberry or whortleberry leaves. The more serious dysentery was relieved by a concoction of blackberry roots, persimmons, and water or salt, vinegar, and water.[28]

Some people preferred stronger remedies. Sallie Lovett of Troup County wrote to her husband about a surefire cure for diarrhea: "My bowels commenced running off, and I had me some red oak bark got and I had it put in a kettle and boiled me some strong tea and put a good dose of laudanum in it, help me right straight. Honey, do try it. Have some strong tea and put laudanum in it and keep drinking it. My bowels is rolling mightily now, but I think I can keep them in check."[29]

While poor whites had only themselves to rely on for medical care, most slaves did have some assistance from their masters when seriously ill. Wealthier slaveholders sometimes contracted with local doctors to treat their slaves. Slaves were certainly glad to get any medical care they could, but they also knew better than to think that owners were motivated by genuine affection. They were cared for in the same way as any valuable livestock. There was an investment to be protected. Celestia Avery, a former Troup County slave, recalled that the "health of slaves was very important to every slave owner for loss of life meant loss of money to them." When one Barbour County slave came down with a serious fever, the owner instructed his wife to "be careful of Jim and see to it that he lacks for nothing; if he dies, I've lost one thousand dollars, good as gold."[30]

In cases of minor illness slaves cared for each other. The slaveholders became involved only if the ailment persisted, and they did most of the doctoring in terms of prescribing home remedies. These palliatives were often less effective than the slaves' own folk medicines, and patients frequently resisted the treatments. One bondsman said that if slaves refused to take medication, they were whipped until they agreed to cooperate. Charlie Pye, a former Muscogee County slave, said that his master called a doctor only in "the last stages of illness." And if the slave was beyond help, no time was wasted on mourning. "When a slave died," Pye recalled, "he was buried as quickly as a box could be nailed together." Avery remembered her owner being so callous that slaves were buried the same day they died: "If [someone] died before dinner," she said, "the funeral and burial usually took place immediately after dinner."[31]

With scarcity and inflation driving store-bought medicines and other goods beyond reach for most southerners, their talent for substitute and industry was taxed to the limit. Hemp was nearly impossible to get so they made ropes from bear grass, sunflower stalks, and cotton. Those who could write made ink from walnut hulls or pokeberries and pens from goose feathers. They wrote on everything from the flyleaves of old books to the margins of their pages. They used old newspapers for envelopes or simply folded the letter and wrote an address on the back. Drinking glasses were made from old bottles. Myrtle, rosin, and chinaberries were used to make soap. Dogwood or willow bark was cut into shavings and mixed with tobacco to make it last longer.

For the more affluent who had a bit of leisure time, homemade pottery began to replace professionally crafted earthenware. For poorer folk who could not afford to waste time on something that might easily break, plates, cups, bowls, and pitchers made of wood had to do. Furniture was made or repaired using hickory or white oak. The better-off who owned kerosene lamps used oil from cottonseed and ground peas or squeezed oil from lard (also used as a hair grease by both men and women). Others made candles out of beeswax, lard, or tallow. In the homes of most slaves and poor whites, burning pine knots or fireplaces were usually the only source of light after the sun went down.[32]

More time went into the production of clothing than perhaps any other home-manufactured items. Retail stocks of cloth began to run out soon after the war started and most new cloth made by the South's textile mills went to the government. What little did go on the open market was so expensive that only the wealthy could afford it. By late in the war even they found it necessary to do without some luxuries.

Making homespun was no easy task and the equipment needed to produce it was scarce. The wide, flat, handheld brushes, known as cotton cards, used to align the fibers for spinning were the hardest to come by. In 1861 cotton cards were only forty cents a pair, but by November of the next year the price was up significantly. One southwest Georgia soldier wrote to his sister that it was "impossible to git a pare of cards in Savannah at this time for less then $10 a pare and i have not got the mony by mee at this time to by them." His salary was only eleven dollars a month. By war's end a pair of cards cost thirty dollars or more.[33]

Cotton cards were among the most valuable items on blockade—runners and the Lincoln administration treated them as contraband of war. Card factories sprang up all over the South, sometimes with state governments leading the way. Inmates at the Georgia state prison in Milledgeville could turn out one pair an hour when they had the leather and steel wire necessary to make them. Wire was the most difficult to obtain and leather was so scarce that dog skins were often used. People could exchange these items at any factory for a pair of cards. Despite state and private efforts the supply of cotton cards was never adequate.[34]

Looms and spinning wheels were nearly as scarce as cotton cards, so much so that people often regarded them as community property. It was not at all uncommon for spinning wheels to be passed from house to house. Neighbors might pitch in to help build a crude wooden loom at someone's home with the understanding that all could use it. One Alabama woman recalled that spinning bees became the most popular means of producing thread in her community. Wheels, cards, and cotton would be hauled by wagon to the hostess's residence on an appointed day, and there might be any number of spinning wheels at these gatherings. According to one account, "sometimes as many as six or eight were whirring at the same time." Some women would spin while others carded or sewed. Children were often included in the work, although, as one Dale County girl admitted, they were not very enthusiastic. But the workers did what they could to keep themselves entertained. A Barbour County woman recalled that "now and then the monotony would be enlivened by snatches of song, merry laughs and jests." Still, she said, "we were glad indeed to see the sun sinking like a huge ball of fire behind the green-topped pines."[35]

To supplement their supply of fabrics some farmers raised sheep for wool production. Wool had been available before the war but most of the supply on hand at its beginning went into making army blankets and uniforms. At one point, Victoria Clayton of Barbour County had about one hundred sheep on her plantation. Wool from these sheep, together with cotton from her fields, supplied fibers for her looms. Most valley residents were not as fortunate. Few poor whites or slaves had woolen garments. They were more difficult to produce and more expensive. Though the spinning could be done at home, cotton cards could not card wool. But for farmers in southeast Alabama the nearest wool carding facility at the beginning of the war was in Eufaula. Some community gristmills, such as Munn's Mill in Dale County, began carding wool to fill the gap.[36]

Poor whites and slaves who could not afford the luxury of wool frequently combined dog hair or cow hair with cotton to produce a material very much like wool that was warmer and more durable than cotton alone. Some people mixed cotton with rabbit fur or raccoon fur to produce a fabric described by one southerner as handsome and sturdy. As fabric of every kind became harder to get, poorer folk used animal fur as coats or cloaks and animal skins for clothing. By the end of the war many slaves were wearing nothing but a long coarse sack with three holes in it—two for the arms and one for the head.[37]

Most people did not bother to dye homespun clothing, but for those who had the time the natural surroundings provided all sorts of substitutes for imported dyes. Barks, leaves, twigs, and berries could all be used to color fabric. Walnut hulls produced what one valley resident described as "a beautiful dark brown," the roots of pine trees yielded a deep, rich garnet, wild indigo gave various shades of blue, and myrtle produced "a nice gray." One southwest Georgia man who owned a small cotton mill sent his wagons into nearby swamps to collect loads of myrtle.[38]

The valley's woodlands also provided the raw materials for making buttons, hats, and bonnets. Buttons were made of nearly any material at hand, including thick leather, gourd shells, and tightly wound thread. Persimmon seeds, sometimes covered with cloth, were also used. Wooden buttons, occasionally polished with sandpaper and varnished, were common too. Some people even used wooden pegs, widely known as "Georgia buttons." Women made bonnets from corn shucks, palmettos, and bulrushes that grew tall in the marshes. Pine straw was woven into hats. At least one man in southeast Alabama continued to make wool hats well into the war, but they were so expensive that only the well-to-do could afford them.[39]

Among the most expensive and scarce items of clothing were shoes. Most shoe factories turned exclusively to supplying the army when the war began, and they could not even do that well. As with so many other things, people had to rely on themselves and their neighbors for footwear. Old shoes were repaired or recycled, some having new uppers put on and others getting new soles. Local tanneries sprang up all over the South, drawing on surrounding communities for supplies of leather. Almost all good cowhides went to the government, so substitutes of horsehide and calfskin or goatskin were used. Any leather could be blackened using a mixture of soot and cottonseed oil or syrup. According to one Dale County resident, horsehide "was very inferior leather as it happened to stretch and was very ugly. It was generally used for making the negroes' workshoes." [40]

Another common material used to make slave shoes was hog skin. As the war dragged on and leather supplies dwindled, even the more affluent whites turned their hogs into shoes. One resident of a Barbour County plantation recalled with disgust that "leather from the hides of swine fell to our lot also, for winter shoes, and many other white families were obliged to use it." Poor whites and slaves went barefoot most of the time, even in winter, and were glad to get whatever shoes they could. But planters and their families considered it a great sacrifice to put on a pair of shoes made from pigskin: "We had consented with some reluctance to have these shoes made," said one plantation girl near Eufaula, "for, although we were willing to immolate ourselves on the altar of our Southern Confederacy, it had fallen rather severely on us to think that we must wear hog-skin shoes!" In the end it was simply too humiliating for her. She refused to wear the shoes and they soon went to one of the house slaves.[41]

Even so basic a thing as food became, like clothing, a mark of social distinction. Of course, the wealthy had eaten much better than the poor even before the war. But now malnutrition and starvation threatened millions of poor whites while planters fed themselves as well as ever. The Clayton plantation in Barbour County boasted "the finest orchard in Southeast Alabama." Victoria Clayton supplied her table from the orchard and exchanged fruit baskets for coffee in Eufaula. Though he continued to grow cotton, John Horry Dent raised enough vegetables and livestock to supply not only his immediate family but members of his extended family as well. And he had plenty left over to sell among those few neighbors who had the money to pay for it.[42]

Slaves were usually at the mercy of their owners when it came to the quality of their diet. Planters typically gave their slaves a ration of cornmeal and lard each week with the occasional privilege of vegetables. Even on farms with only a few slaves where one might have expected a more equitable distribution of food, provisions for the slaves were minimal. Nancy Boudry, one of three slaves on a Georgia farm, recalled how she "sometimes didn't have nothing to eat but a piece of cornbread, but the white folks always had chicken." George Eason, another Georgia freedman, remembered the slaves on his plantation being so hungry that they often made raids on the smokehouse. "This was considered as stealing by the master and the overseer," he said, "but to [the slaves] it was merely taking that which they had worked for." [43]

Poor whites in both urban and rural areas also had a hard time keeping food on the table. By the middle of the war, many yeoman families were cutting back to two meals a day. Some had only one and were lucky to get it. Even before the firing on Fort Sumter, provisions became so scarce in the lower Chattahoochee Valley that a number of merchants gave up on dry goods altogether and shifted to produce and livestock. In March 1861 John Horry Dent recorded in his journal that "a vast amount of Corn, Oats, Flour and Bacon has been imported. And the demand is active and steady and large. The provisions hauled out in the Country is immense. Every wagon goes out loaded down, and the supply is far from being sufficient." Conditions became even worse the next year when a drought wiped out much of the corn crop. [44]

The burden of survival was especially heavy for those families with men in the army. James Crowder wrote to his widowed mother from Virginia in spring 1863 advising her to "plante a heape of corn and other stuf to live on for by nex fall what yo donte have yo cannot get for love nor money." The food situation was often worse for city folk, who were constantly at the mercy of speculators and profiteers. F. C. Humphreys, commanding the Columbus Arsenal, begged local planters to supply his workers with food at reasonable prices. He reminded them that without his arsenal and others like it the Confederacy could not survive. Humphreys even tried to exchange gunpowder and iron for bacon. David Johnston of the Saffold navy yard ran ads in the *Early County News* offering nails and other "iron suitable for plantation purposes" in trade for "pork, lard, bacon, or any kind of provisions." But such appeals to patriotism and humanity were useless. It seemed that having brought the Confederacy into existence, planters were now unwilling to make the sacrifices necessary to maintain it. [45]

Wheat flour was one of the scarcest food products along the lower Chattahoochee. One daughter of a Dale County yeoman remembered that she saw nothing made of wheat flour for more than two years after the war began. Flour was not abundant even among the planters. A Barbour County girl recalled with humor how planters would invite each other for dinner whenever one of them was able to get a barrel of flour. "It was even more amusing," she said, "to have friends sit at the dining-table, and, when a waiter of brown, warm biscuits was passed round, to see them feign ignorance of what they were." [46]

When the blockade made it impossible for southerners to import wheat and other food products, some planters and yeomen tried to meet the demand themselves. In the war's first year small patches of wheat appeared in fields throughout the lower Chattahoochee Valley. Farmers who had land in low-lying areas also planted rice. One planter who lived near Glenville, Alabama, experimented with different amounts of fertilizer on an acre tract that he devoted to wheat. It produced fifty bushels by one account. Edward Garland, a Barbour County planter, raised wheat on a twelve-acre section of hammock land so rich that it needed no fertilizing at all. The Garland children, along with their tutor, Parthenia Hague, rode out one afternoon to see the field for themselves and were struck by the natural beauty of "wave on wave of long amber wheat gently rolling in the wind. A large stream of water bounded two sides of the hammock, and heavy green foliage formed a background in vivid contrast to the golden heads whose every culm seemed on a level. We slid almost unconsciously from our saddles, hitched the horses, and were soon standing in the midst of the wheat, with eyes scarcely able to peer over that vast plain of golden-yellow." [47]

Much of the valley's wheat flour went into homemade bread despite the lack of imported baking soda to make the dough rise. Valley folk quickly discovered that corncob ashes had alkaline properties and made a fine substitute. A small pile of cobs was placed on a stone or clean-swept area and burned. The ashes were then gathered up, sifted, and mixed with a small amount of water for storage in jars or jugs. Red cobs were preferred to white since it was believed they made a better alkali. [48]

Despite some degree of success in isolated areas, wheat production was never widespread along the lower Chattahoochee. One valley yeoman complained that "'rust' or 'smut' or some such plant disease" always infected the crop. Wheat flour thus remained expensive throughout the war. The only available substitute was "bolted" cornmeal, though mill owners insisted that the rough meal had a tendency to tear their bolting cloth when sifting through it. Nonetheless, with some effort this bolted meal was suitable for making piecrusts, muffins, and waffles. It was even used along with homemade brown sugar to make cakes. [49]

Brown sugar became very popular in the valley when the blockade made the importation of refined white sugar impossible. No sugarcane was grown commercially along the lower Chattahoochee before the war and what cane there was had been raised in small patches for making cane syrup. Now it became the main source of sweetener. Other sweetening agents included sorghum and honey. Some people made sugar and syrup from watermelon juice. [50]

Vegetables of all kinds were grown along the lower Chattahoochee to make up for the lack of imported produce. Among the most common were cabbage, peas, beans, squash, and sweet potatoes. One of the most popular food items, rarely grown before the war, was the peanut. Though usually known as *goobers* at the time, peanuts were also called *ground peas* and *pindars*. Whatever the term, people in the valley found all sorts of uses for them. Parched peanuts became a favorite treat among the valley folk. Even more popular was a peanut candy made by stirring raw, shelled peanuts into a pot of boiling syrup and allowing it to cool. Peanut oil was used in lamps, and peanuts could be used as feed for cattle, hogs, and other livestock.[51]

The type and amount of meat available to city dwellers depended, as always, on their social and economic standing. A determining factor for country folk was disease. An 1862 cholera epidemic wiped out so many hogs that ham and bacon were scarce in valley markets for the rest of the war. One daughter of a Dale County yeoman described the family's meat situation as desperate: "The cholera had killed our hogs so there was no fresh pork or bacon or ham. Fresh beef kept such a short time, and we had little of dried beef and chicken. . . . None of it was ever sold; we kept it all for home use; and none could be bought."[52]

What meat slaves received hinged as much on the whims as on the resources of their owners. Many slaves, even on the larger plantations, got little or no meat. Poor, landless whites usually had a few chickens around the house, which they consumed at a rate of perhaps one or two a month. Many had none at all. Most of the yeomen had at least a few hogs. More affluent yeomen and planters usually had a small herd of cattle as well along with an occasional collection of sheep and goats. Livestock killings were frequent among those who could afford them since it was difficult to preserve the meat beyond a few days. Richard Hill, an Early County planter, held six hog killings during winter 1862–63, producing 13,388 pounds of meat.[53]

Most farmers dried or smoked their meat for storage but salt was needed for the best results. Like so many other commodities the salt supply was cut off with the blockade, and there were no substitutes. Within weeks the price of salt went from fifty cents a sack to twelve dollars or more. In December 1861 a Georgia newspaper reflected on the "loud complaints" when the price of salt had gone to ten dollars a sack and noted that "the howls, now that there is none, is terrific." A Chambers County resident reported that salt could not be bought there at any price. "The Salt question," warned the editor of one Georgia paper, "is assuming a greater magnitude than even the war."[54]

Blockade-runners got some salt into Apalachicola. According to one valley citizen, it was the single most important product coming up the Chattahoochee River by 1863. But salt that had been run through the blockade was too expensive for most people. Some valley folk spent several weeks each year on the Gulf Coast making their own by boiling seawater. What they could not use themselves they sold to neighbors for fifteen to twenty-five dollars a bushel. Many could not afford salt even at these prices. Countless farmers recycled salt from the brine left in troughs and barrels where meat had been salted before the war or from the salty dirt of smokehouse floors. In the latter process, dirt was shoveled into a strainer through which boiling water was poured. The resulting liquid brine was then boiled down and left to sit in the sun, where evaporation completed the operation. "The salt made in this way was not white," said one valley farmer, "but it was better than none." Even planters sometimes resorted to this method. One woman on a Barbour County plantation was disappointed that the salt was "never of immaculate whiteness" but "accepted it without complaining." [55]

One hardship that many could not accept without complaint was the lack of coffee. By one account almost every adult in the lower Chattahoochee Valley drank the beverage before the war, some three times a day. But now, with regular coffee imports cut off by the blockade and prices running seventy dollars a pound, few could afford it. One farm family in Dale County, typical of those throughout the valley, did not see or taste real coffee for four years after their supply ran out in summer 1861. Some valley folk reacted to the shortage by declaring themselves better off without it. Most tried all kinds of substitutes to satisfy their craving. Mary Edwards Fleming recalled years later that "because we children heard our elders bemoaning the lack of coffee, even those of us who had never tasted coffee longed for it and drank the substitutes." Parched rye came closer than anything else to real coffee, but rye was almost as scarce as coffee along the lower Chattahoochee. More common substitutes included parched peanuts, parched okra, and parched sweet potato skins. People also used acorns, peas, beans, dandelion roots, and cottonseeds. According to one source, more substitutes for coffee were found than for any other item in the Confederacy. None of these brews were as good as the real thing but for most people they were better than nothing. [56]

Another beverage at least as popular as coffee early in the war was whiskey. Home-distilled spirits had always been common among plain folk. When the blockade shut down imports of rum and other alcoholic beverages, domestic liquor also became popular among the upper classes. But the increased demand for whiskey put tremendous pressure on the corn crop at a time when grain was badly needed as food. Georgia and Alabama, like most other Confederate states, passed laws strictly regulating distillation soon after the war began. In Georgia, Governor Brown even forbade the Confederate government to operate stills producing whiskey for the army. Anyone wishing to make liquor, including Confederate agents, had to get a license from the state. At first, only corn, rye, wheat, and barley were banned from distillation. But people generally ignored the law or found substitutes. Numerous fruits and vegetables were soon added to the list of items prohibited from distillation, including sweet potatoes, pumpkins, peas, and Irish potatoes. The states made exceptions only for medicinal purposes. Not surprisingly, the governors' offices in both Georgia and Alabama were overwhelmed with requests for permission to distill medicinal liquor.[57]

By the middle of the war most people in the Chattahoochee Valley, especially the poorer folk, were much more concerned with food than liquor. Few yeomen had enough land or labor to raise corn for distillation. Landless whites, with only their small gardens to depend on, grew nothing at all commercially, and the urban poor did not even have garden plots. What corn the plain folk did grow had to be used for food. Only wealthier farmers and planters could afford the luxury of converting grain to alcohol.

To make matters worse, planters continued to grow cotton even as plain folk and the army faced starvation. Though the Confederate government had imposed a ban on cotton exports in an attempt to force recognition and intervention by Britain and France, planters stockpiled cotton for future sale. Many simply ignored the embargo and smuggled cotton out of the South. Most did not expect the war to last very long. In August 1861, a Russell County newspaper assured its readers that the war would be over in a few months. But even if the war continued for years, it could not last forever. When it did end, planters hoped to make millions selling their precious fiber to cotton-hungry textile mills in the North and Europe. Confederate Senator Louis Wigfall spoke for thousands of planters when he justified their views in 1862, arguing that "unless we continue to raise the staple in abundance . . . after the war it would be difficult for us to monopolize the markets of the world." With their vision firmly fixed on the promise of future wealth, southern planters failed to heed the warning signs that their shortsightedness was undermining the Confederate cause.[58]

Those signs were clear enough. As early as March 1861 the *Opelika Southern Republic* urged planters to grow less cotton and more grain out of pride as much as necessity: "We have purchased provisions of the North and West until they have concluded that we are dependant upon them for support. It is time for us to learn the gentlemen that we are not compelled to cultivate cotton for a living, but that we have a soil adapted to the growth of all kinds of grain, and can live within ourselves." A LaGrange paper encouraged planters to feel themselves enlisted in the army as food producers just as soldiers were enlisted as the nation's defenders. In a May 1861 letter to a local paper, one southwest Georgian called on planters to plow up that spring's cotton crop and replace it with corn. The editor agreed: "Yes, plow it up, if need be. Look out for corn first, last and all the time." [59]

Few planters took the advice. A year into the war one valley soldier wrote to his wife from Tupelo, Mississippi, "I don't know how the war will be decided if England and France don't interfere and stop the war and if the Confederacy has to gain her independence by fighting. I am afraid she will have to give it up for there are so few provisions in this portion of the Confederacy." Planters certainly recognized the need for more food. Whether they acted on that recognition was another matter. In March 1862 a group of planters meeting in Russell County promised to grow more food than before the war but still insisted on planting enough cotton "for seed and home consumption." A year later, in an open letter to the *Columbus Daily Sun,* one Russell County resident wondered why no similar meeting had been called for spring 1863. John Horry Dent of Barbour County admitted in April 1861 that "as our country is at war, we must plant more for provisions than for cotton." Yet, typical of his class, Dent's greed overcame his reason. He produced more than 40,000 pounds of cotton that year. In January 1862 one disgusted editor wrote that if southerners could not give up cotton and plant more food, they were "not only a blockaded but a block-headed people." [60]

In the face of such criticism, a few planters did at least try to set an example for their more self-interested neighbors. In spring 1862 one Barbour County planter, identified only as "Col. T." in a letter to the *Southern Cultivator,* devoted nearly all his land to food production. Most of it went to growing corn, but he also produced oats, peanuts, millet, apples, and peaches. Not a single acre was planted in cotton. [61] But men like "Col. T." were by far the exception rather than the rule. Few planters followed his lead.

One indignant southwest Georgia man wrote to Brown outlining the problem of cotton overproduction in his region and implored the governor to do something about it: "We are in great danger of *Subjugation* to the hated government that we are resisting, *not* by the army of demons invading our country, but by *avarice* and the *menial Subjects* of King cotton. . . . I here of one planter who is pitching 900 acres in cotton, the overseer of another told me he is going to plant 300 acres, another . . . 90 acres, another, fifteen hand 90 acres, another 300 acres, and two others full crops of cotton. And so it will be all over the state. . . . I hope your Excellency will adopt some plan to stop those internal enemies of the country, for they will whip us sooner than all Lincolndom combined could do it." [62]

Joe Brown was already well aware of the problem. He knew perhaps better than any political leader in the South that support for the Confederacy was fragile. Most Georgians initially had not supported secession. If they were forced to go hungry while wealthy landowners planted cotton, Brown worried about the consequences. In an open letter to the *Southern Cultivator* he was direct and to the point. The question of whether planters could grow less cotton and more food would, more than anything else, determine the war's outcome. [63]

Governor John Gill Shorter of Alabama also knew how strong class antagonism could be. In one Alabama county alone, a mob of about forty enraged women roamed the countryside destroying cotton fields as they went. With hunger on the rise and class resentment already running high, Shorter advised planters that it would be wise to "raise not another crop of cotton beyond the demands for home consumption until this unholy and cruel war shall cease." Even the Confederate Congress passed a series of resolutions condemning those who grew an excess of cotton. But all these pleas to "bury the love of gold," as Governor Shorter put it, fell on deaf ears. [64]

By 1862, planters along the lower Chattahoochee were growing so much cotton that the warehouses could not hold it all. In September of that year the Columbus firm of Dillard, Powell, and Company ran this announcement in the *Enquirer*: "TO PLANTERS: OUR Warehouse being full, Planters will please stop consignments of Cotton to our care until further notice." A year later the situation had hardly improved. In a November 1863 issue of the *Early County News,* editor Grouby expressed anger at seeing local planters growing so much cotton: "It is very strange to us that some men of very large means will plant such cotton crops. . . . But some people do not care a straw *'who sinks, so they swim!'*" Cotton planters, Grouby complained, were doing the South more harm than the Yankees. [65]

When it became clear that the Confederate government would take no direct action against planters, both Georgia and Alabama moved to regulate cotton production themselves. In November 1862 Brown asked the Georgia General Assembly to impose a tax on "each quantity of seed cotton sufficient to make a bale of four hundred pounds . . . produced next year . . . over what is actually necessary for a home supply." The assembly rejected Brown's suggestion. After all, many of the legislators were planters and were not eager to tax themselves. But they did make it illegal for anyone to plant more than three acres in cotton for each slave owned or farmhand employed. Any landowner who violated this law would be fined five hundred dollars for each acre of cotton beyond the limit.[66]

That same year Governor Shorter asked the Alabama legislature to "tax all cotton beyond what may be needed for home consumption . . . to the full extent of its value." Like their counterparts in the Georgia assembly, Alabama legislators were reluctant to tax cotton to its full extent. Instead, they placed a 10 percent tax on those who raised more than 2,500 pounds of seed cotton per hand. Shorter promised "to burn every lock of cotton within the State, if it be necessary," to ensure compliance.[67]

Such threats carried little weight among Alabama planters. Few thought a cotton tax would really be enforced by the state. For the most part, they *were* the state. They knew that the legislature, dominated as it was by slaveholders, would never back serious enforcement efforts. Anti-cotton legislation was little more than a gimmick designed to appease rather than have any real impact. For much the same reason, Georgia planters too had little respect for efforts to curtail cotton production. According to one source, "not one acre in fifty in the best corn district in Georgia was planted in corn." Archsecessionist Robert Toombs, a Confederate congressman and former U.S. senator from Georgia, called regulation of the cotton crop unconstitutional. He pointedly defied the state limit, harvested a full cotton crop, and publicly declared that he would plant as much cotton as he pleased. In frustration, Governor Brown asked Georgia's legislature to restrict the cotton crop to only one-fourth an acre per hand and "make it highly penal" for anyone to exceed that limit. The assembly refused and, despite Brown's continued urging, ignored the issue for the rest of the war.[68]

Some Confederate officials, like Alexander Stephens, suggested that the government might encourage compliance by promising to buy all cotton produced within the limit at fair market value. The plan was never adopted because planters insisted on compensation above market price. Planter intransigence on the issue convinced Martin J. Crawford of Columbus "that our people are not prepared to pay the purchase price of freedom if the planters demand that a poor government . . . shall pay them 2 or 3 cts a pound more for their cotton than the markets afford." [69]

In direct violation of state law and Confederate policy, "planters insisted," as one man put it, "on their right to grow unlimited amounts of cotton; to retain it for sale whenever they chose; and to sell it whenever, and to whomever, they chose." And it did not seem to matter who the buyers were. Planters and cotton merchants would sell to anyone, even the Yankees. According to one estimate, more than half a million bales of southern cotton were smuggled North during the war. J. H. Jones and D. Dudley of Fort Gaines reported to Governor Brown in March 1862 that cotton smuggling was common on the lower Chattahoochee. Steamboats typically made their way upriver, loading cotton bales as they went, with Columbus their supposed destination. But much of the cotton somehow seemed to find its way to Apalachicola, where it was transferred to vessels that took "pleasure excursions" out to see the blockading fleet, always returning with empty cargo holds. [70]

Just as southern cotton was smuggled out of the valley, northern products were smuggled in. John Horry Dent was certain that any number of Eufaula merchants were acting as Yankee agents, an opinion shared by the town's newspaper, *Spirit of the South.* On December 3, 1861, the editor pointed a finger of suspicion at several businessmen who he thought were funneling cotton out and Yankee goods in. The *Opelika Southern Republic* wondered, "How long a war will it require to wean this people from dependence upon the North?" Dent lamented to his friend and fellow planter Mack Wellborn that there was no shortage of corrupt men in the South, calling them "more depraved than the meanest of Yankees." And he insisted that "the severest punishment should be inflicted upon them." [71]

It was not unusual for planters like Dent to criticize unscrupulous cotton speculators for trading with the Yankees, but at the same time the landowners had no qualms about selling their cotton to these merchants. Dent himself sold almost 70,000 pounds of cotton in 1861 and 1862 and was surely aware that much of it wound up in northern textile mills. Two Fort Gaines residents described cotton smuggling as such a fact of economic life for valley planters that no intelligent man in the region could doubt it. Why would the South's planters and merchants provide cotton to clothe northern armies while those of the Confederacy went lacking? The simple fact was that the North paid better and the planters knew it. Some openly bragged that the longer the war went on, the more money they made. With such a lucrative black market in cotton it is little wonder that planters were not anxious to concentrate on growing food. But scarcity forced food prices up and speculation drove them even higher. Rampant inflation inevitably followed, making planters and farmers even less willing to exchange what food they had for increasingly worthless Confederate currency.[72]

By 1863, in what became a turning point for yeoman attitudes toward the war and the Confederacy, the Richmond government determined that what it could not buy it would take by force. That summer the Confederate Congress passed a series of taxes on everything from occupations to incomes. The most significant was a 10 percent confiscation levy on such farm items as livestock, wheat, corn, oats, rye, hay, fodder, buckwheat, sweet potatoes, Irish potatoes, sugar, cotton, wool, tobacco, peas, beans, and peanuts. Even this tax in kind did not provide enough food to meet military needs, so the government began confiscating farm produce and anything else it wanted far beyond the 10 percent level.[73]

The burdens of taxation and impressment, as government confiscation was called, fell heaviest on the small farmers. Though planters resented the levies, they usually had enough food on hand to satisfy the demands of tax collectors and impressment agents. Yeomen were seldom as fortunate. Few could afford even to pay their taxes, much less turn over what little they had to the Confederacy. Government officials were never welcomed at yeoman farms, and as the war went on their jobs became increasingly dangerous. Impressment agents were beaten up, shot at, and sometimes killed. Joe Brown, an avid opponent of Confederate impressment, warned that the practice and its "baneful operations" could only encourage opposition to the central government by producing an "evil spirit, bordering already in many cases upon open disloyalty."[74]

Brown was foremost among southern governors in his hostility to Confederate impressment. As early as 1861, when the Davis administration tried to seize rolling stock on the Western and Atlantic Railroad, Brown threatened military force to stop it. Davis thought it wiser to fight one war at a time and canceled the order. Two years later, when the Confederacy began general impressment, the Georgia General Assembly passed a resolution declaring it unconstitutional.[75]

As hostile as Brown and the legislature were toward Confederate impressment, they did not hesitate to impose it themselves. In fact, Georgia was among the first Confederate states to begin impressment. One citizen wrote to a Georgia newspaper complaining of Brown's hypocrisy, pointing to numerous seizures by the state. "And yet," the man continued, "this same Governor had made more noise about the legal and constitutional rights of the people than all the men in the Confederacy." William Scruggs of the *Columbus Daily Sun* sarcastically observed that impressment "originated in this state with Governor Brown, who, of course, does everything according to the 'Constitutional' square and compass." Even Toombs, who often joined the governor in opposing Confederate policy, wrote of his friend, "I see Brown has got him an impressment law too. How catching is thieving." [76]

Like Brown, Alabama's Governor Shorter criticized Confederate impressment while staunchly defending the state's impressment rights. Nearly a year before Confederate impressment began, Shorter was confiscating leather, shoes, and almost anything else in the name of the state. If anyone voiced objection, the state agent was authorized to take twice the original amount demanded, with no compensation. [77]

Whether by the state or Confederate governments, the issue of compensation for impressment was almost as much a point of argument as its constitutionality. In October 1862 Confederate Secretary of War George Randolph asked Attorney General Thomas H. Watts for an opinion on the legality of impressment. Watts, who would become Alabama's governor less than a year later, concluded that impressment was indeed legal as long as the government paid "just compensation." The problem was that impressment agents and property owners almost never agreed on what "just compensation" was. Davis tried to address the problem by establishing impressment committees to set fair prices, but inflation was so severe and committees met so infrequently that the government's fixed prices were always below market value. By late 1863, the official price allowed for flour was half that paid on the open market, and government corn prices were only a third. Farmers were so afraid their produce would be confiscated on sight that they were reluctant to take it into town for sale, which made the problem of urban hunger even worse. [78]

In most cases, farmers were lucky to get anything at all for their impressed produce. Corruption ran rampant among impressment officers. They pocketed government funds earmarked for farmers, sold confiscated produce on the open market and kept the money for themselves, or both. As governor of Alabama, Watts admitted that many impressment agents cared "neither for God nor man." One Georgia farmer complained bitterly when he discovered that the government was allowing fifty cents a pound for bacon. Confederate agents had given him only thirty-five. Farmers sometimes received promissory notes instead of cash from impressment officers and often did not even get that. Those with notes found them nearly impossible to redeem. When one Georgia man tried to collect on a note that was ten months past due, he was met by a sign "placed up conspicuously in large letters, 'No funds.'" [79]

Sometimes a poor farmer would present a note for redemption only to discover that it had been given to him by an imposter and was therefore worthless. Hundreds of scoundrels posing as impressment officers roamed the southern countryside swindling farmers out of their harvests and livestock. The problem became so bad in Georgia that the General Assembly mandated ten years' imprisonment for anyone engaged in confiscation without authority to do so. Governor Brown favored an additional punishment of "thirty-nine lashes on the bare back," but the legislature thought imprisonment sufficient.[80]

Even when impressment occurred under state or Confederate authority, it was often accompanied by depredations of all sorts. Local agents occasionally used their impressment power to victimize their political or personal enemies. Soldiers' wives or widows were the most frequent targets since their husbands were absent. Sometimes the abuse did not end with simple confiscation. Letters poured into the Alabama governor's office complaining of impressment gangs that "shot down stock, stole horses, tore down fences, and appropriated corn, fodder and other supplies." One Georgian said of Confederate officials, "they devastate the country as much as the enemy." [81]

Such actions were bound to have an impact on attitudes toward the Confederacy. James Bush headed a committee of Early County citizens who warned that corruption among impressment officials was so widespread that it would "ultimately alienate the affections of the people from the government." And they were right. In a letter to her brother, Private Thomas Mann, Nancy Mann of Harris County encouraged him to desert. She did not want to lose a member of her family to a cause she felt was not worth defending. "There is so much rascality carried on in this confedracy," she complained, "untill I think some times I do not no what will be come of the people and nor the confedracy and I do not care much." [82]

Even when confiscated food made it to government depots, it frequently went to waste through incompetence or neglect. It was not uncommon either for produce to rot in government warehouses or for the Quartermaster Department to deliver inedible food to the troops. In March 1863 the *Columbus Times* reported that while thousands faced hunger every day, more than half a million bushels of corn were rotting in government depots throughout southwest Georgia. Albany alone had fifteen storehouses filled with corn, much of it flooded out and all of it certain to spoil.[83]

Though no member of any class held impressment in high regard, yeomen were concerned that the wealthy did not contribute their fair share. As always, impressment agents first sought out the most vulnerable targets—

the farmsteads of poor folk. It seemed that only when yeoman farms were stripped bare did agents turn to plantations. Even then, planters were reluctant to part with their surplus. Some used political connections to avoid impressment while others simply hid their supplies. One valley soldier recalled how planters "would hide their wagons under straw piles, and carry off their horses where you cannot come at them. . . . Some of these men [are] rich—worth fifty thousand dollars." [84]

In Early County one wealthy planter stashed at least a thousand bushels of corn in a large crib hidden deep in the woods near his plantation. "What kind of a man can he be?" asked Grouby. "Is he a friend of the country? No; for no man who is will, at such a time as this, hide his corn from suffering Soldiers and their families." Grouby concluded that the planter ought to be lynched. "He is a meaner man, by far, than any Yankee that ever invaded our country." [85]

As reluctant as the planters were to give up their produce and livestock, they were even more unwilling to part with their slaves. Beginning in 1862 impressment officers confiscated slaves along the lower Chattahoochee for work on the railroads and fortifications at Savannah and Mobile. Two years later impressed slaves were at work on the Columbus defenses. [86]

Slaveholders complained loudly about this practice, many preferring to place their sons at the Confederacy's disposal rather than their slaves. William Castleberry of Clay County wrote to Governor Brown protesting both the impressment of his slaves for work at Savannah and the lack of payment for their services. He wanted to know if these actions were legal and demanded an immediate reply. Across the river in Barbour County, John Horry Dent asked Governor Watts to excuse his slaves from work on fortifications at Mobile. When the forts fell to Union forces in August 1864, Dent condemned its defenders for lacking "resolution or courage." He seemed to have completely forgotten his own meager resolve. [87]

The reluctance of planters to make sacrifices led increasing numbers of yeomen to conclude that the raging conflict was nothing but a rich man's war. When Toombs used political connections to have the slaves on his Stewart County plantation exempted from impressment, Grouby lashed out: "We believe Toombs, because he is rich, does pretty much what he wants . . . if he were a poor man he would be hanged." [88]

Disgusted with the inequities of impressment, Grouby called on the citizens of Early and Miller Counties to organize some form of resistance. Otherwise, he said, "our military officers will soon think they own the whole country." Hundreds of other valley residents agreed. Impressment became so difficult to enforce in southwest Georgia that Secretary of War

James Seddon implored the state's two senators, Benjamin H. Hill and Herschel V. Johnson, to visit the region and "impress on the people the absolute necessity of furnishing and pressing forward the supplies in their possession." Johnson, a longtime opponent of price fixing, refused. Hill thought it a worthy suggestion but knew it would do little good.[89]

Perhaps President Davis now recalled Brown's warning that impressment would cause general disaffection with the Confederacy among common folk. That prediction was prophetic. When a Muscogee County man had his livestock confiscated, he wrote an angry letter to the *Columbus Daily Sun*. Impressment made him "no longer a free agent but a vassal— a slave to those in power over me; therefore I submit *unwillingly* to the behest: whereas, before, I served my country freely, cheerfully and with a *whole heart* enlisted in the cause—now my heart fails me and my patriotism totters and reels . . . to its very base; it must ultimately fall under the crushing weight of arbitrary power."[90] With impressment agents regularly stripping small farmers clean, this man gave voice to the hardships and frustrations of plain folk by the thousands.

So did editor Grouby. After the incident involving Toombs's impressment exemption, Grouby complained, "A *poor* man in this world has no more showing than a blind dog in a meat house with a dozen starving Yankees after him." Three months later, in reflecting on countless inequities suffered by the valley's lower classes, Grouby lamented that "giving poor people their rights in this country has long since 'played out,' and so, we suppose, the poor will have to 'grin and endure' whatever the wealthy are a mind to require. So wags the world!"[91]

Both state and local governments in Alabama and Georgia recognized the dangers of general destitution and took steps to alleviate it. Their efforts, however, were unenthusiastic and ineffective. One major problem was the vast number of people who needed help. In Columbus there were two hundred families on the city's relief rolls by 1864. To the south in Chattahoochee County, an 1862 account listed more than five hundred people on the indigent rolls. Barbour County had 280 families receiving at least half their provisions from the state or county and another 649 families depended completely on government aid. In Dale County nearly half the white population qualified for state aid.[92]

Relief efforts were made even more difficult by thousands of refugees who poured into the valley. Its relative isolation made the lower Chattahoochee a haven for those escaping the ravages of war. Many refugees came from the ranks of the affluent and had friends or family in the valley. Navy Secretary Stephen Mallory's family spent most of the war at Ben

Hill's home in LaGrange. General William J. Hardee also found LaGrange to be a safe haven for his wife. John Guthrie, onetime commander of the gunboat *Chattahoochee,* brought his family to Eufaula from their home on the coast of North Carolina. And the famous fire-eating secessionist Edmund Ruffin of Virginia fled to Eufaula near the end of the war. So many people with money to spend sought refuge in the valley that boarding-houses sprang up to cater specifically to them. F. R. Starr and William Bawn announced in the Columbus papers their establishment of "a safe and pleasant retreat; house, garden, No. 1 cook, washer, ironer." [93]

Most of the valley's refugees could afford no such accommodations. They were, for the most part, common folk driven from their homes and looking for a safe place to spend the remainder of the war. By spring 1862 refugees from as far away as Louisiana were crowding into the lower Chattahoochee Valley. LaGrange alone had sixty families from New Orleans. Hundreds of exiles from Florida began pouring into Bainbridge, Georgia, after the Union navy stepped up its operations on the Gulf Coast. Lumpkin, Georgia, became a popular retreat for many people because the cost of living there was cheaper than in Eufaula or Columbus. Nonetheless, Columbus remained the valley's largest refugee center throughout the war. The city attracted hundreds with a promise of adequate housing and employment in war industries. Most Columbus refugees did find jobs and shelter in 1862, but by 1863 the city's capacity was taxed beyond its limits. When several hundred exiles from New Orleans arrived that year, one Columbus editor urged citizens to take them in, noting that many private homes were not yet "too crowded for comfort." [94]

Such humanitarian appeals generally went unnoticed. Charitable organizations of the well-to-do were virtually nonexistent by the war's third year. Working folk like those in Columbus, many in dire circumstances themselves, sometimes tried to take up the slack. In March 1863 city artisans formed a "Mechanics' Association" in which each member donated one day's wages to a relief fund for indigent families of soldiers. Despite their good intentions, the effort was of little use because salaries were too low and the numbers of indigent too great. [95]

Even local soldiers' aid societies, so active at the war's outset, had almost disappeared. "What has become of the Soldiers' Aid Society of Early County?" asked Grouby. "We havn't heard anything of it lately. We hope our noble ladies have not concluded to cease their efforts to assist our brave Soldiers." This admonishment spurred the society to renewed action, but its efforts were halfhearted at best. A few months later Grouby published a list of the meager contributions received by the Soldiers' Aid Society: "It is with *shame* for our citizens that we publish it," he wrote, "for there are many, *very many*, in our county who are well able to give *bountifully* who have not contributed a cent, while those who have, have given a very small mite." Grouby advised the Soldiers' Aid Society to "hang up the fiddle and the bow, for the people are too infernal hard-hearted and selfish to give a poor Soldier a mouthful to eat." [96]

Confederate currency was so inflated by early 1864 that planters would not even sell food to the poor, much less give it away. James Bush, one of the largest slaveholders in Early County, refused to deal in Confederate money at all. A southwest Georgia soldier's wife wrote to the *Early County News* complaining that planters who had earlier promised to sell meat and corn to soldiers' families now declined to do so. They would, however, take what little the poor had in exchange for food. "This is the only way many Soldiers' families in this county can get anything to eat," wrote the distraught woman. "Love nor Confederate money won't do it." Editor Grouby added that such men "should be drummed out of every respectable community, and sent heels over head to Yankeedoodledum, where they properly belong." [97]

Those few planters who continued to aid soldiers and their families did so grudgingly and even then expected compensation. John Horry Dent occasionally gave food to indigents in Barbour County and allowed soldiers passing through to rest and ration themselves on his plantation. Though he was among the wealthiest planters in the valley, Dent filed for reimbursement every time. [98] One way or the other, primary responsibility for poor relief always fell to state and local governments.

At the county level, Troup became one of the first to act when it levied a tax to help support soldiers' families in July 1861. Alabama was the first state in the Confederacy to address the problem on a larger scale. In November 1861 it authorized county commissioners to use state funds to assist indigent families of soldiers. The state increased relief efforts the next year with a 25 percent property tax to aid poor families. At first the money was distributed only in the county where it was collected, resulting in wide disparities between rich and poor counties. Indigent families in some counties received as little as four dollars a month while those in wealthier counties collected up to sixty-six dollars. And there was always some question about who qualified for assistance. The legislature responded in October 1862 with a two-million-dollar appropriation that was spread evenly across the state. Still, those in wealthier counties received much more. Though Alabama poured nearly twelve million dollars into relief efforts during the war, there was never enough to meet the crisis. Inequities continued and discontent among the poor only became worse.[99]

Attitudes were much the same in Georgia, and Brown recognized early on what kind of impact they would have on the war effort. In November 1862 he asked the state legislature to exempt soldiers with taxable property of less than one thousand dollars from poll and property taxes. He also urged that a one-hundred-dollar bounty be given to their families: "The poor have generally paid their part . . . in military service, exposure, fatigue and blood," he declared. "The rich . . . should meet the money demands of the government." Georgia appropriated two million dollars in relief funds that year and $2.5 million the next. In 1863 it defined the term *indigent* as "wives, mothers, grand mothers, and all who have to leave their ordinary business in the house, and to labor in the fields to support themselves and children, and who are not able to make a sufficient support for themselves and families." Those who qualified were eligible for tax exemption, monetary payments, and direct supplies of food.[100]

Georgia also provided for indigent refugee families of soldiers by making them qualified to receive certificates that they could exchange for food. In 1864 the state extended eligibility to all indigent refugees whether they were soldiers' families or not. By the end of that year Georgia was spending more than half its budget on general relief efforts. Two years earlier that figure had been only .1 percent. In all, Georgia appropriated well over $18 million for poor relief during the war. Still, it was not enough. A major problem was the state's failure to enforce its tax laws. In December 1862 when Georgia placed a tax on cotton and other farm products held as merchandise, speculators simply refused to report their holdings.[101]

Since state relief efforts fell so far short of actual need, many local governments tried to help where they could. As early as August 1861 a Harris County court appointed local men to care for soldiers' families. Most county governments soon realized that their responsibilities could not stop there. By May 1862, only a year into the war, Chambers County had just over five hundred dollars in its treasury and liabilities exceeding $27,000. Nevertheless, a county judge ordered commissioners to collect provisions for the destitute "regardless of cost." Families of dead or wounded soldiers were given an allowance in addition to provisions. Families of four or fewer members received $5.50 per month while larger families got $6.50. By 1864 Early County was allowing two dollars a week for each person in an indigent family no matter how many members it had.[102]

With its greater concentration of indigent families, refugees, and wealth,

Columbus spent more on poor relief than any town in the valley. The city fared better than most areas early in the war. Unemployment was relatively low and wages usually kept pace with inflation. The city council found it necessary to spend only $225 a month on relief efforts through 1862. But the situation changed in 1863, when the great influx of refugees hit and inflation spiraled out of control.

F. G. Wilkins, a wounded veteran of the early battles in Virginia, was elected mayor that year. At his first meeting with the city council Wilkins declared it the city's obligation to care for the families of "brave soldiers who are in the field fighting for our homes, property and independence." He persuaded the council to construct housing on the South Common for indigent families and to provide heating fuel for soldiers' families. The city extended benefits to local workers in 1864 when government industries delayed wages and employees ran out of provisions. The problem became even worse that summer, when a new wave of refugees from north Georgia hit Columbus. Between May and October 1864 the city spent more than $21,000 on food, fuel, and housing for the poor.[103]

To pay for their relief efforts, city and county governments tried to raise taxes on those who could pay. The Columbus city council passed a "personal tax" of five dollars a year in July 1861 that rose steadily as the war went on. Barbour County levied a "special tax" on property for indigent aid, and Dale County enacted an extra 10 percent tax to provide medical relief for the poor. Stewart County levied taxes on personal property at three times the state level for the support of soldiers' families. In Chambers County the commissioners raised taxes by 125 percent in July 1862. Some counties even gave tax breaks to those who contributed directly to indigent relief. Early County issued certificates to local citizens reflecting the value of goods turned over to the indigent, then accepted these documents in lieu of cash payment for taxes. The commissioners in Stewart County exempted from taxation all those who donated at least fifteen dollars in cash or twenty dollars worth of clothing to soldiers.[104]

The "stay laws" represented a further attempt by government to aid the indigent. In 1862, when a drought hit and money ran low, thousands of poor farmers along the lower Chattahoochee went into debt just to feed themselves. A few borrowed money from local banks but many got food and other necessities on credit from neighboring planters. As the war continued and conditions worsened most small farmers found it impossible to repay their debts. It was not uncommon for poor families, many with soldiers at the front, to be forced off their land by planters demanding compensation for unpaid debts. The public outcry against such evictions was so great that state governments passed a series of stay laws making them illegal. Though such laws did not relieve the poor of their debt, they were supposed to allow them to keep their land, at least until the end of the war. Most planters refused to wait that long and used their influence with local law enforcement to continue taking land. Typical of the planter class, John Horry Dent called indebted farmers "worthless and unprincipled" and insisted that the stay laws were unjust and unconstitutional.[105]

It seemed that no matter what form they took, relief efforts of state and local governments were, in the end, useless. Inflation was too high, speculation too rampant, enforcement too lax, and destitution too widespread. Furthermore, planters put up tremendous resistance to taxation, impressment, and debt relief for the poor. They were simply unwilling to sacrifice for the cause even if it meant alienating the plain folk. Corrupt and incompetent officials also alienated the yeomen by taking much more than they should have and failing to deliver promised assistance. Government agents frequently hurt the people they were supposed to help and in the process added to the indigent rolls.

From its beginnings, confusion and corruption plagued the indigent relief system. In May 1862 the state relief agent in Colquitt, Georgia, wrote to Governor Brown asking for clarification on how he should distribute the salt ration: "The salt which by your order was sent to Miller County has come to hand and there is great need of it." But there was "some difference of opinion" over who should receive it. Was it for the families of all soldiers then in service or only those in service when the order was issued? And did the order include both Confederate and state troops, or only one group? If only one, which one? Within a few months, local agents would consider themselves lucky to get any provisions at all.[106]

As always, wealthier counties with more political clout seemed to get more than their share of provisions while others got nothing. In Henry County illiterate soldiers' wives compelled a local man to write to Governor Shorter about their plight. They complained that neighboring Barbour County (the governor's home county) received more aid in one month than Henry got in a year. One Henry woman, the wife of soldier Marion Rudd, was promised up to eighty-five dollars. But "the fact is," said the letter, "she don't git anything." With no means of support, the woman was forced to live on charity. Two of her sons had already been killed in Confederate service and she wanted to know how to collect the pay owed them at the time of their deaths.[107]

All too often, funds that should have been distributed to indigent families wound up in the pockets of corrupt officials. Acting Justice of the Peace

George W. Cleveland of Miller County wrote to Brown in November 1863 accusing the local relief agent of "swindling." Noting that "none of our soldiers families has drawn any money sence the first of August and the agent reports no money on hand," Cleveland asked Brown what the county's appropriation was supposed to be. The state legislature had allocated $2.5 million for aid to soldiers' families statewide but none of that money was getting to Miller County. Cleveland emphasized the urgency of his request: "Some of our brave soldiers families are in very destitute conditions and must soon suffer if not relieved in some way." [108]

More than profiteers and speculators, more than impressment officers and tax collectors, more than corrupt relief agents and hard-hearted planters, the most severe hardship suffered by families in the lower Chattahoochee Valley was the absence of their men. Letters from soldiers to their wives were filled with regret at not being home and advice on what to do until their return. In November 1863 William Asbell wrote to his wife, Sarah, from Camp Cobb in Decatur County, "I have received both of your letters and was glad to hear Through Them that you are all alive but sorry to know that the children are sick on your hands when I cannot be there to assist you with Them." William told Sarah to feed their hogs corn once a day and potatoes the rest of the time. "If the children are not able to dig the potatoes," he said, "fence of a portion of the patch for [the hogs]." As the weather grew colder and food ran low, William wrote to his wife, "You had better try and sell one or other of the horses . . . as you are scarce of Provisions. You will have to do the best you can." [109]

For many women laboring under the burdens of inflation, impressment, sick children, and absent husbands, their best was simply not good enough. Thousands of petitions from women all across the South describing their desperate situation and begging for relief flooded into Richmond. This petition, dated September 8, 1863, from women in Miller County was typical:

> Our crops is limited and so short [that we] cannot reach the first day of march next. . . . But little [illegible] of any sort to Rescue us and our children from a unanamus starveation. . . . We can seldom find [bacon] for non has got But those that are exzempt from service . . . and they have no humane feeling nor patraotic prinsables in thare harts. . . . they care not ef all the South and its effort fail and sink so they swim. . . . an allwise god ho is slow to anger and full of grace . . . will send down his fury and judgement in a very grate manar [on] all those our leading men and those that are in power ef thare is no more

favors shone to those the mothers and wives and of those hwo in poverty has with patrootism stood the fence Battles. . . . I tell you that with out som grate and speadly alterating in the conduckting of afares in this our little nation god will frown on it and that speadly.[110]

These women received no favors from the Davis administration. Worse yet, military officials denied their husbands the opportunity to help. Family starvation was not generally considered a valid reason for granting furloughs. It would have done Miller County's women little good in any case. The day after they signed their petition, the Miller County Wildcats were captured at Cumberland Gap, Tennessee, and spent the rest of the war in an Illinois prison camp.[111]

Abandoned and starving, thousands of women became beggars just to keep their families alive. Leaving children at home for days or weeks at a time, they roamed the countryside pleading for food. Sympathetic railroad conductors and steamboat captains occasionally provided transportation but most often the women made their way on foot. Some planters gave them what they could, others did not. But even the more generous viewed these unfortunates with contempt. One planter called the starving women "perfect nuisances." In a letter to Governor Watts, an Alabama planter questioned whether they deserved assistance at all.[112]

Poor women were occasionally viewed with more than just contempt by men in positions of privilege and power. Such men were not above demanding sexual favors in return for "charity." The frequency with which women complied depended on a variety of economic and personal circumstances. The more desperate their condition, the more submissive they tended to be. And the numbers of desperate women grew ever larger as the war continued. In October 1863, after discussing in vivid terms the hardships suffered by soldiers' wives and widows, one sympathetic Columbus man noted with regret, "they are sometimes offered assistance at the sacrifice of their honor, and that by men who occupy high places both in church and State."[113]

Impressment, taxation, inflation, starvation, and the lack of help from callous elites except "at the sacrifice of their honor" were too much for many women. Hundreds turned to theft rather than see their children starve. So much had been taken from them they saw it as taking back only what was theirs. Many traveling beggars took food from plantations whether the planters offered it or not. Women in Miller County were known to steal livestock on a regular basis. At one point, a group of about fifty soldiers' wives raided the government depot in Colquitt and took a hundred bushels of corn. In a letter to the *Macon Telegraph,* a sympathetic local resident blamed Miller County's inferior court judges for the women's plight: "These gentlemen are more busily engaged in their own business than they are in attending to their judicial duties. In fact, they don't seem to bestow any time at all toward relieving the necessities of suffering families of soldiers, as they are in duty bound by law to do." John Davis, a well-to-do slaveholder and judge of the inferior court, strongly disagreed. Destitution had little to do with the women's actions, he insisted. It was simply in their nature to steal.[114]

Attitudes like this one were common among upper-class folk. Few openly acknowledged the obvious link between desperate circumstances and desperate acts, but ignoring the problems of hunger and speculation only made them worse. By 1863 food riots were breaking out in major cities all across the South, including Macon, Atlanta, and Augusta, Georgia; Salisbury and High Point, North Carolina; Mobile, Alabama; and Richmond, Virginia. One band of starving southwest Georgia women attacked a wagon near Thomasville and made off with three sacks of corn. On April 10, 1863, a mob of about sixty-five Columbus women, some armed with pistols and knives, rallied near the upper bridge (now the Fourteenth Street Bridge) and marched down Broad Street "to raid the stores of speculators."[115]

A few weeks later, Daniel Snell of Harris County wrote home to his wife, Sarah, "You spoke of a riot in Columbus . . . it is no more than I expected. I understand there was also one in Augusta. . . . What will become of the women and children with the food situation."[116] Indeed, thousands of soldiers wondered how their families would get along in their absence. With government corruption out of control and planters unwilling to help, many began to question whether the Confederacy was worth preserving at all, much less fighting for. As the war lumbered on and conditions worsened, more and more soldiers decided it was not.

CHAPTER
5

Fighting the Rich Men's Fight

Hubert Dent had been so enthusiastic for the cause of southern independence that he enlisted in the Eufaula Rifles the same day he learned of Lincoln's election. After nearly a year on active duty, though, his enthusiasm was beginning to wane: "Soldiering does not suit my tastes or inclinations," he wrote to his wife, Nannie, "But unfortunately for me at present it is that or nothing." Elias Register, a farmer in Henry County before the war, found conditions in the army extraordinarily difficult. He was no stranger to hard work, but like Dent, he cared nothing for the life of a soldier. On July 1, 1861, Elias wrote to his wife from the front lines in Virginia, "I never knew what a hard life was before but I know now what it is." He would think even worse of army life just three weeks later when the Yankees came storming across Bull Run.[1]

Thousands of southern soldiers had second thoughts about the wisdom of their enlistment as the realities of war began to take hold. Many advised their friends and relatives not to join the army under any circumstances. James Crowder wrote to his brother in Chambers County, "I wante yo to stay at home." J. H. Jones of Troup County offered the same advice to his brother, and another valley soldier urged his brother not to let recruiting officers "persuade you off. They may tell you great tails . . . and how well we are fixed up here . . . but do not let them excite you into it." G. W. Ross of Macon County told his brother to hire a substitute if he could, "for a life spent in camps is a hard one certain."[2]

By the end of 1861 there had been only one major battle, and it was a Confederate victory. Even so, Dent wrote to his wife, "There seems to be great difficulty in getting men to reenlist. The freshness and first excitement of the war has worn off and men, many of them at least, are tired of the service. . . . Many troops will be entitled to their discharges in the next six months and it will not be easy to supply their places."[3]

Some did not wait six months. After the Battle of Shiloh in April

1862, Dent wrote to Nannie, "Many of our officers are resigning since the fight. . . . Many a man has found out that he could not stand the service on account of health since the fight who to all appearances at least were perfectly healthy before the fight. I tell you my Love they have had enough of battles." And there was no end of battles in sight. Dent thought the war might last for another three years—certainly as long as Lincoln remained in the White House. Private Benjamin Franklin Jackson of the Thirty-third Alabama also knew the war was far from over. Shortly after Shiloh he wrote, "I think we are fixing to do the biggest fighting that has been done yet." [4]

The soldiers were not only weary of battles. Problems with cloth manufacturing and food production were beginning to tell at the front lines. Cold, hunger, and disease, along with military discipline, loneliness, and a rising class consciousness all took their toll on the ranks. One Chattahoochee County soldier wrote home that the men were all "tired of fighting. . . . if it were left to the privates on both sides it would soon be peace everywhere. I hope it will be peace before a great while any how." [5] But, as Dent predicted, for three more years the soldiers would continue to suffer many of the same hardships as their families back home—and worse.

One major burden endured by the soldiers was lack of proper clothing. Within six months most of the soldiers' clothes were wearing out and the Confederacy could supply few replacements. Among the scarcest articles of clothing were shoes. William H. Andrews of Clay County recalled how the soldiers in Robert E. Lee's Army of Northern Virginia made moccasins out of cowhide. They did not "feel much like shoes," he said, "but they [were] better than going barefooted." Even when uniforms were available they almost never fit well. One Chattahoochee Valley soldier wrote home that his pants were too tight in the waist and four inches too long. Letters from boys at the front were full of urgent requests for their families to send clothes. In January 1862, from his post near Manassas, Barnett Cody of Henry County asked his sister, Henrietta, for two pairs of pants and a set of suspenders: "Sister, Send these things at Double quick time for I have only one pr Pants and cannot buy any about here." Benjamin Franklin Jackson asked his wife for two shirts, saying that the ones he had would "last a month longer I reckon." But as the war continued, the home folks found it difficult to clothe themselves, much less relatives who were hundreds of miles away. [6]

When the government would not provide clothing and the folks at home had none to send, dead bodies littering the battlefields were relieved of their raiment. William Andrews recalled that it was "nothing unusual to see yankee clothing in our camps, which was stripped off the dead on the battlefield. Saw Sgt. Alex Clemency of Company G wearing an officer's cap with a slot of his brains sticking to it. Sgt. Bridges of Company M wears a frock coat with a ball hole in the waist of it, and the tails covered in blood where the fellow was shot in the back. Don't think the boys wear them from choice, but from necessity." Andrews complained that the soldiers deserved better and blamed the government for not doing enough to provide adequate clothing.[7]

Confederate soldiers were even more upset about the food situation. The South was renowned for its agricultural productivity, yet its troops were constantly hungry. It was no secret that the main reason for food shortages was planter insistence on growing cotton. In demanding that planters give up cotton and plant more food crops, one Chambers County citizen pointed out that "a starving army cannot long exist." [8]

No one knew that better than Columbus native Raphael Jacob Moses, chief commissary officer in James Longstreet's Corps, Army of Northern Virginia. Thousands of troops looked to him for provisions, but he had none to give. In a desperate attempt to supply his men, Moses journeyed home to Columbus in May 1864 begging for food. "It occurred to me," he later wrote, "that if I could go to Georgia and speak to the people who had sons, brothers, relatives, and friends who were suffering for supplies, I could get supplies." It would not be so easy. When Moses called a meeting at Temperance Hall, only thirty people came. "I thanked them for their presence and stated when I last spoke in this hall it was to urge the people to send their sons and brothers to confront the hazards of war and to redress their country's wrongs, the house was full from pit to gallery with patriotic citizens ready for the sacrifices asked. Now I come from those near and dear to the people here, to appeal to them for bread for the starving army, and I am confronted with empty benches." [9]

Even when the troops received food through official channels, it was often barely edible. Benjamin Jackson wrote from the Tennessee front, "We get a little beef and not a grain of salt to put on it. We have to throw it away for we cant eat it." [10] In their letters home, soldiers begged loved ones to send food as well as clothing. William Stewart wanted his wife to send several dozen eggs: "They will be a great treat to me, since I have been sick if you can send them without their getting broke." Jackson asked his "Dear Companion" to send butter, ground peas, and "the biggest potato you have." As with clothing, it became harder and harder for relatives to comply with requests for food.[11]

When rations could not be obtained from the army or from home, soldiers bought their own food or foraged for it. Many stole it, sometimes from their own comrades. Louis Merz of West Point wrote in his diary of one soldier stealing fifteen pounds of sugar, coffee, bacon, butter, and beef from the company mess tent. Adding insult to injury, the thief left "human dirt" floating in one of the company water buckets. Merz cursed the miscreant with the invocation "May his dirtying machine refuse to do its duty in all time to come." [12]

Most soldiers tried to avoid stealing, especially from their comrades in arms, but keeping food in their bellies was a constant challenge from the war's outset. As early as July 1861, one valley soldier wrote, "I eat nothing only as I buy it myself." I. B. Cadenhead of Russell County told his wife, Luisa, that he paid a dollar and a half for "one half grone Chicken to make mee some supe." In a letter to his wife, Sarah, back home in Hamilton, Daniel Snell wrote from distant Virginia that he caught a catfish and an eel one Saturday and cooked them for breakfast the next morning. He wished he had caught more but wrote, "there's not much fish in this country." [13]

When the soldiers could catch no fish there were always rats, which seemed to infest every camp. Rats followed soldiers like the Pied Piper of Hameln. At Whitmarsh Island, Georgia, wharf rats were so numerous that rations had to be protected constantly. When food ran low, the rats became the rations. William Andrews told in his diary how each morning "rat details" would form, armed with sticks and shovels and prepared to do battle with the rodents: "The rats burrow under a row of cedars near the camps and the boys will dig them out and then let them run for their lives. They don't get far before they are knocked on the head. After the boys kill about 50, they turn too and dress them, each man cooking to suit his taste. Some fry, some stew, while others bake them, and the boys say they eat as well as a cat squirrel." [14]

As hard as it was for soldiers to keep themselves fed, it was even more difficult to keep themselves healthy. Doctors of the time had no idea what caused diseases like dysentery, typhoid, and malaria. Ill fed, ill clothed, living in crowded and unsanitary conditions, it is little wonder that soldiers were susceptible to all kinds of sickness. Twice as many died of disease during the war as were killed or mortally wounded in combat. Not surprisingly, soldiers feared illness more than the enemy. After a severe attack of "bowel disease," Elias Register told his wife, "I had much rather take the risk and fight than the sickness I fell in." [15]

Hardly a letter was written that did not contain some mention of the soldier's health. In September 1861 William Clarke wrote home to Cuthbert that "my health is very bad; I weigh just 95 lbs. . . . I have had chills more or less ever since I started. I want to get stout and sometimes think I am better. I have a very severe cough which I fear this cold mountainous country will not help." William Stewart wrote to his wife in southeast Alabama that a bout with the flu had nearly killed him. He apologized for his poor penmanship but explained, "my hand is so feeble that I can hardly write at all. Dear you don't know what I have suffered since I saw you last." [16]

One poor soldier from Russell County contracted measles, typhoid, and pneumonia at the same time. Another Russell County man summed up the soldiers' condition when he wrote to his sister, "We all look like death on a pale horse." Such misery served only to make the soldiers miss their loved ones and the comforts of home. Private William Turner of Troup County, after a week of chills and high fever, wrote home, "O! mother how I did wish you or sister was here to bathe my aching brow. Dear mother I had no idea how I loved you all at home." [17]

When Russell County soldier James Cantey wrote to his wife in January 1862, he had been suffering with "dyspepsia or indigestion" for nearly two weeks. "I feel a good deal better for the past day or two," he told her, "but have a good deal of sourness in my chest and bowels yet. I live on milk and mush, sometimes rice and toast with tea." Cantey's indigestion was so painful that he was willing to make almost any sacrifice to relieve it. "I mean to use every precaution," he insisted, "to prevent a recurrence by living very light and not using Tobacco any more." [18]

In all too many cases, no precaution was sufficient to overcome the ravages of disease. Elias Register reported his health as "tolerable well" in a letter to his wife but died of disease less than a month later, leaving his beloved Tempa with two young children to raise alone. He had been in the army barely five months. William H. Long of Cuthbert left for the war in May 1861. From his first station in Pensacola he wrote to his wife, "Tell Henry [his son] to attend closely to business and write often and keep me advised of everything pertaining to the crops, etc. Give my love to the children and kiss Frankie and Sallie for me. My best respects to the girls, and be assured, dear Sallie, that I remember you tenderly. May God bless and care for you all." A few months later, Long died of pneumonia.[19]

Private James K. Dowling came from a farm family in Dale County. The youngest son of Noel and Sarah McDonald Dowling, he signed up for the army at Barnes Crossroads in April 1861 and died of measles five months later. In accordance with his dying request, Dowling was buried in Clay-bank Cemetery. His brother, John, recalled how their mother had walked the yard and cried all day when James enlisted: "He returned home a corpse and then the climax came. My father sent for Dr. Plant. . . . He attended Mother all during the night, she fainting away and giving up at the death of her precious boy." [20]

Such heartbreaking scenes were repeated many times along the lower Chattahoochee over the next four years. As one valley resident put it, "this inhuman war is putting our whole country in mourning." [21] Young Barnett Cody of Henry County was severely wounded at the Battle of Gettysburg. Barely eighteen years old, he languished in agony for three weeks before he finally died. I. B. Cadenhead was killed in July 1864 in the Battle of Atlanta. His brother-in-law described Cadenhead's last moments in a letter to Cadenhead's wife, Luisa Faney Cadenhead: "Sister it become my painful duty to inform you that Mr. Cadenhead is nomore he was killed on yesterday, in A charge on the enemy I doonot know where he was struck, but from what I can learn he was shot through the chest with A miney ball, I saw him lying on the field, but we was retreating and there was no time for me to examin him further then to see that he was dead his boddy was left in the hans of the enemy." [22]

Trying to calm his wife's fears, John C. Curtright of Troup County wrote home on October 6, 1862, "My heart is fuller than ever of love to you. . . . Knowing the uneasiness you constantly feel about me, nothing I can write will keep you from feeling so, but I do desire you to try & look on the bright side of the Picture. I know you will say that there is no bright side, but I think there is, & from past protections & safteys we can with confidence ask for a continuation of these." But past protection held no guarantees for the future. Two days later Curtright was killed at the Battle of Perryville. [23]

As if cold, hunger, disease, and death were not enough for the soldiers to endure, there was also the personal humiliation of excessive military discipline. Most of the higher-ranking officers came from the slavehold-ing class and habitually treated those under their command much as they did their slaves. Seventeen-year-old Thomas Lightfoot, whose family had recently moved from Blakely to Henry County, complained in a letter to his cousin, "A soldier is worse than any negro on [the] Chtahooche river. He has no privileges whatever. He is under worse task-masters than any negro. He is not treated with any respect whatever. His officers may insult him and he has no right to open his mouth and dare not do it." William Clarke cared no more than Lightfoot for army discipline. "Military rule," he said, "is perfectly despotic." Most of the enlisted men and many of the lower-ranking officers simply ignored the finer points of military etiquette. When one Georgia soldier on guard duty failed to salute a passing general, the officer demanded to know why. The young man simply replied, "Oh, hell, General, that's played out." [24]

Soldiers also resented the special privileges their officers received. Private Cyrus Jenkins of Troup County complained bitterly that those of his rank, like slaves away from their plantations, had to carry a pass whenever they left their units for any reason. There was no such requirement for officers. Jenkins found the practice humiliating. "Why should a private soldier carry a pass when an officer can go at will," he asked, "for what is an officer but a man!" [25]

The soldiers were especially annoyed with the privileges of rank when it came to more serious issues like medical treatment. Early in the war, William Andrews described the impact of disease on the men and how the officers received exceptional care: "There has been a great deal of sickness in camps and many deaths, especially among the rank and file. . . . The officers always manage to get home or to a hospital. Have never known one to die in camps." But, as one southern private observed, "the officers have all the glory. Glory is not for the private soldier, such as die . . . eaten up with the deadly gangrene, and being imperfectly waited on." It was all too much for many soldiers. Soon after he recovered from wounds received during the Sharpsburg campaign, James Glass of the Miller County Guards was listed on the company rolls as absent without leave. [26]

It should have come as no surprise that common soldiers balked at the rigid authoritarianism of army life and resented special privileges for officers. For years, planters had preached the social equality of all whites in an effort to bolster support for black slavery. Few planters took the notion seriously, and their view of lower-class whites as inferior was obvious in the military. One Georgia planter spoke disdainfully of poor white recruits as "not the men upon whom a brave leader would rely for energetic, heroic action, [but] they will answer as food for powder and understand how to use the spade." [27]

Class consciousness was evident throughout the military, especially in the Confederate navy. Cramped quarters and constant contact with the sailors made naval officers particularly insistent on keeping a social distance. Aboard the *Chattahoochee,* Lieutenant George Gift referred to his fellow officers as "a splendid set: some of them are sons of the old aristocracy, who are carrying on the traditions most creditably." But when describing the sailors under his command, Gift habitually used such terms as *ridiculous, odd, delinquent, buzzard,* and *worser sorts.*[28]

Even more than the contemptuous attitude of officers, soldiers resented the severe physical punishments inflicted on them for the slightest offense. Being whipped, tied up by the thumbs, bucked and gagged, branded, or even shot was not uncommon. Gift had one of his sailors on the *Chatta-hoochee* hung up by his wrists on a hook for four hours just for swearing. Hubert Dent wrote of a man being shot for striking his commanding officer. Barnett Cody saw a young soldier executed for falling asleep on guard duty. The enraged father of one seventeen-year-old soldier from Columbus wrote to Governor Joe Brown complaining that his son had been "most cruelly and inhumanly treated . . . for the most trifling offences." The man recognized the need for military discipline but insisted that "soldiers should not be punished like or worse than slaves."[29]

Their harsh treatment and miserable lifestyle made soldiers all the more lonesome for home. Thomas Barron wrote to his sister at Mill Town in Chambers County, "I often Think of you. . . . I see you in dreams I Think of the blissful hours we have [enjoyed] together . . . in childhood but Those innocent pleasures have pass." Benjamin Stubbs also missed the companionship of his sisters back home in southeast Alabama: "I would be the gladdest person in the world to see you all and talk with you a while, for I see nobody here but men and they appear to be very sorry company for me. I think I could enjoy myself at home better than anywhere else in the world."[30]

The only contact soldiers had with their families was through the mail service, and each letter from home was treated almost as a sacred relic. Harvey Hightower of Muscogee County wrote to his sister, "I had rather have letters now than clothes." In a note to his wife, Benjamin Jackson wrote, "I hope I shall get an answer before long, for it makes me so proud when I get a letter from you. I have to read it over two or three times before I can stop." One Dale County soldier risked his life dodging enemy fire to retrieve a letter from his wife. Another soldier from Troup County told his wife, "I want you to write me 20 letters (in one envelope) each letter twenty pages long." Many a letter home closed with the words "write soon."[31]

If soldiers felt great joy on receiving a cherished letter, they also experienced deep depression when no word came. As young Thomas Lightfoot wrote to his cousin, Hennie, "You cant imagine how bad it makes one feel to see all the boys eagerly seizing on their letters from home—while he is

standing by intently gazing on the package as it gradually grows smaller—
expecting every minute to hear his name—but the last one is gone and his
name has not ben called. He reluctantly turns away with a sad heart while
'Forgotten' 'Forgotten' rings in his ears." Thomas Daniel of Chambers
County felt that way and told his family to write more often: "I have riten
a bout twenty leters to you all and have got the hole a mount of thre I
think you all have forgoten me I wont you all to write to me and let me
no how you all are a geten a long." [32]

Soldiers rarely got as much mail as they would have liked, but seldom
was it because they had been forgotten. Many soldiers' wives were illiterate and had to rely on family or friends for contact with their husbands.
Even among those who could write, some could not afford to buy paper.
In other cases, the burdens of farming and child rearing left little time for
letter writing. Another problem was a lack of personnel to run the postal
service. With so many local militia units called up for service, it was not
unusual for a town to find itself without a postmaster. Sixty people from
the small community of Attapulgus in Decatur County petitioned Governor Brown to have their postmaster, George W. Donalson, discharged
from the army: "If our Post office is permitted to go down for the want of
a P.M. our nearest office will be Bainbridge distant—12 ½ miles." [33]

Sometimes letters were simply lost in the mail. With armies frequently
on the move, it was not uncommon for letters to go missing in transit.
Few of Troup County native Sallie Lovett's letters ever seemed to reach
her husband, Billie. "Honey, what in the world do you reckon is the reason my letters don't go to you?" she asked in May 1862. "This is the
fourth or fifth one I have written to you since you have received one. I
don't know what can be the matter. I have directed some to Chattanooga,
some to Corinth and one to Bethel Springs. I wrote you a letter only four
days ago." She let him know that he was by no means forgotten: "Now,
honey don't you think I don't never write to you, for I do write and put
the letters in the office and what more can I do, though I wish it was so I
could go and put them in your sweet hand, which so oft I have held in
mine." [34]

Along with expressions of love and loneliness, letters from home invariably brought news of hardship and deprivation. Most of the home
folks tried not to burden their soldiers with bad news, but for many families bad news was the only news. As early as July 1861, before the war's
first major battle, the *Opelika Southern Republic* urged its readers not to
write "gloomy" letters. But such letters were inevitable even from the
war's outset and they became more frequent as the war went on. Mary

Brooks was left with three young children, a baby not yet weaned, and a farm to run near Greenville, Georgia. In September 1862 she wrote to her husband, Rhodam, "I never get any rest night or day, and I don't think I will last much longer." She was running low on bacon and salt as well as money with which to purchase them: "It is money for everything so you may know it is getting low with me."[35]

Most soldiers had little or no money to send home. "The private's pay," recalled one southern infantryman, "was eleven dollars per month, if he got it; the general's pay was three hundred dollars per month, and he always got his." Enlisted men went without pay for months at a time. One valley soldier wrote home about how the officers in his regiment received their pay while the soldiers got none. In response, the enlisted men laid down their arms until the payroll arrived. "The [Colonel] and others of our officers said that we were rebelling against our country," he wrote, "but we deny the charge it was not so. We were only rebelling against those haughty officers, for not giving us our rights—and other tyranizeing over us." When payrolls did arrive they usually contained only a fraction of what the soldiers were owed. Benjamin Jackson told his wife in July 1862, "I have not received any money yet and don't know when I shall." Nearly all the enlisted men were constantly in this predicament.[36]

Money was only a secondary concern for soldiers' wives. Most simply wanted their husbands to come home. Mary Jane Curry of Decatur County wrote to her husband, "I had such a pleasant dream last night. I thought you was at home and expected to remain."[37] Sallie Lovett spoke in moving terms of how the days dragged by as she waited for her husband's return.

Troup County, March 26, 1862

My dearest husband:

It is with a sad and heavy heart I take my pen in hand to write you a few lines. I received your very welcome letter last evening, glad indeed to hear from you and hear you was getting along so well. For it is more than I am. Billie, I am in so much trouble this evening. I have looked for you so hard today. I thought you would be sure to come. . . . Every time I hear a train I go to the door. I say, well, I do hope Billie [will] come down on that train. I wait and look until dinner. Then I say, well, I do hope he will come this evening. I wait until dark. No Billie yet. Then I bring a long sigh, perhaps a tear and say, well, I don't know why he don't come. Every time I hear a noise towards the gate I run to the door, but what do I see: nothing but trees and bushes. I strain my eyes almost out of their sockets but no Billie can I see. I turn 'round with a sigh. To think he has forgotten me! . . . I am not living any now, only breathing. It is true I am well in body but not at heart. My heart is grieved, the worst of all diseases. Honey, why don't you come home?[38]

Like so many other southern women, Sallie cared much more for her family than anything else. "I would give a world of Confederacies," she told Billie, "just to be with you." William Brooks of Randolph County wrote for his brother to hurry home as quickly as he could to see his wife. The poor woman was near death on account of illness compounded by her husband's absence: "She ses that she wants you to come home if you ever want to see her eney more fore she has stud it as long as she can. . . . She is growing worse every day." An east Alabama woman, Mrs. T. J. Jarrell, went so far as to threaten suicide unless her husband came home. A family friend wrote Jarrell begging him to "come home just as soon as you can get off for fear Mrs. Jarrell may destroy her self. . . . she says that she will not live unless you come."[39]

Most soldiers' wives were not suicidal over their absent men and stopped short of asking them to desert. Death being the standard penalty, desertion was often more dangerous than remaining on the battle lines. In a letter to his wife, one Dale County soldier wrote as delicately as possible that deserters "suffer a penilty that no body can suffr for them if they air cought." But for many farm women, to have their husbands come home for at least a short time was literally a matter of life or death. One Eufaula soldier told of a woman who wrote that her children were starving to death: "Last night I was aroused by little Eddie's crying. I called and said, 'What is the matter, Eddie?' and he said, 'O, mama, I am so hungry!' And Lucy, Edward, your darling Lucy, is growing thinner every day." The poor woman begged her husband to come home before it was too late. "I would not have you do anything wrong for the world, but before God, Edward, unless you come home, we must die."[40]

The soldiers wanted to come home just as much as their wives wanted them to, but it was nearly impossible for enlisted men in combat units to get furloughs. As early as summer 1862, Benjamin Jackson wrote that he did not know when, if ever, he would be allowed to visit home. Furloughs were rare even for those on garrison duty. William Asbell wrote from his station in Decatur County that none of the men were receiving furloughs and there was no telling when any would be granted. A month later, furloughs remained unavailable.[41]

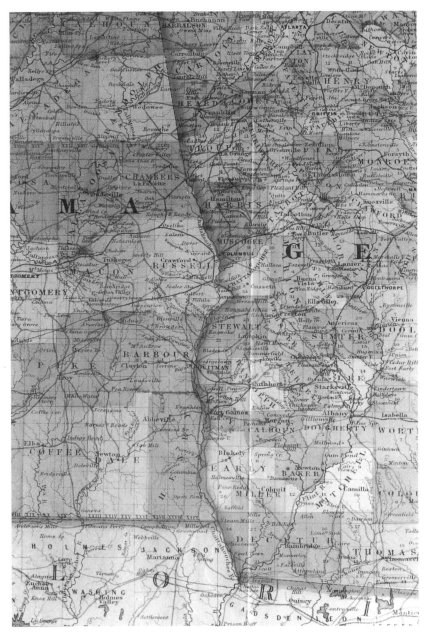

The Lower Chattahoochee River Valley, 1863. A. J. Johnson,
Johnson's Georgia and Alabama, 1863.

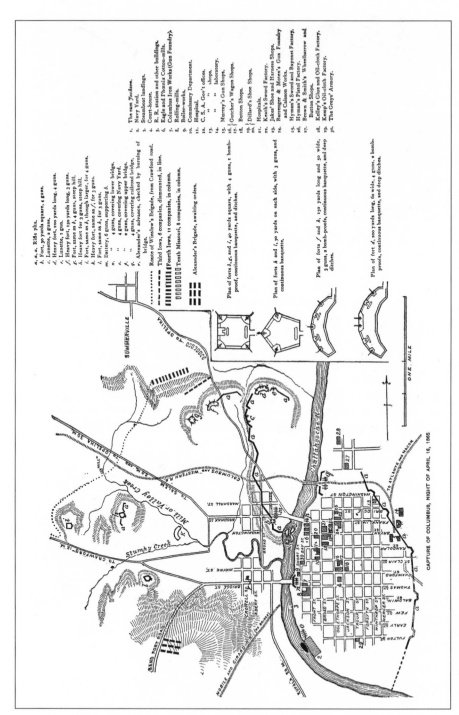

Columbus and Girard (Phenix City), 1865. William Forse Scott, *The Story of a Cavalry Regiment*.

Though he became a senator for Confederate Georgia and was one of Jefferson Davis's most reliable supporters in Congress, Benjamin Harvey Hill of Troup County strongly opposed secession. At Georgia's secession convention, he warned that the South, divided as it was over the wisdom of disunion, could not possibly survive a civil war. The Confederacy would fall, and slavery with it. Hill, *Senator Benjamin H. Hill*.

Like other larger slaveholders, Barbour County planter John Horry Dent expressed misgivings about secession. He feared not only that the prospects of war would disrupt his business but also that class divisions would doom the Confederacy. Slaves, he thought, would seek freedom at the earliest opportunity, and few plain folk would offer sustained support for a slaveholders' republic. Historic Chattahoochee Commission.

Martin J. Crawford, a Columbus lawyer and the district's congressional representative, was among the valley's most ardent fire-eating secessionists. After Lincoln's election, a colleague referred to Crawford as "crazy" and "insane" for secession. Like others of his stripe, Crawford spoke mainly for smaller planters and slaveholders who saw their own advantage in disunion. Kyle, *Images*.

In May 1861, the Democrats and Whigs of Early County held a mass meeting on the Blakely town square. Representing the Democrats, Judge James Bush, the author's great-great-great grandfather, dug a hole under the courthouse steps in which he buried a hatchet as a symbol of unity. Despite his initial enthusiasm for the cause, Bush later warned that Confederate policies tended to "alienate the affections of the people." Courtesy of Helen Kirkland Daniels, Miller County, Georgia.

Salem native Benjamin Franklin Crockett, a great-nephew of the famous Davy Crockett, joined the Confederate army in May 1861 and, though he spent several months in a Macon hospital, served until the army's surrender in April 1865. He died in 1922 at age eighty-three and now lies buried at the Pine Grove Cemetery in Phenix City, Alabama. His father, David Archibald Crockett, moved to what is now Lee County (then part of Russell County), Alabama, in the mid-nineteenth century, drawn by the region's agricultural fertility. Courtesy of Margaret Crockett Crisp, Harris County, Georgia.

Martha Bass Greene's father, Hartwell Bass, was already a man of some means when he left Virginia for Russell County in the 1830s. Her husband, Peter Alexander Greene, was born in Georgia in 1838 and later moved to Russell County, where he set up farming operations not far from Seale. Walker, *Russell County in Retrospect.*

Early in the war, Greene joined the Thirty-first Georgia Regiment as a sergeant with Company G. Shortly thereafter, he was elected first lieutenant of the company, and he served as its commander for the rest of the war since it was never assigned a captain. Walker, *Russell County in Retrospect.*

Valley women volunteered for hospital service by the hundreds in the war's early months. Despite their selfless efforts, community leaders often criticized them for taking on this nontraditional role. Even male doctors objected to their presence, fearing the establishment of a "petticoat government" on the wards. Still, their help was badly needed, and they insisted on their right to serve. Devens, *Pictorial Book*.

Trying to calm his wife's fears, Troup County soldier J. C. Curtright wrote home on October 6, 1862, "Knowing the uneasiness you constantly feel about me, nothing I can write will keep you from feeling so, but . . . from past protections & safteys we can with confidence ask for a continuation of these." Two days later he died at the Battle of Perryville. Rossiter Johnson, *Campfire and Battlefield*.

Barbara McCoy Howell Curtright of Troup County had five sons who fought for the Confederacy. Three did not survive the conflict, John C. Curtright among them. A Dale County woman nearly died herself after learning that her son had been killed in battle. One valley resident lamented that "this inhuman war is putting our whole country in mourning." Georgia Department of Archives and History.

While soldiers were dying at the front, well-to-do women tried to keep up the martial spirit back home. Columbus women were fond of staging choral concerts at Temperance Hall, where they performed such patriotic songs as "Let Me Like a Soldier Fall" and "Southrons, Hear Your Country Call You." They also sponsored benefit concerts by the young slave piano prodigy Thomas "Blind Tom" Bethune. His performances were, said one admirer, "calculated to excite, if not awe, wonderment in the very highest degree." This photo is from an 1860 publicity flyer. Library of Congress.

From the war's outset, the Richmond government recognized Columbus as a natural location for both public and private war-related industries. It was deep in the southern heartland, far from the major theaters of combat; it had rail connections to every major city in the South; it was at the head of navigation on the Chattahoochee River; and it was already a thriving industrial center. So productive were Columbus's textile facilities that prewar promoters called it the Lowell of the South. In this 1868 image, the smokestack to the left of center marks the Columbus Iron Works. *Harper's Weekly.*

A crowning achievement of the valley's industrial effort was the CSS *Chattahoochee,* built at the Saffold Navy Yard in Early County and outfitted at the Columbus naval facilities. But despite the tremendous effort put into its construction and maintenance, the gunboat was of little use to the Confederate war effort. As one of its officers wrote, "if the Yankees can come up the River, the *Chattahoochee* will be no impediment to them." Fortunately for the ship's crew, Yankee officials never felt such an expedition worth the effort. Sketch by Mike Stevens. Mueller, *Perilous Journeys.*

Planters grew much more cotton than was needed for domestic consumption—so much, in fact, that the warehouses could not hold it all. The result was a food shortage so severe that it literally starved the Confederacy out of existence. In March 1862 one southwest Georgia man wrote to Governor Joe Brown urging him to stop the planters in their unrestrained pursuit of profit, "for they will whip us sooner than all Lincolndom combined could do it." *Columbus Enquirer*, September 16, 1862.

State efforts to restrain cotton overproduction had little effect. Even the Confederacy's ban on cotton exports was ignored. Valley planters regularly smuggled cotton downriver on boats like the *Shamrock*, built in Columbus during the war, to Apalachicola, where it was transferred to oceangoing vessels. In 1862 one Fort Gaines resident spoke of cotton smuggling in the valley as such a fact of economic life that no "intelligent man in this section can doubt it." A few planters bragged openly that the longer the war went on, the more money they made. Florida State Archives.

With hunger on the rise, Governor John Gill Shorter of Alabama asked planters to "raise not another crop of cotton beyond the demands for home consumption until this unholy and cruel war shall cease." His advice fell on deaf ears. By the war's second year, the food shortage was taking its toll on soldiers' families, who lived on what little they could grow or beg from men of privilege. One Columbus resident lamented that women were "sometimes offered assistance at the sacrifice of their honor, and that by men who occupy high places in church and State." *Harper's Weekly.*

Hoarding and speculation contributed as much as cotton overproduction to widespread hunger, especially in urban areas. Kate Cumming (*right*), an army nurse who served in several valley hospitals, was sure that the South could sustain itself in spite of the blockade if not for the speculators who were "making *piles* of money out of the misfortunes of their country." Cumming, *Gleanings from Southland.*

While poor families with absent fathers and husbands daily faced the threat of starvation, wealthy southerners enjoyed a lifestyle hardly touched by the war. As late as March 1865, only weeks before the war's end, Kate Cumming wrote of a meal at the Cook House in Columbus where the table was so heavy with food it "actually groaned." Such class disparities were the major cause of disunity among southern whites. *Leslie's Illustrated Newspaper.*

Urban hunger became so serious that food riots, with women as the main participants, broke out in towns throughout the South. One group of about fifty soldiers' wives raided the government depot in Colquitt, Georgia, and took a hundred bushels of corn. In Columbus, a mob of women armed with pistols and knives rallied near the upper bridge and marched down Broad Street "to raid the stores of speculators." *Leslie's Illustrated Newspaper.*

Lack of food was a constant concern for soldiers as well as civilians. Muscogee County native Raphael Moses, chief commissary officer in James Longstreet's Corps, Army of Northern Virginia, traveled home in May 1864 begging for food on behalf of his soldiers. When Moses called a meeting at Temperance Hall in Columbus, to his great disappointment only thirty people showed up. Mueller, *Perilous Journeys*.

When rations could not be gotten from the army or from home, soldiers bought their own food or foraged for it. Many stole it, sometimes from their own comrades. Private Louis Merz of West Point wrote of one soldier stealing fifteen pounds of sugar, coffee, bacon, butter, and beef from the company mess tent. Adding insult to injury, the thief left "human dirt" floating in a water bucket. Merz cursed him with the invocation, "May his dirtying machine refuse to do its duty in all time to come." Cobb Memorial Archives.

(*Opposite, top*) Class-related pressures forced soldiers by the thousands to question their loyalties. The infamous twenty-slave law, which excused planters from the draft, defined the conflict as a rich man's war for the great mass of southern plain folk. One valley paper ran an ad reading "WIFE WANTED—by a young man of good habits, plenty of money, good looking and legally exempt from Confederate Service." *Harper's Weekly.*

Wealthy men could avoid being hauled off by a conscript company by owning at least twenty slaves, paying an exemption fee, hiring a substitute, or bribing the local conscript officer. Plain folk who could afford none of these options had little choice. Editor E. H. Grouby of the *Early County News* wrote, "It is strange to us that the Government allows its officers to conscript poor men who have the appearance of *dead men*, while they turn loose rich ones who are *young, hale and hearty.*" Devens, *Pictorial Book.*

Fearing that they would be drafted, hundreds of men joined the army just before conscription went into effect so that they could get the fifty-dollar enlistment bonus and serve with units of their choice. A small farmer who owned no slaves, John Joseph Kirkland of Early County, the author's great-great grandfather, had a wife and five children when he enlisted with the Early Volunteers a few weeks before the draft began. He was thirty-three, only two years short of exemption. A year later, in May 1863, he lost a leg at the Battle of Chancellorsville. Courtesy of Martha Bush Kirkland, Miller County, Georgia.

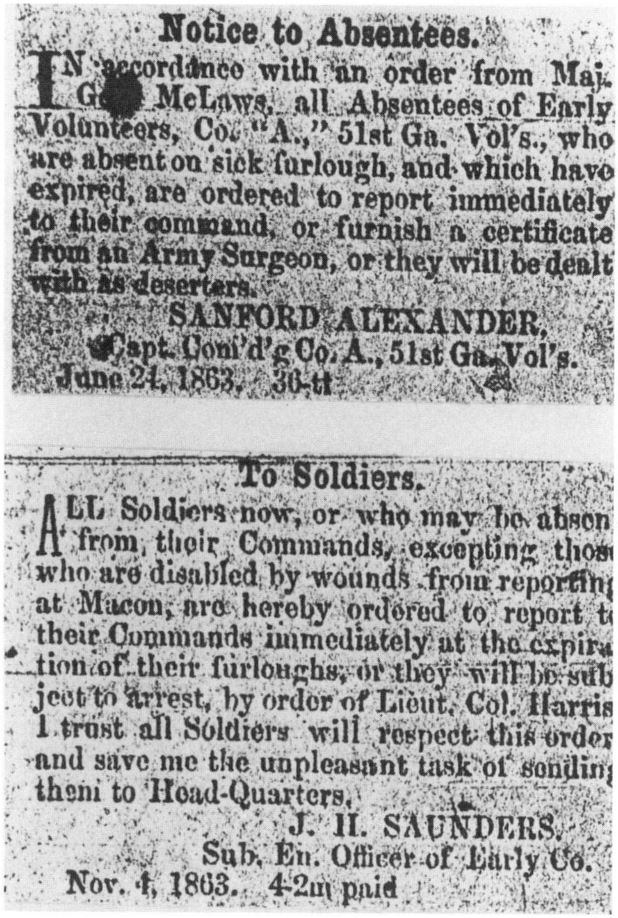

Notice to Absentees.

IN accordance with an order from Maj. Gen. McLaws, all Absentees of Early Volunteers, Co. "A.," 51st Ga. Vol's., who are absent on sick furlough, and which have expired, are ordered to report immediately to their command, or furnish a certificate from an Army Surgeon, or they will be dealt with as deserters.

SANFORD ALEXANDER,
Capt. Com'd'g Co. A., 51st Ga. Vol's.

June 24, 1863. 36-tf

To Soldiers.

ALL Soldiers now, or who may be absent from their Commands, excepting those who are disabled by wounds from reporting at Macon, are hereby ordered to report to their Commands immediately at the expiration of their furloughs, or they will be subject to arrest, by order of Lieut. Col. Harris. I trust all Soldiers will respect this order and save me the unpleasant task of sending them to Head-Quarters.

J. H. SAUNDERS,
Sub. En. Officer of Early Co.

Nov. 4, 1863. 4-2m paid

The year 1863 was not a good one for the Early Volunteers or for any of the county's other military companies. So many Early County men were absent without leave that warnings like these were posted in the *Early County News* encouraging them to return. The effort apparently did not work. Notices like those shown here appeared until the war's end in papers throughout the valley and the South. They were testimony to the rising tide of southern disaffection with the Confederacy. *Early County News.*

Many deserters and draft evaders formed guerrilla bands and attacked Confederate supply wagons, raided local plantations, and harassed impressment and conscription officials. Led by men like John Ward and Joseph Sanders, they virtually eliminated Confederate authority in some parts of the valley. No sessions of the circuit court were held in Dale County during the last two years of the war. *Leslie's Illustrated Newspaper.*

On December 3, 1864, members of Dale County's home guard lynched the Reverend Bill Sketoe on suspicion of riding with John Ward's raiders. In their haste, they tied the rope to a weak branch. When it caught Sketoe's full weight, it bent down just low enough for the condemned man to touch the ground. One of his executioners hurriedly dug a hole under Sketoe's feet, and moments later Sketoe was dead. The hole remains visible to this day. According to local legend, Sketoe's ghost keeps it cleared. Sketch by William A. Dawson. Azbell, "Haunted Hole."

Even southerners who stuck by the Confederacy to its painful end did so with little enthusiasm. William Andrews of Clay County, an enlisted man who joined the army in February 1861 and served through the entire war, wrote in May 1865, "While it is a bitter pill to have to come back into the Union, don't think there is much regret for the loss of the Confederacy. The treatment the soldiers have received from the government in various ways put them against it." Courtesy of Mark Reynolds, Tucker, Georgia.

If white southerners had little love for the Confederacy, black southerners had even less. As the slaves well knew, threats to sell a spouse or child were very real. One valley observer wrote that "such separations as these are quite common, and appear to be no more thought of, by those who enforce them, than the separation of a calf from its brute parent." The slave trade's cruelties became worse as the war dragged on. Rossiter Johnson, *Campfire and Battlefield.*

One of the most terrifying aspects of the slaves' miserable existence was the slave patrol, designed to guard against the possibility of insurrection. In Barbour County, slaves caught off plantations without passes could receive thirty-nine lashes. Still, many slaves fought back, tying ropes or vines neck-high across dark stretches of road just before the patrollers rode by. According to a former slave, these traps were guaranteed to unhorse at least one rider. *Leslie's Illustrated Newspaper.*

The longer the war lasted, the more slaves ran away. Some ran off to join Union military forces; others fled to nearby woods and swamps temporarily or for the war's duration. One Troup County slave hid his family in a cave near the Chattahoochee River until the war was over. Governor John Gill Shorter of Alabama, a Barbour County native, called the Wiregrass a common retreat of runaway slaves. Rossiter Johnson, *Campfire and Battlefield.*

Thousands of slaves deserted their masters in what historian W. E. B. DuBois referred to as a general strike against the Confederacy. And the closer the war came to its conclusion, the more slaves ran away. These notices from the *LaGrange Reporter* of March 3, 1865, testify to how slaves felt about the Confederacy.

When news of approaching Yankee troops spread through Barbour County near war's end, all the slaves on the Garland plantation turned out to greet them. Such scenes were common throughout the valley in April and May 1865. Slaves by the thousands worked and prayed for Union victory as a guarantee of longed-for freedom. Rossiter Johnson, *Campfire and Battlefield.*

Even with Confederate defeat, freedom for former slaves remained more a dream than a reality. As judge of the court of ordinary in Miller County, William B. Daniell, the author's great-great-great grandfather, was empowered by Georgia's legislature to issue "indentures of apprenticeship" that bound freedmen's children to their former masters. Other such Jim Crow laws were contrived by states throughout the former Confederacy to keep black southerners "in their place." Courtesy of Helen Kirkland Daniels, Miller County, Georgia.

Horace Bynum was the oldest living former slave in Russell County when this photo taken shortly before his death in 1948. For a majority of freedmen, as this image suggests, the so-called New South was very much like the Old South. Indeed, cotton and poverty dominated the lives of most valley folk, black and white, well into the twentieth century. Walker, *Russell County in Retrospect.*

If furloughs were hard to get, discharges were nearly impossible to come by. One Georgia private said of his commander, "This damned ginral won't give you a furlough or a discharge till you are dead ten days, and *then* you have to prove it." William Andrews recalled one man who was so desperate to get out of the army that he shot off his left hand. "That," wrote Andrews, "ended his soldiering." [42]

Failing to get permission from the army for their men to come home, thousands of women turned to their governors for help. Susan Thurman of Lumpkin asked Brown to declare her husband exempt from service. All his brothers and brothers-in-law had been killed in the war and he was needed at home to help their widows and children. A Decatur County woman, Mrs. Aliff Williams, wrote to the governor on behalf of her brother, who was home on sick leave suffering with bronchitis and chronic asthma and was unable to return to duty. "Besides," she wrote, "he is a poor man with a wife and a hand full of little children [and] a widowed mother." By October 1863 Mrs. H. N. Jackson of Russell County had suffered the deaths of her husband and eldest son, both killed in battle. She now urged Governor John Gill Shorter to exempt her eldest remaining son, Stephen, from military service so he could help care for his six younger siblings. [43]

Mary Ball of Columbus urged Governor Brown to release her son, William, from Company D of the First Georgia Regiment. "He is under age," she insisted, "and his is all the support i have on earth. . . . if you dont let him com home my self and Children will be turnd out of doors for house rent." Brown received another letter from a poor woman in Stewart County who had lost her husband, two brothers-in-law, and a brother to the war. She had one brother left and he was in the army and sick with typhoid fever, measles, and a "hacking cough." She begged the governor to discharge him so he could recover and care for his three children. "Their Mother is dead," she wrote, "and his Mother is a widow and not able to do anything for them." Despite such heartbreaking pleas, few enlisted men who could walk and carry a rifle were allowed to leave. [44]

One thing that alienated poor soldiers almost as much as the government's inability to care for their families (and its refusal to allow them to do so) was the ease with which wealthy soldiers received furloughs and discharges. The higher one's rank or the greater one's wealth, the easier it was. As a southern private put it, "A general could resign. That was honorable. A private could not resign . . . and if he deserted, it was death." [45] The right to act according to the dictates of one's conscience was a privilege the South's self-styled aristocrats reserved for themselves.

Thousands of southern men faced the dilemma of whether to allow their families to die at home or risk death themselves by deserting, and the risk was very real indeed. In Braxton Bragg's Army of Tennessee, five Alabama men were sentenced to death for an absence of only three days. "If old General Bragg keeps on having them shot like he has been," wrote Benjamin Jackson, "he will certainly thin out the ranks."[46]

On execution day, a condemned man was usually marched or hauled by wagon, sometimes sitting on his coffin, to his burial site, where the bloody work was witnessed by his entire regiment. Few soldiers cared to see the macabre proceedings but were forced to watch as a lesson for would-be deserters. "I saw a site today that made me feel mity bad," one Alabama private wrote of an execution he witnessed. "I saw a man shot for deserting there was twenty fore Guns shot at him thay shot him all to peases. . . . he went home and thay Brote him Back and then he went home again and so they shot him for that Martha, it was one site that I did hate to see it. But I could not helpe my self I had to do Jest as thay sed for me to doo." Executions became so frequent in Bragg's army that Jefferson Davis finally ordered him to stop shooting so many of his men.[47]

Despite the dangers of desertion and clear examples of what would happen if they were caught, soldiers continued to leave by the thousands. Presenting their rifles as furloughs to anyone who dared challenge them, they made their way over hundreds of rugged miles to help their starving families. Some never made it. Many of those who did were dragged back to the army in chains. One valley soldier in Lee's Army of Northern Virginia wrote that it was "an everyday occurrence for men to get letters from home stating that their families are on the point of starvation. Many a poor soldier has deserted and gone home in answer to that appeal, to be brought back and shot for desertion."[48]

The way the soldiers saw it, they had very little choice. If the government could not care for their families, the soldiers had to. Their first duty was to the survival of their wives and children. In a letter to Governor Shorter, James F. Redus asked, "What is independence to a man when those that are most near and dear to him are famished and died for want of his assistance at home?" Another Alabama man concluded, "If I lose all that life holds dear to me, what is my country or any country to me?"[49]

Soldiers who had no starving families at home had great sympathy for those who did. William Andrews, a young bachelor, insisted that if he were faced with the same situation he would desert. "Thank God," he wrote, "I have no wife and children to suffer on account of an ungrateful government." Civilians expressed sympathy as well. In a letter to the *Daily Sun,* one Columbus mechanic wrote that though the city's workers could barely feed themselves, "their condition is much better than the poor soldiers, who are fighting the rich men's fight, for they suffer all of the privations and hardships incident to the life of a soldier, with a prefect knowledge of the sufferings of their families at home."[50]

Family hardships, hunger, cold, disease, and class antagonism all contributed to a general decline of enthusiasm early in the war. Only weeks after First Manassas, men were deserting in droves and there were few volunteers to take their places. In October 1861 an officer wrote to President Davis from Columbus that it was nearly impossible to get new recruits.[51] So weak was support for the Confederacy that officials in Richmond feared the war might soon be lost. The army badly needed men but few would willingly come forward. Willing or not, however, as far as the government was concerned, they had to come.

In April 1862 the Confederate Congress passed an enrollment act, which gave the president authority to force young men into the military with or without their consent. Under the terms of this act, commonly known as conscription or the draft, white males between the ages of eighteen and thirty-five became subject to involuntary enlistment. As an inducement to enlist before the draft went into effect, the government offered a cash bonus to those who volunteered and allowed them to serve with units of their choice. Fearing that they would be drafted anyway, hundreds of reluctant men volunteered in March and early April 1862. One was John Joseph Kirkland of Early County. A small farmer who owned no slaves, Kirkland had a wife and five children when he enlisted with the Early Volunteers. He was thirty-three, only two years short of exemption. A year later he lost a leg, and nearly his life, at the Battle of Chancellorsville.[52]

Not all men who fell into the eighteen-to-thirty-five age group were bound to be drafted. Government officials were exempt, as were employees in key war-related occupations such as riverboat pilots, telegraph operators, and certain kinds of skilled industrial workers. To plain folk, however, the most offensive provisions of the draft act allowed wealthy men to avoid service. Those with enough money could hire a substitute or simply pay the government an exemption fee. Few but the most affluent could take advantage of either loophole. Some wealthy folk signed contracts providing hundreds of pounds of foodstuffs to the government in exchange for exemption. Margaret Huguley, a slaveholder from Macon County, Alabama, signed such a contract to keep her son out of military service.[53]

And then there was the infamous twenty-slave law, which excused planters from the draft outright. Though few elites seemed to realize it at the time, this law defined the nature of the war for plain folk. From 1862 until the conflict's end, for the great mass of southerners, it was a rich man's war. Confirmation of that fact was especially evident in the newspapers. One advertisement for a substitute in the *Columbus Enquirer* offered "a good price" payable "in cash, land, or negro property." Another valley paper ran an ad reading "WIFE WANTED—by a young man of good habits, plenty of money, good looking and legally exempt from Confederate Service." [54]

Reaction to conscription in general and to the twenty-slave law in particular was swift and direct. When several draft evaders in Randolph County, Alabama, were arrested, an angry mob attacked the jail and set the prisoners free. Near Buena Vista, Georgia, a band of draft dodgers armed themselves and swore they would die before being forced into Confederate service. "The people of Georgia regard the draft as disgraceful," Captain George A. Mercer insisted. Another Georgia soldier, Edward R. Harden, wrote from Camp Jackson, "The army here is in great excitement. . . . I find every body opposed to this tyrannical conscription law." William Andrews, along with five other men of his southwest Georgia regiment, hung a conscription officer in effigy as a way to "make our intentions known to them." They erected a gallows, stuffed a uniform with Spanish moss, and hung it up with a sign around its neck reading "Conscript Officer." "It was never found out who done it," Andrews wrote, "and that was the last thing heard of a conscript officer coming to our camps." [55]

Conscription officers were among the most detested men in the South. John Whitner of Troup County wrote to General Howell Cobb, commander of the valley's military district, to complain that "the poppinjays employed as enrolling officers . . . delight in harrassing and putting to expense everybody." According to one account, conscript patrols went "sweeping through the country with little deference either to the law or the regulations designed to temper its unavoidable rigor." A Fort Gaines man wrote that conscript officers were everywhere, "watching for some poor devil who is trying to keep out of the army." He told of soldiers running men down with hounds and dragging the captives off to the army in chains. One draft dodger was caught in Albany disguised as a woman and was chained and delivered to his company wearing the dress in which he was captured. [56]

Among those exempt from the draft were blacksmiths, millers, tanners, shoemakers, telegraph operators, and key industrial workers. Yet citizens complained constantly about conscript officers forcing such people into the army. Thomas Johnson of the Quartermaster Department wrote to Governor Watts that D. M. Banks of Russell County had been drafted. According to Johnson, Banks supplied wood and ran a steam engine at the quartermaster depot in Columbus. He was an essential worker and should be released from duty. David S. Johnston of the Saffold navy yard applied to Governor Brown for the release of R. A. Dykes, one of his engineers. Superintendent Howe of the Columbus telegraph office insisted that if three of his operators, two at Eufaula and one at Columbia, were not relieved of duty, "the line from this point to Tallahassee would have to be abandoned." [57]

Citizens of Russell County petitioned Watts to have their wagon maker and wheelwright, George Jones, discharged. A group of Barbour County residents begged the governor to exempt Robert A. Hatfield, their tanner and shoemaker. From the people of Rocky Head in Dale County came a petition for the release of their community blacksmith. Miller County folk wrote to the War Department that they were suffering "to a great extent" for want of a blacksmith and requested that Joshua L. Brown be discharged to fill the need. Clay County residents likewise called for the release of their blacksmith, W. H. Hunt. Harris County citizens asked to have their miller, William Johnston, relieved of duty, as did the people of Decatur County, who insisted that they were "entirely dependent" on J. W. Reese "for procuring bread for ourselves, families, & many soldiers families, besides many of the indigent & needy of our neighborhood." [58]

There seemed to be no limits beyond which conscript officers would go in quest of recruits. Neither age nor physical condition made any difference to many of them. Kate Cumming wrote in her journal of two Alabama women wandering through the camps looking for their young sons, who had been carried off by conscript officers. One of the boys suffered from a facial cancer that had already eaten an eye out of its socket. "How can our people be guilty of such outrages," Cumming wondered. "There is no punishment too severe for those thus guilty. But," she continued, "I have known conscript officers to take men from their homes whom the surgeons had discharged many times, and sent them to camp. We have had them die in our hospital before reaching the army." [59]

If conscript officers tended to disregard age and infirmity, bribery seemed to carry some weight with them. Men could usually avoid being hauled off by a conscript company if they could hand over enough cash to its commanding officer. An outraged E. H. Grouby wrote in the *Early County News,* "It is strange to us that the Government allows its officers to conscript poor men who have the appearance of *dead men,* while they turn loose rich ones who are *young, hale and hearty.*" [60]

In many cases, extortion rather than recruitment was the conscript officer's primary objective. Even before the draft went into effect, some officers lined their pockets with extorted funds. In March 1862 Abram Kauffman of West Point, Georgia, who was ineligible for military service because of age and affliction, wrote to Governor Brown complaining of his treatment at the hands of local recruiters. The company was led by Captain F. A. Pinkard of Chambers County and was composed of men from Chambers and Troup Counties. According to Kauffman, "they came into my house and seized me with Knives & pistols drawn & took me out by force & threatened to ride me on a rail & Shoot me & when one of the Company proposed that if I would give the Company three hundred dollars they would release me which I did in order to regain my liberty as I felt in great fear for my life." Kauffman offered to send supporting evidence from the city's mayor "and any number of the citizens of this place who witnessed the same & who I am proud to Say wholly disapprove of Such proceedings." [61]

It did not take long for word to reach Jefferson Davis that conscription and the twenty-slave law might be dangerous, even fatal, to the Confederate cause. In December 1862 one prominent Alabamian told the president, "Never did a law meet with more universal odium than the exemption of slave-owners. . . . Its influence upon the poor is most calamitous, and has awakened a spirit and elicited a discussion of which we may safely predict the most unfortunate results." So strong was resentment among the poor, he warned, that the twenty-slave law, "instead of being, as it ought to be, a measure that saved the country, it threatens to be the cause of its subjugation." Joseph Bradford of southwest Georgia agreed, assuring Davis that if the twenty-slave law were not repealed widespread insubordination among the troops was inevitable. [62]

Resentment toward conscription in general was just as evident. One conscript officer was nearly killed when he tried to enforce the draft law at Fort Gaines. Threats to his life were so serious that he fled the state. Draft dodging was rampant throughout the South. Howell Cobb thought it would take the whole Confederate army to enforce conscription. The law, he said, threatened the Confederacy "as fatally as . . . the armies of the United States." Even Vice President Alexander Stephens viewed conscription as "radically wrong in principle and in policy." [63]

The governors of Alabama and Georgia opposed Confederate conscription not only because it alienated the common folk but also because it infringed on their own powers. Brown called the Confederate draft unconstitutional and threatened to use the state militia to resist it. "No act of the government of United States prior to the secession of Georgia," he said, "struck a blow at constitutional liberty so fell as has been stricken by the conscription act." The legislatures of both states took steps to limit the activities of conscript officers operating within their borders. Despite overwhelming opposition from plain folk and state officials, the Confederacy refused to reconsider its draft policy. Georgia Senator Ben Hill fully supported Davis in the matter, and even the supreme courts of Georgia and Alabama upheld the draft as constitutional.[64]

With conscription an established fact, thousands of letters poured into both state and Confederate offices requesting exemptions. Potential draftees cited any number of reasons why they should be excused. Isaac Bush of Colquitt asked for exemption on account of "my ankles swelling." I. M. Horton of Troup County insisted that he should be allowed to remain at home because he was "the most effective patrol & police duty man" in the county. For B. J. Smith of Cuthbert, leaving home would mean leaving his "large warehouse" with three thousand bales of cotton unattended.[65]

E. A. Jenkins of Upatoi in Muscogee County missed qualifying for exemption under the twenty-slave law by only one—he owned nineteen, so he wrote to Brown begging to be excused on other grounds: "I am a small man weighing one hundred and thirty five pounds. I am in bad health and have been aflicted with chronic Diarreah for nearly three years. I am deaf in one of my ears." Jenkins concluded by assuring the governor, "I have always supported you and the Democratic Party."[66]

Those who could not get exemptions outright tried other ways to avoid military duty or at least service on the front lines. When the Confederacy made county officials exempt from the draft, such positions became the focus of heated campaigns. In Early County as many as thirty-seven candidates vied for five seats on the Inferior Court. "But there was no politics in the race," said one county resident. "The candidate just wanted the office to keep him out of the war." In Decatur County, J. A. Zeigler tried to use his position as clerk of court to get a discharge. Dr. Paul DeLacy Baker wrote to Governor Shorter from Eufaula asking for assignment to an army hospital rather than a regimental post because of his asthma. Some draft dodgers even sought refuge among the Yankees. In a letter to the Confederate secretary of war, Shorter lamented that large numbers of south Alabama men were fleeing to Union-held coastal regions in Florida to escape conscription.[67]

One of the most common ways of dodging the draft was to join a home-guard company. Nearly every town and county had home-guard units, which were supposed to be manned primarily by old men, young boys, and the physically disabled. There were a few home-guard companies, like the Nancy Harts of LaGrange, composed entirely of women. Invariably, there were also many healthy men of draft age who joined home-guard units and claimed exemption from the draft on that basis. In January 1864 four young men from Columbus who had just reached draft eligibility organized a home-guard company of local children for the alleged purpose of guarding bridges and performing other light duty. Their real objective, according to one local citizen, was to escape combat service.[68]

Home guards were seldom given any real duties to perform. Even when they were, they often refused to do it. Columbus's post commander was ignored when he called out the city's four companies for guard duty in November 1863. "These men are *terribly* averse to doing guard duty," wrote the editor of a local paper. "We heard of one a few days ago who said that if he had a hundred dollars in gold he would leave the Confederacy before he would perform guard duty." The editor was not surprised by such comments. It was common knowledge that most of the men had become guardsmen to avoid military service.[69]

The increasing reluctance of plain folk to serve the Confederacy reflected a much broader discontent. From its beginnings, many plain folk saw the conflict as a rich man's war. That view became more widely held among them as the months dragged by. Slaveholders brought the Confederacy into existence but would not grow corn enough to feed its soldiers or their families. Speculators were driving prices of even the most basic necessities far beyond the reach of most southerners. The burdens of taxation and impressment fell heaviest on the yeomen, and they and the landless whites bore the brunt of conscription.

As early as 1862 one Georgia paper insisted that "*all classes of the community MUST do their share of the fighting, the high, the low, the rich and poor, and those who have the means MUST pay the expense,* as those who have not the means cannot pay."[70] But they did not. For planters, maintenance of personal profit was the driving force behind secession and it remained their paramount concern throughout the conflict. For the great majority of southern plain folk, the twenty-slave law seemed proof enough that the conflict was nothing more than a rich man's war.

One Alabama farmer believed that the planters only wanted "to git you pupt up and go to fight for their infurnal negroes and after you do there fighting you may kiss there hine parts for o they care." Another Alabamian agreed, saying of the planters, "They think all you are fit for is to stop bullets for them, your betters, who call you poor white trash." One Early County man, who signed himself "An Old Soldier," wrote that one way to get rich in the life-insurance business would be to take "only those applicants who are shouting for their fellow citizens to go to 'the front.' " [71]

Such attitudes produced a class-based political consciousness among plain folk that made itself felt in the 1863 elections, when southern voters ousted nearly half their congressional representatives. Both of Alabama's incumbent senators lost their bids for reelection, as did Governor Shorter, a staunch supporter of the Davis administration. Shorter carried only four counties and lost his home county of Barbour by nearly four hundred votes. Six members of Alabama's new congressional delegation were rumored to be unionists, and one was such an outspoken opponent of the war and the government that Congress expelled him. Georgia voters sent nine new legislators to Congress, eight of them elected on platforms opposing the Davis government. Julian Hartridge of southeast Georgia's First District was the only member of the state's House delegation to retain his seat. [72]

In the five congressional districts of which the lower Chattahoochee Valley was part, only two representatives were reelected. The area's new congressional delegation was much more attuned to concerns of plain folk than was the old. Valley delegates to the First Confederate Congress had supported both impressment and conscription by a five-to-one majority. In the Second Congress, they opposed these measures by the same margin. [73]

Common folk were active in local elections as well. In Columbus they offered their own slate of candidates called the "Mechanics' and Working Men's Ticket" for city office. According to the *Enquirer,* the new party "prevailed by a very large majority" in the October 7 balloting. Its success sent shock waves through the ranks of the city's political establishment. Some went so far as to advocate the exclusion of common folk from future elections by reinstituting extensive property qualifications for voting and holding office. [74]

The *Enquirer*'s editor gave voice to elitist fears just two days after the vote when he chastised workingmen for their "antagonistic" attitude and condemned the "causeless divisions of our citizens into classes." The *Enquirer* conceded that because of their great numbers, the city's plain folk could control any election in which they were united, but he insisted that this fact alone was among the strongest reasons why they should not unite. "Nothing can be more mischievous in any society," he warned, "than antagonistic organizations of its classes. Such divisions are more bitter in their alienations than any other political parties, and are far more apt to produce hurtful collisions." [75]

Reaction to the *Enquirer*'s criticism was swift and direct. On October 13, 1863, a competing paper, the *Daily Sun,* ran a letter it received from a local man signing himself "Mechanic." He argued that mischief had already been done by the elites. Common folk were trying only to protect themselves from further harm.

Voting by Classes

Editor Daily Sun:—I notice in the Enquirer, of Friday evining, an article complaining bitterly of the people voting by classes, in which both classes are accused of clannishness, but the burden of his complaint seems to rest on mechanics and working men. He says, "there is certainly no ground for any antagonism in the city." In this the Enquirer is mistaken; for any man, woman or child can see that the people are dividing into two classes, just as fast as the pressure of the times can force them on. As for example: class No. 1, in their thirst for gain, in their worship of Mammon, and in their mighty efforts to appropriate every dollar on earth to their own account, have lost sight of every principle of humanity, patriotism, and virtue itself, and seem to have forgotten that the very treasures they are now heaping up are the price of blood, and unless this mania ceases, will be the price of liberty itself; for we know something of the feeling which now exits in the army, as well as in our work-shops at home. The men know well enough that their helpless families are not cared for, as they were promised at the beginning of the war. . . . They know, too, that every day they remain from home, reduces them more and more in circumstances, and that by the close of the war a large majority of the soldiery will be unable to live; in fact, many of them are ruined now, as many of their homes and other effects are passing into the hands of speculators and extortioners, for subsistence to their families. Thus you see, that all the capital, both in money and property, in the South, is passing into the hands of class No. 1, while class No. 2 are traveling down, soon to take their station among the descendants of Ham. You can easily see who are class No. 2. The soldiery, the mechanics, and the workingmen, not only of Columbus, but of all the Confederate States. In view of these things, is it not time that our class should awake to a sense of their danger, and in the mildest possible manner begin the work of self-defense, and endeavor to escape a bondage more servile than that imposed by the aristocracy of England on their poor peasantry? Then we claim the right, as the first alternative, to try and avert the great calamity, by electing such men to the councils of the nation as we think will best represent our interests. If this should fail, we must then try more potent remedies.

Efforts to find "more potent remedies" had already given rise to a loosely organized movement, widely known as the Peace Society, to end the conflict with or without southern independence. The Peace Society was one of perhaps half a dozen secret or semisecret organizations that sprang up across the South to oppose the war. Little is known of the society's early days. It probably formed in north Alabama or east Tennessee during spring 1862 and spread from there. Though it was composed mostly of those who wanted nothing more than an end to the fighting, unionists were at the heart of the organization and remained its principal advocates throughout the war.[76]

From the outset of the Civil War, unionism was surprisingly strong in the Confederacy. William Fife of Harris County and John Fuller of Russell were among at least 100,000 white southern unionists who served in northern armies during the war, not counting irregulars never mustered into service, who numbered many more.[77] Unionism found its greatest strength in areas with few slaves such as the southern Appalachians and the pine barrens. But even in regions like the lower Chattahoochee Valley, where slaves made up half the population, there were significant numbers of white unionists.

In March 1862 John O'Connor of Fort Gaines warned Brown of "spies and traitors" operating all along the lower Chattahoochee River. General Cobb was so concerned about pro-Union sentiment in the valley that he began censoring the mail later that year. By late 1862 Henry County unionists were so active that the governor sent in troops with orders to "do or die" in suppressing them. Some Troup County men continued to fly the U.S. flag even after secession. So strong was unionism in some parts of the county that it was dangerous to support the Confederacy openly. Senator Hill, a Troup County native and initial opponent of secession, was well aware of this "class of native men . . . who were always called Union men—they were opposed to secession and to the war and willing at any time to make terms with the United States."[78]

Columbus contained the largest concentration of unionists along the lower Chattahoochee, hardly surprising since many of the city's skilled laborers and industrialists were not native southerners. During the 1840s Columbus industries began attracting craftsmen and entrepreneurs from the more industrialized regions of the North and even from foreign countries. By 1850 at least half the city's skilled workers had been born outside the South.[79]

In late February 1861, almost two months before the firing on Fort Sumter, one Columbus citizen felt certain that city residents would soon be ready to vote themselves back into the Union. Another Columbus man, R. T. Simons, warned Davis, "The yankees of this place hold the controlling power." Simons's statement was almost certainly an exaggeration, but staunch unionists did count powerful Columbus citizens among their number, including such men as William L. Clark, a railroad superintendent; Calvin Statton, a former city official and prominent merchant; Charles N. Terry, another merchant; William R. Brown, proprietor of a local iron foundry; and James Johnson, a former congressman who later became Georgia's provisional governor during Reconstruction.[80]

There were also a number of socially and politically prominent Columbus men who, while not open unionists at the beginning of the war, held strong reservations about secession. At least a few seem to have been closet unionists, including Joseph L. Morton, a former Columbus mayor; William F. Luckie, a cotton broker with an estate valued at more than $17,000; and Joseph B. Hill, a wealthy merchant with assets totaling $50,000.[81]

One of the wealthiest unionists in Columbus was John G. Winter. Though born in New York, Winter had lived in Georgia since 1817. He was involved with enterprises like the Bank of Brunswick, the Bank of St. Mary's, and such local concerns as the Merchant Mills, the Palace Mills, and the Rock Island Paper Mills. He also served as president of both the Girard Railroad Company and the Muscogee Railroad Company. His land holdings alone were valued at $143,000 in 1850. Two years later, he added to his cash assets with the sale of the Palace Mills for $50,000.

Soon after he moved to Columbus in 1842 Winter earned a reputation for civic responsibility. He loaned the financially strapped city $30,000 at simple rather than compound interest, saving his new neighbors a hefty sum. Less than two years later he was elected mayor and was so popular that he ran unopposed for a second term. National politics during the next decade took the South in a direction Winter did not care to go. On February 19, 1861, he wrote to unionist Senator Andrew Johnson of Tennessee calling secession a "diabolical heresy" and assuring him that there were many others in Columbus who felt the same way. He did, however, urge Johnson to keep those sentiments confidential "for this climate is dangerous & I might not be permitted to live to see the rascals brought to Justice." [82]

Winter had good reason to be cautious. "Vigilance committees" were forming all over the South to root out Union sympathizers, and Columbus was no exception. In summer 1861 the city's self-appointed Vigilance Committee began conducting "loyalty hearings." Hardly anyone was safe from the committee's intrusive proceedings, but those born north of the Mason-Dixon line were particularly suspect. If they visited relatives in the North, they were forced to submit to an interview and obtain the committee's permission before they could return to their homes. It was not uncommon for residents to be forced out of the city permanently under pressure from the Vigilance Committee. [83]

Despite these and similar efforts to quash unionist and antiwar sentiment in the valley, discontent continued to grow, especially among the plain folk. Some planters too were beginning to tire of the war. In 1863 one prominent Georgian warned Stephens that many of them saw slavery as finished no matter how the war ended. "These men are willing to give up their slaves tomorrow and go back into the Union with slavery abolished if it will bring peace and security to them in their other property." J. W. Warren, editor of the *Columbus Times,* told Stephens that this feeling was not at all uncommon in eastern Alabama and western Georgia. [84]

So prevalent was antiwar feeling along the lower Chattahoochee that parts of the region became strongholds of the Peace Society. The society held no regular meetings and kept no records, so membership is difficult to determine. Nonetheless, active membership clearly numbered in the thousands, and thousands more were sympathetic to the peace movement. Alabama historian Walter Fleming estimated that by 1863, "at least half the active males left in the state" were associated with the Peace Society. [85]

The Peace Society was only loosely organized. One contemporary wrote from Opelika that the society "has no regular times or places of meeting, and has no organized 'lodges' or 'communities.' Men who have studied the obligations, signs, &c., and who can communicate them well are styled 'eminent,' and pass through the country giving the 'degree' to all whom they regard as fit subjects." Those inducted into the society promised always to aid other members and their families. They also promised never to "cut, carve, mark, scratch, show, &c., upon anything, movable or immovable, under the whole canopy of heaven, whereby any of the secrets of this order might become legible or intelligible." Finally, the inductee concluded with this statement: "I bind myself under no less penalty than that of having my head cut open, my brains taken from thence and strewn over the ground, my body cast to the beasts of the field or to the vultures of the air should I be so vile as to reveal any of the secrets of this order." [86]

Members recognized each other by a variety of complicated signs. One of the most complex was the society's handshake. It was, according to one report, "given by taking hold of the hand as usual in shaking hands, only the thumb is turned with the side instead of the ball to the back of the hand." The following dialogue, which each member committed to memory, would then commence:

What is that?
A grip.
A grip of what?
A constitutional peace grip.
Has it a name?
It has.
Will you give it to me?
I did not so receive it, neither can I so impart it.
How will you impart it?
I will letter it to you.
Letter it and begin.
Begin you.
No, you begin.
Begin you.

Then, starting with any letter but the first, they spelled the word *peace* by calling out letters alternately to each other. [87]

Other signs of recognition included a salute with the right hand closed and the thumb pointed backward over the shoulder, throwing a stick to the right using both hands, and tapping on the toe of the right foot three times with a stick or switch, then waving it to the right. In a crowd, a society member made himself known by three slaps on the right leg. One might also use the phrase "I dreamed that the boys are all coming home." A distress signal was given by using the expression "Oh! Washington!" or "by extending the right hand horizontally and then bringing it down by three distinct motions." Repeating the word *Washington* four times could get a member of the Peace Society released from jail within twenty-four hours if his guard happened to be a brother member. [88]

The society's objectives included the spread of dissension among soldiers as well as civilians. The organization apparently met with considerable success. James Longstreet, Lee's senior corps commander, said that "the large and increasing number of desertions, particularly amongst the Georgia troops, induces me to believe that some such outside influence must be operating upon our men." An officer of the Fifty-ninth Alabama Regiment reported that his men, angered by word from home of impressment abuses, were on the verge of deserting. The entire regiment had been recruited in the Wiregrass region of southeastern Alabama. The Peace Society even claimed credit for Confederate defeat at Vicksburg and Missionary Ridge. These claims were probably exaggerated but it is certain that large numbers of Confederate troops, mostly poor men from Alabama, did desert just before Missionary Ridge.[89]

In December 1863 soldiers under the command of General James Clanton at Camp Pollard in south-central Alabama laid down their arms and refused to fight. The mutineers were all Wiregrass men led by members of the Peace Society. One investigator reported that the men had "bound themselves to each other by solemn oaths never to fight against the enemy, to desert the service of the Confederacy, to encourage and protect deserters, and to do all other things in their power to end the war." More than seventy men were arrested and sent to Mobile for trial. General Dabney H. Maury, commanding at Mobile, wrote to Secretary of War James Seddon that these men were generally from the "poorer classes of people."[90]

For soldiers of the "poorer classes" to lay down their arms was nothing unusual in 1863. By the end of that year, with 278,000 men present for duty out of nearly 500,000 enrolled, close to half the Confederate army was absent with or without leave. When one unsympathetic officer returned from the South Carolina hill country after a failed attempt to talk a band of deserters back into service, he made reference to class as the explanation: "The people there are poor . . . and but little identified with *our* struggle." The same was true for deserters in the lower Chattahoochee Valley. M. A. Baldwin, Alabama's attorney general, confessed ignorance as to what led so many men from the southeast corner of his state to desert, but he knew they all had one thing in common—poverty. For the majority of southern soldiers with starving families and no slaves, loyalty to the Confederacy increasingly seemed misplaced.[91]

It was not uncommon for deserters and draft dodgers (often called "tories" or "lay-outs") to band together in remote areas for better protection against those sent to retrieve them. Local sympathizers supplied these men with food and clothing and did what they could to throw pursuers off the track. Some regions were so hostile to the Confederacy that army patrols dared not enter them, especially to search for deserters. In southeastern Mississippi, Newton Knight led a unionist guerrilla band that controlled most of Jones County. They burned bridges, ran off impressment agents, and ambushed Confederate patrols. For almost three years Knight and his men ruled the county, popularly known as the "Kingdom of Jones." [92]

The Red River Valley of Louisiana was a haven for unionists, deserters, and draft dodgers throughout the war, as was Jackson County in northeast Alabama, where anti-Confederate feeling ran so strong that in March 1864 the county seceded from the Confederacy and rejoined the Union. The pine barrens of southeast Georgia, especially the Okefenokee Swamp, were a favorite hideout for those trying to avoid entanglements with the Confederacy. Soldier Camp Island in the Okefenokee was used both by deserters and by the troops sent in after them. And the Wiregrass region of southwest Georgia and southeast Alabama harbored deserters and draft dodgers by the hundreds. An Early County man noted that there were deserters in "every direction," and an Alabama captain called the Wiregrass "one of the Graitest Dens for Tories and deserters from our Army in the World." [93]

Antiwar feeling in the lower reaches of the valley was so strong by 1863 that state and Confederate officials could do little against it. In June of that year Governor Shorter sent the militia after a band of deserters hiding out in the Pea River swamps of southeast Alabama. Shorter's militia captured only seven men, who were freed when their comrades attacked the command near Abbeville. An enraged Shorter sent more troops into the swamps but they never found the deserters. [94]

Some enterprising Wiregrass residents made a regular business of guiding deserters and draft dodgers to Union lines in north Florida. But most deserters, like those on the Pea River, simply remained in the area. Popular support and innumerable hiding places made it nearly impossible for Confederate authorities to track them down. One deserter band set up camp on an island in the Chattahoochee River near Columbus. Family and friends kept them supplied with food and other necessities until the war was over. Two Dale County deserters lived in a cave near their homes during the last years of the war. According to a local resident they "were peaceable, and did not disturb any one." At one point a military patrol discovered their hideout and found cotton cards and spinning wheels that the men used to help clothe their families, but the deserters themselves were never found. [95]

Many deserters were more outspokenly defiant. In Stewart County several men of the Third Georgia Regiment openly declared that they had no intention of returning to the army. One prominent antiwar resident of Barbour County held a dinner honoring fifty-seven local deserters. Though a subpoena was issued against the host, the sheriff refused to deliver it. Widespread public support for draft dodgers and deserters in Henry County sparked considerable apprehension among the area's remaining pro-Confederates. Local authorities were so ineffectual that four Abbeville men wrote to Governor Watts asking for help in confiscating deserters' property and arresting those who aided them. The Conscript Bureau's superintendent admitted that public opinion made it difficult to enforce the draft act. There was, he lamented, no disgrace attached to desertion or draft evasion.[96]

Judges in the Wiregrass refused to hold court on anyone for antiwar activities without a military escort. According to James Arrington, solicitor of Alabama's eighth circuit, not a single session of the court was held in either Dale or Coffee Counties for the last two years of the war. Even when trials were held, convictions were rare. Juries consistently refused to return guilty verdicts against those who opposed the war. General Cobb conceded in August 1863 that to drag antiwar men into court was "simply to provide for a farcical trial." Besides, it was too dangerous to go after them. When Cobb sent a small force into Henry County to bring out several draft dodgers, it was ambushed by a larger body of local men who freed the prisoners and killed one of the soldiers. One young Wiregrass trooper called tracking down deserters and draft dodgers "the most disagreeable service I was called upon to render."[97]

Frustrated by anti-Confederate sentiment on local juries throughout the South, in February 1864 Congress authorized Davis to suspend the writ of habeas corpus and impose martial law. Officials could now make arrests without warrants and imprison suspects without a trial. The act only made matters worse. One enraged citizen who signed himself "A Georgian" reacted in an open letter to the *Early County News*: "When this war broke out our people thought they had something to fight for, but now they have nothing, but to keep the Yankees checked, so that our own Government may oppress them more." Grouby, the paper's editor, agreed completely. "Our freedom is now gone!" he declared. "May the devil get the whole of the old Congress!" Grouby insisted that if he had the money he would move to Cuba.[98]

Despite empathy from local residents and the growing number of deserters and draft evaders, life for those hiding out in the swamps and bottomlands was precarious at best. They were harassed by army patrols and home-guard units, and, like runaway slaves, some even had a price on their heads. In July 1863 the *Chambers Tribune* published a list of forty-four local deserters, some as young as seventeen. Their commanding officer, Colonel J. W. Jackson of the Forty-seventh Alabama Regiment, offered a thirty-dollar reward for each man captured.[99]

As a last resort, some valley anti-Confederates turned to the Union blockade fleet off Apalachicola for assistance. John Harvey, representing a group of five hundred Wiregrass deserters and draft dodgers, met with Lieutenant George Welch of the USS *Amanda* on February 15, 1863, to discuss placing his friends under federal protection. Armed only with shotguns, the band had been skirmishing with conscript companies for some time and their ammunition was running low. They preferred to be taken into protective custody either as prisoners or refugees but, according to Welch, added "that they would follow me or any other leader to any peril they are ordered to rather than leave their families and go north." Welch was sympathetic but declined, saying he did not have enough manpower to guarantee safe passage for so many men from so deep in enemy territory.[100] However, as Confederate strength along the Apalachicola River declined, the Federals did begin running ammunition and other supplies upriver to anti-Confederate partisans.

As their ranks grew through 1863 some of these stranded groups of deserters formed guerrilla bands, described by one historian as "no longer committed to the Confederacy, not quite committed to the Union that supplied them arms and supplies, but fully committed to survival." They raided plantations, attacked army supply depots, and drove off impressment and conscription officers. Their forays became so frequent in Dale County that one Confederate loyalist, a veteran of the Virginia campaigns, said he felt more uneasy at home than he ever did when he followed Stonewall Jackson against the Yankees. Another Confederate loyalist from Fort Gaines begged Governor Brown to send a cavalry company for protection against raiders in Clay County.[101]

One of the most active layout gangs in the Wiregrass was led by a former soldier of the Thirty-third Alabama Regiment known as "Speckled" John Ward. In September 1864 the Conscript Committee of Dale County notified Ward that he was being called back to service. He immediately went into Newton to see Noah Fountain, chairman of the committee, and said he had no intention of going to the front again. The last thing Ward said to Fountain was, "Don't sic your dogs on me!" Shortly after this confrontation, Ward received word that Fountain was on his way. Ward grabbed his gun and took to the woods with Fountain and his dogs hot on the trail. Not far into the chase, Ward doubled back and killed his pursuer. Within days, Ward had gathered a company of deserters and draft dodgers around him and "Ward's Raiders" became a force to be reckoned with in southeast Alabama.[102]

Perhaps the best organized and most feared band of anti-Confederates in the Wiregrass was led by Joseph Sanders. Early in the war Sanders enlisted with Company C of the Thirty-first Georgia Regiment, a company composed largely of men from the Alabama counties of Barbour, Henry, Dale, and Coffee. Sanders was so admired by his comrades that they elected him one of their company's sergeants. He fought with the Thirty-first Georgia, part of Stonewall Jackson's corps, through the early Virginia campaigns, and by one account "there was not a braver man than he in the unit." The men of Company C eventually elected Sanders their captain, but the regimental commander appointed another man to the post and reduced Sanders to the rank of private. The company's enlisted men encouraged Sanders to return home and raise another company, some surely hoping to join the new unit.

When Sanders arrived, he had some difficulty explaining the situation to local authorities. As far as they were concerned, he was absent without leave and subject to being hanged as a deserter. Faced with the possibility of execution, Sanders fled south to the Gulf Coast and sought refuge with Union forces. Soon after, the Yankees granted him a lieutenant's commission in their First Florida Cavalry.[103]

One of his first missions found Sanders leading the advance guard on a raid into southern Alabama. In November 1864, with Lieutenant Colonel Andrew B. Spurling in command, 450 men of the Second Maine and First Florida Cavalries headed north following the Pensacola-Montgomery rail line. Only eleven miles out of camp, they began picking up sentries from a Confederate cavalry unit. By the time the raid was over, the Federals had captured thirty-eight prisoners, forty-seven horses, three mules, and seventy-five rifles. In his report on the expedition, Spurling spoke highly of Sanders's performance: "It would hardly be doing justice did I not make special mention of Lieut. Joseph G. Sanders, Company F, First Florida Cavalry. He is a worthy officer, and deserves high praise for his meritorious conduct. He was at all times in command of the advance guard, and much of the success is due to the prompt and faithful manner in which all orders were executed."[104]

Not long after this raid, Sanders was placed on detached duty and took charge of a force composed primarily of Union men from the Wiregrass.

Until the end of the war, Sanders and his men conducted raids throughout southeast Alabama. They seized horses and military supplies, plundered well-stocked plantations, and skirmished with Confederate forces. They even stormed Elba in Coffee County and burned down the courthouse.[105]

One of Sanders's most memorable raids took place on the night of March 14, 1865, only weeks before the war's close. Sanders had planned a surprise raid through Dale County, climaxing with an assault on Newton. Early that morning thirty-four of his men met near Campbellton, just across the Florida line, and headed north toward the Dale County seat. Sanders had no clue at the time that he had been betrayed.

That same day, Jesse Carmichael was passing through Newton on his way to Rocky Head in the county's northeast corner. He stopped in to see his father, the local inferior court judge, who told him "on unquestionable authority" that Sanders and his men would reach town by nightfall. Carmichael, a wounded veteran of the Fifteenth Alabama Regiment, decided to remain and help organize a defense. After an early supper with his parents, he went to the town square and asked the handful of men assembled there how they intended to meet the threat. Their only plan was to station a few men around the square. Carmichael had a better idea.

While the others stayed behind to round up more help, he and John McEntyre rode out to meet Sanders's men and warn of their approach. About four miles out of Newton, near the modern site of Pinckard, they heard a sizable body of riders coming up from the southeast. The two men immediately wheeled their mounts and rode hard for town. About thirty old men and boys were gathered at the center of town when they arrived. Carmichael rushed the defenders out to the southeast corner of Newton, lined them up behind a thicket of oak saplings for an ambush, then rode on ahead to sound the alarm when Sanders and his men arrived. Moments later a rider came up from behind and told him that his small troop had decided to go back into town. Carmichael was enraged but had little choice but to follow them.

When he got back to the square, he found the situation utterly confused. Captain Joseph Breare of the home guard had just arrived and placed the defenders on the west side of town. He insisted that he was in charge and refused to listen to anything Carmichael had to say. Carmichael nearly gave up Newton for lost but at the last minute decided to place himself along with his younger brother, Daniel, and two older men, W. H. Kirksey and Samuel E. Fain, at the corner of a hotel east of the square. At the same time, six guardsmen, including the Reverend Pitt M. Callaway, Daniel Duke, and

George Echols, rushed over to the east side of town and positioned themselves in an alley a short distance toward the square from Carmichael's small force. Neither group knew where the other was. Carmichael sent his brother down the road to see if he could catch sight of the raiders, and in a few minutes he was back with news that they were near the Methodist Church. Carmichael later recalled what happened next.

> We waited for them to pass the hotel and get between us and the public square so then we were in their rear. I had to hold the three men back from firing, so anxious were they to open up upon them. Mr. Kirksey rather stuttered a little, and said something like: "Ne-ne-never mind, you villains, we'll show you that there are others here besides you in less than a minute." When I thought that the opportune moment had come, all four of us—some with double-barrel shotguns, and others with muskets charged with buck and ball, turned loose upon them as unexpectedly as if the last trumpet had sounded— we firing so squarely into their rear and at the very same moment Rev. Callaway and his five men, who were secreted between some stores, fired into the head of the column. A more complete surprise was never perpetrated, and in a moment all was confusion, and the bushwhackers stampeded. . . . In much less time than I have been telling about the fight after it began, the enemy was gone, leaving three men dead and dying upon the ground and carrying away five wounded, and not a drop of blood shed by any of our men.

Sanders and his men had not expected armed resistance. They had no idea anyone even knew they were there until Carmichael's men opened fire. In his report on the incident, Lieutenant Colonel Joseph Hough of the Dale County militia wrote, "The scoundrels did no damage to [Newton], but stole much property in the country before they reached here. The repulse was effected wholly by the little squad of militia, Breare's men not having a chance to fire a gun." Sanders's raiding days were not yet finished despite his rout in Newton. Reports of his activities and requests for arms and ammunition to repel him continued to reach Governor Watts's desk through the end of the war.[106]

Urgent petitions from southeast Alabama begging for weapons were nothing new. If contemporary reports are to be taken at face value, it is fortunate for Breare's men that Sanders was driven off so quickly at Newton. The home guard probably did not have enough gunpowder to carry on a sustained fire. Munitions were running so low in winter 1864–65 that Lieutenant J. H. O'Rear of the Dale County reserves wrote to Watts, "If we were visited by the enemy now we would be almost helpless." [107] It was not that the governor cared so little for that part of the state. He had been sending down wagonloads of munitions for some time, but local guerrilla bands were very good at capturing them.

On October 8, 1864, only days after its formation, Ward's gang ambushed a freight wagon filled with ammunition bound for the home guard at Newton. One officer was killed and another soldier, Alex Speller, was wounded. Before the raiders fled back into the woods, they told Speller and his brother, Nat, that the wounds could be dressed at a nearby blacksmith shop owned by Wesley Dowling. The next day, after a futile search for Ward and his men, Breare arrested the fathers of three suspected gang members, dragged them to the ambush site, and threatened to hang them for "harboring the enemy" if they did not tell him where to find Ward's camp. Captain John Dowling, at home recovering from combat wounds, heard the nearby commotion and went to investigate. When he saw what was going on, Dowling threatened Breare with a court-martial if he hanged his prisoners without a proper trial. Having no evidence on which to charge the men, Breare let them go.[108]

Breare was a lawyer by profession and an Englishman by birth. When the war began he enlisted and served with the commissary department until his capture at Gettysburg. He was released in a prisoner exchange shortly thereafter and returned to Dale County, where he formed a cavalry company and offered it for service either with the home guard or as a conscript company. Frontline soldiers generally referred to such units as "Buttermilk Rangers." Breare's victims and their families just called them killers. He and his followers were ruthless when it came to dealing with anyone suspected of anti-Confederate activity or sentiment. Most did not have men like John Dowling around to ensure proper procedure. On November 20, 1864, Breare captured one member of Ward's gang and, after a mock trial, hanged him on the spot. Five days later he hanged from the same tree an old man named Myers who had been accused of sharing food with some of Ward's men.[109]

Breare's most infamous lynching came on December 3, when he and six of his men arrested a Newton preacher named Bill Sketoe on charges of desertion. Sketoe insisted that he had a legitimate furlough, granted so that he could care for his sick wife. He had even paid a man to go back to the front in his place until he could return. But the authenticity of Sketoe's furlough was beside the point. Rumor had it that he was connected with

Ward's gang, which was all Breare needed to convict him. On Breare's orders the men dragged Sketoe from his home and hauled him north of town
to a point near the Choctawhatchee River bridge.

As they were preparing to hang the preacher, Wesley Dowling came
riding across the bridge and tried to stop the lynching. Breare warned
Dowling that if he did not move on he would "get the same medicine."
Breare then turned to Sketoe and asked if he had any last words. The
preacher began to pray aloud, not for himself but for his killers. "Forgive
them, Lord," he said, "Forgive them." Sketoe's pious pleading so enraged
the men that they threw a noose around his neck before he had finished
his prayer. They shoved him onto a buggy, pulled the rope tight over a tree
limb, and slapped the horse, jerking the buggy from under the preacher.
But in their haste to lynch Sketoe, the guardsmen had tied the rope over
a weak branch. When it caught Sketoe's full weight, it bent down just low
enough for the condemned man's toes to touch the ground. One of Breare's
men, George Echols, rushed over and dug a hole under Sketoe's feet with
a crutch. Now swinging freely, Sketoe died within a few minutes. His body
was cut down the next morning and was laid to rest at Mt. Carmel Church
cemetery just outside Newton.

Sketoe's fate became grist for one of Alabama's most famous ghost
stories. As the tale goes, all the men connected with his lynching died
violent or mysterious deaths shortly after the war. Lightning struck one
man. Another was found dead in a swamp. Still another was killed when
a mule ran off with him. Echols was shot in a raid on Sanders's place, and
Breare was killed when a falling limb knocked him from his horse during
a thunderstorm.

As for the hole that Echols dug, legend says that it can never remain
filled. Whenever leaves or dirt cover the spot, it is miraculously cleared
again by Sketoe's ghost. Mary Edwards Fleming, who grew up in Dale
County and saw the hole many times herself, had a more logical explanation. By her account, the hole "was kept raked out by the dead man's
friends who pretended that it was something supernatural." Wash Reynolds, a friend of Sketoe's, was always suspected of keeping the hole clear,
though he insisted that he knew no more about the mystery than anyone
else.[110]

Sketoe's lynching was only one of many incidents that illuminate deep
divisions among southerners in general and people of the lower Chattahoochee Valley in particular. There were, of course, atrocities on both
sides. As E. H. Grouby observed, war makes people meaner, not better.
But atrocities of pro-Confederate zealots like those of Breare served only

to drive more and more plain folk to disaffection with the Confederacy. A few, like Sanders, went so far as to join the Yankees. Of thirteen men who deserted the CSS *Chattahoochee* in May 1863, at least two, J. C. Cook and Elias Lee, fled to the USS *Port Royal* off Apalachicola and took an oath of allegiance to the United States. Lee joined the Union navy and remained on board the *Port Royal* as ship's pilot. Poverty, mistreatment, and a feeling of utter helplessness in the face of speculation, impressment, and conscription all helped turn southerners against the war and the Confederacy.[111]

CHAPTER

6

Us Is Gonna Be Free

Disaffected whites were not the only people to experience poverty, mistreatment, and vulnerability during the war. Nor were they the only ones to resent the planters for it. Slaves had done so for a long time. Now, under a southern government with racism as its cornerstone and holding a promise of freedom should that government fall, slaves had greater reason than anyone to oppose the Confederacy. Comprising a third of the southern population, the black caste's collective antagonism contributed as much as that of whites to Confederate defeat.[1]

Vulnerability had long been a hallmark of American slavery and it persisted through the early war years. Nowhere was that more evident than in the bustling slave trade. From the war's outset, a steady stream of slaves flowed into the valley for auction at increasingly high prices. By 1863 slaves were selling for as much as $3,500. A year later top prices reached $4,700. On January 6, 1864, the *Early County News* reported that "quite a crowd of citizens from all parts of the county were in Blakely yesterday in attendance to the sale and hiring of negroes. The prices paid were exceedingly high." The cost of slaves was rising so fast in Columbus that the *Times's* editor confessed, "we are at a loss to determine upon what basis of reasoning such prices for slaves can be predicted. As slavery is the leading and fundamental principle of the war, of course, the tenure of its existence is as precarious as that of the currency. . . . if our paper money is worthless, so is the institution of slavery; for the solvency of both hinge upon the success of the South in her present struggle." Only in the war's final weeks, when it became clear that slavery's end was inevitable, did prices begin to go down. Along with the collapse of Confederate currency, rising prices brought a virtual end to the slave trade even before the war ended. But in the war's early and middle years, the valley's relative isolation and demand for both industrial and agricultural slave labor made it a magnet for slave traders. The *Columbus Enquirer* feared that there might not be enough work to keep all the slaves busy.[2]

Slave traders were widely regarded as men of low character. Even the planters tended to shun them despite their economic and ideological kinship. The demeanor of slave traders worsened during the war, due at least in part to inflationary pressures and increasingly limited markets. Whatever the reasons, the war served only to intensify the slave trade's cruelties. One former Russell County slave remembered that traders were much less concerned with the condition of their merchandise than with getting as many to market as quickly as they could: "The slaves were driven by men on horses who, at times, drove them on the run until they fell from exhaustion. The drivers also carried whips, 12 to 15 feet long, and made of eight strands of plaited rawhide. These whips were fastened to short, heavy, hickory stocks, and a driver, seated on a horse, could split a Nigger's hide with one of them from a distance of 15 or 20 feet. With such a persuader to impel them along, the Niggers would often travel at a fast gait for hours—until they dropped in the road. All that lagged behind, or didn't keep going at the pace set by the horsemen, were literally slashed to ribbons." Slaves transported by rail were not much better off. One former valley slave recalled seeing slaves packed into boxcars so tightly that there was no room to sit. It was one of his most vivid memories.[3]

The war amplified slavery's miseries in countless ways, most of which involved increased intensity of physical labor. With several hundred thousand whites away at the front, slaves took up much of the slack. They supplied labor for transportation, industry, and constructing fortifications. And as productivity demands increased, slaves were driven beyond the breaking point.[4]

The same was true on the valley's plantations. W. B. Allen, a former Russell County slave, told how the first bell on his master's plantation rang at three o'clock in the morning: "That was a signal for the slaves to rise, get their breakfasts and be ready to go to the fields when the second bell rang—at four o'clock." It was not uncommon during certain times of the year for slaves to work through the night. Frank Menefee of Opelika remembered breaking ground all night with lanterns tied to the front and back of his plow. When harvest time came, he said, "we was picking cotton all night long too." There were severe penalties for less than maximum effort. Graham Martin, another Lee County slave, said that on his plantation, "if you didn't bring up your amount of that cotton you better take to the woods 'cause [the overseer] was sure going to tear you up." As

Menefee recalled, "if you didn't work, they attended to you. They slashed one nigger and he died next week." [5]

That death could come so quickly and arbitrarily illustrates the fear with which blacks lived on a daily basis. "There was no penitentiary for the negro," said one Early County resident. The accused was lucky just to get a hearing. Accusations of murder and rape brought swift execution with or without trial. When word got out that a slave in Henry County had killed his master and raped the man's wife, a local paper insisted that "if the darkey is caught, we should think burning would be too good for him." A Tuskegee mob did just that to one unfortunate slave. Without judicial authority, wrote one eyewitness, the vigilantes "tried him, and sentenced him, and before the sun set, he was burned to ashes. . . . no mercy was shown." [6]

A Barbour County lynch mob broke into the Clayton jail and hanged a slave named Bob even though the Alabama Supreme Court had granted the man a new trial. In Colquitt, a black man jailed on charges of "ravishing" a white woman was lynched by "some of the good citizens" while awaiting trial before the superior court. "Served him right," insisted E. H. Grouby of neighboring Early County. In his view, members of the lynch mob deserved "a great deal of credit for their promptness in this matter." Questions of guilt or innocence were beside the point in most such cases. Mere accusations of murder or rape were more than enough to get blacks lynched. [7]

For lesser offenses slaves were severely beaten, with the overseer serving as judge, jury, and enforcer. It is little wonder that slaves viewed overseers as "the lowest down whites." W. B. Allen spoke for most former slaves when he said, "The regular run of them were trash." The term *overseer,* he said, was synonymous with cruelty and brutality. [8]

If slaves had little love for overseers, they had even less affection for the planters who employed them. Some referred to their owners as kidnappers. Mary Ferguson, a former Muscogee County slave, believed that all who perpetuated slavery would be "burning in hell for they sin." It is hardly surprising that slaves more than anyone else hoped for Confederate defeat and an end to slavery. [9]

Despite efforts to conceal the war's implications from them, many slaves and free blacks were remarkably adept at sorting out the relationship of slavery to the war. In January 1865 the Reverend Garrison Frazier, a black Georgia preacher, expressed that relationship in these terms: "The object of the war was not, at first, to give the slaves their freedom, but the sole object of the war was, at first, to bring the rebellious States back into the Union. . . . Afterward, knowing the value that was set on the slaves by the rebels, the President thought that his proclamation would stimulate them to lay down their arms, . . . and their not doing so has now made the freedom of the slaves a part of the war." Not all southern blacks were as aware of the war's finer points, but they were certain that a northern victory would mean their freedom. When a white minister preached that slavery was a divine institution and prayed aloud for the Lord to drive the Yankees back, one Georgia slave prayed silently to herself, "Oh, Lord, please send the Yankees on." [10]

Slaves had many ways of learning about the war and what it meant for them. Ex-slave Hattie Nettles of Opelika remembered climbing a fence as a young girl to watch Confederate soldiers marching past. She did not know where they were going at first, but it was not long before she found out. Mary Gladdy of Columbus recalled "the whisperings among the slaves—their talking of the possibility of freedom." Anne Maddox heard a great deal of talk about Abraham Lincoln from older slaves on her plantation not far from Opelika. On a nearby plantation, Louis Meadows and his fellow slaves knew that as long as Jefferson Davis was in power they would never be free. "That was why," Meadows said, "everybody hoped Master Lincoln would conquer." [11]

During the war, slaves in the lower Chattahoochee Valley often met in secret to hold prayer meetings for freedom. According to Gladdy, Muscogee County slaves gathered in their cabins two or three nights a week for such meetings. They placed large pots against the doors to keep their voices muffled. "Then," she said, "the slaves would sing, pray, and relate experiences all night long. Their great, soul-hungering desire was freedom." Those few slaves who could read kept up with events through stolen newspapers and spread the word to their neighbors. As news of Confederate reversals became more frequent, excitement grew among the slaves. Young Ella Hawkins of Muscogee County heard older slaves on her plantation whispering among themselves, "Us is gonna be free! Jes as sho's anything. God has heard our prayers; us is gonna be free!" [12]

The more excited slaves became at their approaching freedom, the more difficult they were to control. In areas where most or all of the white men had gone off to war, slaves were particularly defiant. August 1862 found slaveholder Laura Comer writing in her diary, "The servants are so indolent and obstinate it is a trial to have anything to do with them." Slaves typically feigned ignorance or illness, sabotaged equipment, and roamed freely in defiance of laws requiring them to carry passes. Roving slaves became so common that some owners tried to lock them up at night.[13]

What work slaves did, they did grudgingly. Some refused to work at all. A mistress wrote concerning one of her slaves, "Nancy has been very impertinent. . . . She said she would not be hired out by the month, neither would she go out to get work." Another woman wrote to her husband, "We are doing as best we know, or as good as we can get the Servants to do; they learn to feel very independent." Years after the war, in typical Lost Cause fashion, one member of Barbour County's gentry wistfully recalled that the "war was raging all around, both on sea and land, yet in our quiet valley . . . we were happy and contented, both master and slave." But writings from the war years paint a much different picture. In 1863 another Alabamian frankly admitted that "the 'faithful slave' is about played out." [14]

As early as 1861, a Georgia overseer complained to his absentee employer that the slaves would not submit to physical punishment. One slave simply walked away when the overseer told him he was about to be whipped. "I wish you would . . . come down and let the matter be settle," the overseer wrote, "as I do not feel wiling to be runover by him." Another Georgia slave drew a knife on an overseer who tried to whip him. His master locked him up and provided only a bread-and-water diet, but the punishment did little to subdue him. Such actions tended only to make slaves more rebellious. "I am satisfied that his imprisonment has only tended to harden him," one overseer wrote soon after releasing an unruly slave. "I dont think he will ever reform." [15]

Besides being terribly painful, whipping was for slaves a key symbol of their lowly status. It is hardly surprising then that resistance to whipping became one of the main ways slaves sought to demonstrate a measure of independence. Such resistance could, of course, be very dangerous. One Troup County planter was noted for turning his dogs on slaves who refused to be whipped. A slave on the Hines Holt plantation near Columbus was shot after he beat off six men who tried to hold him down.[16]

Despite such dangers, slaves continued to resist. According to former Troup County slave Celestia Avery, Peter Heard whipped his slaves "unmercifully." One day while hoeing the fields, Celestia's grandmother, Sylvia, was told by an overseer to remove her clothes when she got to the end of a fence row. She was going to be whipped for not working fast enough. When the overseer reached for her, she grabbed a wooden rail and broke it across the man's arms. A Russell County slave named Crecie, described as "a grown young woman and big and strong," was tied to a stump by an overseer named Sanders in preparation for whipping. He had two dogs with him just in case Crecie gave any trouble. When the first blow hit Crecie's back, she pulled up the stump and whipped Sanders and his dogs.[17]

Sanders was probably fortunate to escape Crecie's wrath with his life. Some were not so lucky. When one Muscogee County overseer began beating a young slave girl with a sapling tree, one of the older slaves grabbed an axe and killed him. Such violent retaliation was even more common during the war than before. A Fort Gaines slave was hanged for trying to kill two men, one of them his master. Another valley slave named Lash succeeded in killing his master and was burned at the stake.[18]

Slaves sometimes devised or participated in elaborate plots to kill their owners. Occasionally, they even conspired with whites to do it. Two southeast Alabama slaves belonging to Columbus Holley assisted John Ward, leader of a deserter band, in doing away with their owner. Holley made a habit of exposing every deserter he could, and Ward hatched a plan to kill him for it. Holley's slaves eagerly cooperated. On the designated evening, the slaves met Ward at a rendezvous point not far from the plantation and carried him on their shoulders to Holley's residence. They took Ward to a bedroom window that Holley always left open at night and with one shot Ward killed the planter as he slept. The slaves then carried Ward back to his horse and he made a clean getaway. Because his feet never touched the ground there was no scent for bloodhounds to follow. The only tracks near the house were those of the slaves, but no one thought that unusual. Their footprints were all over the plantation. The mystery of Holley's murder remained unsolved until years later, when Ward finally confessed on his deathbed.[19]

To avoid punishment for anything from "insolence" to murder, slaves often fled to nearby woods and swamps temporarily or for the war's duration. Charlie Pye of Columbus said that his mother would hide out in the woods for months at a time rather than be whipped. However, she always returned "when the strain of staying away from her family became too great."[20] Celestia Avery told an especially harrowing story of her grandmother's sadistic treatment at the hands of Peter Heard.

> Every morning my grandmother would pray, and old man Heard despised to hear anyone pray saying they were only doing so that they might become free niggers. Just as sure as the sun would rise, she would get a whipping; but this did not stop her prayers every

morning before day. This particular time grandmother Sylvia was in [the] "family way" and that morning she began to pray as usual. The master heard her and became so angry he came to her cabin, seized and pulled her clothes from her body and tied her to a young sapling. He whipped her so brutally that her body was raw all over. When darkness fell her husband cut her down from the tree. During the day he was afraid to go near her. Rather than go back to the cabin she crawled on her knees to the woods and her husband brought grease for her to grease her raw body. For two weeks the master hunted but could not find her; however, when he finally did, she had given birth to twins. The only thing that saved her was the fact that she was a mid-wife and always carried a small pen knife which she used to cut the navel cord of the babies. After doing this she tore her petticoat into two pieces and wrapped each baby.[21]

After his own severe beating, another Troup County slave named William ran away and dug out a large cave in which he took up residence. Several nights later, under the cover of darkness, he moved his wife and two children to the cave, where they lived until the war ended.[22]

Like deserters and draft evaders, runaway slaves often gathered in small, isolated communities along the Chattahoochee River. So numerous were their settlements in the valley's lower reaches that Governor John Gill Shorter of Alabama referred to the Wiregrass as "the common retreat of deserters from our army, tories, and runaway negroes." Like their white counterparts, groups of runaway slaves sustained themselves by making raids on local towns and plantations. S. S. Massey of Chattahoochee County complained to Georgia Governor Joe Brown that local slaves were "killing up the stock and stealing every thing they can put their hands on." The *Early County News* reported in March 1864 that there had been "more *stealing,* and *rascality generally,* going on in Blakely and Early County, for the past few months, than has ever been known for several years. . . . negroes are doing a great deal of this stealing, burning, &c.,—but," the paper added, "there certainly are some *mean white men* connected with the negroes." In August a white southwest Georgia man named John Vickery was hanged along with three slaves for plotting an insurrection. Two other white men were sought for their part in the scheme.[23]

From the beginning of the war whites feared that individual acts of insubordination might ultimately lead to a general slave uprising. That fear had a devastating impact on the Confederate war effort. While southern armies were constantly outnumbered by their northern counterparts, up to 200,000 southern men were kept at home to guard against the possibility of slave rebellion. As early as May 1861 an Alabama planter urged the men in his district to stay at home and save their families "from the horrors of insurrection." The *Albany Patriot* complained that blacks in southwest Georgia would "congregate together contrary to law, *exhibit their weapons,* and no doubt devise their secret, but destructive plans." [24]

During late spring and early summer 1861 rebellion hysteria swept across southwest Georgia. Especially worried were slaveholders in the large plantation districts along the Chattahoochee and Flint Rivers. Panic spread through Decatur County in June when one of the local slave patrols caught a man named Israel away from his plantation without a pass. Somehow, the patrollers came to believe that a general revolt involving slaves from all over the county was about to begin. Wild rumors spread that blacks in Bainbridge were collecting firearms and planning to "kill all of the men and old women and children and take the younger ones for their wives." Though there was no evidence of such a plot and no guns were ever found, two suspected insurrection leaders were arrested. One local white man swore that they would be killed if they ever got out of jail. [25]

Insurrection mania had died down by midsummer but slaveholder fears of rebellion remained strong. William Mansfield wrote to Governor Brown that owners in Stewart County were terrified of their slaves, fearing that local militiamen were not "prepared to quell any riots that might begin." A Fort Gaines man asked the governor for a company of cavalry to protect southwest Georgia from the slave rebellion that he felt sure was coming. [26]

In an effort to stem the rising tide of rebelliousness among slaves, the Georgia General Assembly made several additions to the state penal code. In December 1861 it stipulated that any black person found guilty of arson would be put to death. It also forbade owners to let slaves hire themselves out and required slaves to reside on their masters' premises. In 1862 the assembly reinforced laws forbidding slaves to travel without passes and canceled all exemptions from patrol duty. The Alabama legislature took steps to restrict liquor sales to free blacks and to prevent any sort of trade with slaves. It also increased fees awarded for the capture of runaway slaves in 1861, in 1863, and again in 1864. [27]

Some city and county governments went further. Officials in Blakely hired extra police for every district in Early County. The editor of the *Early County News* called it "the duty of all good citizens to go out nightly on patrol." The city council in Cuthbert divided the town into three wards and put all available white males between the ages of sixteen and sixty on patrol duty. Each ward was patrolled by at least two men every night. Where there were fewer slaves, patrols were less frequent. In Dale County, where slaves made up less than 15 percent of the population, the patrol made its rounds every Saturday night. That was when the slaves "had their parties, dances, quiltings, etc," according to one resident.[28]

The "patter-rollers," as the slaves called them, severely punished any slave found off of his or her plantation without a pass. In the words of former slave Jennie Kendricks, "a heap of them got whippings for being caught off without these passes." She hastened to add that escapes were not uncommon. One valley slave who had dodged the patrol for some time was finally caught one night. He begged his captors to allow him to say a prayer before they beat him. As the man prayed, he noticed that he was not being watched very closely. He seized the opportunity and added one more escape to his already long list.[29]

Along with the general crackdown on slaves, controls tightened on free blacks as well. Many were literate, and whites viewed them as potential leaders of insurrections. Insisting that "idle negroes are public curses," a Columbus resident suggested that all free blacks be pressed into government service as laborers. He added that they should be closely watched by white supervisors. Many free blacks already worked in government factories, but Georgia did impress free blacks to help construct fortifications.[30]

In November 1863 the Georgia General Assembly seriously considered an act to sell all free blacks into slavery. The proposal never got out of committee, perhaps because it was considered unenforceable. However, the assembly required free blacks to register at their county courthouses and to list white guardians who would be responsible for their actions. Those who had no guardian were subject to being sold into slavery by the state. The registration fee in Randolph County was twenty-five dollars, and there were severe penalties for those who failed to register. In some towns, free blacks, like slaves, had to have a pass from their guardians or employers if they wanted to leave their homes after dark.[31]

Despite such efforts by state and local authorities, blacks continued to take unprecedented liberties. One newspaper reported that Georgia towns were filled with slaves acting "as if they were free people." A southwest Georgia man noted with alarm that the slaves in Fort Gaines were impossible to control: "Many Negroes there are doing as they please, hiring out their time which the law of Georgia forbids." One valley slaveholder, while visiting Columbus, found a runaway slave of his working at a mechanical shop. A Russell County slave hired himself out as a blacksmith and by war's end had a trunk full of money (though in worthless

Confederate bills). To seek work for wages had always been a hallmark of freedom and many southern blacks were taking freedom for themselves long before federal troops arrived.[32]

As early as 1862 one passenger on a southwest Georgia railroad said that "crowds of slaves in gayest attire" were getting on and off the trains at every stop. They held their own picnics, barbecues, dances, and church services. They gathered in the streets on Sunday afternoons to play what one source called "uproarious games." In Blakely, E. H. Grouby reported that blacks were "almost nightly running around where they have no business." A Muscogee County slaveholder feared that the blacks of Columbus were forgetting their second-class status. "It is not uncommon," he wrote, "to see two or three in one whiskey shop."[33]

In summer 1862 the *Columbus Enquirer* complained that the city's black population was becoming difficult to control. Freedom of movement, especially at night, was getting completely out of hand. The editor urged owners to keep a tighter rein on their slaves and suggested increased patrols. Such complaints apparently had little effect. By 1864 Columbus blacks were holding romps almost every night. One city paper called these festivities an "unmitigated nuisance" but could suggest no effective remedy.[34]

Some city residents thought that making concessions to blacks might ease tensions. In March 1865 the *Columbus Times*'s editor suggested returning black churches to their rightful occupants. Like the churches of poor whites, they had been commandeered months earlier for use as hospitals. Furthermore, blacks had been turned away at the well-to-do white churches. "There are comparatively few sick and wounded among us," the *Times* pointed out. "Then why not evacuate these churches at once?"[35] If the editor thought such an act might help calm blacks and make them easier to control, he was very much mistaken.

Even slave patrols were losing their powers of intimidation as the war entered its final year. Slaves were beginning to anticipate their coming freedom and were less likely to see the patrols as a threat. Besides, few white men remained willing to take patrol duty. Most had come to view the struggle as a "rich man's war" and wanted no part in defending slavery at home or on the battlefield. In January 1864 a letter from Harris County reached Governor Brown's desk complaining that only four men in the vicinity of Waverly Hall were riding patrol over seven hundred slaves.[36] Similar complaints came from worried slaveholders throughout the valley.

Whatever the factors involved, by 1864 the patrols clearly inspired little fear among slaves. One slave boy who outran the patrollers made fun of them after he was safely behind his master's fence. Some slaves even fought back. They often tied ropes or vines neck-high across dark stretches of road just before the patrollers rode by. According to a former slave, these traps were guaranteed to unhorse at least one rider. When patrollers raided a prayer meeting near Columbus, one slave stuck a shovel in the fireplace and threw hot coals all over the patrolmen. The room instantly "filled with smoke and the smell of burning clothes and white flesh." In the confusion, every slave got away.[37]

Perhaps the most dramatic way in which southern blacks resisted their enslavement and contributed to Confederate defeat was by running off to join the Union army. Though tens of thousands eventually served with the Federals, there was serious doubt from the beginning whether they would ever be allowed to do so. Many runaway slaves had tried to enlist at the war's start only to be rejected. Some were even returned to the plantations from which they had escaped.

Whatever personal feelings he had on the issue, Lincoln made it clear in the war's first months that his objective was not to free the slaves but to preserve the Union. In his inaugural address of March 1861, the president stated flatly that he had "no purpose, directly or indirectly, to interfere with slavery in the States where it exists." Congress agreed. In a nearly unanimous vote, it passed the Crittenden-Johnson resolution, which assured the nation that the war was being fought not to overthrow or interfere "with the rights or established institutions" of the slave states but only "to defend and maintain the supremacy of the Constitution and to preserve the Union."[38]

The great majority of northerners had never favored emancipation. Many feared that they might be overrun by a wave of black migration should freedom come. Even before the war, some northern states took steps to avoid such an influx. In the 1850s Illinois, Indiana, Iowa, and Oregon closed their borders to free blacks. Other states passed restrictive laws similar to the South's slave codes, making life for free blacks difficult. One Ohio congressman insisted that his state would never allow blacks to settle there: "Three hundred thousand freemen of Ohio would . . . receive them on the points of their bayonets, and drive them from [the] State." It was hardly an exaggeration. When 518 free blacks tried to settle in southern Ohio they were quickly forced out.[39]

With such attitudes prevalent in the North, Lincoln was not eager to make the Civil War a crusade against slavery. Besides, northern business elites wanted only to maintain access to the cotton states' resources. Since slave labor produced most of the cotton, some feared that the end of slavery might mean the end of cheap cotton. So Lincoln and Congress promised that the war would be a white man's war fought by white men. As far as Washington was concerned, neither slavery nor blacks had any part in the conflict.

The situation began to change in 1862. Like their southern counterparts, northern recruiting officers found it increasingly difficult to get volunteers. And like the Confederate army, federal forces began to experience problems with desertion. Homesickness, hardship, and disease all took their toll on the Union ranks. In one year, 995 out of every thousand men suffered from diarrhea and dysentery. By late 1862 nearly a quarter of the Union army was absent without leave.[40]

Something had to be done to get more men into the military, even if they were black. But would large numbers of blacks fight in a war that ignored the slavery question? Probably not. Conversely, making the war a crusade against slavery might cause more white soldiers to desert since many of them supported slavery where it existed and feared competition from free black labor. Freeing the slaves might also cause more states to leave the Union. "I would do it," Lincoln confessed in summer 1862, "if I were not afraid that half the officers would fling down their arms and three more States would rise." Most white northerners also doubted that blacks would make good soldiers. General William Tecumseh Sherman asked, "Can they improvise bridges, sorties, flank movements, etc., like the white man? I say no." But with few whites volunteering and desertion on the rise Lincoln had little choice.[41]

On September 22, 1862, only days after Lee's army was turned back at Antietam, Lincoln announced the Emancipation Proclamation. It was a tentative document that freed only those slaves in Confederate-held territory, but it did introduce an element of abolitionism as a Union war aim. Just as significantly it gave blacks a cause for which to fight.

As Lincoln had feared, thousands of white soldiers deserted over the issue of emancipation. All but thirty-five men of an Illinois regiment went home, saying that they would "lie in the woods until moss grew on their backs rather than help free the slaves." Newspapers across the North encouraged other soldiers to do the same. A group of Kentucky women whose sons were serving in the Union army urged their boys to desert as well. Likening Lincoln to the devil, they said that his Emancipation Proclamation showed "the cloven foot." A midwestern father wrote to his son in the army, "I am sorry you are engaged in this unholy, unconstitutional and hellish war . . . which has no other purpose but to free the negroes and enslave the whites. Come home. If you have to desert, you will be protected."[42]

Though emancipation drove many white soldiers to leave the army, many more blacks came to take their places—nearly 200,000 in all, three-quarters of them from the slave states. By war's end, there were more blacks in Union armies than whites in Confederate armies. The First South Carolina Volunteers counted former Georgia slaves among its ranks. Out of 103 enlisted men in Company B, 138th Colored Infantry Regiment, fifty-four came from Georgia and twenty-nine from Alabama.[43]

These black units, led by white officers, were at first restricted to menial tasks. That policy began to change after the first major engagement of black troops at Milliken's Bend, Louisiana, on June 7, 1863. A white Union officer remarked, "The bravery of the blacks at Milliken's Bend completely revolutionized the sentiment of the army with regard to the employment of Negro troops. I heard prominent officers, who formerly had sneered . . . at the idea of the Negroes fighting, express themselves after that, as heartily in favor of it." The argument that blacks lacked the discipline for soldiering was further damaged in July when the Fifty-fourth Massachusetts led a charge on Fort Wagner near Charleston, South Carolina. Of six hundred men who made the assault, 40 percent did not return. When the order to withdraw came, Sergeant William Carney grabbed the flag and carried it back with him despite wounds to his head, chest, right leg, and arm. He was the first of twenty-three black soldiers awarded the Congressional Medal of Honor during the war.[44]

Battlefield hazards were not the only perils faced by southern blacks who joined the Union military. There were also threats from Confederate zealots who, after the war, roamed the countryside seeking revenge on former slaves who had dared take up arms against them. In one especially brutal incident, a former Georgia slave was raped and beaten nearly to death in retaliation for her husband's service with the Union army. Despite the dangers of war and threats of white retribution, southern slaves flocked to the Union ranks. But whether they went into the Union army or not, thousands of slaves deserted their owners in what historian W. E. B. DuBois referred to as a general strike against the Confederacy. Every slave owned by members of the Troup Artillery fled to Union lines. Eleven slaves held at the saltworks near St. Joseph Bay, Florida, which supplied salt for the lower Chattahoochee Valley, sought refuge with the Union blockading fleet. One southwest Georgia slave was hanged for attempting to organize a mass exodus of local blacks to the Federals on the Florida coast. Slaves ran off individually as well as in groups. One slave who escaped from Conecuh County in southern Alabama made it all the way to Troup County before being captured and taken to the local jail. Other slaves, even while fugitives, stayed much closer to home. A slave named

Bill who escaped from a West Point slave dealer remained in the area for three years before he was finally caught.[45]

Slaveholders were willing to pay considerable sums to have their property returned. Sara Glover of Cuthbert offered one hundred dollars for the return of her slave, Clark. Colonel James Buchannon of Early County advertised a three-hundred-dollar reward for the capture of his slave, Aleinda, who was described as about thirty years of age, weighing 140 pounds, 5'7" in height, and a "copper colored" household servant who left wearing good clothing. No matter how attractive the rewards or detailed their descriptions, determined slaves usually found their way to Union lines.[46]

Some slaves displayed considerable ingenuity in planning and executing their escapes. One Alabama slave may have faked death to cover his tracks. William Stewart wrote home to his wife in southeast Alabama about a slave who disappeared one stormy night from a camp near Mobile. According to Stewart's letter, the slave "got blown off the platform . . . and drowned, or they supposed he is drowned." [47]

The closer the war came to its conclusion, the more slaves tried to escape. It was among the clearest signs of how the general slave population felt about the war. In depriving the Confederacy of much-needed labor, runaways showed how devastating an impact their attitudes could have on the Confederate cause. Mary Chesnut of South Carolina reflected the dread of many planters when she confided to her diary, "If anything can reconcile me to the idea of a horrid failure after all to make good our independence of Yankees, it is Mr. Lincoln's proclamation freeing the negroes. . . . Three hundred of Mr. Walter Blake's negroes have gone to the Yankees." [48]

Such mass desertions were the exception rather than the rule. It was possible and fairly common for slaves on coastal plantations to escape in large groups. But for slaves in the interior like those of the lower Chattahoochee Valley, escape was much more difficult and dangerous. Only when Union armies were near did slave desertions occur on a mass scale. As Sherman's army moved through the heart of Georgia in December 1864, one of his columns reported 17,000 blacks trailing along.[49]

That so many bondsmen and -women took flight to follow Sherman was more a reflection of their desire for freedom than of any love they had for the Yankees. Few were under the illusion that "Uncle Billy," as Sherman's men affectionately called him, held any great affection for them. Any who believed that Sherman did were quickly disappointed. On December 3, 1864, with Confederate cavalry hot on their heels, Sherman's men pulled in their pontoon bridges after crossing Ebenezer Creek near Savannah, leaving more than five hundred terrified refugees stranded on the opposite bank. Some were shot down by the pursuing Rebels. Others, with children clinging to their backs, jumped into the swollen creek and drowned. Survivors were rounded up and carried back to their owners. In reflecting on the callousness of his army's role in the affair, one appalled Union soldier asked, "Where can you find in all the annals of plantation cruelty anything more completely inhuman and fiendish than this?" [50]

Other instances of cruelty to slaves were less violent but just as reflective of the contempt in which blacks were held by most Yankees. When James Harrison Wilson's troopers raided the lower Chattahoochee Valley in April 1865 they ransacked slave cabins along with planters' mansions. Opelika ex-slave Cornelia Robinson told how they stripped her master's plantation clean and "tore up everything they couldn't take with them." Rhodus Walton, a freedman from Stewart County, recalled that the Yankees destroyed nearly everything on his master's place and even pressed slaves into service as cooks.[51]

The harassment did not end with the war. W. B. Allen, a former Russell County slave, told of his family being swindled out of twenty dollars in 1866:

A Yankee took my father down to a beautiful piece of plantation property that lay on the east side of the forks of a road near Summerville and said: "Nigger, the government is going to give every ex-slave 40 acres of land and a mule, but it will cost $20.00 to make out the papers. Meet me here with $20.00 next Monday morning and I'll make over 40 acres of this fine land to you, and give you the mule later." Well, my father got up the $20.00 and met the man and gave it to him and received a paper from him. But father couldn't read, so—just to be on the safe side before taking possession of what he had been given, he took his deed to a local white man to read. And this is the wording of that Yankee's deed: "This is to certify that this Negro has been able to secure a piece of paper called a deed to forty acres and a mule, and I hope that he gets both some day." Of course, my daddy never forgave that Yankee for cheating him.[52]

A similar deception was perpetrated on a Quitman County freedman named Sam. Shortly after the war a Union soldier handed Sam what was supposed to be a deed to forty acres and a mule for $2.50. When Sam presented the document to his former owner as instructed, he was told that it read, "Lift this black rascal out of his boots, I have just lifted him of $2.50." Allen reflected the sentiments of many former slaves when he insisted that "the only time the Northern people ever helped the Nigger was when they freed him." Yankees, he said, were no friends of blacks.[53]

Still, blacks' hatred of slavery was enough to overcome any fear they had of white men in blue uniforms. When news of approaching Yankee troops spread through Barbour County in April 1865, all the slaves on the Garland plantation turned out to greet them. "Large and small left the 'quarter,'" recalled the Garland children's private tutor. By the time she reached the yard, she found herself surrounded by "a surging mass of black humanity." The slaves not only eagerly anticipated the arrival of Yankee troops but also assisted them whenever possible. Percy, a Troup County slave, led a detachment of Wilson's raiders to a nearby swamp where his master had hidden the family's money. On April 16, 1865, a local slave helped Wilson's men locate Confederate defenses just before their attack on Girard and Columbus.[54]

Slaves prayed and worked for a swift Union victory even if the Yankees did handle them badly. At least the war would be over and they would be free. Besides, slaves gave the Yankees little credit for their impending freedom, which they believed to be a gift from God. The Union army was simply God's instrument of deliverance. To the slaves, as one valley freedman recalled, "God was using the Yankees to scourge the slaveholders just as He had, centuries before, used heathens and outcasts to chastise His chosen people—the Children of Israel." Like the ancient Hebrews, blacks saw themselves as a chosen people to whom God was granting a special salvation. "It was God's blessing to the black peoples," said ex-slave Louis Meadows of Russell County, "to come out from bondage; to belong only to theirselves and God."[55]

Slaves were fully aware that whatever form their postwar world might take, whether dominated by North or South, it would still be a white man's world. Nonetheless, they had an abiding faith that conditions would improve with slavery behind them. When a slaveholding couple in Russell County, on the eve of Wilson's raid, asked one of their chattel to pray that God might turn the Yankees back, the young man refused: "I told them flat-footedly that . . . I could not pray against my conscience: that I not only wanted to be free, but that I wanted to see all the Negroes freed!"[56] So precious an ideal was freedom to the slaves that any future with it was preferable to the past they had known without it.

Nevertheless, some slaves remained on their owners' plantations after the Yankees passed through. Such factors as family attachments, limited opportunities, and fear tended to keep slaves close to home just as they had before the war. Furthermore, blacks had learned over the years to distrust all whites, not just those who kept them enslaved. That some whites spoke with a Yankee accent made little difference. It certainly made them no kinder than southern whites. To some slaves, northerners seemed even less intelligent than the whites they knew. Ex-slave Hannah Irwin of Eufaula recalled with amusement how one Yankee soldier asked her about all the "white flowers" he had seen: "You'd think that a gentleman with all them decorations on hisself woulda knowed a field of cotton." [57]

In attempting to understand the variety of ways in which slaves reacted to the war it must be remembered, as historian Paul Escott points out, that "the slave was not a white man, choosing between the North and the South. He belonged to a despised race of people who had never received equal treatment from the white world. Common treatment bred common attitudes, but these were capable of different manifestations. The same basic attitudes moved one man to rebel while they led others to watch cautiously and quietly shake off some of their daily restrictions." [58] No matter what form resistance took, whether subtle or overt, all slaves were trying as best they could to expand their personal liberties and improve their lives in a dangerous and hostile world. And as the war entered its final year, they fervently hoped that the end of chattel slavery would make their world at least a little more tolerable.

CHAPTER

7

I Say Peace

By 1864, few valley folk expected the Confederacy to survive for much longer. Most were so disgruntled with the southern government that they looked forward to its fall. One indignant valley man insisted that the only people pushing to continue the war were those who held "fat Government contracts" and corrupt officials who were "not yet done fleecing the Government. Their voice," he said, "is still for war, war, war!"[1]

For slaves, who made up half the valley's population, Confederate defeat would mean their much-anticipated freedom. For less-affluent whites, it would mean the end of impressment and conscription. It would also mean, so they hoped, an end to planter oppression. One Early County citizen expressed the class-conscious frustration of yeomen and poor whites when he noted that local planters seemed untouched by the plight of their starving neighbors. His pen dripping with sarcasm, the writer asked, "Ain't it a pity but what the Yankees would take every thing such men have, and leave them without a single mouthful of anything? We hope to live to see the day."[2]

Though few were really anxious for Yankee occupation, at least the war would be finished. But it was not over yet. With the Confederacy all but gone and the Davis administration unwilling to let it go, southerners were trapped in a kind of purgatory. Unable to persuade those in power to give up the fight, they could only wait for its inevitable conclusion and try to survive until that time.

Helpless to bring an immediate end to the war, valley folk sunk into a general malaise. Most had given up not only on the Confederacy but on life as they knew it. Kate Cumming noted this feeling of dejection in West Point when she toured the village in 1864: "It is like many other of our small towns—in a forlorn condition. There are in it very nice private dwellings, but no one seems, in these war times, to care how their property is kept." Abbeville left those who passed through with a similar impression. One visitor wrote that the town looked "almost abandoned." In a letter to his fiancée, an army surgeon described Auburn as "a miserable little place almost in ruins." After a visit to his hometown of Columbus, E. H. Grouby remarked that the town had "decreased over two hundred per cent."[3]

Though it was impossible to avoid seeing what years of war had done to their ravaged land, most southerners tried not to think about the damage too much. For some, constant talk of the devastation seemed only to make their emotional depression worse. In a letter to her husband, Pussie Gay of LaGrange expressed deep sadness at how the war had wrecked the South. "But I will not dwell upon this gloomy theme," she promised. "It is one that our hearts ever painfully linger upon and the pain is only augmented by being told."[4]

Despondency was evident even in the churches. Editor Grouby noted that churchgoers in Blakely had lost all enthusiasm for singing. "Before the war," he wrote, "we could say, and truthfully, that here . . . we had as good singing as was ever heard, but such is not the case now." A Columbus newspaper reported that those attending services rarely paid attention to the sermon. Instead they talked, smoked, and chewed tobacco. According to one account they even spat on the carpets. One Columbus preacher complained that "religion used to be the principal topic preached upon; now, it is all rum and niggers!" Many people turned to alcohol in their search for comfort but little liquor was available. Rum had been hard to get since the war began, and now other such beverages were becoming expensive and sometimes were impossible to get at any price. In January 1864 the *Early County News* announced that "whiskey has given out in Blakely, not a drink in the town in over a week."[5]

Like their civilian relatives, soldiers at the front went through the motions of life in a kind of perpetual depression. By 1864, conditions were so bad that most soldiers had long since deserted. Senator Ben Hill estimated that only a third of the army was present for duty. President Jefferson Davis confirmed Hill's suspicions, admitting that two-thirds of the army had deserted. When possible, commanders issued whiskey to the men in an effort to dull their suffering and slow the desertion rate, but alcohol could not make soldiers forget the suffering of their families back home.[6]

Even men stationed hundreds of miles from the front lines deserted. In July 1864 John Winder, commander of southwest Georgia's Andersonville prison, wrote to Howell Cobb begging for reinforcements. Twelve of his men had already deserted and the rest seemed about to follow. "You have not a moment to spare," warned the frustrated commander. "Twenty-four hours may be too late." The desertion rate was so high by August 1864 that Robert E. Lee issued a general amnesty for deserters who returned to their units voluntarily. All others, he warned, would "suffer the extreme penalty of the law." Few responded to Lee's offer. In the war's final year, even the threat of execution was not enough to keep soldiers in line.[7]

Those who remained did so with little enthusiasm. Many would not fight at all. That, said General John Bell Hood, was the reason for his order to evacuate Atlanta in August 1864. The city simply could not be defended with troops who refused to face the enemy.[8] Hubert Dent of Eufaula agreed with his commanding general. In a letter to his wife, Nannie, Dent made it clear that the army's will to fight was gone: "The spirit of our troops is very bad and unless they do better I do not see what is to prevent Sherman from going any where he pleases. If we had been successful at Jonesboro we would have held Atlanta now and there is no reason why we should not have been successful. The men did not fight and Hood ought not to be blamed for that. I feel badly over the result of that fight. It is a new thing for our men to refuse to fight or what is the same thing to fight with no spirit."[9]

That the soldiers fought with so little zeal should not have been surprising. Few thought the Confederacy had any chance of survival. As early as 1862, Private John W. Hodnett of Troup County doubted whether the Confederacy could last without foreign intervention. J. W. Lokey of Muscogee County wrote after the war, "I had been fully convinced in my own mind for twelve months before the surrender that we would never gain our independence." Some soldiers correctly predicted the war's outcome long before that. Joseph H. Truett of Chattahoochee County wrote to his parents in May 1863 that the Yankees were "determined to subjugate us before they stop and I believe that they have nearly done it now. I think that this Confederacy is gone under, though I think peace is a long ways off yet." That notion, common as it was even before the Confederacy's so-called high-water mark at Gettysburg, had its inevitable impact on southern morale. Four months before Gettysburg, John Hogg of Troup County wrote home to his parents, "I would be the best pleased in the world if I could be out of this unrighteous war."[10]

Less than a year later in January 1864, Benjamin Franklin Jackson wrote apologetically to his wife about his company's reenlistment. The men, he told her, had very little choice. If they had not signed up for another tour of duty, they would simply have been drafted back into service.

But Jackson tried to comfort his wife, telling her that the war must soon be over. "I don't think this war will last till our time is out for our army is badly torn up and I think will be worse before two months pass." [11]

Even high-ranking Confederate officials expressed reservations about the government's survival. Though he was one of Davis's most reliable allies in Congress, Hill confided to his wife in February 1864, "The question of the independence of the Confederate States has become a question of secondary importance." He considered Confederate defeat a foregone conclusion and laid primary blame at the feet of fire-eaters, speculators, and corrupt government officials. "This revolution is the result of feeling, not judgment; of passion, not statesmanship. Its whole progress has been distinguished by an utter absence of reason, humanity, and ordinary good motives." The next month, editor Grouby of the *Early County News* expressed a similar opinion in more colorful terms: "We cannot help thinking this is the last year of the war. . . . we have now entirely too many little jackass up-starts filling positions in our government." [12]

The certainty of Confederate defeat became even greater among valley residents after a federal raid through east Alabama in July 1864. Two months earlier, three federal armies under William Tecumseh Sherman had set out from Chattanooga toward Atlanta. Sherman made good progress until he was stalled by Confederate forces under Joseph E. Johnston at Kennesaw Mountain in late June. Soon after, Sherman devised a plan designed to divert Johnston's attention by disrupting his supply lines from the southwest. On June 30, Sherman wrote to Major General Lovell Harrison Rousseau ordering him to gather a force of 2,500 cavalrymen at Decatur, Alabama, and lead it south on a raid against the Montgomery and West Point Railroad. Sherman told Rousseau that his men should hit the line "between Tuskegee and Opelika, breaking up the road and twisting the bars of iron." If they encountered no serious opposition, they should threaten Columbus before turning north along the Chattahoochee to join Sherman near Atlanta. [13]

Rousseau and his men left Decatur on July 10 and made their way south through Somerville and Blountsville. They reached Loachapoka at dusk on July 17 and after a short rest went to work tearing up track. According to Rousseau's report, "The rails and timbers from one side of the road were placed upon those on the other, and fence rails and other combustible material piled on them, and fire applied. The dry pine burned so readily and produced such an intense heat that the iron was warped and rendered worthless, and the ties burned off where the track rested on them, making the destruction complete." [14]

When word of the approaching Federals reached Auburn the next morning, Captain Thomas H. Francis telegraphed Columbus for reinforcements. He also threw together a small force of about eighteen wounded
Texas soldiers who were recovering at a local hospital. He armed them
with shotguns and established a skirmish line along the tracks just west
of town. As Rousseau's Ohio troopers moved toward Auburn, tearing up
track as they went, a group of local blacks hurried out to warn the commander, Colonel W. D. Hamilton, of the Rebel force hidden ahead. When
he reached the outskirts of Auburn around noon, Hamilton ordered the
entire regiment to stop work and mount up. In a charge through the thick-
ets that "could be better heard than seen," the Ohio men rushed the overwhelmed Texans, who, as Hamilton reported, "broke on our first fire and
scattered in every direction." [15] Hamilton sent most of his men back to
work destroying track and then led a small detachment into town to gather
supplies.

After the men took what they needed, Hamilton invited the town's residents to take whatever was left. "This," he said, "changed the excitement.
Women and children, white and black, came rushing to help themselves."
He recalled with some amusement one particular scene: "A well dressed
lady, that I noticed, came with a colored servant, and pointed out some
hams, which she ordered him to take to the house. 'Haint got time, Mis-
sus, haint got time,' replied the negro, eagerly grabbing what he wanted
for himself. The lady then proceeded to help herself as the others were doing." One Auburn resident recalled that not only townsfolk but also
people from the surrounding countryside "broke into stores and carried
off everything movable." [16]

The following day, July 19, Rousseau's men completed their task of destroying track to Opelika and several miles beyond toward West Point
and Columbus. They took all the supplies they could carry at Opelika,
burned the rest, and headed northeast into Georgia. They reached Mari-
etta three days later accompanied by hundreds of black refugees. In a
space of thirty-six hours between July 17 and 19, Rousseau's raiders had
captured or burned nearly everything of military value between Chehaw
Station and Opelika, cut all the telegraph lines, and destroyed more than
thirty miles of track. [17]

By summer 1864, anti-Confederate guerrilla bands had been wreaking
havoc in the valley's lower reaches for some time. Now federal raiders were
doing the same farther north. Valley residents wondered how much more
damage would be done if the war continued. People living near the fall
line feared that Columbus itself might be threatened. As one of the South's

few remaining industrial centers, it would certainly become a prime target for the Union army at some point. With federal troops controlling the northern parts of Georgia and Alabama, some of the most committed Rebels questioned the wisdom of continuing the war. By more than a two-to-one margin, the Georgia General Assembly passed a series of peace resolutions calling for "our Government . . . to put an end to this unnatural, unchristian, and savage work of carnage and havoc." Similar resolutions were introduced in Alabama's legislature.[18]

The people were far ahead of the politicians. A citizen living near Greenville warned Davis in September 1864 that the president had long since lost the confidence of most Georgians: "I assure you Sir that if the question were put to the people of this state whether to continue the war or return to the union, a large majority would vote for a return." One newspaper reported peace meetings throughout southwest Georgia. In a letter to his wife, Howell Cobb confirmed that the state's population was, as he put it, "depressed, disaffected, and too many of them disloyal." Even William F. Samford of Auburn, former editor of the town paper and an ardent secessionist in 1861, asked, "Shall we indeed fight on against the decrees of God, to utter extermination! Shall we shed 'the last drop of blood'? Shall we devote 'the last man' in a vain effort. . . . Is this the will of God?—or the suggestion of the Demon of Pride—the fiery inspirations of our maddened passions? . . . I say Peace!"[19]

With Confederate defeat inevitable, the army's desertion rate continued to rise. Most of those who remained did so halfheartedly. Requests for discharges and extended furloughs flooded Confederate and state offices. Mary Sutton of Harris County wrote to Governor Joe Brown begging him to discharge her son. From Randolph County came a petition to have Private B. F. Brooks relieved of duty. His wife, Julia, headed a list of twenty-six names pleading on his behalf. Already at home on leave, Daniel Chessy of Steam Mill in Decatur County asked for an indefinite extension of his furlough. West Sheffield of neighboring Miller County did the same.[20]

So many soldiers were leaving the ranks that the Confederacy's remaining supporters began to consider seriously what had until then been unthinkable—freeing the slaves and arming them. As early as 1863 high-ranking Confederate officials had begun to advocate such a move. As enthusiasm for the cause waned and prospects for Confederate victory became ever more dim, support for arming slaves began to grow. By late 1864 Davis himself favored the idea.

On January 5, 1865, William Scruggs, editor of the *Columbus Daily Sun,* published a strongly worded editorial in which he attacked Alexander

Stephens's view of slavery as the Confederacy's founding cornerstone. Scruggs called it a shortsighted policy and suggested that freeing the slaves "would excite the sympathy and secure the aid of the Christian world." [21] By March, Scruggs was even more direct in his editorials. The Confederacy's fate, he said, rested entirely in the hands of the slaves: "It is now evident that the negro slave is to be a sort of balance power in this contest, and that the side which succeeds in enlisting the feelings and in securing the active operation and services of the four millions of blacks, must ultimately triumph." [22]

Others too felt that the end of slavery was inevitable no matter which side won. In December 1864 William Samford wrote, "slavery will have to yield, either by Federal emancipation or by Confederate military necessity. The moment we put slaves into the army, the institution is gone— it becomes a question of time only." The Confederacy's most venerated general, Lee, agreed. Though he considered "the relation of master and slave . . . the best that can exist between the white and black races," Lee argued that slaves were already being freed and used by Lincoln to crush the rebellion. Why should the Confederacy not use them in its own defense? He advised Congress to authorize slave enlistments and adopt a plan for "gradual and general emancipation" following the war. [23]

Despite growing support for arming slaves, most slaveholders fiercely resisted any such notion. They feared not only the loss of their property but also what slave conscription would mean for the future of the institution. Howell Cobb summed up slaveholder concerns when he insisted that "you cannot make soldiers of slaves. . . . The day you make soldiers of them is the beginning of the end of the revolution. If slaves will make good soldiers, our whole theory of slavery is wrong." [24]

Slaveholders found strong support in the statehouses of both Alabama and Georgia. In a February 1865 message to the Georgia General Assembly, Governor Brown warned that arming slaves would be "a great error." Governor Thomas Watts of Alabama insisted that it "would be as unconstitutional as it would be destructive." Proponents of slavery's status quo found supporters in the press as well. J. W. Warren, editor of the *Columbus Times,* opposed the idea, as did Grouby of the *Early County News,* who called on his friends and neighbors to lynch anyone who dared "preach abolitionism." [25]

Aside from its threat to the Confederacy's cornerstone, there was the question of whether giving guns to slaves would make them supporters of the Confederacy. It was an unlikely assumption. To Warren, the idea seemed ridiculous. He was certain that slaves would never fight for the

Confederacy even if they were freed. He feared that blacks would join the Yankees upon reaching the front lines. If the slaves were armed, he warned, "we will ourselves, take the best in the country, drill and train them, and then hand them over—ready made warriors—to the enemy."[26]

Despite such fears, on March 13, 1865, at the urging of President Davis and General Lee, the Confederate Congress finally passed legislation authorizing the recruitment of up to 300,000 blacks. There was, however, no promise of freedom for those who agreed to serve. Congress insisted that any change in the legal standing of slave-soldiers must be agreed to both by the states and individual slaveholders. In his General Order no. 14, which implemented the new recruitment program, Davis went a step further by stating that "no slave will be accepted as a recruit unless with his own consent and with the approbation of his master by a written instrument conferring . . . the rights of a freedman."[27]

Reaction in the valley was predictably mixed. Slaveholders raised "a devil of a howl," denouncing the legislation as a direct threat to their property rights. But the *Columbus Enquirer* pushed slaveholders to offer one out of every four of their adult male bondsmen to the Confederate army. And T. E. Speight, who had replaced Grouby as editor of the *Early County News,* condemned the "starch-shirt gentry" who supported military service for everyone but themselves and their slaves. Since they would not fight, said Speight, "we are glad to know that their 'God-blessed niggers' will have to do so."[28] But it hardly mattered one way or the other. By that time it was too late.

Just before Congress approved slave conscription, Senator Hill delivered a fiery oration that his son later called "the last speech made by any southern man in behalf of the Confederacy." The *Columbus Daily Sun* reflected the attitude of most southerners toward such speeches when it said, "A cause that cannot be sustained except by frantic appeals to the passions, cannot be said to be worth the trouble of saving." Faced with mass desertion and virtually no popular support, Davis still refused to let his generals surrender what was left of their armies. Federal troops would have to force the issue.[29]

By March 1865 that issue was not far from its conclusion. Three months earlier, Hood's Army of Tennessee had been decimated at Nashville and Sherman had completed his devastating "march to the sea" through Georgia's heartland. Sherman was now pursuing Johnston's ragged Confederates through the Carolinas. At Petersburg, Virginia, Lee's Army of Northern Virginia was locked in a hopeless standoff with Ulysses S. Grant's forces. Grant, who was general-in-chief of all federal armies, planned to quicken the pace of Confederate defeat by sending a large raiding party through the Deep South. This force would strike at the remaining supply and manufacturing centers of the Confederacy and prevent resupply of Confederate troops. To carry out the assignment, Grant chose Major General James Harrison Wilson, a twenty-seven-year-old cavalry officer. He would lead a mounted infantry corps through Alabama and Georgia in an effort to completely destroy the Confederacy's remaining industrial facilities.

On March 22, 1865, Wilson set out from his base on the Tennessee-Alabama border with more than 13,000 well-trained, well-equipped troopers. His main targets were the manufacturing centers of Selma, Alabama, and Columbus, Georgia. Wilson met little opposition in northern Alabama, but as he approached Selma on April 2 his corps ran into the remnants of Nathan Bedford Forrest's cavalry. Wilson's numerical advantage gave him a swift and thorough victory. With the defeat of the "Wizard of the Saddle" and Selma's subsequent destruction, Wilson was free to advance on Montgomery.[30]

The city had prepared no defenses and surrendered without a struggle on April 12. Governor Watts had fled to Union Springs the day before, planning eventually to move the state capital to Eufaula. Wilson rested his men at Montgomery and prepared for a push toward the rail yard at West Point and the industrial center of Columbus. He well understood Columbus's importance to the Confederate cause, calling Columbus "the door to Georgia." He was convinced that the city's fall would crush the rebellion and bring a quick end to the war.[31]

Still, it was unclear to many in Columbus that their city would be Wilson's next target. As late as April 15, just a day before the Yankees arrived, the *Daily Sun* cautioned its readers to take hearsay information with a grain of salt. Rumors, said the editor, were "as plentiful as blackberries in June. . . . One that the enemy were in Tuskeegee, another that they were within six miles of Union Springs, neither of which do we believe have any foundation in fact." [32]

Others were more certain of Wilson's intentions. Governor Brown ordered all nonengaged state units to rendezvous at Columbus. Two regiments of the Georgia militia, two artillery batteries from General Abraham Buford's forces, and a few reserve units from surrounding Georgia counties were all pressed into service. They were joined by the remains of Alabama's Seventh Cavalry and a handful of reserves from Russell County. Together, these units totaled less than three thousand men.

Even as this small force gathered to meet the invaders, there were those in Columbus who questioned the wisdom of resistance. Many felt that armed opposition was not only useless but would place the city in even greater danger. Its few defenders could not hope to stop Wilson's battle-hardened veterans. The Confederate force might delay the Federals for a short time, but such futile opposition could only antagonize them. The best course of action would be to form a delegation, meet the Yankees before they reached Columbus, and negotiate terms of surrender. General Cobb, the city's ranking military official, quickly dismissed any such suggestions.[33]

As the Federals approached, Cobb and his assistant, Colonel Leon von Zinken, developed a plan of defense for the city. But despite their refusal to negotiate a surrender, they knew the fight would be in vain. On April 15, even as the *Daily Sun* was dismissing rumors of a Yankee attack, Zinken issued a directive warning Columbus citizens to leave the city as soon as possible or "make preparations for their safety."[34] Cobb and Zinken had certainly prepared for their own safety. A train was standing by to speed them away at a moment's notice.

Upriver from Columbus, the people of Troup County were also making preparations to meet the Yankee threat. Wilson had sent a brigade under Colonel Oscar LaGrange up the Montgomery and West Point Railroad, and by nightfall on April 15 it had reached Auburn. Warned by that city's refugees of LaGrange's approach, one-legged General Robert C. Tyler quickly assembled a small force of convalescent soldiers, hospital employees, and local citizens. By morning on April 16 Tyler had placed little more than a hundred men in a small earthen fort guarding the bridges at West Point on the west side of the river.[35]

LaGrange was defended by a small unofficial company of women, the Nancy Harts, named after Georgia's legendary heroine of the American Revolution. Formed for local defense in 1863 by Mrs. J. Brown Morgan, the women armed themselves with old muskets and squirrel rifles, made their own ammunition, and held drills and target practice. From the beginning it was more of a social and service organization. Most of the women's time was spent ministering to wounded soldiers in area hospitals. Until word of advancing Yankee troopers reached them in April 1865, no one ever expected the Nancy Harts to serve a military purpose.[36]

On Easter Sunday, April 16, 1865, the Union cavalry advanced for assaults on Columbus and West Point. Excited by their recent victory over Forrest's cavalry at Selma and the easy surrender of Montgomery, the Yankees looked forward with confidence to the upcoming engagements.

LaGrange's men reached Tyler's fort by midmorning and shelled it before beginning their attack at 1:30. After chasing Rebel skirmishers into the fort, LaGrange left his main force to continue the assault while he led a detachment to capture the bridge into West Point. He and his men had little difficulty driving off the bridge's few defenders. West Point, with its rail center and bridges, was now in Yankee hands.

Back at Fort Tyler, Yankee troopers had torn down several nearby houses, used the planks to bridge the trench, and stormed the fort. An artillery bombardment soon destroyed the fort's three cannons, and with West Point lost, the defenders decided to surrender. General Tyler and seventeen other Confederates were dead; twenty-eight more were wounded. The Union troops suffered a loss of twenty-nine killed and wounded in the assault. After gathering their prisoners, the Federals moved into West Point, where they destroyed nineteen locomotives and 340 rail cars.[37]

The main federal force under Wilson arrived on the outskirts of Girard at two o'clock that afternoon. Wilson hoped that at least one of the three local Chattahoochee bridges could be taken intact. Clapp's Factory bridge, three miles north of Columbus, would be ideal. If the Federals crossed there, they could flank the Rebels and take Columbus from the rear. At Wilson's direction, General Emory Upton, commanding the lead column, ordered two hundred men of the Tenth Missouri to take the bridge. Columbus defenders had anticipated this maneuver and had prepared the bridge for burning. As the Missourians approached, Confederates ignited turpentine-soaked bales of cotton lining the wooden structure. Within seconds, flames engulfed the bridge.[38]

At the same time, Upton sent another force to capture the lower bridge at Dillingham Street. When Upton's men arrived they found that the defenders had torn up the bridge's flooring planks, making a mounted advance impossible. As the Yankees prepared for a dismounted assault, one anxious Confederate gunner set the bridge on fire. According to a federal account, this premature firing of the bridge saved an entire Yankee battalion from certain death. The flames spread too rapidly to have allowed escape. With the bridge at Dillingham Street now gone, only the upper bridge at Broadnax Street (later Fourteenth Street) was left intact.[39]

The Confederate defensive strategy had hinged on the destruction of the Clapp's Factory and Dillingham Street bridges. This done, they could now lure Wilson's men into a heavily protected area around the upper bridge using the bridge itself as bait. Once Yankee cavalry was in range, southern batteries would turn loose a devastating artillery barrage. As a last-ditch defense, the Confederates placed two cannons loaded with grapeshot on the Georgia side of the bridge in case the first line of artillery failed.

The Confederate plan was a good one. The temptation to take the remaining bridge was too great for Wilson even though he had pontoon bridges and might have crossed the river at any point. He decided to aim his attack at the defenders entrenched along the western side of Summerville Road, break the Confederate lines at that point, then make a rush for the bridge. Wilson told his troopers to make coffee, prepare their supper, and rest for the coming battle while he made final preparations.[40]

A Russell County man later recorded his reflections of that Easter Sunday. From his home just west of Girard, he could see smoke rising from the burning bridges and hear the thunder of artillery. "The day was filled with dread and terror," he recalled, "and was so long that it seemed that Joshua had commanded the sun to stand still."[41] With Wilson planning to attack the remaining bridge under cover of darkness, a rare tactic during the Civil War, the night would seem even longer.

The evening of April 16 was, in the words of one soldier, "black as pitch." There was no moon, and the blackness served to heighten tensions on both sides. At 8:00 P.M., six dismounted companies of the Third Iowa Cavalry advanced on the fortifications straddling Summerville Road. They approached with surprising stealth and managed to get within fifty yards of the Rebel works without firing a shot. When they finally saw the Federals coming, Rebel gunners opened fire, but their aim was high and did little to slow the Yankee advance. Within five minutes the road was in federal hands.[42]

Believing that he had broken the main Confederate line, Upton ordered the Tenth Missouri Cavalry to make a dash for the bridge. In a headlong rush down Summerville Road, the troopers quickly found themselves nearing the bridge. To their astonishment, however, they also found themselves behind an unbroken Rebel line. They had met no resistance because they were mistaken for retreating Rebel pickets. The defenders soon realized their error and Confederate artillery began to rain lead down on the Tenth Missouri. Captain Charles Hinricks, a Union cavalryman, later recalled the scene: "All of a sudden there was a shot, another, and in a second 10,000 more. The whole country seemed to be alive with demons. . . . the next second brought the balls of the enemy by thousands over our heads and the shells hurried their way in every direction, leaving a fiery streak behind them. This was the first time that I ever saw shelling during the night time, it is a beautiful but awful spectacle."[43] Close to being trapped, the cavalrymen wheeled around and rushed back through the Rebel lines.

Meanwhile, Upton had turned his troops left in a drive against the entrenchments on Ingersoll Hill. Their progress was slowed to a crawl by thick woods and muddy bogs at the foot of the hill. The Federals doggedly pushed forward but soon became disoriented in the darkness. A few of the advancing troopers yelled "Go to the right," while others cried out "Go to the left." Despite the confusion, they made their way through the underbrush, overwhelmed the outnumbered southerners, and sent them running for the upper bridge.[44]

Wilson's men now regrouped for a final assault on the prized bridge. They hurried over the top of Ingersoll Hill and rushed down toward Broadnax Street. Near Jackson Street, the Fourth Iowa turned right in an attack against Waddell's battery on Red Hill. They overwhelmed Waddell's men and captured ten artillery pieces.[45]

The path to the bridge was now completely clear and Yankee troopers swarmed through the streets of Girard. As they neared their objective, the enthusiastic Federals shouted, "Go for the bridge! Waste no time with prisoners!" The Union soldiers quickly became entangled with a mass of retreating Rebels and confusion reigned. One observer recalled that "horsemen and footmen, artillery wagons and ambulances were crowded and jammed together in the narrow avenue, which was 'dark as Egypt' . . . for that bridge had no gas fixtures and was never lighted. How it was that many were not crushed to death in the tumultuous transit of the Chattahoochee seems incomprehensible." The Yankees pressed on and, to their amazement, managed to cross the bridge without sustaining a single casualty. Southerners guarding the east end of the bridge had refused to fire their two canister-loaded howitzers for fear that the spray of lead would kill friend as well as foe.[46]

The Fourth Iowa was first across the bridge. It fanned out to mop up remaining pockets of resistance on the Georgia side and moved downstream to capture the guns guarding the Dillingham Street Bridge. One detachment rushed to the depot in an effort to prevent high-ranking Confederate officers from escaping. By the time they reached the station, an entire trainload of officers had already gone. General Cobb had been one of the first to leave. Though the top Confederate brass escaped, Columbus was now under Union control. The city's capture had taken little more than an hour.

Panic seized the inhabitants as Yankee troopers swarmed through the city. One eyewitness recalled that "women and children were running through the streets like people deranged, and men, with mules and wagons, [were] driving in every direction." Roads leading east out of the city were packed with soldiers and civilians fleeing the Yankees.[47]

Early the next morning, Mayor F. G. Wilkins issued a statement to the remaining citizens: "The Federals under command of Major Gen. Wilson, having captured our city, I am assured by him that private property will be protected. It is ordered that all citizens remain on their premises until he can have a proper guard for our defense detailed. The Major General further requires of the citizens 30,000 rations, which must be furnished by 12 o'clock noon." [48]

Randolph L. Mott, a longtime Union man, offered his home to Wilson as a temporary headquarters. An active opponent of secession in 1861, Mott reportedly flew the U.S. flag from the cupola of his home throughout the war. Some accorded it the recognition of being the only place in Georgia that had never been out of the Union. [49]

On the morning of April 17, Wilson ordered the destruction of "everything within reach that could be made useful for the continuance of the Rebellion." He placed General Edward Winslow in charge of burning all Confederate warehouses and manufacturing centers in the area. Winslow's brigade torched 125,000 bales of cotton, valued at approximately $62.5 million. The northerners also demolished army stockpiles, including quartermaster stores, which they burned or distributed to the Union troops and area residents. [50]

Not surprisingly, the navy yard and ironworks were hardest hit by the Union occupation. Augustus McLaughlin and James Warner had tried in vain to relocate their facilities before Wilson arrived. They sent a scout down to Bainbridge to select a new site, but by the time he returned it was too late. The Yankees wrecked or dismantled the machinery and burned the ironclad ram *Jackson* to the waterline. Two hundred fifty feet long and boasting six seven-inch Brooke guns, the vessel had nearly been ready for its maiden voyage. The voyage did occur, though not in quite the way intended by its builders. After the Yankees set it afire, the burning hulk drifted thirty miles downriver before sinking. The *Chattahoochee* suffered a similar fate, though not at the hands of the Federals. It was fired and set adrift by navy yard personnel to keep it out of enemy hands. It ran aground at Race Pass, twelve miles south of Columbus. The torpedo boat *Viper* escaped to Eufaula, but this move only delayed its capture by a couple of weeks. [51]

The demolition of Columbus continued all day on April 17. Almost all the mills and factories were razed, including the textile and paper mills, but food-processing mills like those of the Empire grist operations were spared at Wilson's order. Facilities such as the quartermaster depot, the navy yard, the naval ironworks, the arsenal, and Haiman's sword factory were his primary targets. Kate Cumming recalled that the Yankees did little damage to nonmilitary private property. Most of that destruction was done by the people of Columbus themselves. Even before Wilson's men left, local mobs began roaming through the streets, looting businesses and storehouses that still had anything of value. One eyewitness remarked, "It is a strange scene, and it is interesting to watch the free play of human nature. Soldiers are going for the substantials, women for apparel, and the niggers for anything red." He noted that a number of well-dressed women, by all appearances affluent, were also eager for their share of the spoils: "They frantically join and jostle in the chaos, and seem crazy for plunder." [52]

By the morning of April 18, the industrial sections of Columbus lay in ruins. While parts of the city were "still a mass of flame and coals," Wilson made a final check of his men in preparation for their departure. By midmorning, he and his troops were on their way to Macon.[53]

The town of LaGrange suffered its own Yankee occupation, though destruction was much more limited. On the morning of April 17, as Colonel LaGrange approached the town that coincidentally bore his name, the Nancy Harts gathered two blocks west of the town square. From there they moved toward the Female College and met the Yankees in front of the campus. The women agreed to surrender and disperse only after Colonel LaGrange promised not to destroy private homes, which he did not intend to target anyway. That evening the ladies of the town entertained LaGrange and his officers. Next morning, the Yankees burned the tannery, the steam mill, and a tin shop. They tore up railroad track around the town and destroyed the depot. True to their commander's word, however, they stayed out of private dwellings. Their work completed, LaGrange and his men headed east to rendezvous with the rest of Wilson's command.[54]

Two days later, on April 20, Wilson arrived in Macon. He was surprised to learn that Lee had surrendered more than a week earlier, an armistice had been negotiated between Johnston and Sherman in North Carolina, and Abraham Lincoln was dead. Had communications been better, the battles at Girard and West Point could have been avoided. For all practical purposes, the war was over several days before the raids on LaGrange and Columbus. Wilson himself later wrote, "Had we but known what had taken place in Virginia . . . we should certainly have not . . . participated in the injury which was inflicted upon [LaGrange and Columbus] industries." [55]

Eufaula narrowly escaped a similar fate when four thousand Union cavalrymen from Mobile under Major General Benjamin H. Grierson approached the town in late April. Grierson's original target had been Montgomery. On hearing the news of that city's capture by Wilson, he turned east at Greenville and headed for the Chattahoochee River. He divided his force into two columns, sending one through Union Springs while he led the other toward Eufaula.[56]

News of the advancing Federals sent the planters of southeast Alabama into a panic. Near Glenville, Parthenia Hague recalled thinking that now she and her neighbors might know what "Old Virginia" had suffered for four long years. "How vividly I remember that day of suspense," she later wrote, "as the courier heralded from house to house his unwelcome message, 'The Yankees are coming!' The explosion of a bomb in each one's yard could not have created greater excitement." Area planters gathered all the valuables they could and sought refuge in the woods and swamps. A steady stream of wagons and livestock flowed by Hague's residence the day before Grierson arrived. At one point, she was amused in spite of herself to see a featherbed protruding far out the window of one passing carriage. But, as she said, "in our great anxiety, appearances were not regarded."[57]

As the federal cavalry neared the county seat at Clayton on April 29, Grierson finally received word that the war was over. Mayor C. J. Pope of Eufaula along with a committee of the city council rode out to meet Grierson and escorted him into town. One city resident wrote of the Union commander, "Grierson *was* a gentleman. His men deported themselves without committing any depredation." However, he did order his officers to distribute supplies from the Confederate commissary to Eufaula's poor, "many of whom," said Grierson, "were suffering and entirely destitute." He also destroyed the commissary's supply of whiskey so it would not tempt his own soldiers. Grierson's lieutenants knocked holes in the barrel-heads with axes and, much to the horror of many Eufaula residents, allowed the whiskey to run into the streets. Mary Barnett, who lived near the commissary, saw men, both black and white, on their hands and knees lapping up whiskey as it flowed down the ditches. Free-ranging hogs also helped themselves. All through that night and into the next day, men and hogs were seen passed out in the streets or staggering through town in a drunken stupor. The Federals, however, passed through without incident, crossed the river, and spent that evening at Harrison's Mill near Georgetown.[58]

Though valley planters greeted the Federals with apprehension, not everyone was sorry to see them come. For many poor whites, it was a sure sign that the war was finally over. Some even profited from the invasion. One former slave recalled that as the Yankees moved through Troup County, they drove off all the mules on his master's plantation. The animals wandered into neighboring Harris County and, as the old man said, "there was lots of white folks what never had owned nothin' went over there and got theirselves a mule." [59]

For slaves, the Yankees' arrival was a long-anticipated guarantee of freedom. When news that Wilson's troops had overrun Columbus reached the slaves on one Stewart County plantation, they spoke for thousands of valley residents, black and white, with their cry, "It ain't gonna be long now!" [60] And it was not. On May 10, Wilson's men captured Davis near Irwinville, Georgia, as he fled south in a vain effort to get out of the country and establish a Confederate government-in-exile. Hill was arrested ten days later at his home in Troup County. Other Rebel officials were soon in custody, and the Confederate nation ceased to be.

In a sense, though, the Confederacy as a nation never really existed at all. Renowned Georgia historian E. Merton Coulter, enamored as he was with the Lost Cause, still wrote that the Confederacy never became an "emotional reality" to most southerners until long after the war was over. Even at its beginnings, the cause lacked firm backing from its own people. That was the main reason it was lost. Barely half those who bothered to vote on the issue initially favored secession. A majority of Georgians opposed it. As for African Americans, they could feel no abiding loyalty for a government that considered slavery their "natural and normal condition." What support the Confederacy had at its outset eroded quickly as the passions of 1861 died away. [61]

Conscription and impressment only accelerated the decline of enthusiasm for the war. Most devastating to the cause of southern independence were the attitudes of planters and the privileges granted them by the government. Not only were they exempt from the draft, but they continued to grow cotton while their poorer neighbors and Confederate soldiers went hungry. In doing so, planters literally helped starve the Confederacy out of existence.

For those who had not already grasped the war's base reality, it became clear enough by 1862 that the struggle was little more than a rich man's war. Few outside the slaveholding class could enthusiastically support the Confederacy once that realization set in. Some went so far as to take up arms against it. The war continued for three more years only because Lincoln had his own problems with popular support in the North.

Among those who stuck with the Confederacy to its painful end, most did so with little zeal. What loyalty they still felt was more to their commanders and comrades than to the government in Richmond. William

Andrews of Clay County had joined the army in February 1861 and remained through the entire war. Few could match his record of service to the cause of southern independence. Still, only a month after he surrendered with Lee at Appomattox, he wrote, "While it is a bitter pill to have to come back into the Union, don't think there is much regret for the loss of the Confederacy. The treatment the soldiers have received from the government in various ways put them against it." [62]

Many more soldiers—hundreds of thousands, in fact—deserted the Confederate army. Some left to help their starving families or because they themselves were starving. Others laid down their arms because they had no use for a rich man's war. Whatever their reasons, the Confederacy could not survive without an army. As Professor Paul Escott put it, "the decision which common soldiers made with their feet sealed the fate of the Confederacy." [63]

In a larger context, however, the issue had already been decided by the people back home. Lacking a firm base of support from the beginning, the Confederate government was so unpopular by war's end that its collapse was only a matter of time. Aside from the areas it had lost to Union occupation, there were large sections of the South where the Confederacy had no control. Few officials dared enter parts of the lower Chattahoochee Valley for fear of men like John Ward and Joseph Sanders.

Though most valley folk expressed their disaffection less violently than Ward or Sanders, they paid little more than lip service to the Confederacy. Many had voiced their displeasure at the polls in 1863 and, like other southerners, would have done so even more clearly in 1865 had the war not ended before they had the chance. Frank Lawrence Owsley Sr., the leading authority of his generation on the Old South's plain folk, noted that "the Confederacy, even had it not suffered military defeat at the hands of the North in 1865, would have been defeated in the next state and congressional elections, which would have disintegrated its armies and brought peace." That sentiment was reflected shortly after the war by Mary Custis Lee, wife of Robert E. Lee. In a letter to her nephew, she wrote, "The sad truth is that our people got tired of the war." [64]

Much has been made of the North's manufacturing capacity as a cause of Confederate defeat. For many Civil War enthusiasts and even a few professional historians, northern industrial superiority still ranks as the main reason for Union victory. But the rapid development of thriving industrial centers like Columbus together with the Confederate Ordnance Bureau's success in getting munitions to the field points to serious problems with that view. Never did a Confederate army lose a major battle for want of guns or ammunition. Furthermore, as Professor Stanley Lebergott reminds us, a people who saw "a tiny Asian country defeat the world's most powerful nation should not lightly assume that resources or industrial potency guarantees victory in war."[65] The outcome of America's war in Vietnam had much more to do with popular will than military firepower. So it was with America's Civil War.

EPILOGUE:
TEACH THEM THEIR PLACES

Not long after he passed through the lower Chattahoochee Valley in April 1865, General Benjamin Grierson recorded his impressions of the region's people: "The country was filled with armed marauders, composed mostly of deserters from the late rebel armies, who have returned to find their families suffering from the neglect and persecution of the wealthy leaders, at whose instigation they joined the rebel ranks. The poor people, including the returned Confederate private soldiers, are, as a general thing, now loyal, but the far greater portion of the wealthy classes are still very bitter in their sentiments against the Government, and clutch onto slavery with a lingering hope to save at least a relic of their favorite yet barbarous institution for the future." Grierson recommended leniency for the plain folk. They had suffered too much already in a war not of their making. But the spirit of resistance among the planters would have to be broken completely if the slaves were ever to be truly free.[1]

Planter resistance to emancipation was nowhere more evident than in the lower Chattahoochee Valley. One Georgia planter spoke for most of his class when he told a Freedmen's Bureau official, "If we cannot whip the Negro, they and I cannot live in the same country." In Chattahoochee County, Freedman's Bureau agent James McNeil had to order J. H. Wilkinson to release a former slave named Hannah. McNeil noted that federal troops would be arriving shortly to enforce all such orders if necessary. An Opelika woman demanded that occupying federal troops return a young slave girl who had fled to their camp. When told that the girl was now free and could work for wages if she wished, the enraged woman replied, "I will not pay her a cent. I will work my hands to the bone first. She belongs to me."[2]

Other slaveholders were more fearful of doing physical labor themselves. A Dale County woman said that she could not bear the thought of her daughters working in the fields like common folk. Ann Browder of Eufaula wrote in her diary, "I begin to realize poverty now—last week our cook left." John Horry Dent confided to his journal in summer 1865, "Had an ominous dream last night—[I was] pulling fodder."[3]

Some planters did not even tell their slaves that the war was over and that they were free. George Brooks's owner sold him in fall 1865. Only later, when he ran off to Columbus, did Brooks learn that he was legally free. Other masters duped former slaves into making contracts that bound them to service for years after the war.[4]

Planters who held to their old attitudes had a firm friend in the White House. President Andrew Johnson, a former slaveholder from Tennessee, had no commitment to civil rights for former slaves. His only condition for a state's readmission to the Union was ratification of the Thirteenth Amendment, which abolished chattel slavery. Aside from that provision, Johnson was content to leave southern state governments and former slaves in the hands of the planters. They took full advantage of the opportunity.

In October 1865, at the urging of Provisional Governor James Johnson, delegates to the Georgia constitutional convention reluctantly accepted slavery's end. For months Johnson, a Columbus native, had been encouraging Georgians to acknowledge that fact. In plain language he publicly stated, "Slavery is extinguished. It is gone—it is gone forever." Nonetheless, the convention's resolution accepting the end of slavery also defended the institution as "consistent with the dictates of humanity and the strictest principles of morality and religion." And the new constitution, like its 1861 predecessor, left control of the General Assembly in the hands of Black Belt planters.[5]

The Alabama legislature also ratified the Thirteenth Amendment but added that in no way did the action "confer upon Congress the power to legislate upon the political status of freedmen in this State." The legislatures of both Alabama and Georgia reserved that power for themselves. Said Barbour County politician Henry Clayton of the freedman, "We are the only people in the world who understand his character, and hence, the only people in the world capable of managing him." And there was only one way to manage blacks properly, said Clayton: "Teach them their places, and how to keep them." As far as the state legislatures were concerned, their place was not in the voting booth.[6]

Maintaining the old order meant keeping in their places not only blacks but poor whites too. The South's local newspapermen, many of whom had family or financial ties to the planters, proved ready allies in this effort. The *Bainbridge Argus* insisted that anyone who supported voting rights for blacks was either "a fool or a knave." Even the poor white man, insisted the paper's editor, had no business meddling in politics: "He has no time to devote to parties or the discussion of political questions which in no way apply to his condition as a pauper."[7]

Disfranchisement was only the first step in teaching freedmen their places. Under a series of Black Codes, which closely resembled the old slave codes, black freedom became little more than nominal. Blacks could not serve on juries, hold public office, or quit jobs voluntarily. In some states they could not own firearms. Most oppressive were the vagrancy laws. Blacks found "wandering or strolling about in idleness, who are able to work and who have not property to support them," could be arrested for vagrancy and sold into servitude for the price of their fine. They were to perform forced labor only until their custodians were reimbursed. But with the costs of food, clothing, and shelter added to their debt, blacks could be held in bondage for years. Since few blacks owned property of any kind, most were in very real danger of being reenslaved under the vagrancy laws.[8]

Some states went further than that. Both Georgia and Alabama empowered county judges and ordinaries to force black children into "apprenticeship" if their parents could not provide adequate financial support. The definition of adequate support was left entirely to county officials. In Russell County, Judge J. F. Waddell was notorious for apprenticing children on the slightest pretext. Freedwoman Laura Taylor "stole" her two children from the Frank Boyken plantation, but the sheriff tracked her down and took them back. Wadell threatened to throw her in jail if she tried it again. When Ann Richardson tried to get her child from T. W. Mathis of Miller County, she was beaten with a chair. Richardson complained to the local ordinary, who agreed to cancel her child's indenture of apprenticeship, but only if ordered to do so by the Freedman's Bureau. The bureau did just that.[9]

Even employed freedmen sometimes had their children apprenticed or were arrested for vagrancy because they were so often swindled out of their wages. In one month alone, the Freedmen's Bureau agent in Columbus reported one hundred complaints of unpaid wages or crop shares from a single county in his service region. The bureau's agent in Cuthbert said that he spent most of his time trying to collect unpaid wages for black workers. Only half of the labor contracts were being honored by white employers in Randolph County.[10]

If President Johnson cared nothing for black civil rights, Congress certainly did. Its Republican majority naturally assumed that blacks would vote for Republican candidates if given the opportunity. In 1867 Congress took steps to ensure that they got that opportunity. The Reconstruction Act, passed in March over Johnson's veto, divided most of the former Confederacy into five districts and charged their military governors with guaranteeing black voting rights. The next year saw ratification of the

Fourteenth Amendment granting citizenship to "all persons born or nat-
uralized in the United States" and promising them "equal protection of the
laws."[11] Finally, with the Fifteenth Amendment, the Constitution guaranteed the right to vote for all male citizens regardless of race.

Congressional Reconstruction did succeed for a time in extending political rights to blacks. They voted in large numbers and won seats in
southern state legislatures and even in Congress on the Republican ticket.
But electoral supervision was so weak that the planter power structure
soon found ways to control both the black vote and the vote of those whites
who dared cast Republican ballots. As one southwest Georgia planter remarked, "We can control it with little trouble—the only trouble before
was that we did not know how to go about it. . . . Every man who voted
the Radical [Republican] ticket in this county was watched and his ticket
marked and all are now known and they will never cease to regret it, as
long as they live."[12]

And they did not. The Ku Klux Klan saw to that. Operating as the ter-
rorist arm of the Democratic party, bands of hooded night riders spread
panic among both blacks and whites who openly supported the Republicans. The Klansmen broke up prayer meetings, burned homes and
churches, and beat or killed many of their unlucky victims. One particularly vicious Klansman, John Lyons of Lee County, Alabama, frequently
mutilated his victims. According to the Reverend Wade Owens, a former
Lee County slave, Lyons would not hesitate to "cut off a woman's breast
and a man's ear or thumb."[13]

George Ashburn, a white Georgian and Republican politician who
had received warnings from the Klan, was killed in 1868 while visiting
Columbus. Under cover of darkness, a gang of ten to fifteen men broke
into Ashburn's boardinghouse room and shot him dead. Despite eyewitness testimony, civil authorities concluded that Ashburn was killed by
persons unknown. The local military commander intervened and arrested
several suspects, some of them leading Columbus Democrats. But when
Georgia was readmitted to the Union, the accused men were handed over
to local officials, who let the matter drop.[14]

Despite armed resistance to Klan terrorism by blacks themselves, its effects were evident in the presidential campaign of 1868. In Stewart County,
where 752 people had voted for the Republican gubernatorial candidate
in April, the party's candidate for president, Ulysses S. Grant, received
only sixty-three votes in November. More than 1,500 blacks were registered to vote in the county. White voters numbered less than a thousand.
Just to the south in Randolph County, which had nearly 1,200 blacks and
just under a thousand whites registered, Republicans returned nearly seven

hundred ballots for their candidate in April. By November, only one man dared to vote for Grant.[15]

The low Republican turnout reflected not only Klan violence and planter power but also a waning commitment by Congress to secure black civil rights. Blacks certainly could provide northern elites with votes, but landholders could provide something much more important, the very thing for which they had initially gone to war—access to cheap natural resources. Northerners merely had to give their former adversaries a free hand to deal with the South's labor force as they saw fit and riches in the form of lumber, oil, and cotton would flow north. This new economic alliance with the South's elite was much more valuable to northern industrialists than any political alliance they could ever have made with southern blacks. Never enthusiastic about a war against slavery to begin with, much less civil rights for blacks, northerners found the arrangement comfortable. They withdrew their largely ineffective army of occupation and left the freedmen at the mercy of their former owners.

With planters back in control both politically and economically, they moved to reestablish the old order. Southern state governments, like those of the North before them, enacted a series of Jim Crow laws that firmly established social segregation. Blacks were barred from voting by such measures as the grandfather clause, literacy tests, and poll taxes, which kept many poor whites from voting as well. And, despite lip service to the idea of a New South with a diversified economy modeled after that of the North, agriculture remained the region's primary economic activity and cotton was still king. It suited those in power even if it kept most southerners, black and white, in ignorance and poverty.[16]

Poverty was the key element in planter efforts to regain and maintain control. Shortly before the war's end, many slaves had been guaranteed forty acres and a mule once they became free. It would have been little enough compensation for people who had labored all their lives and never received a cent in pay. But the promise was a hollow one. In December 1865 a former Confederate general offered this explanation for continued poverty among southern blacks: "The emancipated slaves own nothing, because nothing but freedom has been given to them." It was an unusually candid recognition, for that or any era, of the relationship between freedom and financial security.[17]

A growing number of landless whites joined the propertyless freedmen throughout the late nineteenth century. Many had owned no land even before the war. Others lost their holdings to neighboring planters during or after the war because they were unable to repay debts. Still others moved from the hill country to the plantation belt looking for economic opportunity. They found none. With few skills other than agricultural abilities and no land of their own to farm, most blacks and many whites fell into tenant farming—as one Georgia historian called it, "the new slavery." [18]

Though usually associated with the post–Civil War era, tenancy and sharecropping were not new at all. In the late 1850s, roughly one in four southern white farmers worked land owned by someone else. In the lower Chattahoochee Valley, landless tenants and sharecroppers made up nearly half the rural white population. Nonetheless, tenancy did see a phenomenal growth after the war. By the turn of the century, two-thirds of all farmers in Georgia and Alabama were tenants. In Barbour County alone, the tenancy rate was more than 75 percent. [19]

Old or new, tenant farming was certainly a kind of slavery. Farmers worked for a share of the crop and borrowed against expected earnings. They had little choice but to make purchases on credit following the war since they had only worthless Confederate money. Once caught in the cycle of debt, tenants were usually trapped for life. With local landholders and merchants (often one and the same) keeping the books, sharecroppers' annual incomes almost never covered their previous year's debt. They remained tied to the land until they could pay off their debt, which was nearly impossible under the circumstances.

Even those farmers who worked their own small holdings were subject to a kind of debt slavery under the oppressive crop-lien system. Poorer yeomen were forced to put up their next year's crop as collateral with local planter-merchants in exchange for supplies. But interest rates were so high, ranging up to 75 percent in some counties, that yeomen, like their tenant neighbors, ended up further in debt than they had been the year before. Many found it impossible to pay off any portion of their debt from one year to the next. These people often fell into tenant farming and lost their land to those who already had large holdings. Tenancy rates continued to rise along the lower Chattahoochee and other parts of the South well into the twentieth century. [20]

A kind of economic slavery was also common among mill workers in company towns like those of Columbus and West Point. Employees worked for company wages, lived in company housing, and were often paid not in cash but in company scrip that could be spent only at the company store or other local establishments where the company had an interest. With the company controlling their salaries, rents, and commodity prices, it is hardly surprising that no matter what the wages, the cost of living was always higher. [21]

Even in the face of overwhelming poverty, most poor whites who bothered to vote at all consistently cast their ballots for the men who kept them poor. To vote otherwise, they were told by the planter-dominated Democratic Party, would mean white subordination to black rule. Though poor whites had no more love for the planters now than during the war, they were as dedicated as ever to the racial caste system. If nothing else, it gave them an artificial status that the reality of their impoverishment denied. In 1884, John Horry Dent confessed to his journal, "This is no country for a man who has to start from the bottom rung of the ladder, no room for enterprise." If the South was not a land of economic opportunity for the poor, the planters did at least promise to keep it a white man's country. That was enough for poor whites. Their racist fears kept their families in poverty and the planters in power for decades after the war.[22]

Some people challenged planter oppression, though not always the caste ideology that supported it. The most serious threat came in the late nineteenth century from the newly formed Populist Party. With its focus on lowering transportation costs and reforming the credit and tax systems, the party was designed to appeal to yeomen and tenants alike. Of course, the Populists had no financial backing from the South's economic elite. To have any chance for success, the Populists needed maximum support from the lower classes to offset the economic advantage of their political opponents. And for that, they needed poor blacks as well as whites.

Georgia Populist Tom Watson was the party's most vocal advocate of black-white cooperation in facing common economic problems. Time and time again, he pointed out that "the accident of color can make no difference in the interests of farmers, croppers, and laborers." Watson often spoke to groups of black and white farmers, always hammering home the message of their shared plight. In an 1892 address, Watson told his audience, "You are kept apart that you may be separately fleeced of your earnings. You are made to hate each other because upon that hatred is rested the keystone of the arch of financial despotism which enslaves you both. You are deceived and blinded that you may not see how this race antagonism perpetuates a monetary system which beggars both."[23]

Try as they might the Populists found it impossible to overcome generations of socially ingrained prejudice. Watson himself recognized the limitations of the Populist approach but could find no way to overcome it. One could get a white farmer's attention, Watson said, with promises to abolish the crop-lien system, provide for more reasonable credit, and reform the regressive tax system. One could even prove to him that this was the way out of his poverty. But at the first cry of "Negro rule!" Watson wrote, "the entire fabric of reason and common sense which you had patiently constructed would fall."[24]

Religion also served as a useful tool in promoting the planter agenda. During the congressional campaigns of 1892, a Georgia Democrat branded his Populist opponent an atheist, saying, "He believes neither in Democracy nor in our God." One of the state's most prominent Methodist preachers told voters that a Populist victory would mean no less than "negro supremacy," "mongrelism," and the "destruction of the Saxon womanhood of our wives and daughters." And there was economic pressure on the voters as well. Merchants frequently refused credit to farmers who would not openly renounce the Populist Party.[25]

Finally, there was the Lost Cause. With white supremacy its creed and Robert E. Lee its Christ, the mythological Lost Cause itself became something of a religion among white southerners. That Confederate soldiers had "cursed the Southern Confederacy" and yeoman farmers had wished for that "damned Government" to fall apart mattered little by the turn of the century. What mattered was that the fiction of kind masters and happy slaves in an idyllic southern past bolstered white supremacy and fit perfectly with postwar planter politics.[26]

Racism, religion, and the Lost Cause all served to perpetuate a system of class and caste that made the New South much like the Old South. In fact, it was not a "new" South at all. Though the Civil War is still viewed by many as *the* turning point in southern history, providing a convenient line of demarcation between Old and New South, very little actually changed as a result of the war. Planters remained the South's ruling class both politically and socially. Cotton agriculture continued as the region's dominant economic force. And while the Civil War ended chattel slavery, the so-called freedmen were simply forced into debt slavery along with millions of poor whites.

Significant change began only in the 1920s after the boll weevil wiped out the South's cotton crop. No longer needed to pick cotton, hordes of tenant farmers, black and white, were driven off the land and released from debt slavery. In a way, the tiny boll weevil freed more slaves in a few seasons of pestilence than Lincoln and the Union army did in four years of war. Over the next few decades, New Deal programs, farm mechanization, expanding markets, and the civil rights movement propelled the region toward becoming a truly new South.

Plain folk came to realize well before the Civil War ended that the immediate postwar South would hardly be a new one. Their lives would go on much as they always had whether the central government was in Richmond or Washington. Either way, the government would be controlled by wealthy elites serving their own interests. Yet the common people were suffering and dying to secure the rights of the rich to become richer. For one young soldier who later in the war worked at a Columbus shoe shop, his army's 1862 victory at Murfreesboro sparked little enthusiasm. "What is gained anyway?" he asked in his journal. "It is a rich man's war and a poor man's fight, at best." [27]

APPENDICES

Population of the Lower Chattahoochee Valley

	White		Free Black		Slave		
	Number	Percent	Number	Percent	Number	Percent	Total
Alabama							
Chambers	11,315	48.74	50	.22	11,849	51.04	23,214
Russell	10,936	41.12	18	.07	15,638	58.81	26,592
Barbour	14,629	47.48	33	.11	16,150	52.41	30,812
Henry	10,464	70.14	21	.14	4,433	29.72	14,918
Dale	10,381	85.11	7	.06	1,809	14.83	12,197
Alabama Total	57,725	53.58	129	.12	49,879	46.30	107,733
Georgia							
Troup	6,223	38.27	37	.23	10,002	61.50	16,262
Harris	5,979	43.53	21	.15	7,736	56.32	13,736
Muscogee	8,966	54.06	173	1.04	7,445	44.89	16,584
Chattahoochee	3,034	52.34	5	.09	2,758	47.58	5,797
Stewart	5,534	41.23	4	.03	7,884	58.74	13,422
Quitman	1,870	53.44	4	.11	1,625	46.44	3,499
Randolph	5,103	53.32	1	.01	4,467	46.67	9,571
Clay	2,626	53.67	14	.29	2,253	46.04	4,893
Early	2,092	34.02	0	.00	4,057	65.98	6,149
Miller	1,151	64.26	0	.00	640	35.73	1,791
Decatur	5,985	50.20	13	.11	5,924	49.69	11,922
Georgia Total	48,563	46.86	272	.26	54,791	52.87	103,626
Combined Total	106,288	50.29	401	.19	104,670	49.52	211,359

Source: United States Census of 1860

APPENDIX 2

Number of Slaveholders in the Lower Chattahoochee Valley

Slaves Held	1–4	5–9	10–19	20–49	50–99	100–199	200–299	300+	Total
Alabama									
Chambers	616	299	227	132	24	—	—	—	1,298
Russell	404	222	175	175	59	8	—	1	1,044
Barbour	444	249	215	170	52	12	1	—	1,143
Henry	237	108	82	56	5	1	—	—	489
Dale	187	70	46	10	1	—	—	—	314
Alabama Total	1,888	948	745	543	141	21	1	1	4,288
Georgia									
Troup	235	193	187	125	25	4	—	—	769
Harris	193	130	124	105	21	2	—	—	575
Muscogee	333	191	148	73	15	2	—	—	762
Chattahoochee	90	55	44	39	5	1	—	—	234
Stewart	231	139	112	106	14	5	1	—	608
Quitman	88	30	29	16	3	1	—	—	167
Randolph	162	130	81	53	8	—	—	—	434
Clay	64	61	39	23	5	1	—	—	193
Early	85	50	39	43	16	3	1	—	237
Miller	25	17	15	7	1	—	—	—	65
Decatur	188	101	89	67	17	2	1	—	465
Georgia Total	1,694	1,097	907	657	130	21	3	—	4,509
Combined Total	3,582	2,045	1,652	1,200	271	42	4	1	8,797

Source: United States Census of 1860

Planters as a Percentage of All Slaveholders, and Percentage
of All Slaves Held by Planters in the Lower Chattahoochee Valley

	Number of Planters[a]	Percentage of All Slaveholders	Number of Slaves Held[b]	Percentage of Slaves Held
Alabama				
Chambers	156	12	5,606	47
Russell	243	23	10,979	70
Barbour	235	21	10,632	66
Henry	62	13	2,070	47
Dale	11	4	335	18
Alabama Total	707	16	29,622	59
Georgia				
Troup	154	20	5,677	57
Harris	128	22	4,711	61
Muscogee	90	12	3,501	47
Chattahoochee	45	19	1,606	58
Stewart	126	21	4,891	62
Quitman	20	12	821	50
Randolph	61	14	2,154	48
Clay	29	15	1,186	53
Early	63	27	2,977	73
Miller	8	12	297	46
Decatur	87	19	3,638	61
Georgia Total	811	18	31,459	57
Combined Total	1,518	17	61,081	58

Source: United States Census of 1860

[a] Slaveholders with twenty or more slaves

[b] Total number of slaves minus approximate number of slaves held by those who owned fewer than twenty calculated from county listings in "Slaveholders and Slaves," in U.S. Census Bureau, *Agriculture of the United States,* 223, 226–27.

Number of Families and the Free
Population in the Lower Chattahoochee Valley

	Free Families	Free Population	Average Family Size[a]
Alabama			
Chambers	1,984	11,365	5.7
Russell	2,098	10,954	5.2
Barbour	2,717	14,662	5.4
Henry	1,843	10,485	5.7
Dale	1,767	10,388	5.9
Alabama Total	10,409	57,854	5.6
Georgia			
Troup	1,193	6,260	5.2
Harris	1,096	6,000	5.5
Muscogee	1,927	9,139	4.7
Chattahoochee	564	3,039	5.4
Stewart	1,026	5,538	5.4
Quitman	335	1,874	5.6
Randolph	907	5,104	5.6
Clay	467	2,640	5.6
Early	471	2,092	4.4
Miller	191	1,151	6.0
Decatur	1,059	5,998	5.7
Georgia Total	9,236	48,835	5.3
Combined Total	19,645	106,689	5.4

Source: United States Census of 1860

[a] Free population divided by number of free families

Estimated Number of Members of Farmholding
Families Owning Three or More Acres in the Lower Chattahoochee Valley

	Number of Farms	Number of Family Members[a]	Percentage of Free Population	Percentage of Total Population
Alabama				
Chambers	1,288	7,342	65	32
Russell	993	5,164	47	19
Barbour	1,529	8,257	56	27
Henry	930	5,301	50	36
Dale	1,066	6,289	60	52
Alabama Total	5,806	32,353	56	30
Georgia				
Troup	648	3,370	54	21
Harris	683	3,756	63	27
Muscogee	337	1,584	17	10
Chattahoochee	325	1,755	58	30
Stewart	598	3,229	58	24
Quitman	147	823	44	23
Randolph	492	2,755	54	29
Clay	222	1,243	47	25
Early	200	880	42	14
Miller	99	594	52	33
Decatur	513	2,924	49	24
Georgia Total	4,264	22,913	47	22
Combined Total	10,070	55,266	52	26

Source: United States Census of 1860

[a] Farms of three or more acres times the average family size (see appendix 4)

Estimated Number of Members of Slaveholding
and Planter Families in the Lower Chattahoochee Valley

	Slaveholding Families[a]	Planter Families[b]
Alabama		
Chambers	7,399	889
Russell	5,429	1,264
Barbour	6,172	1,269
Henry	2,787	353
Dale	1,853	65
Alabama Total	23,640	3,840
Georgia		
Troup	3,999	801
Harris	3,162	704
Muscogee	3,581	423
Chattahoochee	1,264	243
Stewart	3,283	680
Quitman	935	112
Randolph	2,430	342
Clay	1,081	162
Early	1,043	277
Miller	390	48
Decatur	2,650	496
Georgia Total	23,818	4,288
Combined Total	47,458	8,128

Source: United States Census of 1860

[a] Number of slaveholders times average family size (see appendices 2 and 4)

[b] Number of planters times average family size (see appendices 3 and 4)

Estimated Numbers of Members of Slaveholding Families as a Percentage of Free and Total Population in the Lower Chattahoochee Valley

	Members of Slaveholding Families[a]	Percentage of Free Population	Percentage of Total Population
Alabama			
Chambers	7,399	65	32
Russell	5,429	50	20
Barbour	6,172	42	20
Henry	2,787	26	19
Dale	1,853	18	15
Alabama Total	23,640	41	22
Georgia			
Troup	3,999	64	25
Harris	3,162	53	23
Muscogee	3,581	39	22
Chattahoochee	1,264	42	22
Stewart	3,283	59	24
Quitman	935	50	27
Randolph	2,430	48	25
Clay	1,081	41	22
Early	1,043	50	17
Miller	390	34	22
Decatur	2,650	44	22
Georgia Total	23,818	49	23
Combined Total	47,458	44	22

Source: United States Census of 1860

[a] From appendix 6

Estimated Number of Members of Planter Families as a Percentage
of Free and Total Population in the Lower Chattahoochee Valley

	Members of Planter Families[a]	Percentage of Free Population	Percentage of Total Population
Alabama			
Chambers	889	7.8	3.8
Russell	1,264	11.5	4.8
Barbour	1,269	8.6	4.1
Henry	353	3.4	2.4
Dale	65	0.6	0.5
Alabama Total	3,840	6.6	3.6
Georgia			
Troup	801	12.8	4.9
Harris	704	11.7	5.1
Muscogee	423	4.6	2.6
Chattahoochee	243	8.0	4.2
Stewart	680	12.3	5.1
Quitman	112	6.0	3.2
Randolph	342	6.7	3.6
Clay	162	6.1	3.3
Early	277	13.2	4.5
Miller	48	4.2	2.7
Decatur	496	8.3	4.2
Georgia Total	4,288	8.8	4.1
Combined Total	8,128	7.6	3.8

Source: United States Census of 1860
[a] From appendix 6

Bales of Cotton Produced in 1860
in the Lower Chattahoochee Valley

	Cotton Bales (400 pounds per bale)
Alabama	
Chambers	24,589
Russell	38,728
Barbour	44,518
Henry	13,034
Dale	7,836
Alabama Total	128,705
Georgia	
Troup	17,978
Harris	14,906
Muscogee	6,925
Chattahoochee	7,206
Stewart	25,902
Quitman	4,556
Randolph	11,276
Clay	5,292
Early	9,116
Miller	922
Decatur	7,996
Georgia Total	112,075
Combined Total	240,780

Source: United States Census of 1860

Valuation of Estates in the Lower Chattahoochee Valley

	Real	Personal	Aggregate
Alabama			
Chambers	$3,768,818	$15,371,571	$19,140,389
Russell	4,095,020	15,796,185	19,891,205
Barbour	6,721,335	17,265,747	23,987,082
Henry	2,611,009	6,936,350	9,547,359
Dale	1,509,291	3,111,811	4,621,102
Alabama Total	$18,705,473	$58,481,664	$77,187,137
Georgia			
Troup	$2,927,723	$9,048,702	$11,976,425
Harris	1,889,954	8,041,484	9,931,438
Muscogee	5,392,118	9,926,071	15,318,189
Chattahoochee	1,000,678	2,426,505	3,427,183
Stewart	2,749,893	8,200,321	10,950,214
Quitman	703,032	1,973,529	2,676,561
Randolph	2,007,069	4,492,631	6,499,700
Clay	1,038,855	2,638,932	3,677,787
Early	1,358,885	3,126,625	4,485,510
Miller	481,310	635,278	1,116,588
Decatur	2,697,780	5,469,482	8,167,262
Georgia Total	$22,247,297	$55,979,560	$78,226,857
Combined Total	$40,952,770	$114,461,224	$155,413,994

Source: United States Census of 1860

Manufacturing in the Lower Chattahoochee Valley

	Establishments	Employees	Annual Value
Alabama			
Chambers	19	65	$ 63,775
Russell[a]	—	—	—
Barbour	70	241	266,303
Henry	27	65	96,480
Dale	8	18	17,200
Alabama Total	124	389	$443,758
Georgia			
Troup	30	243	$ 344,950
Harris	45	115	325,460
Muscogee	19	955	1,409,711
Chattahoochee	18	21	68,671
Stewart	9	44	57,150
Quitman	6	26	17,948
Randolph	12	41	42,432
Clay	28	84	116,897
Early[a]	—	—	—
Miller[a]	—	—	—
Decatur	15	135	143,100
Georgia Total	182	1,664	$2,526,319
Combined Total	306	1,053	$2,970,077

Source: United States Census of 1860

[a] No returns available

NOTES

PROLOGUE. Sooner Than All Lincolndom

1. Some historians are trying to correct this traditional imbalance by emphasizing the socioeconomic causes of Confederate defeat. One particularly insightful essay is Armstead Louis Robinson, "In the Shadow of Old John Brown." In barely twenty pages, Robinson skillfully weaves the Confederacy's home-front weaknesses, particularly those dealing with class and caste, into a cogent understanding of their impact on Confederate defeat. Escott also focuses a good deal of attention on class issues and their impact in *After Secession*. For overviews of other recent interpretations, see Osher and Wallenstein, "Why the Confederacy Lost"; Glatthaar, "'New' Civil War History"; Vinovskis, *Toward a Social History of the American Civil War*. Freehling argues effectively for more synthesis historiography incorporating recent class-oriented work in *Reintegration of American History*, esp. chapter 10, "The Divided South, the Causes of Confederate Defeat, and the Reintegration of Narrative History."

2. For an excellent introduction to the history of the American class system and its impact, see Zinn, *People's History of the United States*. See also Williamson and Lindert, *American Inequality*. In chapter 7 of *Lies My Teacher Told Me*, Lowen provides an insightful explanation of why class issues are generally ignored in U.S. history texts. For discussions of current American class issues, see Kevin Phillips, *Politics of Rich and Poor*; Hacker, *Two Nations*; Schwarz and Volgy, *Forgotten Americans*; Sennet and Cobb, *Hidden Injuries of Class*; Kozol, *Savage Inequalities*.

3. William C. Oates, *War between the Union and the Confederacy*, 48–49; Dudley, ed., *Civil War*, 107, 109.

4. For an overview of the violence in New York, see Bernstein, *New York City Draft Riots*.

5. In his seminal study, *Lincoln and His Party in the Secession Crisis*, Potter looked at the vote on secession throughout the South and concluded, "At no time during the winter of 1860–1861 was secession desired by a majority of the people of the slave states. . . . Furthermore, secession was not basically desired even by a majority in the lower South, and the secessionists succeeded less because of the intrinsic popularity of their program than because of the extreme skill with which they utilized an emergency psychology, the promptness with which they invoked unilateral action by individual states, and the firmness with which they refused to submit the question of secession to popular referenda" (208). Potter's conclusions are supported by Escott's more recent study, *After Secession*, 23–28, 42–44.

6. Escott, "Southern Yeomen and the Confederacy," 157; A. P. Aldrich to

James H. Hammond, November 25, 1860, in Kibler, "Unionist Sentiment in South Carolina," 358.

7. Watkins, *"Co. Aytch,"* 69; Current, *Lincoln's Loyalists,* 157, 197.

8. Ambrose, "Yeoman Discontent in the Confederacy," 263.

9. Escott, *After Secession,* 111; John W. Hagan to Amanda Roberts Hagan, July 23, 1863, in Wiley, ed., "Confederate Letters of John W. Hagan," 196.

10. Frederick Burtz to Brown, March 29, 1862, in Formwalt, "Planters and Cotton Production as a Cause of Confederate Defeat," 272–75 (original in Georgia, Governor's Correspondence).

11. *War of the Rebellion: A Compilation of the Official Records of the Union and Confederate Armies* (hereafter cited as *O.R.*), ser. 4, vol. 3, pp. 7, 413–14.

12. Cleveland, *Alexander H. Stephens,* 721; Franklin and Moss, *From Slavery to Freedom,* 188.

13. Ward, *Civil War,* 195. While acknowledging the impact of class issues on southern dissension, acclaimed Civil War historian James M. McPherson of Princeton University, author of the Pulitzer Prize–winning *Battle Cry of Freedom,* dismisses dissent as a cause of Confederate defeat. He points out that disaffection with the new U.S. government during the War for Independence was perhaps greater than southern disaffection with the Confederacy. McPherson is probably correct in this assertion. Historian John Shy estimates in *People Numerous and Armed* that only one-fifth of Americans actively supported the cause of independence. The Confederacy enjoyed the support of a third or more of its people, at least in 1861. Yet the fledgling United States survived internal dissent while the Confederate States did not. McPherson fails to note, however, that America's victory over the British was made possible only by French military intervention. The Confederacy had no such foreign troops to supplement its armies and so was forced to depend on domestic support, which simply was not strong enough to maintain southern independence.

In a similar vein, William C. Davis downplays the "loss of will" factor and its impact on Confederate defeat. Arguing that loss of will followed battlefield reverses rather than causing them, Davis suggests that southern enthusiasm for the war began to ebb significantly only after the Confederacy's "high water mark" of Gettysburg was passed in July 1863. Though losses did have an impact on morale, Davis fails to acknowledge divisions of the secession crisis and their long-term effects, and he entirely ignores widespread dissent during the war's first two years. It seems never to have occurred to Davis to ask himself why the Confederacy found it necessary to institute a military draft in April 1862. Davis further ignores the interrelationship and impact of speculation, inflation, cotton overproduction, and home-front hunger. The South's urban riots of early 1863 have little meaning in Davis's Confederacy. Finally, and perhaps most significantly, he dismisses the role of southern blacks in Confederate defeat. Davis seems to feel that the subtle and overt resistance of up to a third of the South's population, not to mention dissent among white folk, is peripheral at most to the war's outcome.

Like Davis, noted Civil War historian Gary W. Gallagher minimizes the impact of divisions within the South. In his recent book, *The Confederate War*, Gallagher maintains that we need look no further than the battlefield to understand the war's outcome. Southerners where whipped—that's why they lost. One might forgive Gallagher his narrow, circular reasoning since he has rarely glanced beyond the battlefield in his scholarly works. *The Confederate War*, Gallagher's first venture behind the lines to the South's social home front, is itself a commentary on existing literature rather than original research.

While acknowledging southern dissent, both black and white, McPherson points out that there was also dissension in the North, which, he argues, offset the impact of dissent in the South. McPherson ignores that Washington was much better equipped to deal with dissenters than was Richmond. And though absolute figures can never be known, it is clear that dissenters as a percentage of population were much more numerous in the South. Since southern dissent had a greater impact on the war's outcome than northern opposition, the key question to be addressed in examining Confederate defeat is this: What was the source of the southern disaffection? This study explores that question.

For the complete text of McPherson's arguments, see his "American Victory, American Defeat" and chapter 8 of *Drawn with the Sword*, entitled "Why Did the Confederacy Lose?" For Davis's views, see *Cause Lost*.

14. For the purpose of this study, the lower Chattahoochee Valley is defined as the region encompassing all or parts of the modern Alabama counties of Chambers, Lee, Russell, Barbour, Henry, Houston, Dale, and Geneva. In Georgia, the modern counties included are Troup, Harris, Muscogee, Chattahoochee, Stewart, Quitman, Randolph, Clay, Early, Miller, Seminole, Decatur, and Grady.

15. Planters are defined by their ownership of twenty slaves or more. The term *yeoman* here refers to small farmers and herdsmen ranging from those who owned at least three acres of land and no slaves to those who held up to four slaves. Tenants, sharecroppers, and farm laborers, generally referred to (along with unskilled urban workers) as *poor whites,* worked land owned by someone else. The designation *plain folk* or *common folk* when used in this study generally means yeomen and poor whites, although most often it includes small merchants and skilled artisans (*mechanics*) as well.

Some of the most insightful works available on the antebellum South's socio-economic types and their interrelationships are Owsley, *Plain Folk of the Old South;* McWhiney, *Cracker Culture;* Boney, *Southerners All;* Collins, *White Society in the Antebellum South;* Oakes, *Slavery and Freedom.* Two of the best such studies focusing on particular regions of the South are Harris, *Plain Folk and Gentry,* and Bolton, *Poor Whites of the Antebellum South.*

16. For treatments of anti-Confederate sentiment in the northern sections of Alabama and Georgia, see Hugh C. Bailey, "Disaffection in the Alabama Hill Country, 1861," and Sarris, "Anatomy of an Atrocity." A more detailed treatment can be found in Sarris's master's thesis, "Madden Branch Massacre." Yeoman attitudes toward the war in the Georgia upcountry and their postwar impact are examined in Hahn, *Roots of Southern Populism.* Among the best studies devoted to

or touching on the question of prewar and wartime social divisions in the South are Fitzgerald, "Poor Man's Fight"; Bonner, "Profile of a Late Ante-Bellum Community" (Hancock County, Georgia); Tripp, *Yankee Town, Southern City;* Fred Arthur Bailey, *Class and Tennessee's Confederate Generation;* Inscoe, *Mountain Masters, Slavery, and the Sectional Crisis in Western North Carolina;* Noe and Wilson, eds., *Civil War in Appalachia;* Ford, *Origins of Southern Radicalism;* Reidy, *From Slavery to Agrarian Capitalism in the Cotton Plantation South,* McCurry, *Masters of Small Worlds;* Faust, *Mothers of Invention;* Paludan, *Victims;* Durrill, *War of Another Kind;* Bynum, *Unruly Women;* Clinton and Silber, eds., *Divided Houses;* Wetherington, *New South Comes to Wiregrass Georgia;* Whites, *The Civil War as a Crisis in Gender;* Bryant, *How Curious a Land.*

17. U.S. Census, 1860; Willoughby, *Fair to Middlin',* 13, 17.

18. U.S. Census, 1860.

CHAPTER 1. Not One Foot Was Owned by a Poor Man

1. U.S. Census, 1860; Mathis, *John Horry Dent,* 145, 193–95, 196.

2. Mathis, *John Horry Dent,* 202, 211, 212.

3. Willoughby, *Fair to Middlin',* 1; Owens, "Sail and Steam Vessels," 195; Cushman, "Blockade and Fall of Apalachicola," 38.

4. *Mobile (Alabama) Daily Herald and Tribune,* Correspondence, November 20, 1849; Beauchamp, "Early Chronicles of Barbour County."

5. Mahan, *Columbus,* 27–28; Standard, *Columbus, Georgia, in the Confederacy,* 11, 12; Willoughby, *Fair to Middlin',* 17.

6. Ware, "Cotton Money," 218; Mears and Company, comp., *Columbus Directory,* 80, 81, 83; DeCredico, *Patriotism for Profit,* 13; Lane, ed., *Rambler in Georgia,* 117. The "Lowell" designation was a reference to the nation's first major textile manufacturing center in Lowell, Massachusetts. See Standard, *Columbus, Georgia, in the Confederacy,* 11.

7. Lane, ed., *Rambler in Georgia,* 105; Olmsted, *Cotton Kingdom,* 213.

8. Featherstonhaugh, *Excursion through the Slave States,* 153; Lane, ed., *Rambler in Georgia,* 105.

9. Lane, ed., *Rambler in Georgia,* 106; *Mobile (Alabama) Daily Herald and Tribune,* Correspondence, November 20, 1849.

10. Thurston, "Apalachicola–Chattahoochee–Flint River Water Route," 201–3.

11. Owens, "Sail and Steam Vessels," 204, 205.

12. John H. Martin, ed., *Columbus,* 2:120; Goff, "Steamboat Period in Georgia," 247; Owens, "Sail and Steam Vessels," 208, 209.

13. Thurston, "Apalachicola–Chattahoochee–Flint River Water Route," 203–4; Coleman, ed., *History of Georgia,* 154.

14. Smith, *History of Troup County,* 108–9; Standard, *Columbus, Georgia, in the Confederacy,* 15–16.

15. Willoughby, *Fair to Middlin'*, 19; John H. Martin, ed., *Columbus*, 2:122. Even the economic panic of 1857, unlike those of 1819 and 1837, had little impact on cotton prices (Cooper and Terrill, *American South*, 1:192).

16. Willoughby, *Fair to Middlin'*, 25, 14.

17. Ibid., 13.

18. For a general study of the antebellum South's pattern of wealth distribution, see Wright, "'Economic Democracy.'"

19. U.S. Census, 1860.

20. Sellers, *Slavery in Alabama*, 30; U.S. Census, 1860.

21. Turner, *Navy Gray*, 14, 15.

22. For a more complete treatment of the planter lifestyle and self-image, see Boney's chapter, "The Aristocrats," in *Southerners All.* One of the most valuable studies of the mythology and reality surrounding the planter image is Taylor's *Cavalier and Yankee.*

23. U.S. Census, 1860.

24. Ibid.

25. Herding was more common in the lower parts of the valley because the soil was less suited to cotton production. Dale and Miller Counties did not approach the cotton output of counties further north until the use of commercial fertilizers became common in the late nineteenth century. Nevertheless, livestock production remained strong in the Wiregrass region. As late as 1979, Miller County had a greater percentage of its land devoted to pasture than any other county in south Georgia (Hodler and Schretter, *Atlas of Georgia*, 91).

26. Olmsted, *Cotton Kingdom*, 213; *Columbus (Georgia) Enquirer*, January 6, 1852.

27. For an in-depth study of farm tenancy patterns in antebellum Georgia, see Bode and Ginter, *Farm Tenancy and the Census in Antebellum Georgia.*

28. Ware, "Cotton Money," 220; Willoughby, *Fair to Middlin'*, 54, 73. In his recent study, *Poor Whites of the Antebellum South*, Bolton argues that although many poor whites immigrated west in search of cheap land, few found any significant degree of upward mobility. Bynum, in her review of Bolton's work, comments that "most poor whites' geographic mobility grew out of class immobility rather than frontier opportunities. . . . Many moved time and again in search of elusive prosperity."

29. Bartley, *Creation of Modern Georgia*, 21. The late antebellum years saw a long-term and accelerating decline in the proportion of slaveholders in the free population, from 36 percent in 1830 to 31 percent in 1850 and finally to 25 percent by 1860 (Wright, *Political Economy of the Cotton South*, 34).

30. *Blakely (Georgia) Early County News*, December 21, 1916; Wright, "'Economic Democracy,'" 30, 84; Barney, *Secessionist Impulse*, 4, 39; Foust, *Yeoman Farmer*, 198.

31. *Columbus (Georgia) Daily Sun*, April 4, 1863.

32. Meriwether, *Slavery in Auburn*, 8–9; Rawick, ed., *American Slave*, ser. 2, vol. 13, pt. 3, p. 1.

33. Stampp, *Peculiar Institution*, 144; Ward, *Civil War*, 9.

34. *Cuthbert (Georgia) Reporter*, September 23, 1856; Sellers, *Slavery in Alabama*, 248.

35. Mueller, *Perilous Journeys*, 28; Lane, ed., *Rambler in Georgia*, 116; Sellers, *Slavery in Alabama*, 246–47, 248. There is some disagreement on the particulars of the *Van Buren* incident. The *Pensacola Gazette* reported that the fire was started by a runaway slave who was being returned to his master. The *Charleston Courier* said that only one person was drowned (Mueller, *Perilous Journeys*, 28, A-2 nn. 55–57).

36. *Reports of Cases in Law and Equity*, 15:542; Lane, ed., *Rambler in Georgia*, 91; Rawick, ed., *American Slave*, ser. 2, vol. 12, pt. 1, pp. 14–15. The most comprehensive overview of the slaves' legal status is Morris, *Southern Slavery and the Law*. For a compilation of the most significant cases dealing with this issue, see Finkelman, *Slavery in the Courtroom*.

37. B. C. Lee to mother, November 11, 1859, in Lee Collection.

38. Rawick, ed., *American Slave*, supplement, ser. 1, vol. 3, pt. 1, pp. 6–7, 71.

39. Ibid., ser. 2, vol. 13, pt. 4, p. 124; supplement, ser. 1, vol. 3, pt. 1, pp. 6–7.

40. Coleman, ed., *History of Georgia*, 182; Oakes, *Slavery and Freedom*, 69.

41. Greene and Lumpkin, *Georgia Justice*, 405; Walker, *Backtracking in Barbour County*, 178.

42. *Blakely (Georgia) Early County News*, December 21, 1916. The term *Buckra* refers to whites.

43. Walker, *Backtracking in Barbour County*, 178–79; Coleman, ed., *History of Georgia*, 182; Rawick, ed., *American Slave*, supplement, ser. 1, 1:255, 6:243, 1:87.

44. Rawick, ed., *American Slave*, ser. 2, vol. 12, pt. 1, p. 26; ser. 2, vol. 13, pt. 3, pp. 16, 187; supplement, ser. 1, vol. 4, pt. 2, p. 4.

45. *Columbus (Georgia) Enquirer*, February 9, 1833; Rawick, ed., *American Slave*, ser. 2, vol. 13, pt. 4, p. 135.

46. Chesnut, *Mary Chesnut's Civil War*, 29, 169; Walker, *Backtracking in Barbour County*, 185.

47. Lane, ed., *Rambler in Georgia*, 163.

48. Rawick, ed., *American Slave*, ser. 2, vol. 13, pt. 3, p. 1. For a record of slave prices in Columbus from 1858 through 1860, see Hatcher and McGehee Account Book. The firm of Hatcher and McGehee was one of three slave-trading companies that operated in Columbus during the late 1850s. For a partial transcription, see McGinnis, "Hatcher and McGehee Negro Book."

49. Stampp, *Peculiar Institution*, 21–22; Morgan, *American Slavery, American Freedom*, 327.

50. Morgan, *American Slavery, American Freedom*, 250–70, 327. See also Washburn, *Governor and the Rebel*.

51. Morgan, *American Slavery, American Freedom*, 269–70.

52. Ibid., 334–35, 344; Zinn, *People's History of the United States*, 57.

53. Jefferson borrowed the phrase from British political philosopher John Locke, who originally penned it as "life, liberty, and property" (*Second Treatise of Government*, 70–71). But because the Declaration of Independence was designed to incite rebellion among the masses, who held little or no land, Jefferson replaced Locke's "property" with "pursuit of happiness."

54. An excellent treatment of changing attitudes toward slavery in the South can be found in Freeman, "Slavery as a Positive Good."

55. Walter L. Fleming, *Civil War and Reconstruction in Alabama,* 10. See also Lamb, "James G. Birney and the Road to Abolitionism."

56. The best overview of the removal of Native Americans from the South remains Foreman, *Indian Removal.* For a treatment of gold's impact on Cherokee removal, see David Williams, *Georgia Gold Rush.*

57. Cleveland, *Alexander H. Stephens,* 721; Stampp, *Peculiar Institution,* 21.

58. Freehling and Simpson, eds., *Secession Debated,* 93; Sellers, *Slavery in Alabama,* 346–47; Cleveland, *Alexander H. Stephens,* 721; Gould, *Mismeasure of Man,* 45. Though a stalwart creationist, Agassiz (along with a number of other prominent scientists of his day), in a break with orthodox Christianity, supported the notion of polygenesis—the separate creation of the races. See chapter 9, "The Unity of Man," in Hovenkamp, *Science and Religion in America.* For a further discussion of antebellum science and race, see Stanton, *Leopard's Spots.*

59. Gould, *Mismeasure of Man,* 70–71. See also Cartwright, "Diseases and Peculiarities of the Negro Race."

60. Cruden, *Many and One,* 204.

61. Hovenkamp, *Science and Religion in America,* 171; Escott and Goldfield, eds., *Major Problems in the History of the American South,* 1:430.

62. Antebellum attempts to reconcile scientific evidence with religious belief among scientists, clergy, and the laity are reviewed in Hovenkamp, *Science and Religion in America.*

63. The question of slavery's morality came to a head among the major denominations when the southern wing of the Presbyterian Church split along sectional lines in 1837–38, followed by the Baptists and Methodists in 1845. For an overview of the controversy, see Snay, *Gospel of Disunion.*

64. *Cuthbert (Georgia) Reporter,* October 28, 1856.

65. Harris, *Plain Folk and Gentry,* 75; *Cuthbert (Georgia) Reporter,* October 7, 1856.

66. Sellers, *Slavery in Alabama,* 346.

67. The most thorough study of antebellum challenges to academic freedom in the South is Eaton, *Freedom-of-Thought Struggle in the Old South.* In his more recent works, Genovese maintains that the South's intelligentsia remained as vibrant as ever but laments that its talents were diverted to the defense of slavery (see his *Southern Front* and *Southern Tradition*).

68. Eaton, *Mind of the Old South,* 238.

69. Freehling and Simpson, eds., *Secession Debated,* 93.

70. For the role of yeomen in antebellum southern politics, see Harry L. Watson, "Conflict and Collaboration"; Genovese, "Yeomen Farmers in a Slaveholders' Democracy"; Thornton, *Politics and Power in a Slave Society;* Bolton, *Poor Whites of the Antebellum South.*

71. Oakes, *Slavery and Freedom,* 80; Standard, *Columbus, Georgia, in the Confederacy,* 20–21; DeBats, *Elites and Masses,* 425; Wallenstein, "Rich Man's War, Rich Man's Fight," 20. In his recent study of poor whites in central North Carolina and northeast Mississippi, *Poor Whites of the Antebellum South,* Bolton draws similar conclusions about the political powerlessness of common folk.

72. Helper, *Impending Crisis,* 42; Oakes, *Slavery and Freedom,* 76.

73. In 1837, Allen signed a pass for an escaping slave named Anthony who was captured near Paris, Kentucky, just short of the Ohio River (George Northcut to postmaster at LaGrange, August 26, 1837, in Slavery in Troup County Folder). For an overview of antislavery sentiment in a single southern state, see Scarborough, *Opposition to Slavery in Georgia.*

74. Helper, *Impending Crisis,* ix, 43.

75. Ibid., 22, 32. For a thorough examination of cotton agriculture's restraint of economic progress, see Dill, "Institutional Possibilities and Limitations of Economic Progress in Antebellum Georgia." Bolton makes much the same point in *Poor Whites of the Antebellum South.*

76. Goodman, "White over White," 451–52.

77. Stirling, *Letters from the Slave States,* 204.

78. Range, *Century of Georgia Agriculture,* 28; Barney, *Secessionist Impulse,* 159; *Eufaula (Alabama) Express,* September 1, 1860; Joseph Paul Johnson, "Southwest Georgia," 57. For an overview of problems with food production in Georgia in the 1850s, see Crawford, "Cotton, Land, and Sustenance."

79. Helper, *Impending Crisis,* 39, 27, 155. For a modern study of the South's antebellum importation of grain, see Lindstrom, "Southern Dependence upon Interregional Grain Supplies."

80. Barney, *Secessionist Impulse,* 42; Harris, *Plain Folk and Gentry,* 40; Walker, *Backtracking in Barbour County,* 177; *Eufaula (Alabama) Express,* December 16, 1858. The foreign slave trade had been closed in 1808 with the backing of slaveholders, who saw it as a opportunity to artificially inflate the value of their slaves.

CHAPTER 2. I Don't Want Any War

1. Wood, *Slavery in Colonial Georgia,* 205–6; Coleman, ed., *History of Georgia,* 54.

2. Ironically, in later life, Jefferson often betrayed the ideals of civil liberty expressed in his youth and lent at least tacit support to slavery's expansion (Finkelman, "Treason against the Hopes of the World"; Levy, *Jefferson and Civil Liberties*).

3. Grant, *Way It Was in the South,* 77.

4. *Eufaula (Alabama) Spirit of the South,* October 15 and November 19, 1850; Schott, *Alexander H. Stephens,* 127.

5. *Eufaula (Alabama) Spirit of the South,* November 5 and October 15, 1850; Griffith, ed., *Alabama,* 368–70. Mayer, "'Leaven of Disunion,'" 106 n. 71, points out that "the younger men—John Gill Shorter, Eli Shorter, James L. Pugh, E. C. Bullock—all practiced law in Eufaula, had numerous kinship ties, and were generally natives of Georgia."

6. Schott, *Alexander H. Stephens,* 127.

7. *Eufaula (Alabama) Spirit of the South,* November 12, 1850; Griffith, ed., *Alabama,* 370–71; *Columbus (Georgia) Enquirer,* February 5, 1850; Samuel W. Flournoy to Howell Cobb, July 18, 1851, in Ulrich B. Phillips, ed., *Correspondence,* 246.

8. Walter L. Fleming, *Civil War and Reconstruction in Alabama,* 16; Grant, *Way It Was in the South,* 78; Mayer, "'Leaven of Disunion,'" 114.

9. Walker, *Backtracking in Barbour County,* 169–70; Mathis, *John Horry Dent,* 193. For an overview, see Walter L. Fleming, "Buford Expedition to Kansas." For a firsthand account of the expedition, see Clayton, *White and Black under the Old Regime,* 62–81.

10. Mathis, *John Horry Dent,* 193. For an overview of the Kansas issue and its national implications, see Gates, *Fifty Million Acres;* Rawley, *Race and Politics.* Kansas was not admitted to the Union until 1861, after most of the slave states had seceded.

11. *Columbus (Georgia) Enquirer,* June 3, 1856.

12. The Republican Party, formed in the wake of Kansas-Nebraska, adopted this position as its primary platform.

13. Proctor, "Slavery in Southwest Georgia," 9; *Albany (Georgia) Patriot,* December 25, 1856. Nat Turner was a black preacher who led an 1831 slave rebellion in Southampton County, Virginia, in which approximately sixty whites were killed (Stephen B. Oates, *Fires of Jubilee,* 126).

14. *Eufaula (Alabama) Express,* November 25, 1858, and October 27, 1859; *Opelika (Alabama) Southern Era,* November 29, 1859.

15. *Columbus (Georgia) Daily Sun,* October 19 and 21, 1859; Hague, *Blockaded Family,* 5.

16. *Blakely (Georgia) Early County News,* December 21, 1916; *Opelika (Alabama) Southern Era,* December 6, 1859, and September 15, 1860; *Columbus (Georgia) Daily Sun,* November 5, 15, and 16, 1859.

17. *Opelika (Alabama) Southern Era,* December 6, 1860.

18. *Columbus (Georgia) Daily Sun,* November 17, 1859; *Opelika (Alabama) Southern Era,* January 3 and 17, 1860.

19. Grant, *Way It Was in the South,* 79; Sellers, *Slavery in Alabama,* 378; *Columbus (Georgia) Daily Sun,* December 7, 1859; U.S. Census, 1860.

20. Mohr, *On the Threshold of Freedom,* 14–15; Walker, *Backtracking in Barbour County,* 179; Sellers, *Slavery in Alabama,* 378–79.

21. In the 1857 case of *Dred Scott v. Sanford,* the U.S. Supreme Court ruled

that the Fifth Amendment, which stated in part that "No person shall . . . be deprived of life, liberty, or property without due process of law," protected slavery not only in the territories but also, by implication, everywhere in the United States. The court had indirectly declared that free states were not, in fact, free at all. In a legal sense, every state was a slave state.

22. *Cuthbert (Georgia) Reporter,* March 23, 1860, argued that southerners should break with the Union on that basis alone: "In a Southern Confederacy, slave holders could have expansion. Soon all Mexico would be ours, and Cuba, the Queen of the Antilles; yes, and Central America, and some of the South American States. Then there would be a chance for us to get the Indian Territory [present state of Oklahoma], Utah [Colorado, Utah, and Nevada], and New Mexico [New Mexico and Arizona]."

23. Norton to cousin Mastin C. Phillips, October 29, 1860, in Phillips Letters; *Columbus (Georgia) Daily Sun,* November 5, 1860; Walker, *Backtracking in Barbour County,* 172; *Columbus (Georgia) Times,* November 5, 1860. Unlike his friend, Alexander Stephens, with whom he had stood for the Union in 1850, Toombs steadily moved away from unionism to become one of Georgia's leading secessionists by 1860.

24. *Columbus (Georgia) Daily Sun,* December 17, 1860. The evidence for active Republican support among whites is very slim. Terrill and Dixon, *History of Stewart County,* 243, hint at the possibility. On October 7, 1856, the *Cuthbert (Georgia) Reporter* indicated that there were a few Republicans in Randolph County that year. There may still have been some in 1860.

25. Rawick, ed., *American Slave,* supplement, ser. 1, 1:255; *Columbus (Georgia) Daily Sun,* September 27, 1860; Walker, *Backtracking in Barbour County,* 173.

26. *Columbus (Georgia) Enquirer,* November 13, 1860.

27. See Ulrich B. Phillips, *Georgia and State Rights;* Barney, *Secessionist Impulse; Columbus (Georgia) Enquirer,* November 13, 1860.

28. Hubert Dent to wife Anna Beall Dent, November 8, 1860, in Dent Confederate Collection; Walker, *Backtracking in Barbour County,* 173; Long, "Unanimity and Disloyalty in Secessionist Alabama," 263; McClendon, *Recollections of War Times,* 7–9. Hubert Dent may have been distantly related to John Horry Dent, but if so, the family connection dated to at least the seventeenth century (Mathis, *John Horry Dent,* 231 n. 3).

29. Bryan, "Churches in Georgia," 284; Walter L. Fleming, *Churches of Alabama,* 4, 5.

30. Sterkx, *Partners in Rebellion,* 28.

31. Hague, *Blockaded Family,* 3–4; Barney, *Secessionist Impulse,* 257 n. 39. Parthenia Hague was governess and tutor on the Edward Garland plantation, located twelve miles north of Eufaula.

32. John H. Martin, ed., *Columbus,* 2:120; Standard, *Columbus, Georgia, in the Confederacy,* 21.

33. Henry L. Benning to Howell Cobb, July 1, 1849, in Ulrich B. Phillips, ed., *Correspondence,* 171; Henry Benning's secession speech, November 19, 1861, in Freehling and Simpson, eds., *Secession Debated,* 115–44. The best overview of Benning's role in the secession crisis is Cobb, "Making of a Secessionist."

34. Evans to Mrs. G. V. French, January 13, 1861, and Evans to Henry L. Benning, January 13, 1861, in Seborn Jones and Henry L. Benning Papers. Born in Columbus in 1835, Augusta Jane Evans became one of the most popular authors of the Civil War era. Taken together, her novels *Beulah* (1859) and *Macaria; or, Altars of Sacrifice* (1864), both of which were reissued by the Louisiana State University Press in 1992, illustrate many of the changes southern white women of the upper classes underwent during the war years. *Beulah* encouraged southern women to remain resolute in the face of opposition, while *Macaria* challenged those who practiced self-indulgence during the war. For a fuller discussion, see Carol T. Williams, "'Power of a True Woman's Heart.'"

35. Adams, "Martin Jenkins Crawford," 229–30; Barney, *Road to Secession,* 197–98; *Albany (Georgia) Patriot,* October 11, 1861; Randall and Donald, *Civil War and Reconstruction,* 166 n. 2. Crawford's reference to the Helper book deals with a circular advertising an abridged edition that was endorsed by sixty-eight Republican congressmen. See McPherson, *Battle Cry of Freedom,* 200.

36. Walker, *Backtracking in Barbour County,* 165; Griffith, ed., *Alabama,* 377–78.

37. Shorter to daughter, December 9, 1860, in Shorter Collection; Sarah Holcombe Bacon to Milton Bacon, January 29, 1861, in Bacon Family Letters.

38. John H. Martin, ed., *Columbus,* 2:120; Mathis, *John Horry Dent,* 196; Bryan, *Confederate Georgia,* 2; Robert M. Howard, *Reminiscences,* 11.

39. Barfield, *History of Harris County,* 292; "Co-Operation Meeting of the Citizens of Stewart County," Stewart County Archives Folder. None of Stewart's "Co-Operation" men won a seat at the secession convention.

40. Standard, *Columbus, Georgia, in the Confederacy,* 21–22; Barney, *Secessionist Impulse,* 285.

41. A. Hood to Howell Cobb, December 19, 1860, in Ulrich B. Phillips, ed., *Correspondence,* 524; Frank S. Jones, *History of Decatur County,* 364–65.

42. Freehling and Simpson, eds., *Secession Debated,* 97, 99.

43. DeBats, *Elites and Masses,* 260.

44. Ibid.; Oakes, *Slavery and Freedom,* 80.

45. Harris, *Plain Folk and Gentry,* 67; Fitzhugh, *Sociology for the South,* 162–63, 225.

46. Barney, *Road to Secession,* 38; Harris, *Plain Folk and Gentry,* 64, 91.

47. *Charleston (South Carolina) Mercury,* October 11, 1860, in the *Atlanta Daily Intelligencer,* October 15, 1860; Barney, *Secessionist Impulse,* 48–49; Levine, *Half Slave and Half Free,* 235.

48. Rawick, ed., *American Slave,* supplement, ser. 1, 1:255.

49. Carey, *Parties, Slavery, and the Union in Antebellum Georgia,* generally

takes exception to this view: "To argue that Georgia seceded primarily because immediate secessionists feared other white Georgians seems to me a drastic overstatement contradicted by far more voluminous evidence" (323 n. 60). That evidence consists mainly of public pronouncements that Carey appears far too willing to take at face value. He too readily discounts less abundant though more revealing and meaningful evidence from private communications exchanged by leading secessionists. The latter speak clearly of fears related to internal dissent generally and threats to slavery in particular. It may be argued with some justification, as Carey does, that those fears were largely unfounded, but they were nonetheless very real and, I believe, had a profound influence on the secession movement.

Carey's comments were made in response to Michael P. Johnson, who most fully explored this issue in his *Toward a Patriarchal Republic*. Johnson argues that most Georgia slaveholders, like those in other Deep South states, saw secession mainly as an opportunity to revise the state constitution in such a way that popular influence would be minimized and Georgia would become more of a "patriarchal republic" than it already was. Viewed in this light, the entire Confederate experience can be seen as essentially an antidemocratic revolution. Many southern plain folk of the period certainly saw it that way, as the widespread "rich man's war" attitude makes clear.

50. Freehling and Simpson, eds., *Secession Debated*, 82. As early as June 1859, a group of citizens organized an opposition party in Hill's home county of Troup, urging southerners to avoid "continued agitation of the slavery question." In pressing for the expansion of slavery, they believed, slaveholders did little more than place the institution in danger where it already existed (*LaFayette (Alabama) Chambers Tribune*, June 10, 1859). For a general discussion of apprehension over disunion among old-money planters, see Alexander and Duckworth, "Alabama Black Belt Whigs during Secession."

51. *Thomaston (Georgia) Upson Pilot*, December 22, 1860.

52. Henry L. Benning to Howell Cobb, July 1, 1849, in Ulrich B. Phillips, ed., *Correspondence*, 171; Milton S. Latham to William S. Shotwell, July 28, 1846, in Latham, "Latham Letter," 145–47. Latham later moved to California, where he found more fertile political fields. He was elected to the U.S. Congress in 1853, to the governorship in 1860, and eventually to the U.S. Senate.

The role of ambitious young slaveholding politicians in the secession crisis is thoroughly reviewed in Rachleff, "Racial Fear and Political Factionalism." Rachleff notes that "many of these firebrands were from east-central Alabama where they found their socioeconomic mobility blocked by the monopolizing tendencies of the [large] planters. By the 1850s the large plantation owners controlled the best cotton lands, and the ultras turned to politics as the best means of enhancing their careers. . . . The ultras politicized racial fears by equating a Republican victory in 1860 with slave rebellions and racial amalgamation [i.e., interracial marriage]. . . . After Lincoln's triumph, Alabama's ultras struck for separate state secession, hoping for political advancement in a southern Confederacy. Thus, chronic racial anxieties were exploited by politicians who provoked Alabama into secession" (v–vi). For further discussion of divisions among planters over secession, see Roark, *Masters without Slaves.*

53. Walter L. Fleming, *Civil War and Reconstruction in Alabama,* 19.

54. Flynt, *Poor but Proud,* 38; Denman, *Secession Movement in Alabama,* 161–65; Michael P. Johnson, *Toward a Patriarchal Republic,* 63; Michael P. Johnson, "New Look," 267–70. The margin against secession in Alabama was probably slightly higher than the figure given since no returns were available from one traditionally unionist county.

Those who ran in opposition to secession usually adopted the label "cooperationist" to indicate their feeling that any southern response to Lincoln's election should be made in cooperation with the slave states as a whole. Beyond that, however, their position was uncertain. More likely, their rhetoric represented an attempt to thwart secession by garnering the undecided vote. For a discussion of the "confused and ambiguous" nature of the cooperationist position see Michael P. Johnson, *Toward a Patriarchal Republic,* 26.

55. Calculation of voter turnout in the valley is based on information from Denman, *Secession Movement in Alabama,* 162; Michael P. Johnson, "New Look," 268–70; and the U.S. Census, 1860. Alexander Stephens estimated that the stormy weather cost the antisecessionists ten thousand votes in Georgia (Michael P. Johnson, *Toward a Patriarchal Republic,* 5–6, 9, 73).

Nowhere was the disparity of secession sentiment between rural and urban areas more apparent than in Columbus and Muscogee County. One antisecessionist noted that "we are gaining ground and outside of the City we can get along well enough." He lamented, however, "we have a hard time in the City" (*Columbus (Georgia) Times,* November 30, 1860).

In their statistical study of the secession vote in the Deep South, McCrary, Miller, and Baum, "Class and Party in the Secession Crisis," 430, 455, confirm both Lipset's and Wooster's earlier findings of a fair degree of regionwide polarization between those who owned slaves and those who did not (see "The Emergence of the One-Party South: The Election of 1860," in Lipset, *Political Man,* 344–54; Wooster, *Secession Conventions of the South*).

56. *Thomaston (Georgia) Upson Pilot,* December 22, 1860.

57. Barney, *Secessionist Impulse,* 302.

58. *Journal of the Public and Secret Proceedings of the Convention of the People of Georgia,* 19–20, 31–39. Of Georgia's forty-one cooperationist delegates who voted for secession, thirty-four (83 percent) were from high slaveholding counties. Almost all of the delegates who stood firm against secession were from the low slaveholding counties of north Georgia and the pine barrens of south Georgia (Michael P. Johnson, *Toward a Patriarchal Republic,* 121).

59. The gap between the delegates and common folk in terms of wealth was just as telling. While the median wealth of the delegates was $24,000, the median

for white Georgians as a whole was less than one thousand dollars (Freehling and Simpson, eds., *Secession Debated*, x; Grant, *Way It Was in the South*, 81; Michael P. Johnson, *Toward a Patriarchal Republic*, 113).

60. *Milledgeville (Georgia) Southern Recorder* in *Thomasville (Georgia) Southern Enterprise*, January 30, 1861; Denman, *Secessionist Movement in Alabama*, 145; Bryan, *Confederate Georgia*, 9.

61. Blanchard Diary; Rhodes Diary.

62. Bryan, *Confederate Georgia*, 11; Hague, *Blockaded Family*, 4; Mathis, *John Horry Dent*, 195.

63. Hubert Dent to Anna Beall Dent, February 14, 1861, in Mathis, ed., *In the Land of the Living*, 2; Rhodes Diary; Dent to granddaughter Minna Wellborn, February 25, 1861, in Wellborn Memorial Collection.

64. Escott, *After Secession*, 39; Dent to Anna Dent, December 5, 1860, in Dent Confederate Collection.

65. Stampp, ed., *Causes of the Civil War*, 68.

66. *Rochester (New York) Union*, quoted in the *Opelika (Alabama) Southern Republic*, January 19, 1861.

67. Mathis, *John Horry Dent*, 198–99; Dennis McQueen Wade Sr., "Some Local History," *Blakely (Georgia) Reporter*, March 22, 1900, in Whitehead, ed., *Collections*, 1:134.

68. Northern, ed., *Men of Mark in Georgia*, 3:57; Chapman, *Georgia Soldier*, 6.

69. Bryan, *Confederate Georgia*, 22; Riley, "Desertion and Disloyalty," 7; Black, "Railroads of Georgia," 517–18; Forrest Clark Johnson III, *Histories of LaGrange and Troup County*, 1:67–68.

70. Standard, *Columbus, Georgia, in the Confederacy*, 24; anonymous letter to Brown, February 19, 1862, in Georgia, Governor's Correspondence; Terrill and Dixon, *History of Stewart County*, 244; Warren, *Henry*, 97; Todd, ed., *History of Clay County*, 10, 174; Shepard, *Quitman Echo*, 18; William Glenn Nunn and Jesse Boring Page, "History of Loachapoka," 17.

71. Brenan to Brown, August 29, 1861, and Flournoy to Brown, November 11, 1861, in Georgia, Governor's Correspondence.

72. Rifles to Brown, March 28, 1861, in Georgia, Governor's Correspondence.

73. Warren, *Henry*, 99–100.

74. Coleman to Brown, September 13, 1861, in Georgia, Governor's Correspondence.

75. *Columbus (Georgia) Enquirer* in *Macon (Georgia) Daily Telegraph*, January 29, 1861; *Clayton (Alabama) Banner*, April 18, 1861; Cleveland, *Alexander H. Stephens*, 721; Mohr, *On the Threshold of Freedom*, 66. It seems improbable that Seals was the sole author of the letter published in the *Clayton (Alabama) Banner*, if he wrote it at all. The writer clearly was well practiced in the rhetoric of racism, the defense of slavery, and the justifications for secession.

76. Barfield, *History of Harris County*, 292; B. H. Cody to Rev. Edmund

Cody, April 18, 1861, in Burnett, ed., "Letters of Barnett Hardeman Cody," 282; Houghton and Houghton, *Two Boys*, 18.

77. *Columbus (Georgia) Daily Sun*, May 27, 1861.

78. Mahan, *Columbus*, 56; *Chattahoochee Trace Historical Markers*, 87; Rhodes Diary. The "Ladies' Defender" was captured at Shiloh on April 6, 1862, but was returned to Columbus by an act of Congress in 1904. It is now on display at the Columbus Government Center.

79. Standard, *Columbus, Georgia, in the Confederacy*, 37; Sterkx, *Partners in Rebellion*, 96; Ladies Relief Society Minutes.

80. Sterkx, *Partners in Rebellion*, 97; Bryan, *Confederate Georgia*, 177, 266 n. 15.

81. Bryan, "Churches in Georgia," 284–85, 287; Walter L. Fleming, *Churches of Alabama*, 3; Key to Brown, March 23, 1862, and Charles Bedell to Brown, June 19, 1861, in Georgia, Governor's Correspondence.

82. *Opelika (Alabama) Southern Republic*, May 18 and June 1, 1861.

83. Gorham Diary.

84. Michael P. Johnson, *Toward a Patriarchal Republic*, 63–64; Freehling and Simpson, eds., *Secession Debated*, xv.

85. *Thomaston (Georgia) Upson Pilot*, December 8, 1860; Rhodes Diary; Mathis, *John Horry Dent*, 201; McClendon, *Recollections of War Times*, 11–12.

86. *Macon (Georgia) Daily Telegraph*, April 23, 1861; S. S. Curry to Matilda Ward Curry, June 22, 1861, in Warren, *Henry*, 98; Botkin, ed., *Lay My Burden Down*, 193, 280.

87. McGee, *Claybank Memories*, 42; Lokey, *My Experiences*, 2.

88. *Eufaula (Alabama) Spirit of the South*, July 30, 1861; Mathis, *John Horry Dent*, 201; *Opelika (Alabama) Southern Republic*, May 18 and 25, 1861; Crawford to Brown, July 31, 1861, in Georgia, Governor's Correspondence; *Albany (Georgia) Patriot*, August 15, 1861. For an overview of how short lived was enthusiasm for war among Civil War soldiers, North and South, and how quickly disillusion set in, see Linderman, *Embattled Courage*.

89. Escott, *After Secession*, 115; Crist and Dix, eds., *Papers of Jefferson Davis*, 7: 361.

90. Escott, *After Secession*, 95.

91. Ibid., 115–16. Governor John Gill Shorter of Alabama received similar warnings (Milo B. Howard Jr., ed., "Governor John Gill Shorter Executive Papers").

CHAPTER 3. For the Benefit of the Aristocrats

1. Allen to Brown, April 7, 1862, and Potter to Brown, June 30, 1861, in Georgia, Governor's Correspondence.

2. Potter to Brown, June 30, 1861, and Zeigler to Brown, November 19, 1862, in Georgia, Governor's Correspondence.

3. Cushman, "Blockade and Fall of Apalachicola," 39, 41–42; Mueller, *Perilous Journeys,* 104–6.

4. Mueller, *Perilous Journeys,* 108; Ware, "Enchantment and Ennui," 416–17; Bryan, *Confederate Georgia,* 72.

5. Todd, ed., *History of Clay County,* 10–11; Mueller, *Perilous Journeys,* 108, 115. The Narrows was a particularly constricted section of the Apalachicola River located about halfway between the Georgia line and the Gulf of Mexico. One of the Fort Gaines cannons is still on display at the small earthen fort.

6. Mueller, *Perilous Journeys,* 108; Ware, "Enchantment and Ennui," 409.

7. Mueller, *Perilous Journeys,* 105.

8. Ibid., 106; *Columbus (Georgia) Daily Sun,* March 4, 1862.

9. *Official Records of the Union and Confederate Navies* (hereafter cited as O.R.N.), ser. 2, 2:208–9; Ware, "Enchantment and Ennui," 415; Whitehead, ed., *Collections,* 2:141.

10. Turner, *Navy Gray,* 128; Ware, "Enchantment and Ennui," 428; Gift to Ellen Shackleford, May 25, 1863, in Castlen, *Hope Bids Me Onward,* 125–26.

11. Daniel and Gunter, *Confederate Cannon Foundries,* 34; Still, *Confederate Shipbuilding,* 38–39.

12. Standard, *Columbus, Georgia, in the Confederacy,* 36–38; DeCredico, *Patriotism for Profit,* 58.

13. Mueller, *Perilous Journeys,* 115; DeCredico, *Patriotism for Profit,* 33; Standard, *Columbus, Georgia, in the Confederacy,* 41.

14. Standard, *Columbus, Georgia, in the Confederacy,* 40; DeCredico, *Patriotism for Profit,* 33, 34.

15. L. Haiman and Brother to Brown, December 3, 1860, in Georgia, Governor's Correspondence; DeCredico, *Patriotism for Profit,* 33–34; Standard, *Columbus, Georgia, in the Confederacy,* 39.

16. DeCredico, *Patriotism for Profit,* 50; Standard, *Columbus, Georgia, in the Confederacy,* 30–31, 32.

17. Bryan, *Confederate Georgia,* 104; DeCredico, *Patriotism for Profit,* 49, 61; Standard, *Columbus, Georgia, in the Confederacy,* 33–34.

18. Standard, *Columbus, Georgia, in the Confederacy,* 29–30.

19. Turner, *Navy Gray,* 10, 144.

20. Smith, *History of Troup County,* 115; Forrest Clark Johnson III, *Histories of LaGrange and Troup County,* 1:69; Turner, *Navy Gray,* 144; *Chattahoochee Trace Historic Markers,* 68; Frank S. Jones, *History of Decatur County,* 325.

21. Fred S. Watson, *Forgotten Trails,* 57; Mary Love Edwards Fleming, "Dale County and Its People," 79; Hendry to Brown, January 7, 1862, and Jackson to Brown, February 17, 1862, in Georgia, Governor's Correspondence.

22. Turner, *Navy Gray,* 133, 145.

23. Black, "Railroads of Georgia," 511, 514–15; Bryan, *Confederate Georgia,* 110; Bowie, *Time of Adversity,* 7–9.

24. Cumming, *Journal,* 210–11; Turner, *Navy Gray,* 146.

25. Massey, *Ersatz in the Confederacy,* 126–27; Black, "Railroads of Georgia," 516–17; Hubert Dent to Anna Beall Dent, December 11, 1862, in Mathis, ed., *In the Land of the Living,* 41.

26. Massey, *Ersatz in the Confederacy,* 127.

27. Bowie, *Time of Adversity,* 9–10.

28. Black, "Railroads of Georgia," 515–16, 520, 522; Bryan, *Confederate Georgia,* 115.

29. *Columbus (Georgia) Times,* September 13, 1861; Turner, *Navy Gray,* 147.

30. Standard, *Columbus, Georgia, in the Confederacy,* 38, 55; Mohr, *On the Threshold of Freedom,* 130, 150; French and French, "Horace King Story," 39. The surgeon in charge at Reid Hospital in West Point seems to suggest that black attendants often worked better than their white counterparts (J. W. Oslin to S. H. Stout, April 13, 1864, in Heard Collection).

31. Mohr, *On the Threshold of Freedom,* 178; Grant, *Way It Was in the South,* 84; Standard, *Columbus, Georgia, in the Confederacy,* 56.

32. Standard, *Columbus, Georgia, in the Confederacy,* 56.

33. Rawick, ed., *American Slave,* ser. 2, vol. 12, pt. 1, p. 14.

34. Mohr, "Slavery and Class Tensions in Confederate Georgia," 65.

35. Ibid.

36. *Columbus (Georgia) Times,* September 13, 1861; Standard, *Columbus, Georgia, in the Confederacy,* 39; *Columbus (Georgia) Times,* quoted in the *Macon (Georgia) Telegraph,* February 24, 1865; *LaGrange (Georgia) Reporter,* March 3, 1865

37. Standard, *Columbus, Georgia, in the Confederacy,* 37; Mueller, *Perilous Journeys,* 115.

38. John H. Martin, ed., *Columbus,* 2:141; Rhodes Diary; Bryan, *Confederate Georgia,* 179; Eliza Frances Andrews, *Wartime Journal,* 141; Sterkx, *Partners in Rebellion,* 157.

39. *Atlanta Southern Confederacy,* April 5, 1863; Standard, *Columbus, Georgia, in the Confederacy,* 50–51. For a collection of interesting primary documents concerning Thomas Greene Bethune, see Norborne T. N. Robinson III, ed., "Blind Tom, Musical Prodigy." Bethune was born Thomas Greene Wiggins but was sold shortly after his birth to James Neil Bethune and became known by his second master's name.

40. Sterkx, *Partners in Rebellion,* 157.

41. Hague, *Blockaded Family,* 106; Barfield, *History of Harris County,* 293–95; Mary Love Edwards Fleming, "Dale County and Its People," 90.

42. *Columbus (Georgia) Daily Sun,* April 27, 1861; Turner, *Navy Gray,* 138.

43. Standard, *Columbus, Georgia, in the Confederacy,* 52; George Douglas to Samuel H. Stout, May 28, 1864, in Schroeder-Lein, "'To Be Better Supplied,'" 829.

44. *Columbus (Georgia) Times,* August 30, 1864.

45. Dr. John S. Meriwether to wife Alice Coleman Meriwether, March 20, 1864, in Meriwether Letters.

46. Baker to Samuel H. Stout, July 24, 1864, in Schroeder-Lein, "'To Be Better Supplied,'" 829–30. For the most complete overview of medical care in the Army of Tennessee, see Schroeder-Lein, *Confederate Hospitals on the Move.*

47. Todd, ed., *History of Clay County,* 11; Suarez, *Source Book;* Forrest Clark Johnson III, *Histories of LaGrange and Troup County,* 1:69; Cherry Papers, folder 1.

48. Douglas to Samuel H. Stout, April 13, 1864, and F. G. Wilkins, mayor, to surgeon general, April 12, 1864, with note on reverse from Douglas, May 2, 1864, in Schroeder-Lein, "'To Be Better Supplied,'" 821.

49. Baker to S. M. Bemiss, March 27, 1864, in Schroeder-Lein, *Confederate Hospitals on the Move,* 104; Nichol to Samuel H. Stout, August 29 and 30, 1864, in Schroeder-Lein, "'To Be Better Supplied,'" 820–21.

50. Sterkx, *Some Notable Alabama Women,* 28; Schroeder-Lein, *Confederate Hospitals on the Move,* 74–75; General Order no. 95, in Confederate States Army, *Regulations for the Medical Department,* 55.

51. *Blakely (Georgia) Early County News,* November 2, 1864.

52. Rable, *Civil Wars,* 126.

53. Ibid., 124; Sterkx, *Some Notable Alabama Women,* 28.

54. Rable, *Civil Wars,* 126, Sterkx, *Some Notable Alabama Women,* 28.

55. Ware, "Enchantment and Ennui," 425.

56. Ibid., 413.

57. DeCredico, *Patriotism for Profit,* 61–62; Standard, *Columbus, Georgia, in the Confederacy,* 53, 54, 70 n. 4.

58. Standard, *Columbus, Georgia, in the Confederacy,* 18.

59. For a treatment of cotton overproduction and its effects on the war's outcome, see Lebergott, "Why the South Lost." Formwalt places a regional spin on this phenomenon in "Planters and Cotton Production as a Cause of Confederate Defeat."

60. Shepard Green Pryor to wife, March 28, 1862, in Bryan, *Confederate Georgia,* 180.

CHAPTER 4. What Will Become of the Women and Children?

1. Dent to Anna Dent, December 5, 1860, in Dent Confederate Collection.

2. Meriwether to Alice Coleman Meriwether, March 29 and April 3, 1864, in Meriwether Letters.

3. Cumming, *Journal,* 244; Chesnut, *Mary Chesnut's Civil War,* 285.

4. Hague, *Blockaded Family,* 110, 113; Massey, *Ersatz in the Confederacy,* 90; Eliza Frances Andrews, *Wartime Journal,* 110–11.

5. *Blakely (Georgia) Early County News,* September 28, 1864.

6. Turner, *Navy Gray,* 135; Flynt, *Poor but Proud,* 39; Bryan, *Confederate Georgia,* 61; Escott, "Joseph E. Brown," 61. The most comprehensive treatment of salt's impact on the Confederate war effort is Lonn, *Salt as a Factor in the Confederacy.*

7. Hague, *Blockaded Family,* 101; Bryan, *Confederate Georgia,* 61; Standard, *Columbus, Georgia, in the Confederacy,* 47; Reiger, "Deprivation, Disaffection, and Desertion in Confederate Florida," 280.

8. Standard, *Columbus, Georgia, in the Confederacy,* 47.

9. DeTreville, "Little New South," 273; *Columbus (Georgia) Enquirer,* April 21, 1863; Standard, *Columbus, Georgia, in the Confederacy,* 47.

10. Standard, *Columbus, Georgia, in the Confederacy,* 46; Columbus Relief Association to secretary of war [James A. Seddon], March 10, 1863, in Confederate Secretary of War, Letters Received, microcopy no. 437, roll 82, 359–60; *Columbus (Georgia) Enquirer,* March 24, 1863; *Columbus (Georgia) Daily Sun,* October 13, 1863; Cumming, *Journal,* 67.

11. Allen to War Department, May 10, 1863, in Confederate Secretary of War, Letters Received, microcopy no. 437, roll 80, 437–38.

12. Bryan, *Confederate Georgia,* 60; *Blakely (Georgia) Early County News,* December 2, 1863, and January 13 and April 27, 1864; *Columbus (Georgia) Daily Sun,* September 24, 1863.

13. Escott, *After Secession,* 114; Frederick Burtz to Brown, March 29, 1862, in Formwalt, "Planters and Cotton Production as a Cause of Confederate Defeat," 273; *Opelika (Alabama) Southern Republic,* December 7, 1861.

14. Jordan to Brown, November 18, 1861, in Georgia, Governor's Correspondence.

15. Walter L. Fleming, *Civil War and Reconstruction in Alabama,* 203; *Blakely (Georgia) Early County News,* April 19, 1865; anonymous to Brown, n.d., in Georgia, Governor's Correspondence.

16. Chapman, *Georgia Soldier,* 5.

17. Davidson, *Brooks of Honey and Butter,* 1:203; *Blakely (Georgia) Early County News,* January 6 and April 6, 1864. So worthless did Confederate currency become by the end of the war that when a Yankee trooper asked one old Alabama woman for a piece of paper to light his pipe, she handed him a dollar bill (Walter L. Fleming, *Civil War and Reconstruction in Alabama,* 183).

18. Massey, *Ersatz in the Confederacy,* 52; Bryan, *Confederate Georgia,* 57, 60; Walter L. Fleming, *Civil War and Reconstruction in Alabama,* 203–4; *Blakely (Georgia) Early County News,* January 20, 1864.

19. Bryan, *Confederate Georgia,* 57, 60–61.

20. Cumming, *Journal,* 67.

21. *Columbus (Georgia) Enquirer,* November 10, 1863.

22. Reiger, "Deprivation, Disaffection, and Desertion in Confederate Florida," 280; Massey, *Ersatz in the Confederacy,* 120; Walter L. Fleming, *Civil War and Reconstruction in Alabama,* 203.

23. Massey, *Ersatz in the Confederacy*, 116.

24. Hague, *Blockaded Family*, 47; Walter L. Fleming, *Civil War and Reconstruction in Alabama*, 240; Massey, *Ersatz in the Confederacy*, 120.

25. Turner, *Navy Gray*, 11.

26. Kitten Erwin to Ann Winston, January 10, 1862, in Thomas DeKalb Harris Family Papers; *LaGrange (Georgia) Reporter*, March 3, 1865; Massey, *Ersatz in the Confederacy*, 121; Mary Love Edwards Fleming, "Dale County and Its People," 100.

27. Rawick, ed., *American Slave*, ser. 2, vol. 12, pt. 1, p. 26; Massey, *Ersatz in the Confederacy*, 121; Hague, *Blockaded Family*, 46–47.

28. Hague, *Blockaded Family*, 46; Massey, *Ersatz in the Confederacy*, 121, 122; Lovett to husband, September 22, 1862, in Lane, ed., *Times That Prove People's Principles*, 104.

29. Lovett to husband, September 22, 1862, in Lane, ed., *Times That Prove People's Principles*, 103.

30. Rawick, ed., *American Slave*, ser. 2, vol. 12, pt. 1, p. 26; Hague, *Blockaded Family*, 120–21.

31. Rawick, ed., *American Slave*, ser. 2, vol. 13, pt. 3, pp. 17, 187; ser. 2, vol. 12, pt. 1, p. 26.

32. Walter L. Fleming, *Civil War and Reconstruction in Alabama*, 234; Mary Love Edwards Fleming, "Dale County and Its People," 97, 98–99; Hague, *Blockaded Family*, 48, 104; *Montgomery (Alabama) Daily Mail*, January 15, 1864; Smith, *History of Troup County*, 204.

33. Wynne and Harrison, eds., "'Plain Folk' Coping in the Confederacy," 106; Massey, *Ersatz in the Confederacy*, 87.

34. Massey, *Ersatz in the Confederacy*, 87.

35. Ibid., 86; Mary Love Edwards Fleming, "Dale County and Its People," 73; Hague, *Blockaded Family*, 83–84.

36. Clayton, *White and Black under the Old Regime*, 117; Hague, *Blockaded Family*, 43; Mary Love Edwards Fleming, "Dale County and Its People," 72.

37. Massey, *Ersatz in the Confederacy*, 91; Rawick, ed., *American Slave*, supplement, ser. 1, vol. 4, pt. 2, p. 476.

38. Hague, *Blockaded Family*, 40–41, 45–46.

39. Ibid., 57–58, 68–70; Mary Love Edwards Fleming, "Dale County and Its People," 98; Fred S. Watson, *Winds of Sorrow*, 5.

40. Hague, *Blockaded Family*, 33, 37–38, 52–54; Mary Love Edwards Fleming, "Dale County and Its People," 79; Fred S. Watson, *Winds of Sorrow*, 4.

41. Rawick, ed., *American Slave*, ser. 1, 6:343; Hague, *Blockaded Family*, 36–37.

42. Clayton, *White and Black under the Old Regime*, 120; Mathis, *John Horry Dent*, 205–6, 207–8.

43. Hague, *Blockaded Family*, 119; Escott, "Context of Freedom," 87.

44. Mary Love Edwards Fleming, "Dale County and Its People," 94; Mathis, *John Horry Dent,* 198; Flynt, *Poor but Proud,* 38.

45. James Crowder to mother, March 3, 1863, in Mathis, ed., *In the Land of the Living,* 51; Standard, *Columbus, Georgia, in the Confederacy,* 42; *Blakely (Georgia) Early County News,* January 6, 1864.

46. Mary Love Edwards Fleming, "Dale County and Its People," 95; Hague, *Blockaded Family,* 24–25.

47. Hague, *Blockaded Family,* 20–21, 26.

48. Mary Love Edwards Fleming, "Dale County and Its People," 97; Hague, *Blockaded Family,* 47–48.

49. Mary Love Edwards Fleming, "Dale County and Its People," 95.

50. Wiley, *Plain People of the Confederacy,* 37; Hague, *Blockaded Family,* 27, 31; Mathis, *John Horry Dent,* 208.

51. Turner, *Navy Gray,* 143; Hague, *Blockaded Family,* 18–19; Mathis, *John Horry Dent,* 208.

52. Mary Love Edwards Fleming, "Dale County and Its People," 95.

53. Mary Cole, ed., "A Transcript of Pages from the Plantation Account Book of Dr. Richard Bradley Hill, Early County, Georgia," in *Collections,* ed. Whitehead, 2:112.

54. Escott, "Joseph E. Brown," 61; Lindsey, *"Reason for the Tears,"* 129.

55. Mary Love Edwards Fleming, "Dale County and Its People," 97; Nellie Cook Davis, *History of Miller County,* 40; Hague, *Blockaded Family,* 38–39.

56. Mary Love Edwards Fleming, "Dale County and Its People," 96–97; Massey, *Ersatz in the Confederacy,* 72–73; Hague, *Blockaded Family,* 101–2.

57. Escott, "Joseph E. Brown," 64; Massey, *Ersatz in the Confederacy,* 48–49; Walter L. Fleming, *Civil War and Reconstruction in Alabama,* 199.

58. *Opelika (Alabama) Southern Republic,* August 17, 1861; Lebergott, "Why the South Lost," 60–61. Restricted access to southern cotton did not have the impact Confederates had hoped. Textile manufacturers in the North and Europe found other sources of cotton, most notably in Egypt and India. That fact was common knowledge by fall 1862. On November 28, 1862, the *Columbus (Georgia) Daily Sun* printed an item from England's *Liverpool Times,* sarcastically entitled "The Cotton Famine—Indian cotton continues to arrive in Liverpool in large quantities."

59. *Opelika (Alabama) Southern Republic,* March 2, 1861; *LaGrange (Georgia) Daily Bulletin,* March 28, 1864; *Thomasville (Georgia) Wire Grass Reporter,* May 11, 1861.

60. Benjamin F. Jackson to Martha Jackson, July 25, 1862, in Jackson, ed., *So Mourns the Dove,* 35; *Opelika (Alabama) Southern Republic,* March 29, 1862; *Columbus (Georgia) Daily Sun,* March 31, 1863; Mathis, *John Horry Dent,* 198; "Cotton—How Much to Plant."

61. "Good Example."

62. Frederick Burtz to Brown, March 29, 1862, in Formwalt, "Planters and Cotton Production as a Cause of Confederate Defeat," 272–75.

63. "Gov. Brown's Letter."

64. McMillan, ed., *Alabama Confederate Reader*, 109–10; Bryan, *Confederate Georgia*, 121.

65. *Columbus (Georgia) Enquirer*, September 16, 1862; *Blakely (Georgia) Early County News*, November 18, 1863.

66. Bryan, *Confederate Georgia*, 121; Gates, *Agriculture and the Civil War*, 18. In "Southwest Georgia," Joseph Paul Johnson concluded that cotton production in the region declined dramatically from 1862 through the end of the war, while the area's corn output rose to more than 1.7 million bushels by the end of 1864. However, the decline was probably not as great as Johnson thought since he based this conclusion mainly on railroad freight records and did not take river freight into account. Even if he had, few records of cotton smuggling would have been found. Smugglers were understandably anxious to keep their activities off the books. However, some hint of cotton smuggling's extent can be gleaned from local accounts and reports from the Union navy of captured cotton. For examples of cotton traffic out of Apalachicola during the war, see Mueller, *Perilous Journeys*, 105–15.

67. Gates, *Agriculture and the Civil War*, 18; McMillan, ed., *Alabama Confederate Reader*, 108, 109.

68. Tatum, *Disloyalty in the Confederacy*, 19; Bryan, *Confederate Georgia*, 122.

69. Bryan, *Confederate Georgia*, 52–53.

70. Lebergott, "Why the South Lost," 69, 71–72; Jones and Dudley to Brown, March 5, 1862, in Lane, ed., *Times That Prove People's Principles*, 122.

71. Dent to Wellborn, December 4, 1861, in Wellborn Memorial Collection; *Opelika (Alabama) Southern Republic*, November 9, 1861.

72. Mathis, *John Horry Dent*, 198, 205; Jones and Dudley to Brown, March 5, 1862, in Lane, ed., *Times That Prove People's Principles*, 122. In 1872, the U.S. Senate estimated that southern planters produced roughly five million bales of cotton during the war. See Senate Report 41, "Affairs in the Late Insurrectionary States," in Griffin, "Cotton Frauds and Confiscations in Alabama," 265.

73. An example of a tax-in-kind form is contained in the George H. Winston Collection. According to this document, George H. Winston of Troup County turned over $432 worth of bacon to the Confederacy in March 1865.

74. Mathis, *John Horry Dent*, 206; Brown to Secretary of War James A. Seddon, November 9, 1863, in O.R., ser. 4, 3:944.

75. Candler, comp., *Confederate Records*, 3:132, 134; Riley, "Desertion and Disloyalty," 27.

76. *Milledgeville (Georgia) Southern Recorder*, March 17, 1863; *Columbus (Georgia) Daily Sun*, November 28, 1862; Toombs to Alexander H. Stephens, March 16, 1861, in Ulrich B. Phillips, ed., *Correspondence*, 660.

77. Walter L. Fleming, *Civil War and Reconstruction in Alabama*, 174.

78. Watts to Randolph, October 17, 1862, in *O.R.*, ser. 4, 2:124–25; John E. Morgan and U. B. Wilkinson, commissioners, to James A. Seddon, May 18, 1863, in *O.R.*, ser. 4, 2:559–62; Joseph E. Brown to Seddon, November 9, 1863, in *O.R.*, ser. 4, 2:944; Bryan, *Confederate Georgia*, 91; Walter L. Fleming, *Civil War and Reconstruction in Alabama*, 197.

79. Watts to James A. Seddon, January 19, 1864, in *O.R.*, ser. 4, 3:37; Christian, "Georgia and the Confederate Policy of Impressing Supplies," 13, 16; P. A. Lawson to Jefferson Davis, December 27, 1864, in *O.R.*, ser. 4, 3:968; Walter L. Fleming, *Civil War and Reconstruction in Alabama*, 176.

80. Walter L. Fleming, *Civil War and Reconstruction in Alabama*, 175; Bessie Martin, *Desertion of Alabama Troops*, 94; Christian, "Georgia and the Confederate Policy of Impressing Supplies," 20.

81. Bessie Martin, *Desertion of Alabama Troops*, 95; Massey, *Ersatz in the Confederacy*, 28.

82. *Blakely (Georgia) Early County News*, April 20, 1864; Nancy Mann to Thomas Mann, January 2, 1864, in Mann Civil War Papers.

83. Christian, "Georgia and the Confederate Policy of Impressing Supplies," 14–15.

84. William A. Clarke to E. Cody, September 7, 1861, in Burnett, ed., "Letters of Barnett Hardeman Cody," 290.

85. *Blakely (Georgia) Early County News*, August 10, 1864.

86. Barfield, *History of Harris County*, 293; Standard, *Columbus, Georgia, in the Confederacy*, 56; Mohr, *On the Threshold of Freedom*, 121, 327 n. 2.

87. Castleberry to Brown, August 1, 1862, in Georgia, Governor's Correspondence; Mathis, *John Horry Dent*, 205.

88. *Blakely (Georgia) Early County News*, March 16, 1864. For more on the impact of impressment on yeoman attitudes, see Wallenstein, *From Slave South to New South*, 120; Christian, "Georgia and the Confederate Policy of Impressing Supplies," 2.

89. *Blakely (Georgia) Early County News*, April 6, 1864; Seddon to Hill and Johnson, September 5, 1864, in *O.R.*, ser. 4, 3:621; Johnson to Seddon, September 18, 1864, in *O.R.*, ser. 4, 3:662; Christian, "Georgia and the Confederate Policy of Impressing Supplies," 28.

90. *Columbus (Georgia) Daily Sun*, October 6, 1863.

91. *Blakely (Georgia) Early County News*, March 16 and June 15, 1864.

92. Standard, *Columbus, Georgia, in the Confederacy*, 49; N. K. Rogers, *History of Chattahoochee County*, 43; Flynt, *Poor but Proud*, 40; Bessie Martin, *Desertion of Alabama Troops*, 130.

93. Turner, *Navy Gray*, 145; Massey, *Refugee Life in the Confederacy*, 85.

94. Massey, *Refugee Life in the Confederacy*, 85.

95. *Columbus (Georgia) Daily Sun*, March 31, 1863.

96. *Blakely (Georgia) Early County News*, March 30 and August 24, 1864.

97. Ibid., May 4, 1864, and March 8, 1865.

98. Mathis, *John Horry Dent*, 206, 209.

99. Troup County Inferior Court Minutes, July 1861; Massey, *Ersatz in the Confederacy,* 47; Bessie Martin, *Desertion of Alabama Troops,* 180–81; Flynt, *Poor but Proud,* 40; Walter L. Fleming, *Civil War and Reconstruction in Alabama,* 197.

100. Escott, "Joseph E. Brown," 65; Lonn, *Desertion during the Civil War,* 115; Wallenstein, *From Slave South to New South,* 102.

101. Wallenstein, *From Slave South to New South,* 102; Wallenstein, "Rich Man's War, Rich Man's Fight," 24, 29; Lonn, *Desertion during the Civil War,* 115.

102. Barfield, *History of Harris County,* 293; Lindsey, *"Reason for the Tears,"* 129; *Blakely (Georgia) Early County News,* April 6, 1864.

103. Standard, *Columbus, Georgia, in the Confederacy,* 49; John H. Martin, ed., *Columbus,* 2:168.

104. Standard, *Columbus, Georgia, in the Confederacy,* 48–49; Bryan, *Confederate Georgia,* 63; Bessie Martin, *Desertion of Alabama Troops,* 183; Lindsey, *"Reason for the Tears,"* 129; Wallenstein, *From Slave South to New South,* 116.

105. Mathis, *John Horry Dent,* 202.

106. J. B. Guest to Brown, May 20, 1862, in Georgia, Governor's Correspondence.

107. Flynt, *Poor but Proud,* 38–39.

108. Cleveland to Brown, November 3, 1863, in Georgia, Governor's Correspondence; Wallenstein, *From Slave South to New South,* 102.

109. Asbell to wife Sarah, November 1 and 19, 1863, in Wynne and Harrison, eds., "'Plain Folk' Coping in the Confederacy," 115, 117.

110. Petition from women of Miller County, Georgia, to James Seddon and Jefferson Davis, September 8, 1863, in Confederate Secretary of War, Letters Received, microcopy no. 437, roll 80, 776–80.

111. *O.R.,* ser. 1, vol. 30, pt. 2, pp. 629–31, 635–36; Henderson, comp., *Roster,* 5:775–86.

112. Flynt, *Poor but Proud,* 41.

113. *Columbus (Georgia) Daily Sun,* October 13, 1863.

114. Nellie Cook Davis, *History of Miller County,* 171, 395; *Blakely (Georgia) Early County News,* January 25 and February 8, 1865; *Macon (Georgia) Daily Telegraph,* February 24 and March 8, 1865.

115. Krug, "The Folks Back Home," 138; Riley, "Desertion and Disloyalty," 33; *Columbus (Georgia) Daily Sun,* April 11, 1863.

116. Barfield, *History of Harris County,* 758.

Chapter 5. Fighting the Rich Men's Fight

1. Dent to Nannie Dent, December 7, 1861, in Mathis, ed., *In the Land of the Living,* 11; Register to Tempa Register, July 1, 1861, in Fred S. Watson, *Winds of Sorrow,* 19.

2. James P. Crowder to G. M. Crowder, March 13, 1864, in Mathis, ed., *In the Land of the Living*, 86; James H. Jones to S. C. Jones, May 20, 1862, J. H. Jones Letter; J. Boyd to brother, February 16, 1862, in Boyd Letters; G. W. Ross to J. W. Ross, April 29, 1862, in Ross Civil War Letters.

3. Dent to Nannie Dent, December 7, 1861, in Mathis, ed., *In the Land of the Living*, 11.

4. Dent to Nannie Dent, April 23, 1862, in ibid., 23; B. F. Jackson to Martha Jackson and James Thomas Jackson, July 25, 1862, in Jackson, ed., *So Mourns the Dove*, 34.

5. N. K. Rogers, *History of Chattahoochee County*, 49.

6. William H. Andrews, *Footprints of a Regiment*, 93; Barnett H. Cody to Fransinia Cody McGarity, February 2, 1863, and Cody to Henrietta Cody Burnett, January 26, 1862, in Burnett, ed., "Letters of Barnett Hardeman Cody," 367, 363; Jackson to Martha Jackson, August 12, 1862, in Jackson, ed., *So Mourns the Dove*, 40.

7. William H. Andrews, *Footprints of a Regiment*, 93–94.

8. Lindsey, *"Reason for the Tears,"* 129. Lack of adequate transportation also contributed to food shortages in the army. In summer 1863, Captain A. M. Allen of Columbus wrote that he had 300,000 bushels of corn ready for delivery to Robert E. Lee's army, but he needed help getting the corn to Richmond: "The Corn is ready," he said. "Transportation is the great difficulty." But even had there been no problem with transportation, the underproduction of food would have remained. By Allen's own calculations, his corn would have met the demands of Lee's army for barely a month. And in an earlier letter to the War Department, Allen complained that the corn crop in southwest Georgia was nearly exhausted (Allen to R. R. Cuyler, August 12, 1863, and Allen to War Department, May 10, 1863, in Confederate Secretary of War, Letters Received, microcopy no. 437, roll 80, 713–14).

9. Moses, "Southern Romantic," 1:185–86. See also Young, ed., *Last Order of the Lost Cause*, 232.

10. Jackson to Martha Jackson, August 12, 1862, in Jackson, ed., *So Mourns the Dove*, 40.

11. Stewart to wife, December 8, 1862, in Fred S. Watson, *Winds of Sorrow*, 25; Jackson to Martha Jackson, November 2, 1863, in Jackson, ed., *So Mourns the Dove*, 70.

12. Merz, "Diary," 19.

13. Elias Register to Tempa Register, July 1, 1861, in Fred S. Watson, *Winds of Sorrow*, 19; Cadenhead to Luisa F. Cadenhead, 1862, in Cadenhead, "Some Confederate Letters," 571; Daniel W. Snell to Sarah Snell, April 22, 1863, in Barfield, *History of Harris County*, 758.

14. William H. Andrews, *Footprints of a Regiment*, 151.

15. McPherson, *Ordeal by Fire*, 385; Register to Tempa Register, May 29 and July 1, 1861, in Fred S. Watson, *Winds of Sorrow*, 18–19.

16. Clarke to Edmund Cody, September 7, 1861, in Burnett, ed., "Letters of Barnett Hardeman Cody," 289; Stewart to wife, December 8 and 14, 1862, in Fred S. Watson, *Winds of Sorrow*, 24–25.

17. J. M. Dickinson to John W. Solomon, June 20, 1862, in Solomon Papers; Larkin Weaver to Lou Weaver, July 23, 1862, in Gary Papers; Turner to mother, August 17, 1861, in Turner Letters.

18. Cantey to wife, January 5, 1862, in Mathis, ed., *In the Land of the Living*, 18.

19. Register to Tempa Register, August 21, 1861, in Fred S. Watson, *Winds of Sorrow*, 20–21; Long to wife Sallie, May 14, 1861, in Suarez, *Source Book*, 160–61.

20. McGee, *Claybank Memories*, 42.

21. N. L. Atkinson to wife, April 12, 1863, in Atkinson Collection.

22. C. Dicken to Luisa Faney Cadenhead, July 23, 1864, in Cadenhead, "Some Confederate Letters," 567–68.

23. Curtright to wife Mary Evans Curtright, October 6, 1862, and J. U. Lennard to Mrs. J. Curtright, October 27, 1862, in Curtright Papers. John Curtright was buried near the Perryville battlefield. Years after the war, a nephew discovered the grave and had Curtright moved to LaGrange, where today he lies buried next to his wife in Hillview Cemetery (*War Was the Place*, 4).

24. Lightfoot to Henrietta S. Cody, May 29, 1861, in Burnett, ed., "Letters of Three Lightfoot Brothers," 389; Clarke to E. Cody, September 7, 1861, in Burnett, ed., "Letters of Barnett Hardeman Cody," 290; Escott, *After Secession*, 103.

25. Jenkins Diary.

26. William H. Andrews, *Footprints of a Regiment*, 26; Watkins, "*Co. Aytch*," 194; Henderson, comp., *Roster*, 5:396.

27. Ward, *Civil War*, 201.

28. Castlen, *Hope Bids Me Onward*, 96.

29. Benjamin F. Jackson to Matilda Jackson, July 1862, in Jackson, ed., *So Mourns the Dove*, 29; William H. Andrews, *Footprints of a Regiment*, 20; Ware, "Enchantment and Ennui," 418; Dent to Nannie Dent, November 7, 1861, in Mathis, ed., *In the Land of the Living*, 9; Cody to Edmund Cody, August 20, 1861, in Burnett, ed., "Letters of Barnett Hardeman Cody," 287; Garret Hallenbeck to Brown, November 20, 1863, in Lane, ed., *Times That Prove People's Principles*, 134.

30. Barron to sister, April 19, 1863, in Mathis, ed., *In the Land of the Living*, 53; Stubbs to Martha Stubbs Jackson and sisters, July 1862, in Jackson, ed., *So Mourns the Dove*, 31–32.

31. Hightower to Martha S. Hightower, August 8, 1862, in Grantham, ed., "Letters from H. J. Hightower," 176; Jackson to Martha Jackson, July 13, 1862, in Jackson, ed., *So Mourns the Dove*, 32–33; David M. Denny to wife Sinai and children, August 24, 1864, Denny Confederate Letters Collection; J. C. Curtright

to wife, October 6, 1862, Curtright Papers; Thomas Daniel to sister Amy Daniel, September 6, 1862, in Lindsey, *"Reason for the Tears,"* 132.

32. Lightfoot to Henrietta S. Cody, October 10, 1861, in Burnett, ed., "Letters of Three Lightfoot Brothers," 399; Daniel to family, September 6, 1862, in Lindsey, *"Reason for the Tears,"* 132.

33. Citizens of Attapulgus and Vicinity to Brown, August 1863, in Georgia, Petitions to the Governor.

34. Lovett to husband, May 7, 1862, in Lane, ed., *Times That Prove People's Principles,* 98–99. The regular postal service was so unreliable that soldiers preferred to send letters by friends who were going home on furlough (Hammond Diary, December 18, 1861).

35. *Opelika (Alabama) Southern Republic,* July 20, 1861; Brooks to husband, September 3, 1862, in Katherine M. Jones, ed., *Heroines of Dixie,* 183.

36. Watkins, *"Co. Aytch,"* 194; J. Boyd to brother, February 16, 1862, in Boyd Letters; Jackson to Martha Jackson, July 25, 1862, in Jackson, ed., *So Mourns the Dove,* 35. Pay for soldiers did go up to eighteen dollars a month in June 1864, but as before, it was rarely delivered (Bessie Martin, *Desertion of Alabama Troops,* 142–43).

37. Mary Jane Love Curry to Duncan Curry, December 9, 1862, in Curry Hill Plantation Records.

38. Lovett to husband, March 26, 1862, in Lane, ed., *Times That Prove People's Principles,* 97.

39. Lovett to husband, February 14, 1864, in ibid., 105; William Brooks to brother, n.d., Brooks Civil War Letter; D. G. Crowder to T. J. Jarrell, December 12, 1861, in Crowder Family Papers.

40. T. T. Bigbie to wife, February 13, 1864, in Bigbie Collection; Bessie Martin, *Desertion of Alabama Troops,* 148; Thomas, *History of the Doles-Cook Brigade,* 593–95. Edward Cooper later died in battle.

41. Benjamin Jackson to father Amariah B. Stubbs and family, August 26, 1862, in Jackson, ed., *So Mourns the Dove,* 44; Asbell to wife Sarah, October 19 and November 19, 1863, in Wynne and Harrison, eds., "'Plain Folk' Coping in the Confederacy," 114, 116–17.

42. Ward, *Civil War,* 201; William H. Andrews, *Footprints of a Regiment,* 20.

43. Thurman to Brown, October 11, 1864, and Williams to Brown, June 20 1864, in Georgia, Governor's Correspondence; R. E. Covington, justice of the peace, for Mrs. H. N. Jackson to Shorter, October 10, 1863, in Alabama, Governor's Correspondence.

44. Ball to Brown, April 10, [n.d.], and Mrs. S. E. Cook to Brown, August 16, 1864, in Georgia, Governor's Correspondence.

45. Watkins, *"Co. Aytch,"* 194.

46. Bessie Martin, *Desertion of Alabama Troops,* 17; Jackson to Martha Jackson, July 13, 1862, in Jackson, ed., *So Mourns the Dove,* 32.

47. Ward, *Civil War,* 201; *Columbus (Georgia) Enquirer,* November 10, 1863.

48. Owsley, "Defeatism in the Confederacy," 449; William H. Andrews, *Footprints of a Regiment,* 39.

49. Bessie Martin, *Desertion of Alabama Troops,* 149.

50. William H. Andrews, *Footprints of a Regiment,* 39; *Columbus (Georgia) Daily Sun,* October 13, 1863.

51. Crist and Dix, eds., *Papers of Jefferson Davis,* 7:361.

52. Kirkland, Compiled Service Records; Henderson, comp., *Roster,* 5:372; Union Missionary Baptist Church Cemetery Records.

53. Fraser Collection.

54. *Columbus (Georgia) Enquirer,* August 26, 1862; *Blakely (Georgia) Early County News,* May 4, 1864.

55. John Gill Shorter to James A. Seddon, December 23, 1862, in *O.R.,* ser. 4, 2:258; Bryan, *Confederate Georgia,* 142; William H. Andrews, *Footprints of a Regiment,* 121–23.

56. Whitner to Cobb, August 12, 1862, in Ulrich B. Phillips, ed., *Correspondence,* 603; Purcell, "Military Conscription," 104; William H. Andrews, *Footprints of a Regiment,* 110.

57. Johnson to Watts, January 10, 1865, in Alabama, Governor's Correspondence; Johnston to Brown, August 5, 1863, and Howe to Brown, October 10, 1863, in Georgia, Governor's Correspondence.

58. Richard J. Tillery and others to Watts, December 1863, citizens of Barbour County to Watts, March 13, 1864, and citizens of Rocky Head to Watts, March 21, 1864, in Alabama, Governor's Correspondence; petition from Miller County to "Gineral Commander and Secretary of the Southern Army," April 14, 1863, in Confederate Secretary of War, Letters Received, microcopy no. 437, roll 82, 448; citizens of Clay County to Brown, August 1864, in Georgia, Petitions to the Governor; William Hudson, J. J. Biggers, and J. G. Davis to Brown, October 10, 1864, in Georgia, Governor's Correspondence; citizens of Decatur County to Brown, January 25, 1864, in Georgia, Petitions to the Governor.

59. Cumming, *Journal,* 243.

60. *Blakely (Georgia) Early County News,* March 30, 1864.

61. Abram Kauffman to Brown, March 31, 1862, in Georgia, Governor's Correspondence.

62. James Phelan to Davis, December 9, 1862, in *O.R.,* ser. 1, vol. 17, pt. 2, p. 790; Bradford to Davis, February 18, 1863, in Confederate Secretary of War, Letters Received, microcopy no. 437, roll 81, 81.

63. Prescott Reminiscences; Bryan, *Confederate Georgia,* 90; Cleveland, *Alexander H. Stephens,* 765.

64. Moore, *Conscription and Conflict,* 256, 278; Walter L. Fleming, *Civil War and Reconstruction in Alabama,* 96–98; Bryan, *Confederate Georgia,* 87; Pearce, *Benjamin H. Hill,* 67. In keeping with the state sovereignty written into the Con-

federate constitution, there was neither a centralized Confederate judicial system nor a supreme court. Each state's supreme court was the ultimate arbiter of constitutionality within its boundaries.

65. Bush to Brown, October 16, 1863, Anderson [last name illegible] for Horton to Brown, February 8, 1864, and Mrs. B. J. Smith to Brown, August 13, 1864, in Georgia, Governor's Correspondence.

66. Jenkins to Brown, February 27, 1863, in Georgia, Governor's Correspondence.

67. Dennis McQueen Wade Sr., "Some Local History," *Blakely Reporter,* March 22, 1900, in *Collections,* ed. Whitehead, 1:134; Baker to Shorter, March 12, 1862, Baker Letter; Massey, *Refugee Life in the Confederacy,* 21.

68. James Campbell to Brown, January 16, 1864, in Georgia, Governor's Correspondence.

69. *Columbus (Georgia) Enquirer,* November 10, 1863.

70. Escott, *After Secession,* 117.

71. Hugh C. Bailey, "Disloyalty in Early Confederate Alabama," 525; Bessie Martin, *Desertion of Alabama Troops,* 122; *Blakely (Georgia) Early County News,* December 14, 1864.

72. Bessie Martin, *Desertion of Alabama Troops,* 138–39; Beals, *War within a War,* 53; Escott, *After Secession,* 155; McMillan, *Disintegration of a Confederate State,* 68; Martis, *Historical Atlas,* 87. See also Percy, "Localizing the Context of Confederate Politics."

73. Martis, *Historical Atlas,* 87, 110–13.

74. *Columbus (Georgia) Enquirer,* October 9, 1863; *Columbus (Georgia) Daily Sun,* October 13, 1863.

75. *Columbus (Georgia) Enquirer,* October 9, 1863.

76. Tatum, *Disloyalty in the Confederacy,* 26. Other such organizations included the Peace and Constitutional Society and the Order of the Heroes of America.

77. Fife, Compiled Service Records; Fuller, Compiled Service Records; Current, *Lincoln's Loyalists,* 218.

78. O'Connor to Brown, March 10, 1862, in Georgia, Governor's Correspondence; Mueller, *Perilous Journeys,* 109; *O.R.,* ser. 1, vol. 52, pt. 2, pp. 403–4; Tatum, *Disloyalty in the Confederacy,* 73; Riley, "Desertion and Disloyalty," 3; Degler, *Other South,* 169. For overviews of unionism and peace activities in Georgia and Alabama, see Dodd, "Unionism in Confederate Alabama"; Doherty, "Union Nationalism in Georgia"; Talmadge, "Peace-Movement Activities in Civil War Georgia."

79. U.S. Census Bureau, *Seventh Census of the United States, 1850;* Turner, *Navy Gray,* 9. For a typescript of Muscogee County's 1850 census, see Otto, comp., *1850 Census of Georgia.*

80. John G. Winter to Andrew Johnson, February 28, 1861, in Graf and

Haskins, eds., "Letters of a Georgia Unionist," 392, 400–401; Simons to Davis, received September 25, 1861, in Crist and Dix, eds., *Papers of Jefferson Davis,* 7:349; Cook, "James Johnson"; Shadgett, "James Johnson." Though opposed to secession, few unionists seem to have had serious reservations when it came to doing business with the Rebs. William R. Brown, for example, made ordnance and boilers for the Confederacy (Turner, *Navy Gray,* 149, 162).

81. Graf and Haskins, eds., "Letters of a Georgia Unionist," 401.

82. Ibid., 385–91. Winter's concern for his neighbors' financial well-being had its limits. During the 1850s, he issued personal currency (change bills) that could be redeemed only in Charleston or New York (Willoughby, *Fair to Middlin',* 58–61). Winter fled north shortly after the war began, but he always considered Columbus home. His body was returned to the city for burial in the 1870s.

83. Standard, *Columbus, Georgia, in the Confederacy,* 25, 66 n. 18.

84. Schott, *Alexander H. Stephens,* 384.

85. Walter L. Fleming, *Civil War and Reconstruction in Alabama,* 138. Fleming's estimate was probably exaggerated, although it can be said that most were sympathetic to the Peace Society's goals.

86. *O.R.,* ser. 4, 3:393–95.

87. Ibid., 397.

88. Ibid., ser. 1, vol. 32, pt. 3, pp. 682–83; ser. 4, 3:397.

89. Longstreet, *From Manassas to Appomattox,* 651; W. G. Swanson to J. H. Clanton, December 26, 1863, in *O.R.,* ser. 1, vol. 26, pt. 2, pp. 549–50; Tatum, *Disloyalty in the Confederacy,* 68–69.

90. *O.R.,* ser. 1, vol. 26, pt. 2, pp. 548–57.

91. Escott, *After Secession,* 127; Ward, *Civil War,* 201. Baldwin wrote, "What private griefs they have to take their present status [as deserters] I know not, except they are generally poor men, and there was much difficulty in the way of having their families provided for in their absence" (Baldwin to Jones M. Withers, January 30, 1865, in *O.R.,* ser. 4, 3:1043–44).

92. Ward, *Civil War,* 201. See also Leverett, *Legend of the Free State of Jones.*

93. Mills, *Southern Loyalists,* viii; McMillan, ed., *Alabama Confederate Reader,* 393; Bryan, *Confederate Georgia,* 146; *O.R.,* ser. 1, vol. 28, pt. 2, p. 411; Riley, "Desertion and Disloyalty," 46; Bessie Martin, *Desertion of Alabama Troops,* 51, 52; *Blakely (Georgia) Early County News,* January 20, 1864.

94. McMillan, *Disintegration of a Confederate State,* 62.

95. Allen W. Jones, "Unionism and Disaffection in South Alabama," 124–25; Houghton and Houghton, *Two Boys,* 237–41; Mary Love Edwards Fleming, "Dale County and Its People," 92.

96. John W. Riley to Brown, July 22, [n.d.], in Georgia, Governor's Correspondence; Bessie Martin, *Desertion of Alabama Troops,* 233; M. A. Bell, John E. Price, A. C. Gordon, J. W. L. David, and H. E. Owens to Watts, March 23, 1864, in Alabama, Governor's Correspondence.

97. Arrington to General J. M. Withers, January 30, 1865, in *O.R.,* ser. 4, 3:1042–43; Cobb to Thomas Jordon, August 11, 1863, in *O.R.,* ser. 1, vol. 28, pt. 2, p. 273; Turner, *Navy Gray,* 131.

98. *Blakely (Georgia) Early County News,* February 10 and 24, 1864. For an excellent overview of the habeas corpus issue, see Robbins, "Confederacy and the Writ of Habeas Corpus."

99. *LaFayette (Alabama) Chambers Tribune,* July 30, 1863.

100. Turner, *Navy Gray,* 130–31, 325 n. 6.

101. Ibid., 130; Bessie Martin, *Desertion of Alabama Troops,* 196; [illegible] to Brown, October 5, 1864, in Georgia, Governor's Correspondence.

102. McGee, *Claybank Memories,* 44–45, 50–51.

103. Sanders, Compiled Service Records; McGee, *Claybank Memories,* 53. See also McGee, "Confederate Who Switched Sides."

104. McGee, *Claybank Memories,* 53; *O.R.,* ser. 1, 44:419.

105. McGee, *Claybank Memories,* 54, 55–56; Bessie Martin, *Desertion of Alabama Troops,* 190.

106. Bessie Martin, *Desertion of Alabama Troops,* 195; McGee, *Claybank Memories,* 55–58. For Jesse Carmichael's firsthand account, see "A War Incident: The Bushwhackers in Southeast Alabama," *Ozark (Alabama) Southern Star,* April 12, 1899 (also in Alabama–Barbour County Letters Folder).

When the war ended, Sanders settled in Dale County and resumed his trade as a millwright. Shortly thereafter, a band of riders led by Confederate veteran George Echols showed up, called Sanders a turncoat, and demanded that he come out. He refused and yelled back that he would kill the first man who tried to come in and get him. Echols rushed the door, and Sanders carried out his threat. Sanders then fled to southwest Georgia and again tried to settle down in peace, but a few days later, an anonymous band of riders crossed the Chattahoochee River by ferry from the Alabama side one night and, according to the ferryman, returned a couple of hours later. The next morning, Sanders was found shot to death in his home. According to one historian, the killers were led by George Echols's father, a former probate judge in Dale County (McGee, *Claybank Memories,* 63–64).

107. O'Rear to Watts, December 26, 1864, in Alabama, Governor's Correspondence.

108. McGee, *Claybank Memories,* 51.

109. Ibid., 51–52.

110. The hole is today located near a modern bridge and is marked by four small concrete posts. Fred S. Watson, *Piney Woods Echoes,* 183–86; Fred S. Watson, *Winds of Sorrow,* 28–31; McGee, *Claybank Memories,* 52; Mary Love Edwards Fleming, "Dale County and Its People," 92; Azbell, "Haunted Hole."

111. *Blakely (Georgia) Early County News,* November 2, 1864; *O.R.N.,* ser. 1, 17:474–75.

CHAPTER 6. Us Is Gonna Be Free

1. The contribution of blacks to the downfall of slavery and the Confederacy is explored in Armstead Louis Robinson, "Day of Jubilo."

2. *Atlanta Southern Confederacy,* February 14, 1863; *Blakely (Georgia) Early County News,* January 6, 1864; *Columbus (Georgia) Times,* January 22, 1864; Mohr, *On the Threshold of Freedom,* 164.

3. Rawick, ed., *American Slave,* supplement, ser. 1, vol. 3, pt. 1, p. 5; ser. 2, vol. 13, pt. 4, p. 123.

4. Bryan, *Confederate Georgia,* 73; A. H. Chappell to daughter, December 5, 1862, in Chappell Collection.

5. Rawick, ed., *American Slave,* supplement, ser. 1, vol. 3, pt. 1, p. 9; ser. 1, 6:279; supplement, ser. 1, 1:170.

6. *Blakely (Georgia) Early County News,* December 21, 1916; Sellers, *Slavery in Alabama,* 247, 264.

7. Sellers, *Slavery in Alabama,* 263–64; *Blakely (Georgia) Early County News,* October 12 and 19, 1864.

8. *Blakely (Georgia) Early County News,* December 21, 1916; Rawick, ed., *American Slave,* ser. 2, vol. 12, pt. 1, p. 14.

9. Rawick, ed., *American Slave,* supplement, ser. 1, vol. 3, pt. 1, p. 45; ser. 2, vol. 12, pt. 1, p. 330.

10. *O.R.,* ser. 1, vol. 47, pt. 2, p. 40; Rawick, ed., *American Slave,* ser. 2, vol. 12, pt. 1, p. 258.

11. Rawick, ed., *American Slave,* ser. 1, 6:297; ser. 2, vol. 12, pt. 2, p. 17; ser. 1, 6:272; supplement, ser. 1, 1:257.

12. Ibid., ser. 2, vol. 12, pt. 2, pp. 26–27; supplement, ser. 1, vol. 3, pt. 1, p. 315.

13. Bryan, *Confederate Georgia,* 125; Grant, *Way It Was in the South,* 83.

14. Bryan, *Confederate Georgia,* 125; Hague, *Blockaded Family,* 119; John F. Andrews to Mrs. Clement Claiborne Clay, July 10, 1863, in Clay Papers.

15. Bryan, *Confederate Georgia,* 124–25.

16. Rawick, ed., *American Slave,* ser. 2, vol. 12, pt. 1, p. 24; ser. 2, vol. 12, pt. 2, p. 17.

17. Ibid., ser. 2, vol. 12, pt. 1, p. 25; ser. 2, vol. 9, pt. 4, p. 18.

18. Ibid., ser. 2, vol. 13, pt. 3, pp. 5, 186; Bryan, *Confederate Georgia,* 126.

19. Fred S. Watson, *Winds of Sorrow,* 13–14.

20. Rawick, ed., *American Slave,* ser. 2, vol. 13, pt. 3, p. 187.

21. Ibid., ser. 2, vol. 12, pt. 1, pp. 24–25.

22. Ibid., 24.

23. Shorter to James A. Seddon, January 14, 1863, in *O.R.,* ser. 1, 15:947; Massey to Brown, March 9, 1865, in Georgia, Governor's Correspondence; *Blakely (Georgia) Early County News,* April 6, 1864; *Milledgeville (Georgia) Southern Recorder,* August 30, 1864. The plot involving Vickery is examined in Meyers, "'Wretch Vickery.'"

24. Beals, *War within a War,* 142–43; George W. Gayle to Davis, May 22, 1861, in Crist and Dix, eds., *Papers of Jefferson Davis,* 7:175; *Albany (Georgia) Patriot,* May 23, 1861.

25. Mohr, *On the Threshold of Freedom,* 51, 310 n. 86; Bryan, *Confederate Georgia,* 127.

26. Mansfield to Brown, May 26, 1864, and [illegible] to Brown, October 5, 1864, in Georgia, Governor's Correspondence.

27. Bryan, *Confederate Georgia,* 126; Denson, *Slavery Laws in Alabama,* 10–11, 55.

28. *Blakely (Georgia) Early County News,* March 16, 1864; Suarez, *Source Book,* 130–31; Mary Love Edwards Fleming, "Dale County and Its People," 102.

29. Rawick, ed., *American Slave,* ser. 2, vol. 13, pt. 3, p. 5.

30. Mohr, *On the Threshold of Freedom,* 164; Bryan, *Confederate Georgia,* 131.

31. Bryan, *Confederate Georgia,* 131; Suarez, *Source Book,* 125.

32. Bryan, *Confederate Georgia,* 132; Whitehead, ed., *Collections* 2:160; *Columbus (Georgia) Enquirer,* April 9, 1862; Rawick, ed., *American Slave,* ser. 2, vol. 12, pt. 1, p. 12.

33. Bryan, *Confederate Georgia,* 132; *Blakely (Georgia) Early County News,* March 16, 1864; B. W. Clark to Brown, January 30, 1864, in Georgia, Governor's Correspondence.

34. *Columbus (Georgia) Enquirer,* August 12, 1862; Bryan, *Confederate Georgia,* 132.

35. *Columbus (Georgia) Times,* March 17, 1865.

36. John R. Edwards to Brown, January 8, 1864, in Georgia, Governor's Correspondence.

37. Rawick, ed., *American Slave,* ser. 2, vol. 13, pt. 3, p. 5; supplement, ser. 1, vol. 3, pt. 1, pp. 4–5.

38. McPherson, *Ordeal by Fire,* 264.

39. Barney, *Road to Secession,* 66.

40. Ward, *Civil War,* 184.

41. Ibid., 150, 247.

42. J. C. Curtright to wife, October 6, 1862, in Curtright Papers; Ward, *Civil War,* 187.

43. Grant, *Way It Was in the South,* 87; Glatthaar, *Forged in Battle,* 273.

44. Ward, *Civil War,* 248.

45. Berlin et al., *Free at Last,* 537–38; Grant, *Way It Was in the South,* 83, 87; *Columbus (Georgia) Enquirer,* September 18, 1862; Bryan, *Confederate Georgia,* 127; *LaGrange (Georgia) Reporter,* March 3, 1865.

46. *LaGrange (Georgia) Reporter,* February 13, 1863; *Blakely (Georgia) Early County News,* July 13, 1864.

47. Fred S. Watson, *Winds of Sorrow,* 26.

48. Chesnut, *Mary Chesnut's Civil War,* 407.

49. Escott, "Context of Freedom," 85.

50. Glatthaar, *March to the Sea and Beyond,* 64. See also Burke Davis, *Sherman's March,* 91–94; Kennett, *Marching through Georgia,* 290–91.

51. Rawick, ed., *American Slave,* ser. 1, 6:331; ser. 2, vol. 13, pt. 4, p. 127; ser. 2, vol. 13, pt. 3, p. 187.

52. Ibid., supplement, ser. 1, vol. 3, pt. 1, pp. 8–9.

53. Thompson, *Barbour County,* 233; Rawick, ed., *American Slave,* ser. 2, vol. 12, pt. 1, p. 13.

54. Hague, *Blockaded Family,* 152–53; Rawick, ed., *American Slave,* ser. 2, vol. 12, pt. 1, p. 26; Scott, *Story of a Cavalry Regiment,* 492.

55. Rawick, ed., *American Slave,* ser. 2, vol. 12, pt. 1, p. 26; supplement, ser. 1, 1:257.

56. Ibid., ser. 2, vol. 12, pt. 1, p. 13.

57. Ibid., ser. 1, 6:219.

58. Escott, "Context of Freedom," 85.

CHAPTER 7. I Say Peace

1. *Blakely (Georgia) Early County News,* October 5, 1864.

2. Ibid., April 5, 1865.

3. Cumming, *Journal,* 209; *Blakely (Georgia) Early County News,* November 11, 1863, and September 21, 1864; Hamilton M. Weedom to Mary (Mollie) Young, March 26, 1865, in Weedom Papers.

4. Pussie Gay to John T. Gay, April 4, 1865, in Gay Letters.

5. *Blakely (Georgia) Early County News,* January 20 and November 2, 1864; Bryan, "Churches in Georgia," 296.

6. Bryan, *Confederate Georgia,* 150, 263 n. 74; Grant, *Way It Was in the South,* 82.

7. Winder to Cobb, July 9, 1864, in Ulrich B. Phillips, ed., *Correspondence,* 644–45; *Blakely (Georgia) Early County News,* September 14, 1864.

8. Hood, *Advance and Retreat,* 206. McNeill, "Survey of Confederate Soldier Morale," 13, confirms Hood's assessment. One Union soldier who witnessed the voluntary surrender of 173 Confederates noted that "they say they are sick of war and want peace on any terms."

9. Hubert Dent to Nannie Dent, September 7, 1864, in Mathis, ed., *In the Land of the Living,* 109.

10. Hodnett to brother William Hodnett, July 28, 1862, in *War Was the Place,* 61; Lokey, *My Experiences,* 24; Truett to parents, May 23, 1863, in Truett Civil War Letters; Hogg to parents, March 3, 1863, in Hogg Papers.

11. Jackson to Martha M. Jackson, January 24, 1864, in Jackson, ed., *So Mourns the Dove,* 77.

12. Hill, *Senator Benjamin H. Hill,* 87; *Blakely (Georgia) Early County News,* March 30, 1864.

13. *O.R.*, ser. 1, vol. 38, pt. 2, pp. 909–11.

14. Ibid., 904–7.

15. Ibid., pt. 3, pp. 973–74; Hamilton, *Recollections of a Cavalryman*, 137.

16. Hamilton, *Recollections of a Cavalryman*, 137; *O.R.*, ser. 1, vol. 38, pt. 3, pp. 973–74.

17. *O.R.*, ser. 1, vol. 38, pt. 2, pp. 908–9; Joseph H. Harris, Oak Bowery Journal, July 19, 1864. For overviews of Rousseau's raid, see Bearss, "Rousseau's Raid"; Fretwell, "Rousseau's Alabama Raid." See also "The Yankee Raid into Alabama," *Columbus (Georgia) Times* in *Thomasville (Georgia) Weekly Times*, August 4, 1864.

18. Bass, "Attack upon the Confederate Administration," 243; Hall, "Alexander H. Stephens," 60; Walter L. Fleming, "Peace Movement in Alabama," 121–22.

19. F. Kendall to Davis, September 16, 1864, in Berlin et al., *Free at Last*, 151; William Warren Rogers, *Thomas County*, 96; Cobb to wife, January 19, 1865, in Cobb Papers; Samford to General Henry A. Wise, December 16, 1864, in Petrie Collection. In 1860, Samford had opined that there were "greater calamities" than disunion: "I value our rights above ANY FORM OF GOVERNMENT WHATEVER" (*Opelika (Alabama) Southern Era*, September 1, 1860).

20. Sutton and others to Brown, July 25, 1864, and Julia A. Brooks and others to Brown, June 22, 1864, in Georgia, Petitions to the Governor; Chessy to Brown, October 7, 1864, and Sheffield to Brown, September 30, 1864, in Georgia, Governor's Correspondence.

21. *Columbus (Georgia) Daily Sun*, January 5, 1865.

22. Ibid., March 22, 1865.

23. Samford to Henry A. Wise, December 16, 1864, in Petrie Collection; Lee to Andrew Hunter, January 11, 1865, in Nolan, *Lee Considered*, 175–77.

24. Cobb to James A. Seddon, January 8, 1865, in *O.R.*, ser. 4, 3:1009–10.

25. Candler, comp., *Confederate Records*, 2:832–35; *Columbus (Georgia) Daily Sun*, November 20, 1864; *Blakely (Georgia) Early County News*, January 18, 1865.

26. *Columbus (Georgia) Times*, February 15, 1865. There seem to have been at least a few blacks who served unofficially in the Confederate armies (Jordan, *Black Confederates and Afro-Yankees in Civil War Virginia*).

27. Mohr, *On the Threshold of Freedom*, 283. For the most complete treatment of emancipation as an issue in the South, including the question of arming the slaves, see Durden, *Gray and the Black*. An excellent study of how the issue of arming slaves developed at the local level in Georgia is Dillard, "Arming the Slaves."

28. Mohr, *On the Threshold of Freedom*, 283–84; *Blakely (Georgia) Early County News*, April 5, 1865.

29. Hill, *Senator Benjamin H. Hill*, 273; Standard, *Columbus, Georgia, in the Confederacy*, 58.

30. James Pickett Jones, *Yankee Blitzkrieg,* 28.

31. McMillan, ed., *Alabama Confederate Reader,* 418; Wilson, *Under the Old Flag,* 2:265.

32. *Columbus (Georgia) Daily Sun,* April 15, 1865.

33. Candler, comp., *Confederate Records,* 3:712; Telfair, *History of Columbus, Georgia,* 134. The Peace Society may have contributed to difficulties in getting local men to answer the call to arms (Winn, "Columbus' Last Battle").

34. Zinken, Notice to the Citizens of Columbus.

35. Johnson and Buel, eds., *Battles and Leaders,* 4:761; M'Farland, "Battle of West Point," 353; Smith, *History of Troup County,* 78.

36. Bryan, *Confederate Georgia,* 185; Forrest Clark Johnson III, *Histories of LaGrange and Troup County,* 1:71. For concise overviews of the Nancy Harts, see Cleaveland, "Nancy Harts of LaGrange" and "Southern Girls with Guns."

37. *O.R.,* ser. 1, vol. 49, pt. 1, pp. 428–29; Scott, *Story of a Cavalry Regiment,* 481; M'Farland, "Battle of West Point," 354; Black, *Railroads of the Confederacy,* 287–90. See also Stanley, "A True Story of the Last Battle at West Point, Georgia," United Daughters of the Confederacy Collection.

38. *O.R.,* ser. 1, vol. 49, pt. 1, p. 480; Michie, ed., *Life and Letters of Emory Upton,* 166. For a brief overview of the action at Girard and Columbus, see Cantrell and Williams, "Battle for the Bridges."

39. Curry, comp., *Four Years in the Saddle,* 223, 224.

40. Ibid., 259, 261.

41. Ellison Letter.

42. *O.R.,* ser. 1, vol. 49, pt. 1, pp. 474, 481; Wilson, *Under the Old Flag,* 2:261.

43. Hinricks Diary, April 16, 1865, in James Pickett Jones, *Yankee Blitzkrieg,* 136.

44. Ibid., 137; *O.R.,* ser. 1, vol. 49, pt. 1, pp. 493–94.

45. *O.R.,* ser. 1, vol. 49, pt. 1, p. 481.

46. Wilson, *Under the Old Flag,* 264; James Pickett Jones, *Yankee Blitzkrieg,* 138.

47. James Pickett Jones, *Yankee Blitzkrieg,* 139.

48. Cantrell and Williams, "Battle for the Bridges," 43.

49. Swift, *Last Battle of the Civil War,* 27.

50. Wilson, *Under the Old Flag,* 2:266; Swift, *Last Battle of the Civil War,* 31; *O.R.,* ser. 1, vol. 49, pt. 1, p. 487.

51. *O.R.,* ser. 1, vol. 49, pt. 1, p. 485; Carnes Memoirs, 204–5; McLaughlin Letterbook, April 16, 1865; Ware "Enchantment and Ennui," 431–32; Turner, *Navy Gray,* 233–34, 142–45.

52. Cumming, *Journal,* 279; James Pickett Jones, *Yankee Blitzkrieg,* 142–43; DeCredico, *Patriotism for Profit,* 114–15.

53. Ingersoll, *Iowa and the Rebellion,* 438.

54. Bryan, *Confederate Georgia,* 185; Forrest Clark Johnson III, *Histories of LaGrange and Troup County,* 1:73; *Augusta (Georgia) Chronicle and Sentinel,* May 10, 1865; Horton, "Story of the Nancy Harts," 14. For a firsthand account of LaGrange's occupation and the Nancy Harts's role, see Morris, Personal Recollections of the War, Nancy Harts Folder, Troup County Archives.

55. James Pickett Jones, *Yankee Blitzkrieg,* 144.

56. *O.R.,* ser. 1, vol. 49, pt. 1, p. 300.

57. Hague, *Blockaded Family,* 144–45.

58. *O.R.,* ser. 1, vol. 49, pt. 1, pp. 300–301; Thompson, "Occupation of Eufaula"; Walker, *Backtracking in Barbour County,* 205; Thompson, *History of Barbour County,* 232–33; Shepard, *Quitman Echo,* 19.

59. "Uncle Lon" Winston Interview.

60. Rawick, ed., *American Slave,* ser. 2, vol. 13, pt. 4, p. 126.

61. Coulter, *Confederate States of America,* 105; Cleveland, *Alexander H. Stephens,* 721.

62. William H. Andrews, *Footprints of a Regiment,* 184.

63. Escott, *After Secession,* 128.

64. Owsley, "Defeatism in the Confederacy," 456; Mary Custis Lee to Edward Lee Childe, May 5, 1865, in Flood, *Lee,* 56. Owsley was the first prominent historian to argue that the causes of Confederate defeat were primarily internal. In his seminal work, *State Rights in the Confederacy,* Owsley emphasized the concept of state sovereignty written into the Confederate constitution and the weakness it imparted on the central government as the leading factor in the Confederacy's collapse.

65. Beringer et al., *Why the South Lost the Civil War,* 13; Lebergott, "Why the South Lost," 58–59. The Confederate Ordnance Bureau's operation under Josiah Gorgas is most fully explored in Vandiver, *Ploughshares into Swords.*

EPILOGUE. Teach Them Their Places

1. *O.R.,* ser. 1, vol. 49, pt. 1, p. 301.

2. Grant, *Way It Was in the South,* 92; McNeil to Wilkinson, n.d., folder 3, Wilkinson Family Papers; Alexander Nunn, ed., *Lee County and Her Forebears,* 255.

3. Mary Love Edwards Fleming, "Dale County and Its People," 80; Pruett, ed., "Diary of Ann Browder," 51; Mathis, *John Horry Dent,* 213.

4. Rawick, ed., *American Slave,* ser. 2, vol. 12, pt. 1, pp. 133–34; Escott, "Context of Freedom," 99; Rawick, ed., *American Slave,* ser. 2, vol. 13, pt. 3, p. 6.

5. *Macon (Georgia) Daily Telegraph,* July 18, 1865; Wynne, *Continuity of Cotton,* 2–4.

6. Walker, *Backtracking in Barbour County,* 225; Clayton, *White and Black under the Old Regime,* 162.

7. *Bainbridge (Georgia) Argus,* June 19 and 26, 1869.

8. Grant, *Way It Was in the South*, 95–96; Flynn, *White Land, Black Labor,* 35–37; Drago, *Black Politicians and Reconstruction in Georgia*, 103.

9. Georgia General Assembly, *Acts*, 6–8; Kolchin, *First Freedom*, 63–65; U.S. Bureau of Refugees, Freedmen, and Abandoned Lands, Records of the Assistant Commissioner for the State of Georgia, register of letters received, M798, roll 12, 4:318, register of endorsements sent, M798, roll 10, 5:153.

10. Grant, *Way it Was in the South*, 117, 99.

11. Both the federal and state governments understood the amendment to apply only to males. Voting rights for women, black or white, were not guaranteed by constitutional amendment until 1920.

12. Drago, *Black Politicians and Reconstruction in Georgia*, 148.

13. Rawick, ed., *American Slave*, ser. 1, 6:308. For specific instances of violence against freedmen in the valley's Georgia counties in 1868, see Tift, *Condition of Affairs in Georgia*, 124–35.

14. Conway, *Reconstruction of Georgia*, 158–60; Drago, *Black Politicians and Reconstruction in Georgia*, 145–46. See also Daniell, "Ashburn Murder Case."

15. Drago, *Black Politicians and Reconstruction in Georgia*, 149. For a discussion of armed resistance to the Klan by freedmen in Stewart, Randolph, Quitman, and Clay Counties, see Cimbala, *Under the Guardianship of the Nation*, 209–10. For details concerning fraud, intimidation, and violence at the polls in November 1868, see Tift, *Condition of Affairs in Georgia*, 64, 67–69. One of the worst instances of election-day violence occurred in Eufaula when a number of freedmen were shot down by an "unofficial white militia" as they stood in line at the polls (Hennessey, "Reconstruction Politics and the Military").

16. Two of the best overviews of how and to what extent the planters regained power in the South are Wynne, *Continuity of Cotton*, and Wiener, *Social Origins of the New South*. For an excellent local study, see Formwalt, "Planter Persistence in Southwest Georgia."

17. Sherman, *Memoirs*, 2:250–52; Foner, *Reconstruction*, 70–71; Foner, *Nothing but Freedom*, 6. Well into the twentieth century there were former slaves who still felt the injustice of working without pay. In 1936, Mary Carpenter of Harris County asked one special favor of the person interviewing her for the Federal Writers Project: "All us old slave-time darkies oughta be pensioned, and I wish you'd tell Governor [Eugene] Talmadge that I said that" (Rawick, ed., *American Slave*, supplement, ser. 1, vol. 3, pt. 1, p. 145).

18. Grant, *Way It Was in the South*, 137. For a review of the postwar life of poor whites, see Flynt, "Spindle, Mine, and Mule"; Gilmour, "Other Emancipation."

19. Coleman, ed., *History of Georgia*, 259; Loveman, *Historical Atlas*, 58.

20. Coleman, ed., *History of Georgia*, 259.

21. Opposing company oppression was dangerous work. When the United Textile Workers held a rally near Columbus's Bibb Manufacturing Company in

1919, company operatives fired on the crowd, killing one man, crippling a twelve-year-old boy, and wounding four other people. After the shooting, Bibb made sure "that the law would not touch its men" (Byrne, "Wartime Agitation and Postwar Repression," 366–68).

22. Flynn, *White Land, Black Labor,* 150. Just as before the war, a poll tax worked to keep the poorest citizens away from the polls (Wallenstein, "Rich Man's War, Rich Man's Fight," 40).

23. Woodward, *Tom Watson,* 190. Watson later adopted an "if you can't beat 'em, join 'em" strategy, becoming one of the most racist campaigners in Georgia's political history. It worked. In 1920, he was elected to the U.S. Senate.

24. Ibid., 191.

25. Ibid., 195.

26. Watkins, *"Co. Aytch,"* 69; O.R., ser. 4, 3:413. For the most complete treatment available on the rise of the Lost Cause, see Foster, *Ghosts of the Confederacy.*

27. Rutledge, "Stephen W. Rutledge," 108.

BIBLIOGRAPHY

Primary Sources

ARCHIVAL MATERIAL, MANUSCRIPT COLLECTIONS,
AND CEMETERY RECORDS

Alabama. Governor's Correspondence, 1861–65. Alabama Department of Archives and History. Montgomery.

Atkinson, Joe. Collection. Cobb Memorial Archives. Valley, Alabama.

Bacon Family Letters. Troup County Archives. LaGrange, Georgia.

Baker, Paul DeLacy. Letter, Alabama–Barbour County Letters Folder. Carnegie Library. Eufaula, Alabama.

Bigbie, Thomas T. Collection. Alabama Department of Archives and History. Montgomery.

Blanchard, Thomas Eliel. Diary. Columbus Museum Collection. Columbus State University Archives. Columbus, Georgia.

Boyd Letters. Columbus Museum Collection. Columbus State University Archives. Columbus, Georgia.

Brooks, William. Civil War Letter. AC 00-268. Georgia Department of Archives and History. Atlanta.

Carmichael, J. M. "A War Incident: The Bushwhackers in Southeast Alabama." Alabama–Barbour County Letters Folder. Carnegie Library. Eufaula, Alabama.

Carnes, William Watts. Memoirs. Confederate Naval Museum. Columbus, Georgia.

Chappell Collection. Columbus State University Archives. Columbus, Georgia.

Cherry, Francis LaFayette. Papers. Alabama Department of Archives and History. Montgomery.

Clay, Clement Claiborne. Papers. Records of Ante-Bellum Southern Plantations from the Revolution through the Civil War, Series F, Part 1, Roll 21. Auburn University Library. Auburn, Alabama.

Cobb, Howell. Papers. University of Georgia Library. Athens.

Confederate Secretary of War. Letters Received. National Archives. Washington, D.C.

"Co-Operation Meeting of the Citizens of Stewart County" (broadside). Stewart County Archives Folder, File 2, Counties. Georgia Department of Archives and History. Atlanta.

Crockett, Benjamin Franklin. Compiled Service Records. National Archives. Washington, D.C.

Crowder Family Papers. Auburn University Archives. Auburn, Alabama.

Curry Hill Plantation Records. Georgia Department of Archives and History. Atlanta.

Curtright, Mary Charles Evans. Papers. Troup County Archives. LaGrange, Georgia.

Denny, D. M. Confederate Letters Collection. Auburn University Archives. Auburn, Alabama.

Dent Confederate Collection. Auburn University Archives. Auburn, Alabama.

Ellison, F. A. Letter. Hurtsboro Folder, Russell County Clippings File. Alabama Department of Archives and History. Montgomery.

Fife, William. Compiled Service Records. National Archives. Washington, D.C.

Fraser, Alexander. Collection. Auburn University Archives. Auburn, Alabama.

Fuller, John. Compiled Service Records. National Archives. Washington, D.C.

Gary, Charles Mack. Papers. Alabama Department of Archives and History. Montgomery.

Gay, John T. Letters. Nix-Price Collection. Troup County Archives. LaGrange, Georgia.

Georgia. Governor's Correspondence, 1861–65. Georgia Department of Archives and History. Atlanta.

Georgia. Petitions to the Governor, 1861–65. Georgia Department of Archives and History. Atlanta.

Gorham, Anna Fannie. Diary. Columbus State University Collection. Columbus State University Archives. Columbus, Georgia.

Hammond, Hiram Warner. Diary. Civil War Collection. Cobb Memorial Archives. Valley, Alabama.

Harris, Joseph H. Oak Bowery Journal. Cobb Memorial Archives. Valley, Alabama.

Harris, Thomas DeKalb. Family Papers. Georgia Department of Archives and History. Atlanta.

Hatcher and McGehee Account Book. Columbus State University Archives. Columbus, Georgia.

Heard, Janie Lovelace. Collection. Cobb Memorial Archives. Valley, Alabama.

Hogg, John J. Papers. Troup County Archives. LaGrange, Georgia.

Jenkins, Cyrus F. Diary. Troup County Archives. LaGrange, Georgia.

Johnson, A. J. (Alvin Jewett). *Johnson's Georgia and Alabama, 1863*. New York: Johnson and Ward, 1863. Auburn University Special Collections. Auburn, Alabama.

Jones, J. H. Letter. Chattahoochee Valley Historical Society Collection. Cobb Memorial Archives. Valley, Alabama.

Jones, Seborn, and Henry L. Benning. Papers. Columbus State University Archives. Columbus, Georgia.

Kirkland, John Joseph. Compiled Service Records. National Archives. Washington, D.C.

Ladies Relief Society Minutes. Chattahoochee Valley Historical Society Collection. Cobb Memorial Archives. Valley, Alabama.

Lee, B. C. Collection. Auburn University Archives. Auburn, Alabama.

Mann, Nancy O., and Thomas A. Mann. Civil War Papers. Georgia Department of Archives and History. Atlanta.

McLaughlin, Augustus. Letterbook and Confederate Navy Yard Log and Accounts. Confederate Naval Museum. Columbus, Georgia.

Meriwether, John S. Letters. Alabama–Barbour County Letters Folder. Carnegie Library. Eufaula, Alabama.

Mobile (Alabama) Daily Herald and Tribune. Correspondence. Alabama–Barbour County Letters Folder. Carnegie Library. Eufaula, Alabama.

Morris, Leila C. Personal Recollections of the War. Nancy Harts Folder. Troup County Archives. LaGrange, Georgia.

Petrie, George. Collection. Auburn University Archives. Auburn, Alabama.

Phillips Letters. Alabama–Barbour County Letters Folder. Carnegie Library. Eufaula, Alabama.

Pine Grove Cemetery Records. Phenix City, Alabama.

Prescott, Emma J. Slade. Reminiscences. Atlanta Historical Society Archives. Atlanta.

Rhodes, Elizabeth. Diary. Auburn University Special Collections. Auburn, Alabama.

Ross Civil War Letters. Confederate Collection. Auburn University Archives. Auburn, Alabama.

Sanders, Joseph G. Compiled Service Records. National Archives. Washington, D.C.

Shorter, John Gill. Collection. Alabama Department of Archives and History. Montgomery.

Slavery in Troup County Folder. Troup County Archives. LaGrange, Georgia.

Solomon, John W. Papers. Alabama Department of Archives and History. Montgomery.

Stanley, Isham. "A True Story of the Last Battle at West Point, Georgia." United Daughters of the Confederacy Collection. Cobb Memorial Archives. Valley, Alabama.

Troup County Inferior Court Minutes. Troup County Archives. LaGrange, Georgia.

Truett, Joseph H. Civil War Letters. Minnie Robertson Smith Collection. Georgia Department of Archives and History. Atlanta.

Turner, William W. Letters. Troup County Archives. LaGrange, Georgia.

Union Missionary Baptist Church Cemetery Records. Miller County, Georgia.

Union Primitive Baptist Church Cemetery Records. Miller County, Georgia.

U.S. Bureau of Refugees, Freedmen, and Abandoned Lands. Records of the Assistant Commissioner for the State of Georgia. National Archives Microfilm Publication M798. National Archives. Washington, D.C.

Weedom, H. M. Papers. Auburn University Archives. Auburn, Alabama.

Wellborn Memorial Collection. Auburn University Archives. Auburn, Alabama.

Wilkinson Family Papers. Manuscripts Section. AC 68-080. Georgia Department of Archives and History. Atlanta.

Winston, George H. Collection. Cobb Memorial Archives. Valley, Alabama.

Winston, "Uncle Lon." Interview (c. 1940). "Little Valley Stories: Slavery Days." Margaret Parker Milford Collection. Cobb Memorial Archives. Valley, Alabama.

Zinken, Leon von. Notice to the Citizens of Columbus, April 15, 1865. Columbus State University Archives. Columbus, Georgia.

GOVERNMENT PUBLICATIONS

Candler, Allen D., comp. *The Confederate Records of the State of Georgia*. 6 vols. (vol. 5 never published). Atlanta: State Printing Office, 1909–11.

Confederate States Army. *Regulations for the Medical Department of the Confederate States Army*. Richmond, Va.: Richie and Dunnavant, 1863.

Georgia General Assembly. *Acts of the General Assembly of the State of Georgia Passed in Milledgeville, at an Annual Session in December 1865, and January, February, and March, 1866*. Milledgeville, Ga.: Boughton, Nisbet, Barnes, and Moore, 1866.

Journal of the Public and Secret Proceedings of the Convention of the People of Georgia, 1861. Milledgeville, Ga.: Boughton, Nisbet, and Barnes, 1861.

Official Records of the Union and Confederate Navies in the War of the Rebellion. 31 vols. Washington, D.C.: Government Printing Office, 1894–1927.

Reports of Cases in Law and Equity Argued and Determined in the Supreme Court of the State of Georgia from Macon Term to Americus Term, 1854, Inclusive. Thomas R. R. Cobb, reporter. Vol. 15. Athens, Ga.: Reynolds and Brother, 1855.

Tift, Nelson. *The Condition of Affairs in Georgia: Statement of Hon. Nelson Tift to the Reconstruction Committee of the House of Representatives, Washington, February 18, 1869*. Freeport, N.Y.: Books for Libraries Press, 1971.

U.S. Census Bureau. *Agriculture of the United States in 1860*. Washington, D.C.: Government Printing Office, 1864. Reprint, New York: Norman Ross, 1990.

———. *Eighth Census of the United States, 1860*. Washington, D.C.: Government Printing Office, 1864.

———. *Manufactures of the United States in 1860*. Washington, D.C.: Government Printing Office, 1864. Reprint, New York: Norman Ross, 1990.

———. *Population of the United States in 1860*. Washington, D.C.: Government Printing Office, 1864. Reprint, New York: Norman Ross, 1990.

———. *Seventh Census of the United States, 1850*. Washington, D.C.: Robert Armstrong, 1853. Reprint, New York: Norman Ross, 1990.

———. *Statistics of the United States in 1860.* Washington, D.C.: Government Printing Office, 1866. Reprint, New York: Arno Press, 1976.

War of the Rebellion: A Compilation of the Official Records of the Union and Confederate Armies. 128 parts in 70 vols. Washington, D.C.: Government Printing Office, 1880–1901.

NEWSPAPERS

Albany (Georgia) Patriot, 1856, 1861.
Augusta (Georgia) Chronicle and Sentinel, 1865.
Atlanta Daily Intelligencer, 1860.
Atlanta Southern Confederacy, 1863.
Bainbridge (Georgia) Argus, 1869.
Blakely (Georgia) Early County News, 1863–65, 1916.
Clayton (Alabama) Banner, 1861.
Columbus (Georgia) Daily Sun, 1859–65.
Columbus (Georgia) Enquirer, 1833, 1850, 1852, 1856, 1860, 1862–63.
Columbus (Georgia) Times, 1860–61, 1864–65.
Cuthbert (Georgia) Reporter, 1856, 1860.
Eufaula (Alabama) Express, 1858–60.
Eufaula (Alabama) Spirit of the South, 1850, 1861.
LaFayette (Alabama) Chambers Tribune, 1859, 1863.
LaGrange (Georgia) Daily Bulletin, 1864.
LaGrange (Georgia) Reporter, 1863, 1865.
Macon (Georgia) Daily Telegraph, 1861, 1865.
Milledgeville (Georgia) Southern Recorder, 1863–64.
Mobile (Alabama) Daily Herald and Tribune, 1849.
Montgomery (Alabama) Daily Mail, 1864.
Opelika (Alabama) Southern Era, 1859–60.
Opelika (Alabama) Southern Republic, 1861–62.
Ozark (Alabama) Southern Star, 1899.
Thomaston (Georgia) Upson Pilot, 1860.
Thomasville (Georgia) Southern Enterprise, 1861.
Thomasville (Georgia) Weekly Times, 1864.
Thomasville (Georgia) Wire Grass Reporter, 1861.

PUBLISHED DOCUMENTARY SOURCES

Andrews, Eliza Frances. *The Wartime Journal of a Georgia Girl.* Edited by Spencer Bidwell King Jr. Atlanta: Cherokee Publishing Co., 1976.

Andrews, William H. *Footprints of a Regiment: A Recollection of the First Georgia Regulars, 1861–1865.* Introduction by Richard M. McMurry. Atlanta: Longstreet Press, 1992.

Berlin, Ira, Barbara J. Fields, Steven F. Miller, Joseph P. Reidy, and Leslie S. Rowland, eds. *Free at Last: A Documentary History of Slavery, Freedom, and the Civil War.* New York: New Press, 1992.

Botkin, B. A., ed. *Lay My Burden Down: A Folk History of Slavery.* Athens: University of Georgia Press, 1989.

Burnett, Edmund Cody, ed. "Letters of Barnett Hardeman Cody and Others, 1861–1864." *Georgia Historical Quarterly* 23 (1939): 265–99, 362–80.

———, ed. "Letters of Three Lightfoot Brothers, 1861–1864." *Georgia Historical Quarterly* 25 (1941): 371–400; 26 (1942): 65–90.

Cadenhead, I. B. "Some Confederate Letters of I. B. Cadenhead." *Alabama Historical Quarterly* 18 (1956): 564–71.

Cartwright, Samuel A. "Diseases and Peculiarities of the Negro Race." In *The Cause of the South: Selections from* De Bow's Review, *1846–1867,* edited by Paul R. Paskoff and Daniel J. Wilson, 26–43. Baton Rouge: Louisiana State University Press, 1982.

Castlen, Harriet Gift. *Hope Bids Me Onward.* Savannah, Ga.: Chatham Printing Co., 1945.

Chapman, R. D. *A Georgia Soldier in the Civil War, 1861–1865.* Houston, Tex.: n.p., 1923.

Chesnut, Mary. *Mary Chesnut's Civil War.* Edited by C. Vann Woodward. New Haven: Yale University Press, 1981.

Clayton, Victoria V. *White and Black under the Old Regime.* Milwaukee, Wis.: Young Churchman Co., 1899. Reprint, Freeport, N.Y.: Books for Libraries Press, 1970.

Cleveland, Henry. *Alexander H. Stephens in Public and Private with Letters and Speeches, before, during, and since the War.* Philadelphia: National Publishing Co., 1866.

"Cotton—How Much to Plant." *Southern Cultivator* 20 (January 1862): 13.

Crist, Lynda Lasswell, and Mary Seaton Dix, eds. *The Papers of Jefferson Davis.* Vol. 7. Baton Rouge: Louisiana State University Press, 1992.

Cumming, Kate. *Gleanings from Southland: Sketches of Life and Manners of the People of the South before, during, and after the War of Secession.* Birmingham, Ala.: Roberts and Son, 1895.

———. *The Journal of Kate Cumming—A Confederate Nurse, 1862–1865.* Edited by Richard Harwell. Savannah, Ga.: Beehive Press, 1975.

Curry, W. L., comp. *Four Years in the Saddle: History of the First Regiment, Ohio Volunteer Cavalry.* Jonesboro, Ga.: Freedom Hill Press, 1898.

Devens, Richard M. *The Pictorial Book of Anecdotes and Incidents of the War of the Rebellion.* Hartford, Conn.: Hartford Publishing Company, 1866.

Dudley, William, ed. *The Civil War: Opposing Viewpoints.* San Diego, Calif.: Greenhaven Press, 1992.

Evans, Augusta Jane. *Beulah.* New York: Derby and Jackson, 1859; Baton Rouge: Louisiana State University Press, 1992.

————. *Macaria; or, Altars of Sacrifice.* New York: J. Bradburn, 1864; Baton Rouge: Louisiana State University Press, 1992.

Featherstonhaugh, G. W. *Excursion through the Slave States.* New York: Harper and Brothers, 1844. Reprint, New York: Negro Universities Press, 1968.

Fitzhugh, George. *Sociology for the South, or the Failure of Free Society.* New York: Burt Franklin, 1854.

Fleming, Mary Love Edwards. "Dale County and Its People during the Civil War." *Alabama Historical Quarterly* 19 (1957): 61–109.

Freehling, William W., and Craig M. Simpson, eds. *Secession Debated: Georgia's Showdown in 1860.* New York: Oxford University Press, 1992.

"A Good Example." *Southern Cultivator* 20 (May–June 1862): 114.

"Gov. Brown's Letter." *Southern Cultivator* 20 (March–April 1862): 68.

Graf, LeRoy P., and Ralph W. Haskins, eds. "The Letters of a Georgia Unionist: John G. Winter and Secession." *Georgia Historical Quarterly* 45 (1961): 385–402.

Grantham, Dewey W., Jr., ed. "Letters From H. J. Hightower, a Confederate Soldier, 1862–1864." *Georgia Historical Quarterly* 40 (1956): 174–89.

Greene, Rhodom A., and John W. Lumpkin. *The Georgia Justice: Being a Convenient Directory for the Justices of the Peace.* Milledgeville, Ga.: P. L. and B. H. Robinson, 1835.

Griffith, Lucille, ed. *Alabama: A Documentary History to 1900.* Tuscaloosa: University of Alabama Press, 1972.

Hague, Parthenia A. *A Blockaded Family: Life in Southern Alabama during the Civil War.* Cambridge, Mass.: Riverside Press, 1888. Reprint, Freeport, N.Y.: Books for Libraries Press, 1971.

Hamilton, William Douglas. *Recollections of a Cavalryman of the Civil War after Fifty Years, 1861–1865.* Columbus, Ohio: F. J. Herr Printing Co., 1915.

Helper, Hinton Rowan. *The Impending Crisis of the South.* New York: Burdick Brothers, 1857. Reprint, Cambridge: Harvard University Press, 1968.

Henderson, Lillian, comp. *Roster of the Confederate Soldiers of Georgia, 1861–1865.* 6 vols. Hapeville, Ga.: Longina and Porter, 1959–64.

Hill, Benjamin H., Jr. *Senator Benjamin H. Hill of Georgia: His Life, Speeches and Writings.* Atlanta: H. C. Hudgins and Co., 1891.

Hood, John Bell. *Advance and Retreat: Personal Experiences in the United States and Confederate Armies.* New Orleans: G. T. Beauregard, 1880.

Houghton, W. R., and M. B. Houghton. *Two Boys in the Civil War and After.* Montgomery, Ala.: Paragon Press, 1912.

Howard, Milo B., Jr., ed. "Governor John Gill Shorter Executive Papers." *Alabama Historical Quarterly* 23 (1961): 278–88.

Howard, Robert M. *Reminiscences.* Columbus, Ga.: Gilbert Printing Co., 1912.

Jackson, Alto Loftin, ed. *So Mourns the Dove: Letters of a Confederate Infantryman and His Family.* New York: Exposition Press, 1965.

Johnson, Robert U., and Clarence C. Buel, eds. *Battles and Leaders of the Civil War.* 4 vols. New York: Century, 1887–88.

Johnson, Rossiter. *Campfire and Battlefield: A History of the Conflicts and Campaigns of the Great Civil War in the United States.* New York: Knight and Brown, 1896.

Jones, Katherine M., ed. *Heroines of Dixie: Spring of High Hopes.* St. Simons Island, Ga.: Mockingbird Books, 1983.

Lane, Mills, ed. *The Rambler in Georgia.* Savannah, Ga.: Beehive Press, 1973.

————, ed. *Times That Prove People's Principles: Civil War in Georgia—A Documentary History.* Savannah, Ga.: Beehive Press, 1993.

Latham, Milton S. "Latham Letter." *Alabama Historical Quarterly* 19 (1957): 145-47.

Locke, John. *The Second Treatise of Government.* Indianapolis: Bobbs-Merrill, 1979.

Lokey, J. W. *My Experiences in the War between the States.* Tishomingo, Okla.: n.p., 1959.

Longstreet, James. *From Manassas to Appomattox: Memoirs of the Civil War in America.* Philadelphia: J. B. Lippincott Co., 1896.

Martin, John H., ed. *Columbus, Georgia, from Its Selection as a Trading Town in 1827 to Its Partial Destruction by Wilson's Raid in 1865.* 2 parts. Columbus, Ga.: Thomas Gilbert, 1874–75. Reprint, Easley, S.C.: Georgia Genealogical Reprints, 1972.

Mathis, Ray, ed. *In the Land of the Living: Wartime Letters by Confederates from the Chattahoochee Valley of Alabama and Georgia.* Troy, Ala.: Troy State University Press, 1981.

McClendon, William Augustus. *Recollections of War Times by an Old Veteran while under Stonewall Jackson and Lieutenant General James Longstreet: How I Got in, and How I Got Out.* Montgomery, Ala.: Paragon Press, 1909. Reprint, San Bernardino, Calif.: California Church Press, 1973.

McGinnis, Callie B. "Hatcher and McGehee Negro Book." *Muscogiana* 4 (summer 1993): 8–16.

McMillan, Malcolm C., ed. *The Alabama Confederate Reader.* Tuscaloosa: University of Alabama Press, 1963.

Mears and Company, comp. *The Columbus Directory, for 1859–1860.* Columbus, Ga.: Sun Book and Job Printing Office, 1859.

Merz, Louis. "Diary of Private Louis Merz, C.S.A., of the West Point Guards, 1862." *Chattahoochee Valley Historical Society Bulletin* 4 (1959): 17–45.

M'Farland, L. B. "The Battle of West Point." *Confederate Veteran* 23 (1915): 353-55.

Michie, Peter, ed. *The Life and Letters of Emory Upton.* New York: D. Appleton, 1885.

Moses, Jacob Raphael. "A Southern Romantic." In *Memoirs of American Jews,*

1775–1865, compiled by Jacob Rader Marcus, vol. 1. Philadelphia: Jewish Publication Society of America, 1955.

Oates, William C. *The War between the Union and the Confederacy and Its Lost Opportunities, with a History of the Fifteenth Alabama Regiment and the Forty-eight Battles in Which It Was Engaged.* New York and Washington, D.C.: Neale Publishing, 1905.

Olmsted, Frederick Law. *The Cotton Kingdom: A Traveler's Observations on Cotton and Slavery in the American Slave States.* New York: Alfred A. Knopf, 1953.

Otto, Rhea Cumming, comp. *1850 Census of Georgia, Muscogee County.* Savannah, Ga.: Otto, 1977.

Phillips, Ulrich B., ed. *The Correspondence of Robert Toombs, Alexander H. Stephens, and Howell Cobb.* Washington, D.C.: Government Printing Office, 1913.

Pruett, Dorothy Sturgis, ed. *The Diary of Ann Browder, 1858–1859, 1866–1867.* Macon, Ga.: Pruett, 1984.

Rawick, George P., ed. *The American Slave: A Composite Autobiography.* Series 1 and 2, 19 vols. Supplement, Series 1, 12 vols. Westport, Conn.: Greenwood Press, 1972 and 1977.

Robinson, Norborne T. N., III, ed. "Blind Tom, Musical Prodigy." *Georgia Historical Quarterly* 51 (1967): 336–58.

Rutledge, Stephen W. "Stephen W. Rutledge: His Autobiography and Civil War Journal." *East Tennessee Roots* 6 (fall 1989): 101–12.

Scott, William Forse. *The Story of a Cavalry Regiment: The Career of the Fourth Iowa Veteran Volunteers from Kansas to Georgia, 1861–1865.* New York: Knickerbocker Press, 1893.

Sherman, William T. *Memoirs of General William T. Sherman.* 2 vols. New York: D. Appleton and Co., 1875.

Stampp, Kenneth M., ed. *The Causes of the Civil War.* Englewood Cliffs, N.J.: Prentice Hall, 1974.

Stirling, James. *Letters from the Slave States.* London: John W. Parker and Son, 1857.

Thomas, Henry W. *History of the Doles-Cook Brigade, Army of Northern Virginia, C.S.A.* Atlanta: Franklin Publishing, 1903.

Volck, Adalbert John. *Sketches from the Civil War in North America.* London: Volck, 1863–64.

"War Was the Place: A Centennial Collection of Confederate Soldier Letters." *Chattahoochee Valley Historical Society Bulletin* 5 (1961).

Watkins, Sam R. *"Co. Aytch."* Nashville: Cumberland Presbyterian Publishing House, 1882. Reprint, Wilmington, N.C.: Broadfoot Publishing Co., 1987.

Wiley, Bell Irvin, ed. "The Confederate Letters of John W. Hagan." *Georgia Historical Quarterly* 38 (1954): 170–200, 268–89.

Wilson, James Harrison. *Under the Old Flag.* 2 vols. New York: D. Appleton and Co., 1912.

Wynne, Lewis N., and Guy Porcher Harrison, eds. "'Plain Folk' Coping in the Confederacy: The Garrett-Asbell Letters." *Georgia Historical Quarterly* 72 (1988): 102–18.

Young, Mel, ed. *Last Order of the Lost Cause: The Civil War Memoirs of a Jewish Family from the "Old South," Raphael Jacob Moses, Major, C.S.A., 1812–1893.* Lanham, Md.: University Press of America, 1995.

Secondary Sources

Adams, O. Burton. "Martin Jenkins Crawford." In *Dictionary of Georgia Biography,* edited by Kenneth Coleman and Stephen Gurr, 229–30. Athens: University of Georgia Press, 1983.

Alexander, Thomas B., and Peggy J. Duckworth. "Alabama Black Belt Whigs during Secession: A New Viewpoint." *Alabama Review* 17 (1964): 181–97.

Ambrose, Stephen E. "Yeoman Discontent in the Confederacy." *Civil War History* 8 (1962): 259–68.

Azbell, Joe. "The Haunted Hole Where They Hanged the Spaniard." *Montgomery Advertiser,* February 29, 1952.

Bailey, Fred Arthur. *Class and Tennessee's Confederate Generation.* Chapel Hill: University of North Carolina Press, 1987.

Bailey, Hugh C. "Disaffection in the Alabama Hill Country, 1861." *Civil War History* 4 (1958): 183–93.

———. "Disloyalty in Early Confederate Alabama." *Journal of Southern History* 23 (1957): 522–28.

Barfield, Louise Calhoun. *History of Harris County, Georgia, 1827–1961.* Columbus, Ga.: Columbus Office Supply Co., 1961.

Barney, William L. *The Road to Secession: A New Perspective on the Old South.* New York: Praeger Publishers, 1972.

———. *The Secessionist Impulse: Alabama and Mississippi in 1860.* Princeton: Princeton University Press, 1974.

Bartley, Numan V. *The Creation of Modern Georgia.* 2d ed. Athens: University of Georgia Press, 1990.

Bass, James Horace. "The Attack upon the Confederate Administration in Georgia in the Spring of 1864." *Georgia Historical Quarterly* 18 (1934): 228–47.

Beals, Carleton. *War within a War: The Confederacy against Itself.* Philadelphia and New York: Chilton Books, 1965.

Bearss, Edwin C. "Rousseau's Raid on the Montgomery and West Point Railroad." *Alabama Historical Quarterly* 25 (1939): 7–48.

Beauchamp, Green. "Early Chronicles of Barbour County." *Alabama Historical Quarterly* 33 (1971): 37–74.

Beringer, Richard E., Herman Hattaway, Archer Jones, and William N. Still. *Why the South Lost the Civil War.* Athens: University of Georgia Press, 1986.

Bernstein, Iver. *The New York City Draft Riots: Their Significance for American Society and Politics in the Age of the Civil War.* New York: Oxford University Press, 1990.

Black, Robert C. *Railroads of the Confederacy.* Chapel Hill: University of North Carolina Press, 1952.

———. "The Railroads of Georgia in the Confederate War Effort." *Journal of Southern History* 18 (1947): 511–34.

Bode, Frederick A., and Donald E. Ginter. *Farm Tenancy and the Census in Antebellum Georgia.* Athens: University of Georgia Press, 1986.

Bolton, Charles C. *Poor Whites of the Antebellum South: Tenants and Laborers in Central North Carolina and Northeast Mississippi.* Durham, N.C.: Duke University Press, 1994.

Boney, F. N. *Southerners All.* Macon, Ga.: Mercer University Press, 1984.

Bonner, James C. "Profile of a Late Ante-Bellum Community." *American Historical Review* 49 (1944): 663–80.

Bowie, Marshall L. *A Time of Adversity—and Courage: A Story of the Montgomery and West Point Rail Road, 1861–1865.* N.p.: n.d.

Bryan, T. Conn. "The Churches in Georgia during the Civil War." *Georgia Historical Quarterly* 33 (1949): 283–302.

———. *Confederate Georgia.* Athens: University of Georgia Press, 1953.

Bryant, Jonathan M. *How Curious a Land: Conflict and Change in Greene County, Georgia, 1850–1885.* Chapel Hill: University of North Carolina Press, 1996.

Bynum, Victoria E. Review of *Poor Whites of the Antebellum South,* by Charles C. Bolton. *Journal of Southern History* 61 (1995): 601–2.

———. *Unruly Women: The Politics of Social and Sexual Control in the Old South.* Chapel Hill: University of North Carolina Press, 1992.

Byrne, Frank J. "Wartime Agitation and Postwar Repression: Reverend John A. Callan and the Columbus Strikes of 1918–1919." *Georgia Historical Quarterly* 81 (1997): 345–69.

Cantrell, Kimberly Bess, and H. David Williams. "Battle for the Bridges." *America's Civil War* (March 1991): 38–44.

Carey, Anthony Gene. *Parties, Slavery, and the Union in Antebellum Georgia.* Athens: University of Georgia Press, 1997.

Chattahoochee Trace Historical Markers. Eufaula, Ala.: Historic Chattahoochee Commission, 1983.

Christian, Rebecca. "Georgia and the Confederate Policy of Impressing Supplies." *Georgia Historical Quarterly* 28 (1944): 1–33.

Cimbala, Paul A. *Under the Guardianship of the Nation: The Freedmen's Bureau and the Reconstruction of Georgia, 1865–1870.* Athens: University of Georgia Press, 1997.

Cleaveland, R. Chris. "The Nancy Harts of LaGrange." *Georgia Journal* (fall 1991): 8–9, 19.

————. "Southern Girls with Guns: Georgia's Nancy Harts." *Civil War Times Illustrated* 33 (May–June 1994): 44–45.

Clinton, Catherine, and Nina Silber, eds. *Divided Houses: Gender and the Civil War.* New York: Oxford University Press, 1992.

Cobb, James C. "The Making of a Secessionist: Henry L. Benning and the Coming of the Civil War." *Georgia Historical Quarterly* 60 (1976): 313–23.

Coleman, Kenneth, ed. *A History of Georgia.* Athens: University of Georgia Press, 1977.

Collins, Bruce. *White Society in the Antebellum South.* London and New York: Longman House, 1985.

Conway, Alan. *The Reconstruction of Georgia.* Minneapolis: University of Minnesota Press, 1966.

Cook, James F. "James Johnson." In *Dictionary of Georgia Biography,* edited by Kenneth Coleman and Stephen Gurr, 1:536–37. Athens: University of Georgia Press, 1983.

Cooper, William J., and Thomas E. Terrill. *The American South: A History.* 2 vols. New York: McGraw-Hill, 1991.

Coulter, E. Merton. *The Confederate States of America, 1861–1865.* Baton Rouge: Louisiana State University Press, 1950.

Crawford, George B. "Cotton, Land, and Sustenance: Toward the Limits of Abundance in Late Antebellum Georgia." *Georgia Historical Quarterly* 72 (1988): 215–47.

Cruden, Robert. *Many and One: A Social History of the United States.* Englewood Cliffs, N.J.: Prentice-Hall, 1980.

Current, Richard Nelson. *Lincoln's Loyalists: Union Soldiers from the Confederacy.* Boston: Northeastern University Press, 1992. Reprint, New York: Oxford University Press, 1994.

Cushman, Joseph D., Jr. "The Blockade and Fall of Apalachicola, 1861–1862." *Florida Historical Quarterly* 41 (1962–63): 38–46.

Daniel, Larry J., and Riley W. Gunter. *Confederate Cannon Foundries.* Union City, Tenn.: Pioneer Press, 1977.

Daniell, Elizabeth Otto. "The Ashburn Murder Case in Georgia Reconstruction, 1868." *Georgia Historical Quarterly* 59 (1975): 296–312.

Davidson, William H. *Brooks of Honey and Butter: Plantations and People of Meriwether County, Georgia.* 2 vols. Alexander City, Ala.: Outlook Publishing Co., 1971.

Davis, Burke. *Sherman's March.* New York and Toronto: Random House, 1980.

Davis, Nellie Cook. *The History of Miller County, Georgia, 1856–1980.* Colquitt, Ga.: Colquitt Garden Club, 1980.

Davis, William C. *The Cause Lost: Myths and Realities of the Confederacy.* Lawrence: University Press of Kansas, 1996.

DeBats, Donald A. *Elites and Masses: Political Structure, Communication, and Behavior in Ante-Bellum Georgia.* New York and London: Garland Publishing, 1990.

DeCredico, Mary A. *Patriotism for Profit: Georgia's Urban Entrepreneurs and the Confederate War Effort*. Chapel Hill: University of North Carolina Press, 1990.

Degler, Carl. *The Other South: Southern Dissenters in the Nineteenth Century*. New York: Harper and Row, 1974. Reprint, Boston: Northeastern University Press, 1982.

Denman, Clarence Phillips. *The Secession Movement in Alabama*. Freeport, N.Y.: Books for Libraries Press, 1971.

Denson, John V. *Slavery Laws in Alabama*. Auburn: Alabama Polytechnic Institute Historical Studies, 1907.

DeTreville, John R. "The Little New South: Origins of Industry in Georgia's Fall-Line Cities, 1840–1865." Ph.D. diss., University of North Carolina at Chapel Hill, 1986.

Dill, Floyd Richard. "The Institutional Possibilities and Limitations of Economic Progress in Antebellum Georgia: A Social Systems Approach." Ph.D. diss., Cornell University, 1973.

Dillard, Philip David. "Arming the Slaves: Transformation of the Public Mind." Master's thesis, University of Georgia, 1994.

Dodd, Donald Bradford. "Unionism in Confederate Alabama." Ph.D. diss., University of Georgia, 1969.

Doherty, Herbert J., Jr. "Union Nationalism in Georgia." *Georgia Historical Quarterly* 37 (1953): 18–38.

Drago, Edmund L. *Black Politicians and Reconstruction in Georgia: A Splendid Failure*. Baton Rouge: Louisiana State University Press, 1982. Reprint, Athens: University of Georgia Press, 1992.

Durden, Robert F. *The Gray and the Black: The Confederate Debate on Emancipation*. Baton Rouge: Louisiana State University Press, 1972.

Durrill, Wayne K. *War of Another Kind: A Southern Community in the Great Rebellion*. New York: Oxford University Press, 1990.

Eaton, Clement. *The Freedom-of-Thought Struggle in the Old South*. New York: Harper and Row, 1964.

———. *The Mind of the Old South*. Baton Rouge: Louisiana State University Press, 1964.

Escott, Paul D. *After Secession: Jefferson Davis and the Failure of Confederate Nationalism*. Baton Rouge: Louisiana State University Press, 1978.

———. "The Context of Freedom: Georgia's Slaves during the Civil War." *Georgia Historical Quarterly* 58 (1974): 79–104.

———. "Joseph E. Brown, Jefferson Davis, and the Problem of Poverty in the Confederacy." *Georgia Historical Quarterly* 61 (1977): 59–71.

———. "Southern Yeomen and the Confederacy." *South Atlantic Quarterly* 77 (1978): 146–58.

Escott, Paul D., and David R. Goldfield, eds. *Major Problems in the History of the American South*. 2 vols. Lexington, Mass.: D. C. Heath, 1990.

Faust, Drew Gilpin. *Mothers of Invention: Women of the Slaveholding South in the American Civil War.* Chapel Hill: University of North Carolina Press, 1996.

Finkelman, Paul. *Slavery in the Courtroom: An Annotated Bibliography of American Cases.* Washington, D.C.: Library of Congress, 1985.

————. "Treason against the Hopes of the World: Thomas Jefferson and the Problem of Slavery." Paper presented at the National Museum of American History Colloquium, Washington, D.C., March 23, 1993.

Fitzgerald, Michael W. "Poor Man's Fight." *Southern Exposure* 18 (spring 1990): 14–17.

Fleming, Walter L. "The Buford Expedition to Kansas." *Transactions of the Alabama Historical Society* 4 (1900): 167–92.

————. *The Churches of Alabama during the Civil War and Reconstruction.* Montgomery, Ala.: W. M. Rogers and Co., 1902.

————. *Civil War and Reconstruction in Alabama.* New York: Columbia University Press, 1905. Reprint, New York: Peter Smith, 1949.

————. "The Peace Movement in Alabama during the Civil War." *South Atlantic Quarterly* 2 (1903): 114–24, 246–60.

Flood, Charles Bracelen. *Lee: The Last Years.* Boston: Houghton Mifflin, 1981.

Flynn, Charles L., Jr. *White Land, Black Labor: Caste and Class in Late Nineteenth-Century Georgia.* Baton Rouge: Louisiana State University Press, 1983.

Flynt, Wayne. *Poor but Proud: Alabama's Poor Whites.* Tuscaloosa: University of Alabama Press, 1989.

————. "Spindle, Mine, and Mule: The Poor White Experience in Post–Civil War Alabama." *Alabama Review* 34 (1981): 243–86.

Foner, Eric. *Nothing but Freedom: Emancipation and Its Legacy.* Baton Rouge: Louisiana State University Press, 1983.

————. *Reconstruction: America's Unfinished Revolution, 1863–1877.* New York: Harper and Row, 1988.

Ford, Lacy K., Jr. *Origins of Southern Radicalism: The South Carolina Upcountry, 1800–1860.* New York: Oxford University Press, 1988.

Foreman, Grant. *Indian Removal.* Norman: University of Oklahoma Press, 1932.

Formwalt, Lee W. "Planter Persistence in Southwest Georgia, 1850–1870." *Journal of Southwest Georgia History* 2 (1984): 40–58.

————. "Planters and Cotton Production as a Cause of Confederate Defeat: Evidence from Southwest Georgia." *Georgia Historical Quarterly* 74 (1990): 269–76.

Foster, Gaines M. *Ghosts of the Confederacy: Defeat, the Lost Cause, and the Emergence of the New South, 1865 to 1913.* New York: Oxford University Press, 1987.

Foust, James Donald. *The Yeoman Farmer and Westward Expansion of U.S. Cotton Production.* Chapel Hill: University of North Carolina Press, 1967.

Franklin, John Hope, and Alfred A. Moss, Jr. *From Slavery to Freedom: A History of African Americans.* 7th ed. New York: McGraw-Hill, 1994.

Freehling, William W. *The Reintegration of American History: Slavery and the Civil War*. New York: Oxford University Press, 1994.

Freeman, Leon Howard, Jr. "Slavery as a Positive Good: The Change in the Southern Defense of Slavery, 1819–1832." Master's thesis, Valdosta State University, 1973.

French, Thomas L., Jr., and Edward L. French. "The Horace King Story: Building Bridges across Rivers and between Cultures." *Columbus and the Valley Magazine* (spring 1994): 34–40.

Fretwell, Mark E. "Rousseau's Alabama Raid." *Alabama Historical Quarterly* 18 (1956): 526–51.

Gates, Paul W. *Agriculture and the Civil War*. New York: Alfred A. Knopf, 1965.

————. *Fifty Million Acres: Conflicts over Kansas Land Policy, 1854–1890*. Ithaca: Cornell University Press, 1954.

Genovese, Eugene D. *The Southern Front: History and Politics in the Cultural War*. Columbia: University of Missouri Press, 1995.

————. *The Southern Tradition: The Achievement and Limitations of an American Conservatism*. Cambridge: Harvard University Press, 1994.

————. "Yeomen Farmers in a Slaveholders' Democracy." *Agricultural History* 49 (1975): 331–42.

Gilmour, Robert Arthur. "The Other Emancipation: Studies in the Society and Economy of Alabama Whites during Reconstruction." Ph.D. diss., Johns Hopkins University, 1972.

Glatthaar, Joseph T. *Forged in Battle: The Civil War Alliance of Black Soldiers and White Officers*. New York: Free Press, 1990.

————. *The March to the Sea and Beyond: Sherman's Troops in the Savannah and Carolinas Campaigns*. New York: New York University Press, 1985.

————. "The 'New' Civil War History: An Overview." *Pennsylvania Magazine of History and Biography* 115 (1991): 339–69.

Goff, John H. "The Steamboat Period in Georgia." *Georgia Historical Quarterly* 12 (1928): 236–54.

Goodman, Paul. "White over White: Planters, Yeomen, and the Coming of the Civil War: A Review Essay." *Agricultural History* 54 (1980): 446–52.

Gould, Stephen Jay. *The Mismeasure of Man*. New York: Norton, 1981.

Grant, Donald L. *The Way It Was in the South: The Black Experience in Georgia*. Edited with an introduction by Jonathan Grant. New York: Birch Lane Press, 1993.

Griffin, Richard W. "Cotton Frauds and Confiscations in Alabama, 1863–1866." *Alabama Review* 7 (1954): 265–76.

Hacker, Andrew. *Two Nations*. New York: Scribner's, 1992.

Hall, Mark. "Alexander H. Stephens and Joseph E. Brown and the Georgia Resolutions for Peace." *Georgia Historical Quarterly* 64 (1980): 50–63.

Hahn, Steven. *The Roots of Southern Populism: Yeoman Farmers and the Transformation of the Georgia Upcountry, 1850–1890*. New York: Oxford University Press, 1983.

Harris, J. William. *Plain Folk and Gentry in a Slave Society: White Liberty and Black Slavery in Augusta's Hinterlands.* Middletown, Conn.: Wesleyan University Press, 1985.

Hennessey, Melinda M. "Reconstruction Politics and the Military: The Eufaula Riot of 1874." *Alabama Historical Quarterly* 38 (1976): 112–25.

Hodler, Thomas W., and Howard A. Schretter. *The Atlas of Georgia.* Athens, Ga.: Institute of Community and Area Development, 1986.

Horton, Mrs. Thaddeus. "The Story of the Nancy Harts." *Ladies Home Journal* (November 1904): 14.

Hovenkamp, Herbert. *Science and Religion in America, 1800–1860.* Philadelphia: University of Pennsylvania Press, 1978.

Ingersoll, Lurton Dunham. *Iowa and the Rebellion.* Philadelphia: J. B. Lippincott and Co., 1866.

Inscoe, John C. *Mountain Masters, Slavery, and the Sectional Crisis in Western North Carolina.* Knoxville: University of Tennessee Press, 1989.

Johnson, Forrest Clark, III. *Histories of LaGrange and Troup County, Georgia.* Vol. I, *A History of LaGrange, Georgia, 1828–1900.* LaGrange: Family Tree, 1987.

Johnson, Joseph Paul. "Southwest Georgia: A Case Study in Confederate Agriculture." Master's thesis, University of Georgia, 1992.

Johnson, Michael P. "A New Look at the Popular Vote for Delegates to the Georgia Secession Convention." *Georgia Historical Quarterly* 56 (1972): 259–75.

———. *Toward a Patriarchal Republic: The Secession of Georgia.* Baton Rouge: Louisiana State University Press, 1977.

Jones, Allen W. "Unionism and Disaffection in South Alabama: The Case of Alfred Holley." *Alabama Review* 24 (1971): 114–32.

Jones, Frank S. *History of Decatur County, Georgia.* Spartanburg, S.C.: Reprint Co., 1980.

Jones, James Pickett. *Yankee Blitzkrieg: Wilson's Raid through Alabama and Georgia.* Athens: University of Georgia Press, 1976.

Jordan, Ervin L. *Black Confederates and Afro-Yankees in Civil War Virginia.* Charlottesville: University of Virginia Press, 1995.

Kennett, Lee. *Marching through Georgia: The Story of Soldiers and Civilians during Sherman's Campaign.* New York: HarperCollins, 1995.

Kibler, Lillian A. "Unionist Sentiment in South Carolina in 1860." *Journal of Southern History* 4 (1938): 346–66.

Kolchin, Peter. *First Freedom: The Responses of Alabama's Blacks to Emancipation and Reconstruction.* Westport, Conn.: Greenwood Press, 1972.

Kozol, Jonathan. *Savage Inequalities: Children in America's Schools.* New York: Crown, 1991.

Krug, Donna Rebecca Dondes. "The Folks Back Home: The Confederate Homefront during the Civil War." Ph.D. diss., University of California at Irvine, 1990.

Kyle, F. Clason. *Images: A Pictorial History of Columbus, Georgia.* Norfolk, Va.: Donning Co., 1986.

Lamb, Robert Paul. "James G. Birney and the Road to Abolitionism." *Alabama Review* 47 (1994): 83–134.

Lebergott, Stanley. "Why the South Lost: Commercial Purpose in the Confederacy." *Journal of American History* 70 (1983): 58–74.

Leverett, Rudy H. *Legend of the Free State of Jones.* Jackson: University Press of Mississippi, 1984.

Levine, Bruce C. *Half Slave and Half Free: The Roots of Civil War.* New York: Hill and Wang, 1991.

Levy, Leonard W. *Jefferson and Civil Liberties: The Darker Side.* Cambridge: Harvard University Press, 1963.

Linderman, Gerald F. *Embattled Courage: The Experience of Combat in the American Civil War.* New York: Free Press, 1987.

Lindsey, Bobby L. *"The Reason for the Tears": A History of Chambers County, Alabama, 1832–1900.* West Point, Ga.: Hester Printing Co., 1971.

Lindstrom, Diane. "Southern Dependence upon Interregional Grain Supplies: A Review of the Trade Flows, 1840–1860." *Agricultural History* 44 (1970): 101–13.

Lipset, Seymour Martin. *Political Man: The Social Bases of Politics.* Garden City, N.Y.: Doubleday, 1960. Expanded ed., Baltimore: Johns Hopkins University Press, 1981.

Long, Durward. "Unanimity and Disloyalty in Secessionist Alabama." *Civil War History* (1965): 257–73.

Lonn, Ella. *Desertion during the Civil War.* New York: Century Co., 1928.

———. *Salt as a Factor in the Confederacy.* Tuscaloosa: University of Alabama Press, 1965.

Loveman, Louis Vandiver. *Historical Atlas of Alabama, 1519–1900.* Gadsden, Ala.: Loveman, 1976.

Lowen, James W. *Lies My Teacher Told Me: Everything Your American History Textbook Got Wrong.* New York: New Press, 1995.

Lupold, John S. *Chattahoochee Valley Sources and Resources: An Annotated Bibliography.* Vol. 1, *The Alabama Counties.* Eufaula, Ala.: Historic Chattahoochee Commission, 1988.

———. *Chattahoochee Valley Sources and Resources: An Annotated Bibliography.* Vol. 2, *The Georgia Counties.* Eufaula, Ala.: Historic Chattahoochee Commission, 1993.

Mahan, Joseph B. *Columbus: Georgia's Fall Line "Trading Town."* Northridge, Calif.: Windsor Publications, 1986.

Martin, Bessie. *Desertion of Alabama Troops from the Confederate Army: A Study in Sectionalism.* New York: AMS Press, 1966.

Martis, Kenneth C. *The Historical Atlas of the Congresses of the Confederate*

States of America, 1861–1865. Gyula Pauer, cartographer. B. Reed Durbin, research assistant. New York: Simon and Schuster, 1994.

Massey, Mary Elizabeth. *Ersatz in the Confederacy.* Columbia: University of South Carolina Press, 1952.

———. *Refugee Life in the Confederacy.* Baton Rouge: Louisiana State University Press, 1964.

Mathis, Ray. *John Horry Dent: South Carolina Aristocrat on the Alabama Frontier.* Tuscaloosa: University of Alabama Press, 1979.

Mayer, Henry. "'A Leaven of Disunion': The Growth of the Secessionist Faction in Alabama, 1847–1851." *Alabama Review* 22 (1969): 83–116.

McCrary, Peyton, Clark Miller, and Dale Baum. "Class and Party in the Secession Crisis: Voting Behavior in the Deep South, 1856–1861." *Journal of Interdisciplinary History* 8 (1978): 429–57.

McCurry, Stephanie. *Masters of Small Worlds: Yeoman Households, Gender Relations, and the Political Culture of the Antebellum South Carolina Low Country.* New York: Oxford University Press, 1995.

McGee, Val L. *Claybank Memories: A History of Dale County, Alabama.* Ozark, Ala.: Dale County Historical Society, 1989.

———. "The Confederate Who Switched Sides: The Saga of Captain Joseph G. Sanders." *Alabama Review* 47 (1994): 20–28.

McMillan, Malcolm C. *The Disintegration of a Confederate State: Three Governors and Alabama's Wartime Home Front, 1861–1865.* Macon, Ga.: Mercer University Press, 1986.

McNeill, William J. "A Survey of Confederate Soldier Morale during Sherman's Campaigns through Georgia and the Carolinas." *Georgia Historical Quarterly* 55 (1971): 1–25.

McPherson, James M. "American Victory, American Defeat." In *Why the Confederacy Lost,* edited by Gabor S. Boritt. New York: Oxford University Press, 1992.

———. *Battle Cry of Freedom: The Civil War Era.* New York: Oxford University Press, 1988.

———. *Drawn with the Sword.* New York: Oxford University Press, 1996.

———. *Ordeal by Fire: The Civil War and Reconstruction.* 2d ed. New York: McGraw-Hill, 1992.

McWhiney, Grady. *Cracker Culture: Celtic Ways in the Old South.* Tuscaloosa: University of Alabama Press, 1988.

Meriwether, Harvey. *Slavery in Auburn, Alabama.* Auburn: Alabama Polytechnic Institute Historical Studies, 1907.

Meyers, Christopher C. "'The Wretch Victory' and the Brooks County Civil War Slave Conspiracy." *Journal of Southwest Georgia History* 12 (1997): 27–38.

Mills, Gary B. *Southern Loyalists in the Civil War: The Southern Claims Commission.* Baltimore: Genealogical Publishing Company, 1994.

Mohr, Clarence L. *On the Threshold of Freedom: Masters and Slaves in Civil War Georgia*. Athens: University of Georgia Press, 1986.

———. "Slavery and Class Tensions in Confederate Georgia." *Gulf Coast Historical Review* 4 (1989): 58–72.

Moore, Albert B. *Conscription and Conflict in the Confederacy*. New York: MacMillian Co., 1924.

Morgan, Edmund S. *American Slavery, American Freedom: The Ordeal of Colonial Virginia*. New York: W. W. Norton and Co., 1975.

Morris, Thomas. *Southern Slavery and the Law, 1619–1860*. Chapel Hill: University of North Carolina Press, 1996.

Mueller, Edward A. *Perilous Journeys: A History of Steamboating on the Chattahoochee, Apalachicola, and Flint Rivers, 1828–1928*. Eufaula, Ala.: Historic Chattahoochee Commission, 1990.

Noe, Kenneth W., and Shannon H. Wilson. *The Civil War in Appalachia: Collected Essays*. Knoxville: University of Tennessee Press, 1997.

Nolan, Alan T. *Lee Considered: General Robert E. Lee and Civil War History*. Chapel Hill: University of North Carolina Press, 1991.

Northern, William J., ed. *Men of Mark in Georgia*. 7 vols. Atlanta: A. B. Caldwell, 1907–12. Reprint, Spartanburg, S.C.: Reprint Co., 1974.

Nunn, Alexander, ed. *Lee County and Her Forebears*. Montgomery, Ala.: Herff Jones, 1983.

Nunn, William Glenn, and Jesse Boring Page. "History of Loachapoka." Master's thesis, Auburn University, 1929.

Oakes, James. *Slavery and Freedom: An Interpretation of the Old South*. New York: Vintage, 1990.

Oates, Stephen B. *The Fires of Jubilee: Nat Turner's Fierce Rebellion*. New York: HarperCollins, 1990.

Osher, David, and Peter Wallenstein. "Why the Confederacy Lost: An Essay Review." *Maryland Historical Magazine* 88 (1993): 95–108.

Owens, Harry P. "Sail and Steam Vessels Serving the Apalachicola-Chattahoochee Valley." *Alabama Review* 21 (1968): 195–237.

Owsley, Frank L. "Defeatism in the Confederacy." *North Carolina Historical Review* 3 (1926): 446–56.

———. *Plain Folk of the Old South*. Baton Rouge: Louisiana State University Press, 1949.

———. *State Rights in the Confederacy*. Chicago: University of Chicago Press, 1925. Reprint, Gloucester, Mass.: Peter Smith, 1961.

Paludan, Phillip Shaw. *Victims: A True Story of the Civil War*. Knoxville: University of Tennessee Press, 1981.

Pearce, Haywood J., Jr. *Benjamin H. Hill: Secession and Reconstruction*. Chicago: University of Chicago Press, 1928. Reprint, New York: Negro Universities Press, 1969.

Percy, William Alexander. "Localizing the Context of Confederate Politics: The

Congressional Election of 1863 in Georgia's First District." *Georgia Historical Quarterly* 79 (1995): 192–209.

Phillips, Kevin. *The Politics of Rich and Poor.* New York: Random House, 1990.

Phillips, Ulrich B. *Georgia and State Rights.* Washington, D.C.: Government Printing Office, 1902. Reprint, n.p.: Antioch Press, 1968.

Potter, David M. *Lincoln and His Party in the Secession Crisis.* New Haven: Yale University Press, 1942.

Proctor, William G., Jr. "Slavery in Southwest Georgia." *Georgia Historical Quarterly* 49 (1965): 1–22.

Purcell, Douglas Clare. "Military Conscription in Alabama during the Civil War." *Alabama Review* 34 (1981): 94–106.

Rable, George C. *Civil Wars: Women and the Crisis of Southern Nationalism.* Urbana: University of Illinois Press, 1989.

Rachleff, Marshall J. "Racial Fear and Political Factionalism: A Study of the Secession Movement in Alabama, 1819–1861." Ph.D. diss., University of Massachusetts, 1974.

Randall, J. G., and David Herbert Donald. *The Civil War and Reconstruction.* 2d ed. Lexington, Mass.: D. C. Heath, 1969.

Range, Willard. *A Century of Georgia Agriculture: 1850–1950.* Athens: University of Georgia Press, 1954.

Rawley, James A. *Race and Politics: "Bleeding Kansas" and the Coming of the Civil War.* Philadelphia: Lippincott, 1969.

Reidy, Joseph P. *From Slavery to Agrarian Capitalism in the Cotton Plantation South: Central Georgia, 1800–1880.* Chapel Hill: University of North Carolina Press, 1992.

Reiger, John F. "Deprivation, Disaffection, and Desertion in Confederate Florida." *Florida Historical Quarterly* 48 (1969–70): 279–98.

Riley, James A. "Desertion and Disloyalty in Georgia during the Civil War." Master's thesis, University of Georgia, 1951.

Roark, James L. *Masters without Slaves: Southern Planters in the Civil War and Reconstruction.* New York: W. W. Norton, 1977.

Robbins, John B. "The Confederacy and the Writ of Habeas Corpus." *Georgia Historical Quarterly* 55 (1971): 83–101.

Robinson, Armstead Louis. "Day of Jubilo: Civil War and the Demise of Slavery in the Mississippi Valley, 1861–1865." Ph.D. diss., University of Rochester, 1976.

———. "In the Shadow of Old John Brown: Insurrection Anxiety and Confederate Mobilization, 1861–1863." *Journal of Negro History* 65 (1980): 279–97.

Rogers, N. K. *History of Chattahoochee County, Georgia.* Columbus, Ga.: Columbus Office Supply Co., 1933. Reprint, Easley, S.C.: Southern Historical Press, 1976.

Rogers, William Warren. *Thomas County during the Civil War.* Tallahassee: Florida State University, 1964.

Sarris, Jonathan Dean. "Anatomy of an Atrocity: The Madden Branch Massacre and Guerrilla Warfare in North Georgia, 1861–1865." *Georgia Historical Quarterly* 77 (1993): 679–710.

———. "The Madden Branch Massacre: Loyalty and Disloyalty in North Georgia's Guerrilla War, 1860–1865." Master's thesis, University of Georgia, 1994.

Scarborough, Ruth. *The Opposition to Slavery in Georgia prior to 1860.* Nashville, Tenn.: George Peabody College for Teachers, 1933. Reprint, New York: Negro Universities Press, 1968.

Schott, Thomas E. *Alexander H. Stephens of Georgia.* Baton Rouge: Louisiana State University Press, 1988.

Schroeder-Lein, Glenna R. *Confederate Hospitals on the Move: Samuel H. Stout and the Army of Tennessee.* Columbia: University of South Carolina Press, 1994.

———. "'To Be Better Supplied Than Any Hotel in the Confederacy': The Establishment and Maintenance of the Army of Tennessee Hospitals in Georgia, 1863–1865." *Georgia Historical Quarterly* 76 (1992): 809–36.

Schwarz, John E., and Thomas J. Volgy. *The Forgotten Americans: Thirty Million Working Poor in the Land of Opportunity.* New York: Norton, 1992.

Sellers, James Benson. *Slavery in Alabama.* 2d ed. Tuscaloosa: University of Alabama Press, 1964.

Sennet, Richard, and Jonathan Cobb. *The Hidden Injuries of Class.* New York: Vintage Books, 1973.

Shadgett, Olive Hall. "James Johnson, Provisional Governor of Georgia." *Georgia Historical Quarterly* 36 (1952): 1–21.

Shepard, Jacquelyn. *The Quitman Echo.* Georgetown, Ga.: Shepard, 1991.

Shy, John. *A People Numerous and Armed: Reflections on the Military Struggle for American Independence.* New York: Oxford University Press, 1976.

Smith, Clifford L. *History of Troup County.* Atlanta: Foote and Davies, 1933.

Snay, Mitchell. *Gospel of Disunion: Religion and Separatism in the Antebellum South.* New York: Cambridge University Press, 1993.

Stampp, Kenneth M. *The Peculiar Institution: Slavery in the Ante-Bellum South.* New York: Vintage Books, 1956.

Standard, Diffee William. *Columbus, Georgia, in the Confederacy: The Social and Industrial Life of the Chattahoochee River Port.* New York: William-Frederick Press, 1954.

Stanton, William. *The Leopard's Spots: Scientific Attitudes toward Race in America, 1815–59.* Chicago: University of Chicago Press, 1960.

Sterkx, H. E. *Partners in Rebellion: Alabama Women in the Civil War.* Cranbury, N.J.: Associated University Presses, 1970.

———. *Some Notable Alabama Women during the Civil War.* Tuscaloosa: Alabama Civil War Centennial Commission, 1962.

Still, William N. *Confederate Shipbuilding.* Athens: University of Georgia Press, 1969.

Suarez, Annette McDonald. *A Source Book on the Early History of Cuthbert and Randolph County, Georgia*. Atlanta: Cherokee Publishing Co., 1982.

Swift, Charles Jewett. *The Last Battle of the Civil War*. Columbus, Ga.: Gilbert Printing Co., 1915.

Talmadge, John E. "Peace-Movement Activities in Civil War Georgia." *Georgia Review* 7 (1953): 190–203.

Tatum, Georgia Lee. *Disloyalty in the Confederacy*. Chapel Hill: University of North Carolina Press, 1934. Reprint, New York: AMS Press, 1970.

Taylor, William R. *Cavalier and Yankee: The Old South and American National Character*. New York: Harper and Row, 1961.

Telfair, Nancy. *A History of Columbus, Georgia, 1828–1928*. Columbus, Ga.: Historical Publishing Co., 1929.

Terrill, Helen Eliza, and Sara Robertson Dixon. *History of Stewart County, Georgia*. Vol. 1. Columbus, Ga.: Columbus Office Supply Co., 1958.

Thompson, Mattie Thomas. *History of Barbour County, Alabama*. Eufaula, Ala.: n.p., 1939.

———. "Occupation of Eufaula by Union Cavalry Was Quiet and Orderly." *Birmingham News*, February 10, 1929.

Thornton, J. Mills, III. *Politics and Power in a Slave Society: Alabama, 1800–1860*. Baton Rouge: Louisiana State University Press, 1978.

Thurston, William N. "The Apalachicola–Chattahoochee–Flint River Water Route System in the Nineteenth Century." *Georgia Historical Quarterly* 57 (1973): 200–212.

Todd, Priscilla Neves, ed. *The History of Clay County*. Fort Gaines, Ga.: Clay County Library Board, 1976.

Tripp, Steven Elliott. *Yankee Town, Southern City: Race and Class Relations in Civil War Lynchburg*. New York: New York University Press, 1997.

Turner, Maxine. *Navy Gray: A Story of the Confederate Navy on the Chattahoochee and Apalachicola Rivers*. Tuscaloosa: University of Alabama Press, 1988.

Vandiver, Frank E. *Ploughshares into Swords: Josiah Gorgas and Confederate Ordnance*. Austin: University of Texas Press, 1952.

Vinovskis, Maris A., ed. *Toward a Social History of the American Civil War: Exploratory Essays*. Cambridge and New York: Cambridge University Press, 1990.

Walker, Anne Kendrick. *Backtracking in Barbour County: A Narrative of the Last Alabama Frontier*. Richmond, Va.: Dietz Press, 1941. Reprint, Eufaula, Ala.: Eufaula Heritage Association, 1967.

———. *Russell County in Retrospect: An Epic of the Far Southeast*. Richmond, Va.: Dietz Press, 1950.

Wallenstein, Peter. *From Slave South to New South: Public Policy in Nineteenth-Century Georgia*. Chapel Hill: University of North Carolina Press, 1987.

———. "Rich Man's War, Rich Man's Fight: Civil War and the Transformation of Public Finance in Georgia." *Journal of Southern History* 50 (1984): 15–42.

Ward, Geoffrey C. *The Civil War.* New York: Alfred Knopf, 1992.

Ware, Lynn Willoughby. "Cotton Money: Antebellum Currency Conditions in the Apalachicola/Chattahoochee River Valley." *Georgia Historical Quarterly* 74 (1990): 215–33.

———. "Enchantment and Ennui: The Experiences of the Crew of the CSS *Chattahoochee.*" *Georgia Historical Quarterly* 70 (1986): 409–32.

Warren, Hoyt M. *Henry: The Mother County, 1816–1903.* 3d printing rev. Abbeville, Ala.: Henry County Historical Society, 1981.

Washburn, Wilcomb E. *The Governor and the Rebel: A History of Bacon's Rebellion in Virginia.* Chapel Hill: University of North Carolina Press, 1957.

Watson, Fred S. *Forgotten Trails: A History of Dale County, Alabama.* Birmingham, Ala.: Banner Press, 1968.

———. *Piney Wood Echoes: A History of Dale and Coffee Counties, Alabama.* Elba, Ala.: Elba Clipper, 1949.

———. *Winds of Sorrow: Hardships of the Civil War, Early Crimes and Hangings, and War Casualties of the Wiregrass Area.* Dothan, Ala.: Hopkins Printing Co., 1986.

Watson, Harry L. "Conflict and Collaboration: Yeomen, Slaveholders, and Politics in the Antebellum South." *Social History* 10 (1985): 273–98.

Wetherington, Mark V. *The New South Comes to Wiregrass Georgia, 1860–1910.* Knoxville: University of Tennessee Press, 1994.

Whitehead, Mary Grist, ed. *Collections of Early County Historical Society.* 2 vols. Colquitt, Ga.: Automat Printers, 1971; Tallahassee, Fla.: Rose Printing, 1979.

Whites, Lee Ann. *The Civil War as a Crisis in Gender: Augusta, Georgia, 1860–1890.* Athens: University of Georgia Press, 1995.

Wiener, Jonathan M. *Social Origins of the New South: Alabama, 1860–1885.* Baton Rouge: Louisiana State University Press, 1978.

Wiley, Bell Irvin. *The Plain People of the Confederacy.* Baton Rouge: Louisiana State University Press, 1943. Reprint, Gloucester, Mass.: Peter Smith, 1971.

Williams, Carol T. "'The Power of a True Woman's Heart': Augusta Jane Evans and Feminine Civil War Values." *Journal of Southwest Georgia History* 8 (1993): 39–46.

Williams, David. *The Georgia Gold Rush: Twenty-Niners, Cherokees, and Gold Fever.* Columbia: University of South Carolina Press, 1993.

———. "'Rich Man's War': Class, Caste, and Confederate Defeat in Southwest Georgia. *Journal of Southwest Georgia History* 11 (1996): 1–42.

Williamson, Jeffrey G., and Peter H. Lindert. *American Inequality: A Macroeconomic History.* New York: Academic Press, 1980.

Willoughby, Lynn. *Fair to Middlin': The Antebellum Cotton Trade of the Apalachicola/Chattahoochee River Valley.* Tuscaloosa: University of Alabama Press, 1993.

Winn, Bill. "Columbus' Last Battle: Peace Society May Have Aided City's Fall." *Columbus Ledger-Enquirer,* April 19, 1987.

Wood, Betty. *Slavery in Colonial Georgia, 1730–1775*. Athens: University of Georgia Press, 1984.

Woodward, C. Vann. *Tom Watson*. 2d ed. Savannah, Ga.: Beehive Press, 1973.

Wooster, Ralph A. *The Secession Conventions of the South*. Princeton: Princeton University Press, 1962.

Wright, Gavin. "'Economic Democracy' and the Concentration of Agricultural Wealth in the Cotton South, 1850–1860." *Agricultural History* 44 (1970): 63–93.

———. *The Political Economy of the Cotton South: Households, Markets, and Wealth in the Nineteenth Century*. New York: Norton, 1978.

Wynne, Lewis Nicholas. *The Continuity of Cotton: Planter Politics in Georgia, 1865–1892*. Macon, Ga.: Mercer University Press, 1986.

Zinn, Howard. *A People's History of the United States*. New York: Harper and Row, 1980.

INDEX